EARLY MODERN DYNASTIC MARRIAGES AND CULTURAL TRANSFER

Toward the end of the fifteenth century, the Habsburg family began to rely on dynastic marriage to unite an array of territories, eventually creating an empire as had not been seen in Europe since the Romans. Other European rulers followed the Habsburgs' lead in forging ties through dynastic marriages. Because of these marriages, many more aristocrats (especially women) left their homelands to reside elsewhere. Until now, historians have viewed these unions from a primarily political viewpoint and have paid scant attention to the personal dimensions of these relocations. Separated from their family and thrust into a strange new land in which language, attire, religion, food, and cultural practices were often different, these young aristocrats were forced to conform to new customs or adapt their own customs to a new cultural setting.

Early Modern Dynastic Marriages and Cultural Transfer examines these marriages as important agents of cultural transfer, emphasizing how marriages could lead to the creation of a cosmopolitan culture, common to the elites of Europe. These essays focus on the personal and domestic dimensions of early modern European court life, examining such areas as women's devotional practices, fashion, patronage, and culinary traditions.

Transculturalisms, 1400–1700

Series Editors:
Mihoko Suzuki, University of Miami, USA,
Ann Rosalind Jones, Smith College, USA, and
Jyotsna Singh, Michigan State University, USA

This series presents studies of the early modern contacts and exchanges among the states, polities and entrepreneurial organizations of Europe; Asia, including the Levant and East India/Indies; Africa; and the Americas. Books will investigate travelers, merchants and cultural inventors, including explorers, mapmakers, artists and writers, as they operated in political, mercantile, sexual and linguistic economies. We encourage authors to reflect on their own methodologies in relation to issues and theories relevant to the study of transculturism/translation and transnationalism. We are particularly interested in work on and from the perspective of the Asians, Africans, and Americans involved in these interactions, and on such topics as:

- Material exchanges, including textiles, paper and printing, and technologies of knowledge
- Movements of bodies: embassies, voyagers, piracy, enslavement
- Travel writing: its purposes, practices, forms and effects on writing in other genres
- Belief systems: religions, philosophies, sciences
- Translations: verbal, artistic, philosophical
- Forms of transnational violence and its representations.

Also in this series:

Early Modern Exchanges
Dialogues Between Nations and Cultures, 1550–1750
Edited by Helen Hackett

Aesthetic Hybridity in Mughal Painting, 1526–1658
Valerie Gonzalez

Commedia dell' Arte *and the Mediterranean*
Charting Journeys and Mapping "Others"
Erith Jaffe-Berg

The Chinese Impact upon English Renaissance Literature
A Globalization and Liberal Cosmopolitan Approach to Donne and Milton
Mingjun Lu

Early Modern Dynastic Marriages and Cultural Transfer

Edited by

JOAN-LLUÍS PALOS
University of Barcelona, Spain

MAGDALENA S. SÁNCHEZ
Gettysburg College, USA

ASHGATE

Published by
Ashgate Publishing Limited
Wey Court East
Union Road
Farnham
Surrey, GU9 7PT
England

Ashgate Publishing Company
110 Cherry Street
Suite 3-1
Burlington, VT 05401-3818
USA

www.ashgate.com

British Library Cataloguing in Publication Data
A catalogue record for this book is available from the British Library

The Library of Congress has cataloged the printed edition as follows:
Early modern dynastic marriages and cultural transfer / edited by Joan-Lluís Palos and Magdalena S. Sánchez.
pages cm. -- (Transculturalisms, 1400-1700)
Includes index.
ISBN 978-1-4724-4321-2 (hardcover: alk. paper) -- ISBN 978-1-4724-4322-9 (e-book) -- ISBN 978-1-4724-4323-6 (e-pub)
1. Europe--Civilization--16th century. 2. Europe--Civilization--17th century. 3. Europe--Civilization--18th century. 4. Europe--Court and courtiers--History. 5. Royal houses--Europe--History. 6. Marriages of royalty and nobility--Europe--History. 7. Upper class women--Europe--History. 8. Culture diffusion--Europe--History. I. Palos, Joan-Lluís, editor of compilation. II. Sánchez, Magdalena S., editor of compilation.

CB401.E17 2015
940.2'32--dc23

2015020322

ISBN: 9781472443212 (hbk)
ISBN: 9781472443229 (ebk—PDF)
ISBN: 9781472443236 (ebk—ePUB)

MIX
Paper from responsible sources
FSC® C013985
www.fsc.org

Printed in the United Kingdom by Henry Ling Limited, at the Dorset Press, Dorchester, DT1 1HD

Contents

List of Illustrations

List of Tables

Notes on Contributors

Bethany Aram is a Ramón y Cajal Research Professor at the Pablo de Olavide University in Seville and the Principal Investigator of European Research Council Consolidator Grant 648535, "An ARTery of EMPIRE. Conquest, Commerce, Crisis, Culture and the Panamanian Junction (1513–1671)." She is the author of *Juana the Mad: Sovereignty and Dynasty in Renaissance Europe* (2005) and *Leyenda negra y leyendas doradas en la conquista de América: Pedrarias y Balboa* (2008) and has edited *Global Goods and the Spanish Empire, 1492–1824: Circulation, Resistance, and Diversity* (2014) with Bartolomé Yun Casalilla.

Leticia de Frutos is Museum Curator at the Ministry of Education, Culture, and Sports of the Spanish Government. Her interdisciplinary research is focused on the study of cultural relationships, collections, and the spread of images and cultural models between Spain and Italy during the early modern era. She is the author of *El Templo de la Fama: Alegoría del marqués del Carpio* (2009) and of *Cartas del navegar pintoresco: Correspondencia de pinturas con Venecia* (2011).

Laura Oliván Santaliestra is IEF Marie Curie Fellow at the University of Vienna (2014–16), where she is working on the project *Imperial Ambassadresses between the Courts of Madrid and Vienna (1650–1700): Diplomacy, Sociability and Culture*. In particular her work focuses on the image, power, and the body of women at Baroque courts. She has published *Mariana de Austria: Imagen poder y diplomacia de una reina cortesana* (2006) and, with Pilar Pérez Cantó and Esperanza Mó Romero, *Rainhas de Portugal e Espanha: Margarida de Austria. Isabel de Bourbon* (2012).

Joan-Lluís Palos is Professor of Modern History at the University of Barcelona where he directs the research group *Poder y Representaciones en la Época Moderna* (www.ub.edu/poderirepresentacions). His current research focuses on cultural relations in the Mediterranean world. His most recent book is *L'impero di Spagna allo specchio: Storie e propaganda nei dipinti del Palazzo Reale di Napoli* (2015). His chapter in this book is part of a book-length project on Eleonora Álvarez de Toledo, Duchess of Florence.

María de los Ángeles Pérez Samper is Professor of Modern History at the University of Barcelona. She is past president of the Fundación Española de Historia Moderna. She is a founding member of the European Institute of History and Cultures of Food. She has researched and published on the Spanish monarchy, the female presence in the world of power, the queens of Spain, the history of food, and the history of everyday life in early modern Europe. She is the author of *Isabel de Farnesio* (2003) and *Isabel la Católica* (2004).

Magdalena S. Sánchez is Professor of History at Gettysburg College, Pennsylvania. She is the author of *The Empress, the Queen, and the Nun: Women and Power at the Court of Philip III of Spain* (1998). She has published several essays on women at the court of Philip II and Philip III, and is the author of "'Lord of My Soul': The Letters of Catalina Micaela, Duchess of Savoy, to Her Husband, Carlo Emanuele I," in *Early Modern Habsburg Women*, edited by Anne J. Cruz and Maria Galli Stampino (2014). She is at work on a book-length project on the *Infanta* Catalina Micaela.

Anna Santamaría López received her BA in history from the University of Barcelona and is finishing her Master's degree at the University Pompeu Fabra (Barcelona). She is an intern at the National Archive of Catalonia and has also collaborated on several research projects on patrimonial organizations. Her research is primarily on the institutional history of Catalonia in the early modern period and on the cultural exchange between Spain and England in the sixteenth century.

Mafalda Soares da Cunha is Professor of History at the University of Évora. She is vice-director of the Interdisciplinary Center for History, Culture and Society of the University of Évora (CIDEHUS-UE) and co-editor of the *e-Journal of Portuguese History*. She has researched Portuguese and imperial social elites in Portugal under the Habsburgs, focusing particularly on the Portuguese nobility as well as on governmental and political communication in the early modern period. She is the author of *A Casa de Bragança (1560–1640): Práticas Senhoriais e Redes Clientelares* (2000) and, with Leonor Freire Costa, co-authored the book *D. João IV* (2008).

Mark de Vitis is a lecturer in the Department of Art History at the University of Sydney. His current research project focuses on the capital of cultural hybridity at the courts of early modern Europe. Besides his contribution to this volume, other publications resulting from the project include "Sartorial Transgression as Socio-Political Collaboration: Madame and the Hunt," *Konsthistorisk Tidskrift*, 82, no. 3 (2013): 205–18, which examines the sartorial choices of Elisabeth Charlotte von der Pfalz, duchesse d'Orléans (1652–1722). The wider project, including material in this volume, has been realized through the support of the National Art School, Sydney, Australia and the Getty Research Institute, Los Angeles.

Bartolomé Yun Casalilla is Professor of Early Modern History at the Pablo de Olavide University in Seville and is a member of the Academia Europaea. For ten years he was Professor of the European University Institute in Florence where he directed the Department of History and Civilization. He has published widely on global, comparative, and transnational history. His latest book, co-edited with Bethany Aram, is *Global Goods and the Spanish Empire, 1492–1824: Circulation, Resistance, and Diversity* (2014).

Acknowledgments

This book has its origins in a conference titled *A New Life in a Foreign Country. Dynastic Marriages and Cultural Transfers in Early Modern Europe*, organized by the research group *Power and Representations: Cultural Transfers in the Early Modern Age* and held at the University of Barcelona in October 2010. Our principal thanks go to the authors, some of whom took part in the Barcelona meeting while others become involved in the project later, broadening its perspectives and enriching its content. Despite other commitments, these scholars have responded in every case with generosity and diligence to the editors' requests.

Anna Santamaría López coordinated the original meeting and the compilation of the contributions. Davide van Vlijmen and Anna Saxby translated, proofread, and copyedited early versions of several of the chapters. Phil Banks and Melissa Calaresu read a number of the original contributions and suggested improvements. To all of these we wish to express our sincere appreciation.

This book has been conceived within the framework of the following research projects based at the University of Barcelona (www.ub.edu/Poderirepresentacions): *Power and Representations in the Modern Age: The Spanish Monarchy as Cultural Field (1500–1800)* (HAR12-39516-C02-01), sponsored by the Spanish government; *Power and Representations in the Modern Age: Diplomatic Networks and Cultural Encounters in the Spanish Monarchy (1500–1700)* (HAR2012-39516-C02-02) sponsored by the Spanish government; and *Grup d'Estudis d'Història del Mediterrani Occidental* (GEHMO), sponsored by the Generalitat de Catalunya through the Agency for Management of University and Research Grants (AGAUR) (Ref. 2014SGR173). We are grateful to the institutions which funded these research projects.

We are also indebted to Ruth MacKay who translated several of the chapters from Spanish to English and copyedited the entire manuscript with speed, accuracy, and professionalism. Her help was invaluable. A generous grant from Gettysburg College allowed us to pay for Ruth's editorial work and we are especially grateful to the Faculty Development Committee at the College for awarding the grant. Erika Gaffney at Ashgate Publications has been a model editor—patient, generous, and encouraging. Finally, Magdalena would like to thank her family for their patience and support, as well as María José del Río Barredo and Anne J. Cruz for their advice and assistance. Joan-Lluís would like to dedicate this book to the memory of Davide van Vlijmen, who helped so generously in the preparation of many of the chapters.

Introduction
Bargaining Chips: Strategic Marriages and Cultural Circulation in Early Modern Europe

Joan-Lluís Palos

Bella gerant alii, tu, felix Austria, nube, nam quae Mars aliis, dat tibi regna Venu …

Many scholars have attributed the Habsburg family's rapid attainment of hegemony in early sixteenth-century Europe to the application of the motto which Emperor Maximilian I (1493–1519) borrowed from Ovid: "Let others wage war, but thou, O happy Austria, marry; for those kingdoms which Mars gives to others, Venus gives to thee." Maximilian's grandson and faithful disciple, the emperor Charles V (1520–55), followed this advice to the letter, managing to weave a web of family connections that spanned the entire continent, from Spain to England and from the Low Countries to Italy, and including, of course, his patrimonial lands in Central Europe.

In subsequent generations not only his relatives and heirs, but also many other European elites chose to benefit from such a useful example: monarchs of France, England, Poland, or Sweden; governors of small states, particularly Italian and German ones; or nobles with aspirations to maintain or expand their territories and influence all followed Maximilian's example. They negotiated marriages for themselves and their offspring, primarily for political or economic gain. As a consequence, young princes (and, above all, princesses) were sent from one side of the continent to another, in the hope that Venus would achieve that which Mars could not.

Of course, elites had great expectations for these marriage negotiations, but this was a field in which the final outcome was in the hands of divine providence, something that not even the most powerful rulers of the world could control. Some of these unions, however, produced results that even the most optimistic could not have imagined: that of Philip of Burgundy and Juana of Castile in 1495, which Bethany Aram analyzes in this book, was the basis of the creation of the universal empire of the Habsburgs; that of Cosimo de' Medici and Eleonora de Toledo in 1539, studied by Joan-Lluís Palos, was decisive for the consolidation of the Medici family in the governance of Tuscany during the subsequent two centuries; and that of Louis XIV of France and the Spanish Habsburg princess, María Teresa, in 1660, which Mark de Vitis examines, resulted in the ascent of the Bourbon family to the Spanish throne at the beginning of the eighteenth century. Others resulted in resounding failure: that of Philip II of Spain to Mary

Tudor in 1554, discussed by Anna Santamaría López, far from consolidating the alliance which should have allowed the Habsburgs to dominate the north of Europe, contributed instead to creating anti-Spanish sentiment in England for centuries. It is difficult for historians, perhaps precisely because they have the advantage of hindsight to see the long-term consequences of certain decisions, to put themselves in the place of early modern people and assess their goals objectively.

Furthermore, one must take into account that the outbreak of the Protestant Reformation in the first decades of the sixteenth century considerably limited the marriage market. Except in a few cases, the heads of confessional dynasties could not marry their children to someone who did not profess the same religion. Naturally, this considerably limited the options, which in some cases, particularly that of the Habsburgs, caused growing endogamy, which produced the disastrous genetic degradation which is all too well known.

Until now historians have viewed the proliferation of these marriages of convenience primarily from a political perspective, and as such have assessed their importance through the effects they had on the maintenance or modification of the political status quo in Europe. As a result we still know very little about the experiences that these marriages brought to their young protagonists, who were often uprooted in mid-adolescence from their family environment and transplanted into strange, even hostile, new surroundings in which everything from language to food, from style of dress to forms of prayer, was different. Transformed into queens or princesses consort, some girls had to watch as their husbands declared war on their fathers and brothers, while they themselves were distrusted or humiliated in their new country. This human dimension of dynastic marriage is precisely the perspective that the authors of this volume undertake.

Perhaps in the hopes of alleviating the effects of so drastic an uprooting, but also primarily to protect their dynastic interests, the fathers of these young princesses and noblewomen adopted the practice of newly married spouses moving to their new home accompanied by a sizeable retinue of ambassadors, soldiers, clerics, tutors, writers, musicians, pages, ladies-in-waiting and numerous servants. This entourage was supposed to help create living conditions as similar as possible to that of their homeland. Many of those in these entourages lived out their lives in their new country, where they aspired to maintain their original ways of life, transferring devotional practices and festive rituals from their home country, as well as rules of etiquette, style of dress, and culinary tastes. The creation of a household for the displaced consort attracted ambitious aristocrats who saw service to a ruler as a way to gain power and influence. Not surprisingly, these aristocrats often established lasting relationships with nobles in their adopted countries, forming connections which often survived the death of their sovereign. As Bartolomé Yun highlights in the epilogue of the book, a royal marriage was often accompanied by marriages between lower-ranking aristocrats from the two countries. So, for example, intermarriage between the royal families of Portugal and Castile led to the intermingling of the Portuguese and Castilian nobility during the sixteenth and seventeenth centuries, as Mafalda Soares da Cunha discusses in her chapter on the Soares de Alarcão family. In this manner, dynastic marriages became one of the principal channels for the circulation of people, correspondence, and diverse objects between European countries throughout the early modern period.

While the cultural circulation derived from these unions principally followed the direction of the displaced individuals, it also frequently occurred in the opposite direction. For example, during the period of prenuptial discussions, numerous gifts—particularly portraits of the future spouses—circulated between the two negotiating courts. This factor alone is the reason that to this day the Kunsthistoriches Museum in Vienna and the Prado Museum in Madrid have so many paintings of Spanish and Austrian princes and princesses respectively. After a marriage a princess corresponded regularly with her birth family, informing them of personal matters but also sometimes reporting political or military developments. Through their correspondence, women played a crucial role in transmitting news and knowledge from their spouses' territories to their original homes. For their part, some of the members of their entourage acted as active agents in the acquisition of paintings, books, maps, and luxury objects, later sent to friends and relatives in their country of origin. In some cases, princesses returned to their paternal homes after being widowed, bringing with them objects and cultural practices acquired during their years abroad.

Another of the focal points of this book is how marriage negotiations and agreements brought about intense cultural exchange; literature, theatre, painting, music, architecture—in short, no small part of a country's artistic tastes, as well as its scientific knowledge and techniques—came to be known and either assimilated or adapted in other cultures. This cultural flow produced a true cosmopolitan environment characterized by the integration of experience and knowledge coming from very diverse locations.

Royal families were not the only ones fostering this cosmopolitan culture. Numerous unions between princely and noble houses also contributed to the creation of an international culture. The consequence of these unions was that the elites of distinct European countries came to speak a similar cultural language, which in turn gradually trickled down the social ladder.

This phenomenon allows us to trace the genealogy of certain defining features of our own society, such as cultural hybridization or transcultural practices, directly related to the process of globalization. Sociologist Manuel Castells describes this process by saying that

> The space of flows is a technological system that allows the ruling elites of all societies to live and work in permanent contact, connecting across the entire world and travelling via global routes to those places where the power of

> decision is established, and [where they have] the enjoyment of the results of this power.[1]

We can apply Castells's theory to sixteenth-century Europe in order to understand how, in the words of Pierre Chaunu, a "planetary unlocking" allowed cultures previously fixed in place and isolated from one another to enter into a dynamic of intense exchange.[2]

Through the exploration of several specific case studies, this book aims to examine the concept and the practice of cultural transfer. The notion of "*transfert culturel*," first coined and applied by French and German historians such as Michel Espagne, Michael Werner or Serge Gruzinski, has since spread through the Anglo-American world in the context of the renovation of cultural history.[3] *Transfert culturel* is a particularly useful concept in analyzing the interactions between diverse cultures and societies in their historical context. Our objective in this volume is to analyze how through dynastic marriages, certain cultural practices were transferred to other places, and how these practices were received, interpreted, and spread in different cultural settings.

The authors of the chapters in this book seek to understand better how ideas and values were transferred and adapted to diverse local environments. To what degree were these values and knowledge used as instruments in the reinforcement of certain political objectives and social practices? What reactions did these provoke in the local culture in which they were received? In what way did the various systems of communication condition the information and knowledge that were transferred from one place to another?

On the whole, a shared vision of the world, as well as a shared system of values, aided the cultural circulation of artifacts, correspondence, and people in early modern Europe. Our book sheds light on the distinguishing features of these cultural transfers in the era in which they occurred, to capture their specificity and their otherness (their *Fremdartigkeit*), without simply reducing their practices and discourses to today's approaches.

Our analysis of cultural transfer is distinctive, insofar as in most of the cases we consider, the principal agents were women. As has been shown repeatedly in recent years, women's approach to culture was in some respects quite distinct from that of men. For example, women were particularly involved in devotional practices, everyday matters, and household culture. They also showed an increased receptivity to certain foreign customs and practices, such as recipes, style of dress,

---

1 Mayte Pascual and Manuel Castells, *En qué mundo vivimos: conversaciones con Manuel Castells* (Madrid: Alianza, 2006), 131–32.

2 Pierre Chaunu, *L'expansion européenne du XIIIe au XVe siècle* (Paris: Presses Universitaires de France, 1969), 176.

3 Michel Espagne and Michael Werner, eds., *Transferts. Les relations interculturelles dans l'espace franco-allemand (XVIIIe–XIXe siècles)* (Paris: Ed. Recherche sur les civilisations, 1988); Serge Gruzinski, *La pensée métisse* (Paris: Fayard, 1999).

and cosmetics, which at that time would have been seen primarily as part of the female universe. The chapters dedicated to Marie Mancini and Johanna Theresia Lamberg, by Leticia de Frutos and Laura Oliván Santaliestra respectively, highlight how women shaped cultural transfers in ways different from that of men, indicating that cultural transfer had definite gendered characteristics.

The contributions to this volume concentrate primarily on territories connected to the Spanish monarchy. This focus is easily justified because from the beginning of the sixteenth century, the Spanish Habsburgs more than any other European dynasty used marriage to realize their goals. To this end they contributed to the creation of a *modus operandi* later imitated by minor rulers and noble families within their zone of influence, in places such as Portugal, Castile, Austria, and Italy. Moreover, the Habsburg family governed a global empire, making its policies felt worldwide. Many of this book's conclusions are equally applicable to other European territories not directly governed by the Habsburgs or related families. So, for example, in discussing the case of Elisabetta Farnese, Maria de los Ángeles Pérez Samper demonstrates that at the beginning of the eighteenth century, the Bourbon family, who replaced the Habsburgs on the Spanish throne, had learned their predecessors' lessons well.

The book is divided into three sections. The first one focuses on three women directly related to the Spanish crown: the first two to the Habsburg family and the third to the Bourbons. The case of the Infanta Catalina Micaela of Spain, studied by Magdalena Sánchez, illustrates what was expected of the daughter of the most powerful monarch in Christendom, King Philip II of Spain. Hers appeared to be anything but an ascendant marriage, seeing as her chosen husband, Carlo Emanuele I of Savoy, was no more than the ruler of a small state in the north of Italy, although one strategically important to Spanish interests. Under these circumstances, everything was arranged before the wedding so that Catalina Micaela could use her superior rank to full effect. Contrary to the usual practice, Carlo Emanuele went to Spain to marry Catalina and accompany her on the journey to her new residence in Turin. Philip II made sure to send along meticulous instructions concerning the manner in which she and her attendants should conduct themselves in a manner befitting a princess and a royal household. In order to ensure that everything proceeded in accordance with these expectations, Philip II insisted on the presence in Turin of a number of his trusted servants.

The most conscientious of these was without doubt Cristóbal de Briceño, who as Catalina's *mayordomo* (steward), watched over her day and night to ensure she was treated as the daughter of a king and not merely as the wife of a duke. Briceño needed but a few days in the *infanta*'s service to conclude that standards at the Savoyard court were lower than those in Madrid. In his first letters written to Philip II's ministers, he complained about what he considered a "*gran indecencia*" (great indecency) during court festivities in Turin, precisely because the Spanish rules of etiquette were not being followed.

Briceño was outraged by the behavior of Carlo's courtiers and worked to change their customs: by October of 1586, when he reported the problems to Philip II's secretary, Mateo Vázquez, he could happily add that the duke had agreed to modify practices so as to conform to the "order that was brought from Spain." Although it appears that the duke was more than willing to accept these demands because they lent royal character to his court, not everyone reacted in the same way. Briceño reported that people in Turin complained about changes in the rules of etiquette that restricted access to the court and made it especially difficult for the public to observe women or court festivities. While Briceño saw these changes as positive, the Savoyards failed to appreciate it.

The *mayordomo*'s chief concern, however, was Catalina's conduct. If he is to be believed, even the *infanta* was disregarding Spanish etiquette at the court in Turin. Briceño, who started out criticizing Carlo's courtiers for what he considered an inappropriate degree of contact, ended up directing his invective at Catalina herself for failing to conform to Spanish rules of etiquette, noting on at least one occasion that she had become lax: "she grows careless." With time Catalina did conform to Spanish etiquette but she also adapted quickly to life with the duke. Such cultural adaptation was essential for a princess and Catalina performed this task well. The example of Catalina Micaela suggests that despite the rigid rules in which they had been educated, the Spanish *infantas* sent to other countries displayed a remarkable capacity for adaptation to their new environment, perhaps because their future was now tied to that of their spouse, their offspring, and their new land. A move to a different country could thus at times be rather liberating for a young princess.

The same conclusion can also be drawn in part from Mark de Vitis's study of Catalina Micaela's great-niece, María Teresa of Austria, daughter of Philip IV, King of Spain. María Teresa's marriage to Louis XIV sealed the 1659 Treaty of the Pyrenees between Spain and France, and almost immediately French propagandists adapted her image for political purposes. As Mark de Vitis shows, María Teresa symbolized both the peace between the Habsburgs and the Bourbons as well as the power of the Bourbons in France. While she herself might not have intervened directly in political decision making, she still played a crucial role in the use of symbolism and imagery to build the power of the Bourbon monarchy. De Vitis demonstrates how early descriptions of María Teresa, when she first entered France, emphasized the Spanish aspects of her attire, such as the farthingale, but also that she gradually began to incorporate French elements. One telling description noted that while she wore a Spanish dress, her hair was "half coiffed" in the French style. In her body and attire, she blended Habsburg and Bourbon culture and symbolically unified two countries which had previously been at war.

De Vitis also examines royal entries into key cities, especially in areas that had been in revolt against Bourbon dominance during the Fronde (1548–53) and, in some cases, had cooperated with the Spanish Habsburgs. By entering with and displaying his Spanish bride, Louis XIV was demonstrating his victory over the rebels and over Spain. The imagery used in the entries also intermingled Habsburg and Bourbon symbols to emphasize unification and peace. For example, on the triumphal arch of Faubourg Saint-Antoine, the queen was shown holding an olive branch in order to highlight the role she played in cementing the peace between the two royal houses.

The portraits of the queen done by the Beaubrun cousins also served to point out how in her person, María Teresa combined Spanish and French culture. De Vitis argues that the Bourbons chose the Beaubruns to paint official portraits of the queen precisely because they had long been patronized by the Bourbon family and had done many portraits of the nobles at the Bourbon court. It was important for María Teresa to be incorporated into this visual tradition. However, the Beaubruns broke with French tradition and painted the queen in a less idealized fashion, emphasizing her distinctive facial features, such as the protruding "Habsburg" jaw. Thus the portraits—painted by artists who had executed portraits of several generations of nobles at the French court—recognized and accentuated her Spanish and Habsburg features while employing settings and poses used frequently in French portraits. The portraits of the queen served to blend Spanish and French artistic traditions and emphasize how, in her person, María Teresa brought together the two countries. Ultimately then, cultural symbols could have significant political power, and a woman's display of these cultural signifiers could be of great importance to the building of a monarch's and a dynasty's power.

Surely Elisabetta Farnese, Princess of Parma and Queen of Spain from 1717 thanks to her marriage to Philip V, also blended different cultural traditions. Her process of adaptation was easier than, or at least different from, that of her predecessors on the Spanish throne. After all, her husband, a Bourbon prince and grandson of Louis XIV, born and educated in Versailles, was nearly as foreign to his kingdom as Elisabetta herself.

Philip V's accession to the Spanish throne in 1700, following the death of the last Habsburg king of Spain, Charles II, who died without a direct heir, heralded the rapid and intense transformation of the Crown and of government, culture, and arts, as well as the gradual transformation of the country's society and customs. French culture became dominant throughout Europe, and Versailles the model for European courts, nowhere more so than at the Spanish court. If Philip V was a symbol of the French in Spain, Elisabetta would represent Italian culture. Almost surreptitiously, both monarchs competed to impose the cultural tastes of their respective countries, and it could well be argued that in the end, Elisabetta triumphed.

The setting of Elisabetta's formative years was a small, circumscribed world filled with natural and artistic beauty. Her earliest scenes and landscapes were the Farnese duchies of Parma and Piacenza: the great Palazzo della Pilotta and the beautiful summer home of Colorno. After her arrival in Spain, she drew major Italian artists to the Spanish court: the architects Filippo Juvarra and Giovanni Battista Sachetti, the painters Andrea Procaccini and Francesco Pavona, the scenographer Giuseppe Bibbiena, the poet Ottavio Baiardi, and musicians and singers such as Paolo Antonio Foresi, Domenico Scarlatti, and Carlo Broschi, the famous castrato better known as Farinelli. One of the most visible results of the imposition of Italian fashions was the palace of La Granja de San Ildefonso, situated in the Guadarrama mountains to the north of Madrid, a highly personal project, modeled closely after the palace at Colorno. However, her great building project was undoubtedly the new royal palace in Madrid, replacing the Real Alcázar of the Habsburg kings, which had gone up in flames on Christmas Eve in 1734. As a Bourbon, Philip always remembered the splendor of Versailles and sought to duplicate many of its features, but Elisabetta, wishing to remain true to her Italian roots, successfully pushed for Italian architects. The new palace would be the heir to two grand traditions: the French style exemplified by Louis XIV's Versailles and Bernini's Louvre in Paris, and the Italian style seen in many palaces in Rome, Venice, Parma, and, above all, Turin. In some respects, the new palace in Madrid also incorporated certain architectural aspects of Spanish Habsburg structures such as the Real Alcázar and the Escorial. Nevertheless, even though French and Spanish features were visible in the Palacio Real de Madrid, Italian traditions predominated thanks to Elisabetta's influence.

While living and ruling in Spain, and without ever forgetting Italian cultural traditions or disregarding the French styles so dear to her husband, Elisabetta also dedicated herself to discovering Spanish art forms, paying special attention to painting, without doubt the art *par excellence* in Spain.[4] In these and many other ways explored by María de los Ángeles Pérez Samper in her chapter, Elisabetta Farnese exercised considerable cultural influence in Spain, but also in other parts of Europe, such as to Naples and Sicily where her son Charles ruled. She successfully blended the cultural traditions of Spain, Italy, and France.

The second part of the book explores three cases in which dynastic marriages demanded the relocation of men—a rare occurrence in early modern Europe. Bethany Aram examines the experience of Philip of Burgundy, son of Emperor Maximilian I; Anna Santamaría López considers that of Philip II of Spain, Maximilian's great-grandson; and Mafalda Soares da Cunha that of the Spanish nobleman Juan Suárez de Alarcón whose name became João Soares de Alarcão after moving to Portugal as a part of the retinue of the infanta María of Aragon. All three of these cases raise the issue of gender and cultural adaptation by considering whether it was particularly problematic for men to adapt to cultural and political conditions that made them subordinate to their spouse.

At the end of the fifteenth century, Emperor Maximilian I's skillful wielding of marriage as a political strategy was matched by Ferdinand of Aragon and Isabel of Castile, better known as the Catholic Monarchs. Not surprisingly, when these

[4] José Miguel Morán Turina, *El arte en la corte de Felipe V* (Madrid: Fundación Caja Madrid, 2002); Jonathan Brown, *Kings and Connoisseurs: Collecting Art in Seventeenth-Century Europe* (Princeton, NJ: Princeton University Press, 1995).

parties sat down to negotiate, the result was not one but two unions at a single stroke: on the one hand, that of Juana of Castile and Philip of Burgundy, also known as Juana la Loca and Philip the Handsome, and on the other that of Juan, Prince of Asturias and heir to the throne of Castile, and Margaret of Austria.

As Bethany Aram demonstrates in her study of Juana and Philip, the nuptial agreement included a visit by each of the new spouses to the other's country. In the first instance, Juana was the one to make the journey because when they married in 1496, she ranked lower than Philip; unlike her spouse, she was second-born and not in the immediate line of succession to her parents' thrones. Cultural differences between Castile and the Low Countries caused problems for Juana during her trip, but these problems would not be as serious as those that characterized the subsequent trip of her spouse, Philip, to Castile. Juana's case suggests that perhaps women adapted better than men to cultural differences.

When it was Philip's turn to travel in 1502, more critical issues surfaced. One of his most illustrious Burgundian subjects, Desiderius Erasmus, expressing his prejudices about the Spanish kingdoms, worried that the trip to Spain would make Philip more provincial and even tyrannical. In turn prominent Castilians such as Gutierre Gómez de Fuensalida voiced their concerns that Philip would bring undesirable practices to their territories, noting that Burgundian practices were "as different from Castilian customs as good is from evil." Cultural tension and hostility certainly characterized Philip's trip through Castile and Aragon. The many festivities which accompanied the diverse stages of the itinerary through the principal cities of Castile, with their banquets, dances, and bullfights, soon became a competition to see who was more capable of impressing or astonishing the other.

All indications are that, at least at the outset, Philip made a genuine effort to adapt to Castilian customs, and even showed signs of enjoying them, appearing publicly "gorgeously dressed in Castilian style." Things began to change dramatically during the stay in Toledo, where bitter disputes occurred between the members of the two retinues. The mysterious death of various members of Philip's retinue, among them his tutor, the Bishop of Besançon, gave rise to suspicions that they may have been poisoned.

When in 1506 Philip once again returned to the Iberian Peninsula, the political circumstances had changed dramatically: his wife had unexpectedly become Queen of Castile following the death of her mother and the premature loss of her elder siblings Juan and Isabel. Indeed, the prince arrived with the lesson well learned regarding the correct way in which to deal with his former hosts—now his subjects—but now had a new obstacle to overcome: the suspicions concerning his attempts to impose his own authority over Juana's. His sudden death on September 25 of that same year prevented the escalation of hostilities. He never had the chance to demonstrate whether, as his adversaries supposed, he intended to impose Flemish customs and traditions in Castile. Years later, however, his experience, was of great use to his son Charles (the future emperor Charles V) on inheriting his mother's crowns of Castile and Aragon. Just as the journey of 1502 provided training for that of 1506, Philip I's entourage in 1506 laid the political and cultural groundwork for Charles V's succession in 1518. The servants who returned to Flanders after Philip's death had gained experience in Spain; they could put this experience to good use in the service of Charles V. Their story suggests how those who served the Habsburgs began to acquire and develop cultural habits which made them extremely valuable to a dynasty that had courts throughout Europe. These habits were at the center of the cosmopolitan culture shared by aristocrats at Habsburg courts.

Philip of Burgundy's grandson, Philip II, also traveled to a distant land to be the consort of a foreign queen. When in 1553 the English crown passed to Mary Tudor, daughter of Henry VIII and Catherine of Aragon, Emperor Charles V decided the moment had arrived to realize his aspirations to restore Catholicism to the island and to expand his family's sphere of influence. To this end, he immediately proposed the marriage of his niece Mary to his son Philip, a young widower since the death of his first wife, Maria Manoela of Portugal. It mattered little that she was 11 years his senior, and at an age where her hopes of procreation had diminished considerably. Mary's obsession with bearing an heir who would be educated in Catholicism ended up overcoming her initial reluctance to marry. Philip's feelings were an entirely different matter.

In a reversal of roles, the English queen personally controlled the negotiation of the wedding agreement while her future spouse was marginalized completely, despite being the male and the direct heir to the immense dominions of his father. Seemingly hurt and frustrated at his father's failure to consult him about the marriage agreement, his only response to Charles's proposition was: "If you wish to arrange a marriage for me, know that I am an obedient son who has no other wish than yours." Accepting his father's wishes and marrying Mary Tudor did not mean that Philip had to welcome his new wife warmly. In fact, the coldness he displayed towards her, referring to her sometimes in private as "aunt," did not go unnoticed by anyone. Neither did his resentment at having been obliged to accept nuptial clauses that he considered offensive, both to his rank and to his dignity as a man. This resentment is clearly evident in a remark he made to one of his closest companions as they travelled to England. Comparing his suffering to that of Jesus Christ in the garden of Gethsemane, Philip commented that "Great faith is necessary to drink from this chalice" ("*Mucho Dios es menester para tragar este cáliz*"). The agreement was signed in his name by the count of Egmont. Who knows whether Philip remembered this when, years later, he ordered the count's head cut off.

As Anna Santamaría López highlights in her chapter, the first encounter between the new spouses was indicative of the difficulties they would have communicating with each other: because Philip did not speak a word of English, he addressed Mary in Spanish, a language that she was able to understand but not to speak. She responded in French, a tongue which Philip understood, but again could not speak. They lived together for only one and a half years of their four-year marriage, and even then only intermittently. The confirmation of Mary's inability to conceive only made matters worse. Rumors began to circulate at court that Philip would all too often find his way to the bedrooms of Mary's ladies-in-waiting rather than to that of his spouse. In September of 1555, he decided, quite without warning, to abandon England.

His discomfort was not only limited to linguistic and biological problems. His difficulties in adapting to a cultural environment that was entirely alien to him only made matters worse. In truth, however, nobody could accuse him of not trying. From the outset, he ordered his courtiers to dress according to English tastes, and to replace the wine on their tables with the beer so unattractive to Spanish palates. He himself made a noteworthy effort to conform to English practices: in the nuptial ceremony he tolerated the humiliation of renouncing the outfit of purple velvet he had brought from Spain for another in white and gold, even though these colors were reserved for queen consorts. He strove to learn the history of England and the peculiarities of its system of government. The library at the Escorial to this day holds the majority of the manuscripts and prints that he acquired during these months. He abandoned the popular Spanish "game of lances" (*juego de cañas*) and took part whenever required in jousts and tournaments in the English style. Soon, however, it became apparent that Philip alone could not shoulder the entire task: the disputes between the Spanish nobles who accompanied him and the English courtiers began to take on an alarming tone. "Every day in the palace there are knife fights between English and Spaniards," declared one eyewitness.

In her work, Anna Santamaría López openly questions the scholarly opinion that cultural and religious incompatibility between Castile and England led to these confrontations. In fact, the two kingdoms had a long history of mutual collaboration, which had led to many matrimonial links between their ruling houses. Philip's own great-aunt, Catherine of Aragon (Mary Tudor's mother), had been a very popular queen until her husband's split with Rome had left her in an untenable position. Far from having negative prejudices towards his new country, Philip, along with the majority of his retinue, had an idealized vision of England nourished by the books of knights and chivalry which they so admired: it was the land of the intrepid literary hero, *Amadís de Gaula*. They admired the beauty of its countryside, the exuberance of its nature, and the sublime charms of the young ladies of its court.

What, then, of the English attitude toward Philip and his retinue? The religious explanation for the rejection of the Spaniards scarcely withstands detailed scrutiny, because as historians have shown, the England which Philip knew continued to be a culturally Catholic country despite Henry VIII's break with Rome. Furthermore, Philip intervened several times to mitigate his wife's persecution of Protestants. The time had yet to arrive when the Black Legend, which presented him as the Catholic ogre, would take root among English Protestants.

There are many indications that English opposition to Mary's marriage with Philip was not cultural but rather political in nature. Many people in England had trouble accepting a woman on the throne, especially because her chosen spouse was a Habsburg. They feared that Mary, who as a woman was supposedly weak in nature, would have trouble governing England and would hand over authority to her husband, who was a powerful Habsburg prince. In this way England would essentially be governed by a foreign monarch. In order to assuage these fears, Mary and her advisers at first tried to emphasize her sovereignty by relegating Philip to a secondary role in public, which made it difficult for him to gain the respect of his new subjects. Only after they perceived that this strategy was counter-productive did they begin to incorporate Philip's image alongside that of the queen in paintings and on coins. The struggle to find a workable balance in the symbolic presentation of Mary's and Philip's political roles also reflected the difficulties these two had in their marriage. The experience of Philip in England, like that of Philip the Handsome, confirms that displacing men could be even more complicated than displacing women.

The chapter which closes the second part of the book, written by Mafalda Soares da Cunha, is dedicated to João Soares de Alarcão and his family, the Soares de Alarcão or Suárez de Alarcón. Were they Portuguese or Spanish? Their experience clearly illustrates the manner in which the intensity of the dynastic marriages between the two kingdoms could result in the creation of an international nobility, for whom political borders lost their meaning.

From 1490 and continuing throughout the first half of the sixteenth century, five Spanish princesses crossed the border to marry members of the Portuguese royal family: Isabel and María of Aragon (both daughters of the Catholic Monarchs); Leonor and Catalina of Austria (granddaughters of Ferdinand and Isabel and sisters of Charles V); and finally, Juana of Austria (daughter of Charles V and sister of Philip II). The flow in the opposite direction was by no means so pronounced. Only two Portuguese princesses made their way to the Spanish court: Isabella of Portugal, daughter of Manoel I, who married Charles V, and María Manuela, daughter of João III, to wed Prince Philip (later Philip II of Spain). However, the number evens out if we take into account that Leonor of Austria returned to Spain in 1523 and Juana de Austria in 1554 after the death of her young husband. Intermarriage between the Portuguese and the Castilian lines had in fact begun during the fifteenth century, when there were two more dynastic marriages: Joana of Portugal, sister of Alfonso V, who became queen consort to Henry IV of Castile in 1455, and Princess Juana of Castile (known as Juana la Beltraneja) who arrived in Portugal in 1475 to become queen consort to the aging Alfonso V. What distinguishes Portugal and Spain in this process is the precocity and frequency of these movements, and the fact that royal intermarriage eventually led to Portugal's integration into the Spanish kingdom in 1580.

The presence of Spanish queens in Portugal and Portuguese queens in Castile had great repercussion in the royal households and in turn brought great potential for aristocrats to intermarry and form new alliances. João Soares de Alarcão exemplifies well how aristocrats took advantage of these new alliances. Although born in Castile, as a young boy Juan de Alarcón moved to Portugal in 1500 when his recently widowed mother, doña Elvira de Mendoza, was named an attendant to María, wife of King Manoel. Unlike the other women in the queen's retinue, Elvira decided to stay in Portugal after the death of Queen María in 1517. Elvira continued to enjoy royal favor, serving first as *aya* (governess) to the princesses Isabel and Beatríz and afterwards as lady in the household of the new queen (who was also Spanish), Leonor de Austria. Nevertheless, after the death of King Manoel and Leonor's move to France to wed Francis I, Elvira decided to return to Castile. Her son, Juan, who by then had adopted the Portuguese version of his name, João de Alarcão, decided to stay in the country where he had been raised and educated. A strong incentive was his marriage in 1515 to Margarida Soares de Melo, daughter of one of the Portuguese king's closest advisers. This marriage was a crucial step in João rapid social advancement. Nevertheless, João never forgot his Castilian roots nor did he disregard his interests in his ancestral lands, and neither did his descendants who in subsequent generations became a transnational family.

The case of the Soares de Alarcão family illustrates how important the queen and her household were for aiding in the assimilation of nobles into a new culture and environment, and for fostering marriages between Portuguese and Castilian nobles. The Soares de Alarcão's story also demonstrates how the queen controlled a significant patronage network and how service in the queen's household could be a crucial step toward improving the fortunes of a noble family. By serving the queens well, the Soares de Alarcãos received household offices for other family members. In turn court service helped the family negotiate marriages for their sons and daughters with the offspring of influential Portuguese families. The story of the Soares de Alarcão also suggests that on the whole, Portuguese courtiers were receptive to intermarriage and to forging ties with Castilian aristocrats.

Whereas the first two parts of the book focus on royal men and women, and on one aristocratic man and his family, the third section considers how the example of royalty influenced the nobility. Of course, nobles enjoyed much less freedom than monarchs to determine their matrimonial strategies. Furthermore, their marriages often formed part of the crown's political strategy.

This occurred in a most obvious form with the marriage of Eleonora of Toledo to Cosimo I de' Medici, devised as part of the Italian policies of Emperor Charles V. After conquering Florence in 1530, Charles had restored to power a member of the Medici family, Alessandro, to whom he granted the title of duke. To ensure that the new ruler remained loyal to imperial interests, Charles also offered him his daughter Margaret in marriage. The marriage did not last long, as Alessandro was assassinated a few months after the wedding took place. His successor, his cousin Cosimo, tried to inherit not only his ducal title but also his widow. The Farnese Pope Paul III, however, arranged for Margaret to be given to a member of his own family, Ottavio. Cosimo had to agree to what *a priori* seemed a lesser marriage: the daughter of don Pedro de Toledo, Spanish Viceroy of Naples and the emperor's principal agent in Italy. Although Charles V intended for the union to serve as a means to control Cosimo through Eleonora's father, and thus to guarantee Cosimo's loyalty to the interests of the empire, the marriage proved very advantageous for the duke. Joan-Lluís Palos examines Eleonora's role in the consolidation of the Medicis' power and while historians still debate her influence, the evidence suggests that her contributions were decisive. She journeyed to Florence in 1539 surrounded by Spaniards, many of them members of her own family, and in the following years became one of the most efficient agents for the integration of Castilian, Neapolitan, and Florentine cultures, which until then had been quite distinct.

The day that she made her solemn entrance into the city, the Florentines were struck by Eleonora's beauty, but also by other details, such as her style of dress. In the following months, they had occasion to witness the extent to which Eleonora behaved in a very different way from Florentine women, including those of high society: her haughty character, her love of luxury, her religious practices, her aesthetic tastes, and her independent opinions soon became the object of widespread debate. Some admired her while others detested her. One of the latter went so far as to call her a "Spanish barbarian, enemy of her husband's homeland." To what extent was this true? Certainly, Eleonora had been born in Castile and belonged to one of the most reputed Castilian noble lines. As a young girl, however, she had moved to Naples, where she was educated by a devout Jewish woman with whom Eleonora maintained a close relationship for the rest of her life. Furthermore, in Naples she had learned the cultural habits of high-ranking women of southern Italy, who followed different practices from those in other parts of the Italian peninsula. In a manner comparable to that of Elisabetta Farnese, Eleonora experienced three different cultural traditions: the Castilian, the Neapolitan, and the Florentine. While Florentines might have seen Eleonora as "Spanish," she did not necessarily identify herself with one specific place or nationality. Her identity was far more complex, illustrating precisely how dynastic marriages could contribute to the formation of a cosmopolitan culture.

Another example of a woman with a complex cultural identity was Marie Mancini, studied in this volume by Leticia de Frutos. To Marie's misfortune, her life would cross with that of María Teresa of Austria (the subject of Mark de Vitis's chapter) at the most inopportune moment. Marie had been born in Rome in 1639. Her mother was the sister of the powerful Prime Minister of France, Cardinal Mazarin, as attuned to the monarch's concerns as to those of his own family. Initially destined for the religious life, while still a young girl Marie exchanged the strict lifestyle of the Benedictine nunnery of Campo Marzio in Rome for the much more relaxed Convent of the Visitation in Paris. There she was carefully educated in a manner designed more towards introducing her to the world than distancing her from it. In addition to the French language, she acquired the basic skills required to move with confidence among high society. She was, without doubt, an outstanding student, and soon came to the attention of the young King Louis XIV, who apparently fell head over heels in love with her.

This, though, was not an era of marrying for love. Thus, when the marriage of Louis XIV with the Spanish infanta María Teresa was arranged in 1659, Marie was considered a nuisance in Paris. Her uncle, Cardinal Mazarin, arranged for her to return to Rome to marry Lorenzo Onofrio Colonna, the firstborn of one of the most prestigious Roman families, one that had a long history of collaboration with the Spanish. She soon began to feel suffocated in her new city, where women served merely as ornaments at the pontifical court. Only her trips to Venice, to celebrate Carnival and attend the opera, afforded her a measure of relief. Her French manner of dressing, evident in her décolletage and uncovered shoulders, provoked immediate condemnation in the city of the popes. Yet Marie had many admirers, with whom she organized meetings reminiscent of those of the "blue room" of Madame de Rambouillet's Parisian *hôtel*, where she had learned so much about the world. With scarcely time to catch her breath, she gave birth to three sons: Filippo, Marcantonio, and Carlo. Soon afterwards, following the example of her sister Hortensia, she decided to leave her husband, whose infidelities were notorious throughout the city. Their matrimonial disagreements had become a matter of state, and her situation in Rome had become unbearable.

In 1672 she abandoned everything, husband and children, and left the city. "All these reasons together … obliged me to accelerate the execution of the intention I had formed to retire to France, the country of my education," she wrote years later to justify her decision. She attempted to return to Paris, but the king forbade it. She moved from one French city to another, staying in one convent after another but still closely watched by her husband, who refused to grant her full liberty. Eventually, both partners reached an agreement: Marie would move to Madrid to live under the surveillance of her husband's brother-in-law, Paolo Spinola Doria.

After numerous unforeseen incidents, she took up residence in a modest apartment alongside the convent of Santo Domingo el Real in Madrid, close to the royal palace. She still received occasional visitors, although far fewer than she would have liked. Among them was the imperial ambassador, the count of Harrach. She did what she could to adapt to the customs of the country, dressing in the Spanish style (*a la española*), with the heavy farthingale (*guardainfante*) that she so despised. But she deeply missed certain objects that she was unable to find in Madrid, especially those related to her personal care, hygiene and beauty, such as Arras powders or *spermaceti* (whale oil) for her hair. She wrote incessantly to her Italian friends, requesting object after object: gloves, fans, and crowns as gifts to the ladies who visited her, and relics for the nuns who gave her lodging. The most valuable gifts she reserved for the queen, such as the agate medal sent by her husband and which Marie found the most precious of all. She requested money to buy chocolate, which she hoped to lavish upon the visitors she received during Lent. These gifts were her primary medium of interaction with her environment. To the ladies, she gave first and foremost the Neapolitan fans so highly prized at the time. To her sons she sent tobacco cases and decorative boxes insisting that Pippo, her firstborn whom she adored, should choose first. In these ways, she acted as an agent for the transfer of objects among several European courts.

One of Marie's most appreciated visitors during her reclusion was the imperial ambassador to Madrid, the count of Harrach, with whom she had many interests in common. The count's wife, Johanna Theresia Lamberg, the focus of Laura Oliván Santaliestra's chapter, like Marie, loved the most refined objects: furniture, paintings, clothing, portable escritoires from America, and books. Yet what Johanna Theresia truly loved were culinary recipes (especially if they had medicinal effects) and perfumes. There was, however, a substantial difference between the two women: while Marie always expressed a certain disdain for the lack of refinement at the Spanish court, Johanna Theresia became of the most passionate admirers and promoters of Spanish court culture.

Johanna Theresia first arrived in Madrid in 1654 at the age of 14, when her father, Maximilian Lamberg, was named ambassador of Emperor Ferdinand III to the King of Spain, Philip IV. She was soon named lady-in-waiting to her compatriot, Queen Mariana of Austria, only five years her senior, with whom she struck up a friendship which was to last throughout their lives. In fact, Queen Mariana played a crucial role in arranging the marriage of Johanna to Ferdinand, Count of Harrach, when he was serving as an imperial ambassador to Madrid. Eight months pregnant, Mariana attended the union of the two Austrian nobles in the palace's chapel, and the newlyweds returned to Vienna after celebrating the wedding.

In the imperial capital Johanna discovered a climate enthusiastically receptive to Spanish objects and culture. Not in vain were the negotiations for the marriage of the new emperor, Leopold I, to the infanta Margarita, the daughter of Philip IV whom Diego Velázquez would immortalize in *Las Meninas*. Against this backdrop Johanna acted as a true Spanish cultural ambassador in Vienna, introducing everything from culinary habits to style of dress. When, in 1666, the infanta Margarita arrived at the imperial court in Vienna, Johanna became her principal protector, although not for long as Margarita died in 1673. That same year, the count of Harrach was named ambassador to Madrid and Johanna once again set off for the capital of Spain, where she remained for three years.

Having returned to Vienna, Johanna Theresia demonstrated that her inclinations towards Spanish tastes were not due only to political circumstance. Although the imperial court was now much more receptive to French fashion, she remained committed to promoting and disseminating Spanish culture to the end of her days. Only a few days before her death on February 2, 1716, at 77 years of age, Johanna ordered various medicines from the *Apotheke zum Weissen Engel*, the famous pharmacy in Vienna. Among these were essence of ambergris, the biliary secretion of the sperm whale, found floating in exotic seas and used to make medicinal perfumes. Together with clay and chocolate, ambergris was one of the products that the countess of Harrach helped introduce into the Viennese court. Throughout her life, she continued to enjoy a restorative chocolate drink in the mornings, and to entertain her afternoon guests with a chocolate beverage that she herself prepared, following various recipes she had compiled during her stays in Madrid. Johanna Theresia also collected *búcaros*, small vases of lightly baked clay which held perfumed waters or chocolate and which, once the contents had been drunk, could be eaten piece by piece, a custom widely practiced by the court ladies of Spain. Chocolate, clay, and ambergris, whose flavors and perfumes were thought to ennoble the bodies of courtiers, appeared as ingredients among the pages of two recipe manuscripts, written in Spanish and preserved by the countess of Harrach, perhaps in one of the escritoires from America that she brought from Madrid. She spent her life traveling between Vienna and Madrid, serving as an important cultural mediator between the two courts.

All the contributions to this book raise interesting questions about the construction of political and regional identity in the early modern period. The Soares de Alarcãos continuously crossed the lines literally and figuratively between Castile and Portugal, identifying perhaps more with the monarchs they served than with a specific country. In a similar fashion, the cases discussed by Joan-Lluís Palos or Bethany Aram indicate that while observers and critics might be quick to label specific dress or practice as "Spanish" or "Burgundian" or "Florentine," those people being observed did not always identify themselves along these lines. Instead they might more readily see themselves as members of a dynasty or a family, adopting cultural practices from several different regions and in some cases adapting these practices to fit a new cultural setting. The ability of a ruler, a queen, or a noble family to blend cultural traditions could have clear political advantages.

Historians have argued that during the early modern period, the internationalization of the nobility increased the geographic scale of aristocrats' circuits of cultural consumption. Our book adds to this scholarly debate by concentrating primarily on women as agents of cultural transfer. The research presented here indicates that as they traveled to take up residence in new countries, women sought to maintain their cultural identity and attempted to carve out an autonomous space for themselves. They were avid consumers and collectors, engaging fully in the culture of consumption which characterized European courts. Many of these women exercised great power and influence at their new courts or in their new country, serving as cultural mediators and even exercising political influence. They often maintained close links to their natal families, promoted cultural and political circulation between both countries, sometimes allying with other women who found themselves in the same situation.

Despite their efforts to adapt to their new country and to forge cultural links between their natal and their adopted lands (or, perhaps, precisely because of this), many of these women were considered foreigners at their husband's court and were made to endure severe criticism and, on occasion, active opposition. This was the price they had to pay to maintain their composite identities.

The analyses in this volume also raise further questions and present avenues for future research. For example, what conditions were required to allow these women to develop their own cultural identities, preserving specific elements from their original upbringing? To what degree did a woman's social status, relative to that of her husband, determine her ability to act as a cultural agent? Did specifically feminine channels of cultural mediation exist? To what extent were these women able to communicate with each other to share their experiences? Were some cultural forms and manifestations more easily exported than others? In short, how did women contribute to the construction of this cosmopolitan European elite culture of the early modern period, so frequently mentioned in this book?

When it comes to answering these and other questions, it would be advisable to avoid the same error which has so often been made in the study of men, namely that of considering the women in isolation, separate from the initiatives of their husbands. We should not forget that what was expected of these women was, above all else, that they make use of their skills and judgment to assist the latter in completing their various objectives. We should therefore ask ourselves about women's power to control their own activity, and the extent to which this was conditional upon the interests of their husbands. How may we distinguish the cultural initiatives of the women and the artworks created for their personal use from those which reflect their spouses' cultural agenda? The next step will be, as Bartolomé Yun Casalilla suggests in the epilogue, to move from the consideration of specific cases to broader conceptualization and firmer conclusions. This book will hopefully stimulate further research on cultural transfer, the circulation of goods, the creation of a cosmopolitan culture in the early modern world, and particularly women's role in all of these activities.

A Note on Names

We have maintained the form of a person's name customary in his or her country of origin. So, for example, we refer to the daughter of Philip IV of Spain as María Teresa and not as Marie-Thérèse, as she was known in France. The only exceptions are when the person's name is well recognized in English; so, for example, we have used Philip II, Charles V, Ignatius of Loyola and not Felipe II, Carlos V, Ignacio de Loyola.

Bibliography

Brown, Jonathan. *Kings and Connoisseurs: Collecting Art in Seventeenth-Century Europe*. Princeton, NJ: Princeton University Press, 1995.

Chaunu, Pierre. *L'expansion européenne du XIIIe au XVe siècle*. Paris: Presses Universitaires de France, 1969.

Espagne, Michel, and Michael Werner, eds. *Transferts. Les relations interculturelles dans l'espace franco-allemand (XVIIIe–XIXe siècles)*. Paris: Ed. Recherche sur les civilisations, 1988.

Gruzinski, Serge. *La pensée métisse*. Paris: Fayard, 1999.

Morán Turina, José Miguel. *El arte en la corte de Felipe V*. Madrid: Fundación Caja Madrid, 2002.

Pascual, Mayte, and Manuel Castells. *En qué mundo vivimos: conversaciones con Manuel Castells*. Madrid: Alianza, 2006.

PART I
Princesses across Borders

CATALINA MICAELA (1567–97),
DUCHESS OF SAVOY

MARÍA TERESA (1638–83),
QUEEN OF FRANCE

ELISABETTA FARNESE (1692–1766),
QUEEN OF SPAIN

Chapter 1
"She Grows Careless": The *Infanta* Catalina and Spanish Etiquette at the Court of Savoy*

Magdalena S. Sánchez

When the *infanta* Catalina Micaela (1567–97), younger daughter of Philip II of Spain, married Carlo Emanuele I, Duke of Savoy, in 1585, she went to Turin and never returned to Spain. (See Figure 1.1 for her portrait and Figure 1.2 for their joint portraits executed in or soon after 1585.) How did she adjust to the court in Turin, and what does her case tell us about the cultural exchange that occurred through dynastic marriages? Despite cultural differences between a royal Spanish court and a ducal Savoyard court, Catalina quickly grew accustomed to life in Turin and to married life with Carlo. No doubt their common aspirations and their strong mutual affection helped Catalina adapt culturally to a new court. Nevertheless, her arrival at the court in Turin brought an initial clash between a rigid Spanish court etiquette and a much less formal etiquette at the Savoyard court. In the end, Spanish etiquette won out in Catalina's household in Turin, but not without challenges.

The Etiquette Watchdog: Cristóbal de Briceño

My main source for documenting the conflicts over court etiquette is the correspondence of one of Catalina's Spanish stewards (*mayordomos*), Cristóbal de Briceño, with Juan de Zúñiga (1536–86), *mayordomo mayor* (chief steward) of Philip II's children, councilor of state, and a principal advisor to Philip II.[1]

* I would like to thank Gettysburg College and especially the Faculty Development Committee for awarding me a Research and Professional Development grant as well as a Mellon grant to fund the research for this contribution. This chapter forms part of the research project Poder y Representaciones en la Edad Moderna: la Monarquía Hispánica como campo cultural (1500–1800) (HAR12-39516-C02-01), financed by the Spanish government.

[1] I learned of Briceño's letters through Mercedes Fórmica's *La infanta Catalina Micaela en la corte alegre de Turín* (Madrid: Fundación Universitaria Española, 1976). Fórmica found the Briceño letters in the Bibliothèque Publique et Universitaire in Geneva, and she discussed them in her short, fascinating book. For this chapter, I have consulted the 13 Briceño letters in Geneva as well as four others found in the Instituto

Figure 1.1 Juan Pantoja de la Cruz (attributed), The *Infanta* Catalina, ca. 1585, oil on canvas, 112 × 98 cm. Museo Nacional del Prado, Madrid.

Figure 1.2 Johan Wierix, Portrait of Catalina Micaela and her husband, Carlo Emanuele I, Duke of Savoy, ca. 1585, pen and brown ink on vellum, 61 × 46 cm and 61 × 48 cm respectively (on same sheet of vellum). Fondation Custodia, Frits Lugt Collection, Paris. Inv. 6097A and 6097B.

From December 1585 until July 1586, Briceño wrote Zúñiga once or twice a month informing him of difficulties at Catalina and Carlo's court. Zúñiga had been instrumental in preparing Catalina's household for Turin and in seeing to the written version of the *etiquetas* which she took with her. In addition to writing to Zúñiga, Briceño also wrote letters defending his actions and voicing his complaints to Mateo Vázquez, Philip II's secretary. His first two letters to Vázquez are from August and September 1585, and his two other surviving letters are from May and October 1586. Collectively, then, Briceño's letters to Zúñiga and Vázquez cover roughly Catalina's first year at the court in Turin.[2]

Briceño was a *comendador* (knight commander) in the Knights of Saint John and had served in the Spanish embassy in Rome from 1580 to 1585.[3] In 1585 he had been named *caballerizo* (groom) for Prince Philip (later Philip III), but he did not take up that court office; instead he was appointed *mayordomo* to the *infanta*.[4] As such, he was only one of several *mayordomos* in Catalina's household, but as a Spaniard he clearly saw himself as chiefly responsible for implementing Spanish etiquette within Catalina's household—and for establishing greater order, even over fiscal matters (not usually under the purview of a *mayordomo*) at the court. In Briceño's view, Catalina's court in Turin often fell short.

In writing to Zúñiga and Vázquez, Briceño was hoping to inform Philip II so that what he saw as the court's disorder in Turin would be remedied, or at the very least, he—Briceño—would not be blamed. Briceño's voice is decidedly cranky and long-winded (at an audience with Carlo and Catalina to voice his concerns about court life, Briceño "read and discussed his report" for more than an hour and a half and still had not finished making all his

Valencia de Don Juan in Madrid. For another discussion of some aspects of Briceño's letters, see Elisa García Prieto, "La infanta Isabel Clara Eugenia de Austria, la formación de una princesa Europea y su entorno cortesano" (PhD diss., Universidad Complutense, Madrid, 2012), 180–87.

[2] For a discussion of the gifts exchanged at Catalina's marriage and of the festivities that took place at the court in Turin from 1585 to 1587, see Almudena Pérez de Tudela, "La vida festiva de la infanta Catalina en la corte de Turín en la correspondencia del Baron Paolo Sfondrato," *Ars & Renovatio*, no. 1 (2013): 148–66. I would like to thank Vanessa de Cruz Medina for bringing this article to my attention.

[3] He might have met Juan de Zúñiga earlier in Italy because Zúñiga served as Spanish ambassador in Rome from 1568 to 1579 and then as viceroy of Naples from 1579 to 1582. On Juan de Zúñiga y Requeséns's years as Spanish ambassador in Rome, see Michael J. Levin, *Agents of Empire. Spanish Ambassadors in Sixteenth-Century Italy* (Ithaca, NY: Cornell University Press, 2005), 83–105, 108–12.

[4] See María José del Río Barredo, "De Madrid a Turín: el ceremonial de las reinas españolas en la corte ducal de Catalina Micaela de Saboya," *Cuadernos de historia moderna*, Anejo [supplement] 2 (2003), 117n44.

points), but the councilors of Philip II listened to his complaints and took them seriously.[5] His concerns found a ready audience at the Spanish court.[6]

For Briceño, Spanish court etiquette gave royal status to the court in Turin; Catalina needed to be treated as the daughter of Philip II, not merely as the wife of a duke.[7] Briceño's views about Spanish etiquette were not original. In fact, he merely articulated the opinion of Philip II and his councilors. When Catalina married the duke of Savoy and left Spain, Philip II sent with her a copy of the rules of etiquette governing the household of Spanish queens. Under Philip II's orders, the marquis of Ladrada, *mayordomo mayor* of Philip's fourth wife, Anna de Austria, had painstakingly elaborated this etiquette from 1570 to 1575 and the rules were then applied to Anna's household.[8] This etiquette codified regulations governing the queen's household as well as that of the royal children, since the two households were joined. The rules mandated very strict enclosure for the queen and her female household, sharply limiting access to her apartments and restricting interaction between the queen's ladies and outsiders. Moreover, the etiquette included detailed instructions on how the queen and her ladies were supposed to behave both within the palace and outside, so that the queen's household might be a model of decorous behavior. Finally, the rules established the queen's *mayordomo mayor* as the overseer of her household—the person who would ensure that these rules were followed closely. The *camarera mayor* (chief lady-in-waiting), the feminine counterpart to the *mayordomo mayor*, helped monitor the queen's rooms, sleeping (with several additional ladies) in the queen's bedroom when the king was absent.

---

[5] Baron Paolo Sfondrato to Philip II, Archivo General de Simancas (hereafter AGS), Estado (hereafter E) 1262, fol. 129, March 18, 1587: "… el cual fue leyendo su relación y discutiendo sobre ella lo que le pareció … Quedaban por tractar algunos puntos tocantes más a la buena orden y disciplina que no al gasto, pero como había durado aquella junta más de hora y media remitió nos el duque a otra." I would like to thank María José del Río Barredo for bringing this document to my attention and for sharing her notes with me.

[6] For a brief discussion of the correspondence between Philip II and Sfondrato about the problems in Catalina's household, see José Martínez Millán, "La casa y los servidores de la infanta Catalina Micaela en Turín," in *L'Infanta. Caterina d'Austria, duchessa di Savoia (1567–1597)*, ed. Blythe Alice Raviola and Franca Varallo (Rome: Carocci, 2013), 402–05.

[7] Letter of Cristóbal Briceño to Mateo Vázquez, Instituto Valencia de Don Juan (hereafter IVDJ), Envío 5, T. III, fol. 256, August 14, 1585.

[8] On this issue, see Río Barredo, "De Madrid a Turín," 97–122. See also Magdalena S. Sánchez, "Privacy, Family, and Devotion in the Spain of Philip II," in *The Politics of Space: European Courts, ca. 1500–1750*, ed. Marcello Fantoni, George Gorse, and Malcolm Smuts (Rome: Bulzoni Press, 2009), 363–69; Martínez Millán, "La casa y los servidores," 398–402; Félix Labrador Arroyo, "From Castile to Burgundy: The Evolution of the Queens' Households during the Sixteenth Century," in *Early Modern Habsburg Women. Transnational Contexts, Cultural Conflicts, Dynastic Continuities*, ed. Anne J. Cruz and Maria Galli Stampino (Burlington, VT: Ashgate, 2013), 137–41.

Philip intended that this etiquette—designed for a queen's household—be implemented in the ducal court at Savoy, helping to lend it royal status and enhance Catalina's and the duke's prestige.[9]

Catalina had grown up with this etiquette and was undoubtedly thoroughly familiar with its complicated features. Nevertheless, she herself was not charged with personally ensuring that her household conform to the rules; instead, her *mayordomo mayor* was charged to see to its implementation.[10] Catalina's *mayordomo mayor* was Baron Paolo Sfondrato, a Lombard.[11] Sfondrato had served as Emanuele Filiberto's (Carlo's father) ambassador in Milan and then as the Spanish ambassador to the court in Turin. In 1585, he was appointed Catalina's *mayordomo mayor* (making him, in effect, Briceño's boss), even as he continued to serve as Philip II's ambassador in Turin. As *mayordomo mayor*, Sfondrato was supposed to implement Spanish etiquette and enforce its rules in Catalina's household, yet he was not fully familiar with it (never having served at the court in Madrid), nor did he necessarily understand or appreciate its finer points. It is not surprising, therefore, that Briceño had frequent confrontations with Sfondrato, whom Briceño thought was overlooking crucial aspects of Spanish etiquette. Once, faced with specific criticism from Briceño, an annoyed and frustrated Sfondrato replied that he had to check the rules.

When he was appointed *mayordomo mayor*, Sfondrato asked for clarification of numerous issues of etiquette; no doubt he realized his lack of familiarity with

---

[9] See Río Barredo, "De Madrid a Turín," especially 102, 114, and 122. For the rules for Catalina's household, see Biblioteca del Palacio Real de Madrid, II/3127, fol. 59–155, "La orden que es nuestra voluntad que guarden los criados y criadas de la Serenísima Infanta Doña Catalina mi muy cara y muy amada hija, en lo que toca a su servicio, uso y ejercicio de sus oficios." For the rules governing the Spanish queen's household, see Archivo General de Palacio, Madrid (hereafter AGP), Sección Histórica, Caja 49, expediente 3, "Hordenanzas y Etiquetas que el Rey Nuestro Señor Don Phelipe Segundo Rey de las Españas mando se guardasen por los criados y criadas de la Real Casa de la Reyna Nuestra Señora, dadas en treinta y uno de diziembre de mil quiniento y setenta y cinco años y referendadas por su secretario de estado Martin de Gaztelu."

[10] The officials of a queen's household seem to have been the ones chiefly familiar with how the rules of etiquette worked. When Philip II charged the marquis of Ladrada with codifying the rules governing the queen's household, Ladrada talked with people who had served in the queen's household who were able to tell him what the rules were. For Ladrada's correspondence with Philip II, see British Library, Additional Manuscript 28354. For the oral transmission of the rules of etiquette, see Carlo Gómez-Centurión Jiménez, "La herencia de Borgoña: el ceremonial real y las casas reales en la España de los Austrias (1548–1700)," in *Las sociedades ibéricas y el mar a finales del siglo XVI*, vol. 1, *La corte. Centro e imagen del poder* (Madrid: Sociedad Estatal para la Conmemoración de los Centenarios de Carlos V y Felipe II, 1998), 11–31.

[11] Sfondrato married Sigismonda D'Este, was baron of Valassina, and was named count of Riviera by Philip II. He was the brother of Niccolo Sfrondato, who became Pope Gregory XIV in 1590.

Spanish court practices. Sfondrato had been shown the rules from 1575 from the Spanish queen's household, but he wanted a copy of the rules signed by Philip II, specifically addressing the special case of the court in Turin because "the manners and customs" (*trato y costumbres*) in Savoy were so different from those in Spain.[12] Sfondrato, who accompanied Carlo to the wedding with Catalina in Zaragoza, received the instructions before he left Spain in June 1585, but he did not issue them to members of Catalina's household until December 1585—six months after he had received them and four months after Catalina and the duke's official entrance into Turin.[13] This delay caused Briceño to write to Philip II's secretary, Mateo Vázquez, in September 1585, complaining that Catalina's servants still did not have any written directives from Sfondrato detailing the responsibilities of their specific office.[14]

His assignment to Catalina's household was the first time that Sfondrato had served as *mayordomo mayor*. He was perhaps too preoccupied with juggling two offices (*mayordomo mayor* and Spanish ambassador) and with questions of precedence between himself and the duke's *mayordomo mayor* to be overly concerned about the minutiae of Spanish etiquette within the *infanta*'s household. Briceño noted, for example, that Sfondrato's ambassadorial responsibilities kept him from attending the *infanta*'s meals—a feature of court life that in Spain was heavily governed by strict rules, which stipulated that Catalina's ladies would serve the food.[15] In Turin, however, the duke's male servants put the meat on the table. Briceño was appalled by this irregularity and insisted that these male servants give the food to pages (*meninos*), who in turn would hand it to the *infanta*'s ladies, ensuring that men did not enter the room while Catalina was dining. Briceño told the duke that the practice of male servers was inappropriate (*no parecía cosa decente*), and the duke remedied it in order to conform to the instructions which Catalina had brought from Spain.[16] Although Sfondrato had received a copy of the written rules, he had clearly not paid sufficient attention to them, either because he was too busy with his ambassadorial duties or because he did not think them important enough.

---

[12] Consulta of Juan de Zúñiga to Philip II, AGS, E1260, fol. 184, May 25, 1585, "Consulta del Comendador mayor de Castilla sobre cosas del cargo del Baron Sfondrato"; Río Barredo, "De Madrid a Turín," 112.

[13] Letter of Cristóbal de Briceño to Juan de Zúñiga, Bibliothèque Publique et Universitaire de Genève (hereafter BPG), Collection Edouard Favre (hereafter CEF), MS 23, fol. 402v, December 13, 1585.

[14] Letter of Cristóbal de Briceño to Mateo Vázquez, IVDJ, Envío 5, T. III, fol. 257, September 15, 1585.

[15] Ibid.

[16] Letter of Cristóbal Briceño to Mateo Vázquez, IVDJ, Envío 5, T. III, fol. 258, October 20, 1586. "… que comiendo su Alteza con la infanta sirviendo damas no parecía cosa decente que llegasen sus criados a ponerle la vianda en la mesa sino que la diesen a los meninos para que la sirviesen las damas y ansí el duque vino que fuese confirme a la orden que se halla de España y se he hecho desde entonces …."

The difference in customs between Savoy and Spain, noted originally by Sfondrato and reported angrily by Briceño, would sometimes make Briceño seethe; his actions, in turn, would provoke a great deal of consternation at Catalina's new court. Nevertheless, Sfondrato must not initially have anticipated problems with Briceño, because when the Spanish government suggested possible candidates to serve in Catalina's household, Philip II's councilors noted that Sfondrato was in favor of Briceño's appointment. Sfondrato wanted a Spanish *mayordomo* and favored Briceño both because he had financial resources and because he was familiar with life at the Spanish court.[17] No doubt Sfondrato thought that Briceño would help him in understanding and implementing Spanish etiquette in Catalina's household, but Sfondrato did not know how difficult a character Briceño would be. (Sfondrato learned his lesson. When Briceño died, Sfondrato urged the Spanish government to find another Spanish *mayordomo*, but one with a milder character than that of Briceño.[18]) Interestingly enough, the Spanish government *did* foresee problems, not with Briceño in particular, but with a Spanish *mayordomo*. In suggesting people for Catalina's household, Spanish councilors noted that no Spaniard would want to serve under an Italian *mayordomo mayor*.[19] Although Sfondrato was Philip II's ambassador to the court in Turin and might have seen himself as more Spanish than Italian, the Spanish court (and Briceño) saw him as decidedly Italian.[20]

Curbing Breaches of Etiquette in Catalina's Household

Briceño's problematic relationship with Sfondrato is indicative of the larger cultural conflict between Spaniards and Italians at the court in Turin. Briceño argued with many of Carlo's and Catalina's Italian courtiers over how Catalina and the women of her household were treated. In some cases, however, the conflict was between Spaniards who differed in their understanding of how a Spanish *infanta*'s household should be run.[21] The turmoil at the court in

---

17 Biblioteca Francisco de Zabálburu (hereafter BFZ), Altamira 85, GD 4/Altamira, 85, D. 70/1. "A Su Majestad se ha representado cuanto convendría que la señora infanta doña Catalina llevase un mayordomo español y el barón Esfrondato hace en ello gran instancia … el barón desearía mucho a Briceño, o a don Alonso, porque tienen de comer y son pláticos en las cosas de palacio."

18 AGS, E1262, fol. 128, March 17, 1587. "… pero sobre todo blando de condición para que se eviten los inconvenientes pasados."

19 BFZ, Altamira, 85, GD. 4/Altamira, 85, D.29/4. "Serán menester dos, y así se habrían de escoger entre los vasallos y criados del duque porque españoles de las partes y calidades que convienen no se hallarán quizás que querrán ir, y obedecerán de mala gana al mayordomo mayor siendo italiano."

20 On this issue, see Río Barredo, "De Madrid a Turín," 118.

21 I use the terms "Spaniards" or "Italians" to describe everyone in Catalina's entourage, but in fact, people identified themselves with a specific region rather than

Turin, so readily detailed by Briceño, further reveals that it took some time for Carlo and Catalina to establish and organize their household. Their youth and inexperience clearly comes through in Briceño's correspondence.

One major issue of conflict at the court in Turin was upholding the hierarchy within Catalina's female household. Briceño complained that the distinctions between the ladies-in-waiting (*dueñas de honor* or *damas*, who were widows for the most part) and the women of the chamber (*mozas de la cámara*, unmarried women who served the *infanta* but were lower in status to the *dueñas de honor*) were not being maintained.[22] According to Briceño, the problems had begun almost immediately after arriving at Nice, when the women of the *cámara* (referred to as *camaristas* by Briceño), faced with an insufficient number of carriages, wanted to travel in carriages reserved for the *infanta*'s *damas*.[23] Briceño tried to stop them, but when the women complained, the *infanta* took their side, and allowed them to ride in the *damas*' carriages.[24] For the last leg of the journey, the *infanta* and her *damas* rode on boats on the Po, but in this case the *camaristas*—thanks to Briceño's intervention—were not allowed to do so. As the *infanta* and her household settled into the palace in Turin and began to hold court entertainments, other breaks with Spanish etiquette occurred. Briceño complained that the women of the *cámara* were allowed to enter the *sala* to watch musical performances, whereas in Spain they would have watched from the doorway. Moreover, at these performances in Turin, the *camaristas* were given rugs to sit on, a privilege reserved in Spain for the *infanta*'s *damas*.[25]

Briceño blamed one of the *infanta*'s *damas*, Luisa de Mexia (who held the court office of Catalina's *guarda menor*), for these breaches of etiquette, because Mexia had several nieces who were in the *cámara* and she did not want them

---

with a country. It is clear from Catalina's letters, for example, that the Savoyards did not consider themselves "Italians." Catalina often used the term "Italian" disparagingly (and not for those of Savoy) when she wrote to Carlo, which suggests that Carlo shared her sentiments. Similarly, the Spaniards at Catalina's court would have had some common identity from previous court service; they formed an elite with cosmopolitan connections. However, they, too, would have identified with their regions of origin rather than with a national entity. Finally, there was a decidedly pro-French element at the court in Turin, which is not necessarily reflected in this rather facile separation between Spaniards and Italians.

[22] See also Fórmica, *La infanta Catalina Micaela*, 13–15.

[23] Letter of Cristóbal de Briceño to Juan de Zúñiga, BPG, CEF, MS 23, fol. 438v, June 11, 1586.

[24] For a discussion of the restrictions placed on who could travel in carriages as well as a discussion of carriages as a social privilege reserved for those designated by the king, see Alejandro López Álvarez, *Poder, lujo y conflicto en la Corte de los Austrias. Coches, carrozas y sillas de mano, 1550–1700* (Madrid: Polifemo, 2007), 156–67.

[25] Letter of Cristóbal de Briceño to Juan de Zúñiga, BPG, CEF, MS 23, fol. 438v–439, June 11, 1586. See also Fórmica, *La infanta Catalina Micaela*, 16.

treated as if they were lower in rank than the *damas*.[26] In fact, Briceño claimed that when the women of the *cámara* had not been allowed to ride in boats on the Po, Mexia complained to the *infanta*, telling her that the *camaristas* came from the principal families of Spain; that the *infanta*'s mother (Isabel de Valois) had never been served by women from such important families; and that the *infanta* would never learn to be a woman if she allowed the women of the *cámara* to be treated in this fashion.[27] (Apparently Mexia was indicating that in order to assume her role as duchess, the *infanta* needed to assert herself vis-à-vis people like Briceño—or at least that she should not follow the rules of etiquette blindly.) In these cases, therefore, Briceño claimed that the problem was not that Italian or Savoyard customs ("local" customs, as he wrote) clashed with Spanish practice, but rather that the *infanta*'s strong-willed lady-in-waiting took advantage of the distance from Spain to disregard or revise court etiquette. For Mexia, evidently, the move to Turin allowed for some modification in strict rules of etiquette which might benefit her own kin. Her case indicates that on a princess's arrival at a foreign court, the opportunity existed to introduce changes—to modify behavior or customs not only to suit local practice and conditions but also to advance the interests of specific individuals. Perhaps some courtiers (both female and male) even expected that a princess would make these changes as a step toward self-assertion and maturity.

Briceño, on the other hand, firmly believed that the rules of etiquette could not be relaxed in the least. For example, he quarreled with one of Catalina's Italian *mayordomos*, Count Alfonso de la Mota, over questions of etiquette. De la Mota, whose wife was pregnant, gave her a crimson velvet pillow (*terciopelo carmesí*) to sit on during an evening reception at the palace. On another occasion, de la Mota had a small chair brought in for his pregnant wife. Briceño complained that this was unseemly because there were other women of higher status present who had not been given the same privilege and who might be insulted by this breach of etiquette.[28] Briceño (who was not a count) thought that de la Mota was taking advantage of his noble title, and quipped to Zúñiga that neither de la Mota nor his parents or brothers possessed the household of a count.[29] Briceño was suggesting that in Spain, de la Mota and his family would not enjoy the status of counts; they lacked the entourage and de la Mota had no experience in managing

[26] Río Barredo, "De Madrid a Turín," 119. The *guarda menor* was responsible for opening and closing the windows and doors to the women's apartments. She thus played a key role in ensuring that the *infanta*'s women were enclosed. See Biblioteca Nacional, Madrid, MS 18720, no. 37, "La orden que es nuestra voluntad guarden los criados y criadas de las sermas. infantas mis muy caras y muy amadas hijas," Section 1.

[27] Letter of Cristóbal de Briceño to Juan de Zúñiga, BPG, CEF, MS 23, fol. 438v, June 11, 1586.

[28] Letter of Cristóbal de Briceño to Juan de Zúñiga, BPG, MS 23, CEF, fol. 412, February 17, 1586.

[29] Ibid., fol. 413v. "Conde Alfonso ni tiene la casa de Conde ni sus padres ni hermanos."

a household, making him singularly unfit to serve as Catalina's *mayordomo*. When Briceño attempted to stop a chair from being brought into the room for de la Mota's wife, he was told that Catalina's *camarera mayor*, Sancha de Guzmán, had ordered it. The following day Briceño spoke with Guzmán explaining to her the ramifications of allowing a woman to be seated in a room when women of higher status did not have the privilege, and Guzmán accepted his reasoning. At the next evening party, de la Mota's wife was given a chair without arms or back (*un taburete*), which was placed in the entranceway to the room among the women of lower status. This incident caused some animosity between Briceño and de la Mota, precisely because Briceño insisted that more formal rules of etiquette be applied at the Turinese court despite de la Mota's understandable solicitude for his pregnant wife. Nevertheless, some accommodation was made—de la Mota's wife was given a chair to sit on and not forced to stand—though the chair had to be placed in an inconspicuous location. In practice, the rules of etiquette could be modified to accommodate illness, age, or temporary circumstances such as pregnancy, even if Briceño was unwilling to tolerate any flexibility.[30] His firm application of the rules of etiquette did not win him many friends at the court in Turin.

Spanish etiquette governing a queen's household had strict guidelines for limiting access to the ladies of the household, to protect both their honor and reputation and those of the queen. Briceño argued that restricted access to Catalina's ladies and their decorous behavior was the defining feature of a royal court and was in fact the only regal aspect of Catalina and Carlo's court. He was therefore determined to enforce rigorously these aspects of Spanish court etiquette. Briceño complained that several men had too much access to the apartments of the *infanta* and her ladies. Dr. Madera, for example, the Spanish medical doctor for the *infanta* and her ladies, entered the *infanta*'s and the ladies' rooms unaccompanied and at all hours, often staying to chat and play cards with the ladies.[31] Acacio de Loaisa—a servant of the *infanta*'s *camarera mayor*, Sancha de Guzmán—had a key to the ladies' rooms, which allowed him to stay until late in the evening, spending two or three hours chatting before letting himself out through doors usually reserved for those living in the palace. Once again, Spaniards took advantage of a new cultural setting to bend the rigid rules of etiquette.

[30] The rules of etiquette at the Spanish court were sometimes modified. For example, they stipulated that when she accompanied the queen on an outing, the *camarera mayor* was not supposed to ride in the carriage with the queen or even on horseback, but rather on a mule. However, if she was old or infirm, she could ride a horse, in a carriage, or on a litter. See M.V. López-Cordón Cortezo, "Entre damas anda el juego. Las camareras mayores de Palacio en la edad moderna," *Cuadernos de historia moderna*, Anejo [supplement] 2 (2003), 130; and Sánchez, "Privacy, Family, and Devotion," 369.

[31] Letter of Cristóbal de Briceño to Juan de Zúñiga, BPG, MS 23, CEF, fol. 405, Turin, January 7, 1586. For Fórmica's discussion of these incidents, see *La infanta Catalina Micaela*, 21–22.

Briceño claimed that these offenses were possible because the physical layout of the palace in Turin was not designed for Spanish court etiquette; the apartments of the *infanta*'s ladies, for example, were not physically connected to those of the *infanta*, making it more difficult to cordon off the women's quarters in the palace. A few architectural changes had been made to accommodate the needs of Catalina's large Spanish entourage. For example, a *pasadizo* (covered passageway) was constructed between the house of the countess of Racconigi, wife of one of the duke's advisors, and the palace.[32] Briceño also explained that in order for Sancha de Guzmán to go easily and freely to her servants' house, which was adjacent to the palace, a door was made from the rooms of the *damas* to the servants' house. When one of the *infanta*'s ladies gave birth, she did so in the house of Guzmán's servants in order to be as close as possible to the palace and so that others could pass easily from the palace to see her. However, Briceño noted that while women of the palace entered through the newly constructed door, women and men not connected to the palace entered to visit the new mother from the street entrance.[33] Briceño worried that in visiting the new mother, the *infanta*'s ladies mixed too freely with these others and were not as enclosed and restricted as was mandated by the Spanish rules of etiquette. Indeed, Philip II's councilors shared Briceño's concerns. They reminded Sfondrato that he had to be sure that the apartments of the palace women were strictly enclosed ("*muy recogidos*") and that the doors and windows were secured firmly.[34] Briceño blamed these problems in part on architecture—the alterations to accommodate a large household—but also on the *infanta*'s *camarera mayor*, whose influence and power was such that no one dared contradict her. More than anything, however, Briceño believed that the changes resulted from a different ethos in Turin.

In Turin, according to Briceño, courtiers were accustomed to freer access to court women and to less formal rules governing their actions than in Madrid. As he noted, "manners [in Turin] are more liberal and with greater license" ("*El trato es con mas largueza y licencia*"). He reported, for example, that one of the duke's courtiers, the lord of Scalenghe, spent too much time with the *infanta*'s women. This degree of contact was inappropriate, and after Briceño complained,

---

[32] The duke of Savoy instructed several of his courtiers to vacate their houses close to his palace in order to house Catalina's servants. The Racconigi house was one of those designated for the *infanta*'s ladies. See Franca Varallo, ed., *Da Nizza a Torino: I festeggiamenti per il matrimonio di Carlo Emanuele I e Caterina d'Austria: Relatione degli apparati e feste fatte nell'arrivo del serenissimo signor duca di Savoia con la Serenissima Infante sua Consorte in Nizza, nel passaggio del suo Stato, e finalmente nella entrata in Turino 1585* (Turin: Centro Studi Piemontesi, 1992), 19n28, 20n29, 22.

[33] Letter of Cristóbal de Briceño to Juan de Zúñiga, BPG, MS 23, CEF, fol. 404v, January 7, 1586.

[34] Consulta of Juan de Zúñiga, AGS, E1260, fol. 184, May 25, 1585, "Consulta del Comendador mayor de Castilla sobre cosas del cargo del Baron Sfondrato."

the duke curbed Scalenghe's access to Catalina's apartments.[35] Worse yet, Briceño lamented, the duke's half-brother, don Amadeo, and other courtiers wanted to spend time with the ladies when Catalina was not present. Briceño claimed that this free mixing of the sexes had been the practice at the court of Carlo's mother, but that it needed to be changed. Most shocking to Briceño was that the duke's men had the habit of helping the *infanta*'s ladies as they descended from horses, "putting their hands on their arms and [committing] other vulgarities" ("*groserías*").[36] Spanish court etiquette allowed only the *mayordomo* to assist the court ladies from their carriage. Briceño was outraged by the behavior of Carlo's men and worked to change this practice; and, by October 1586, when he reported the problems to Philip II's secretary, Mateo Vázquez, he could add happily that the duke had agreed to modify practices so as to conform to the "order that was brought from Spain."[37]

Briceño's complaints extended to the male officials of Catalina's household. He complained that household officials (specifically, the *contralor*, who was in charge of overseeing court expenses; the *grafiel*, who worked alongside the *contralor* and functioned as his secretary; and the *dispensero mayor*, who oversaw the distribution of goods in the palace) entered the *infanta*'s antechamber at all times, not just at mealtimes; this should have been a privilege reserved for the *caballerizo mayor* (master of the stables) or *mayordomo*, he asserted, so perhaps his complaint was motivated as much by defense of his own privileges as by maintenance of Spanish etiquette. In any case, his complaints echoed those of Philip II's closest advisors, who urged Philip to tell Sfondrato as well as the duke of Savoy that especially in *saraos* (soirées) and *festines* (banquets), the rules ("*forma y orden*") governing a Spanish queen's household had to be followed in Turin. According to Zúñiga, who was probably echoing Briceño's complaints, there was "great indecency" ("*gran indecencia*") during court festivities in Turin precisely because the rules were not being followed. Because Italians seemed to have more relaxed rules, Briceño argued that it was essential that Spaniards retain certain offices in the *infanta*'s household. These included the guards at the women's rooms (*guarda damas*); the *ugeres* (who controlled the doors as well, and so determined who had access); and the *reposteros de camas*—all offices which allowed the holder to enter the inner

---

35 Letter of Cristóbal de Briceño to Juan de Zúñiga, BPG, CEF, MS 23, fol. 434v, June 6, 1586.

36 Letter of Cristóbal de Briceño to Mateo Vázquez, IVDJ, Envío 5, T. III, fol. 258, October 20, 1586. "... fue menester ir a la mano a las horas que don Amadeo y otros caballeros querían ir a entretenerse con las damas no estando presente la infanta mi señora como se hacía en la casa de las duquesas de Saboya y también fue menester apartarlos de que al tiempo que las damas se ponían o bajaban de los cuartagos no las ayudasen tomándolas de los brazos y otras groserías que acá usaban que sentían les privasen de ellas y ansí hube menester resolverme de acudir con cuidado a todo para ponerlo en el estilo de España."

37 Ibid.

apartments of the *infanta*'s household. If Italians held these positions, they might not be as strict as Spaniards in controlling access.[38] Briceño claimed that there was no one in Turin suitable for these offices, and the implication was that no Savoyard would understand or enforce the rules.[39]

So, for example, Briceño reported that on one wintry occasion, the duke and Amadeo wanted the ladies to go on a sleigh ride with them. Briceño found it unseemly for the ladies to go unchaperoned with men through the streets, racing in sleighs.[40] As *mayordomo*, he was supposed to accompany the ladies to the door and see them to the sleighs, but he refused to do so, believing that the Spanish ladies should not go outside unaccompanied. His refusal effectively prevented the sleigh ride, but he worried that if Savoyards served as guards they would allow the ladies to have more open contact with male courtiers.[41] On another occasion, Sfondrato invited the ladies to the midday meal at his house when his wife was away, which provoked Briceño's protestations.[42] He was horrified at the scandalous prospect, especially because as *mayordomo mayor* Sfondrato should have known better. Briceño complained to several members of the *infanta*'s household, knowing that his complaints would reach Catalina. His protest was again successful—the *camarera mayor*, Sancha de Guzmán, told the *infanta*, who changed the plans. Instead, the duke and *infanta* held a midday meal at a house they owned on the outskirts of town, and invited the court, including Sfondrato. At the end of the evening, when the ladies were going to return to the palace by way of boats on the Po, the duke jokingly questioned Sfondrato—well in reach of Briceño's ears—whether he thought Spanish etiquette had rules for river travel (or for how court ladies entered and rode on *barcas*) as well.[43]

This luncheon suggests that the duke had told Sfondrato that Spanish etiquette did not permit the *infanta*'s ladies to visit Sfondrato's house when his wife was absent. It also demonstrates that neither the duke nor Sfondrato was fully familiar with this etiquette, nor did they necessarily take it as seriously as they might have. In Sfondrato's case, this presented a particular problem because

---

38 Letter of Cristóbal de Briceño to Juan de Zúñiga, BPG, CEF, MS 23, fol. 415–415v, March 6, 1586.

39 Interestingly, Zúñiga, voicing the opinion of Philip II and the other councilors, responded that when certain offices fell vacant, they could be filled by Italians, but their salaries would be lower. Two offices—that of *contralor* and *tesorero*—had to be held by Spaniards. See AGS, E1260, fol. 184, May 25, 1585.

40 Letter of Cristóbal de Briceño to Juan de Zúñiga, BPG, CEF, MS 23, fol. 408–408v, February 5, 1586. For Fórmica's discussion of the sleigh ride, see *La infanta Catalina Micaela*, 23–4.

41 Letter of Cristóbal de Briceño to Juan de Zúñiga, BPG, CEF, MS 23, fol. 415v, March 6, 1586.

42 For Fórmica's discussion of this incident, see *La infanta Catalina Micaela*, 19–20.

43 Letter of Cristóbal de Briceño to Juan de Zúñiga, BPG, CEF, MS 23, fol. 436, June 6, 1586.

Spanish etiquette gave special importance to the *mayordomo mayor*, making him the enforcer of the rules governing the *infanta*'s household. Yet Briceño's letters indicate that Sfondrato was still getting used to this etiquette and did not really understand all its ramifications.

Conforming to Local Practice

Sfondrato's invitation to the ladies to dine with him is particularly interesting because Briceño reported that the locals were thrilled that the *infanta* and the *damas* were going to Sfondrato's house. At last, there would be dancing and festivities outside the palace. They recalled earlier times when the duke's mother was alive and her ladies attended parties given by nobles during *carnestolendas* (Carnival) and danced in public. The *infanta*'s ladies had never done this, but seeing that they were now going to go to visit Sfondrato's house, the locals were hopeful that the *infanta* and her ladies were going to conform to local practice, i.e., the practice of the duke's mother. As Briceño explained:

> during past carnival seasons they say that when there was a party at important houses, the ladies of the late duchess would go to dance and they wondered why her highness's [Catalina's] ladies did not go. Seeing this [Sfondrato's invitation to dine at his house], they thought that the treatment of the ladies was being lowered to that of over here [in Savoy], which is what they desire.[44]

Briceño's word choice was charged with cultural assumptions, clearly indicating his belief that standards at the Turinese court were lower than those in Madrid. His comments suggest that locals were critical of a court culture that confined dancing to interior court spaces and did not allow the public to observe court women and court festivities often. Spanish etiquette was directly responsible for this confinement of women. While Briceño saw this seclusion as positive and even regal, the Savoyards failed to appreciate it.

Nevertheless, although Spaniards such as Briceño might generalize about customs at the court in Turin, these customs were not as homogeneous as they supposed. Marguerite of Valois (1523–74), Carlo's mother—whose ladies supposedly had danced in public—was not Savoyard, but French. She had introduced in Turin a French court culture that was much more open and less rigid than that of her husband, and their son—Carlo Emanuele—adopted these

[44] Letter of Cristóbal de Briceño to Juan de Zúñiga, BPG, CEF, MS 23, fol. 435v, June 6, 1586: "... porque en el tiempo de las carnestolendas pasadas decían que cuando había algún festín en casas principales iban a danzar a el las damas de la duquesa pasada que como no iban las de su Alteza y viendo esto les parecía se iba reduciendo el trato de las damas a lo de acá que es lo que desean."

customs from his mother.[45] Furthermore, by 1570, Carlo's mother had established her own court, separate from that of her husband, because of the latter's frequent infidelities.[46] If Briceño had indeed understood correctly what the "locals" wanted, it is unclear to what earlier practices these Savoyards were referring, and whether these cherished customs were Savoyard or, more likely, French. Moreover, the locals might have been referring to practices from early in the reign of Carlo's father, when his relationship with Marguerite was still good. Briceño obviously did not care to analyze local nostalgia; he cared only to have Catalina and her ladies follow the practices of the Spanish court.

The duke of Savoy apparently allowed his closest advisors still other privileges at court that seemed to grate on Briceño. He complained that when the *infanta* first arrived in Turin, only the duke's half-brother, don Amadeo, and an occasional ambassador were allowed to remain with their head covered in the *infanta*'s presence, but that less than a year later, at least four other men who served the duke were allowed the privilege.[47] Briceño worried that when men with the same social standing as these four passed through Turin and visited the *infanta*, they would demand the same privilege, thereby lessening the respect shown to a Spanish *infanta*. In fact, Sfondrato, no doubt anticipating this issue, had requested the privilege of keeping his hat on in the *infanta*'s presence, and Philip II decided to allow it because several of the duke's entourage already had the privilege and he wanted Sfondrato—the representative of the Spanish king—to have the same status as the duke's men. However, Philip instructed Sfondrato to use the privilege sparingly and to remove his hat when a Spaniard with equal rank (but without the privilege of keeping his head covered) visited. Thus, faced with a more relaxed etiquette at the court in Turin—an etiquette that allowed more courtiers to wear their hat in the presence of the duchess—Philip II and his advisors decided to relax the rules a bit, especially since the honor and status of the Spanish ambassador in Turin was at stake.[48]

In some cases, the clash of etiquette was not solely cultural but stemmed at least partially from adjustments made to accommodate a ducal, rather than a royal, court. Briceño noted, for example, that at the midday meal only 10 courses (*platos*) were served, which was a sharp reduction from a royal meal. Also, since the household personnel was smaller, in a few cases one person had to hold two different offices.

---

[45] Pierpaolo Merlin, *Tra Guerre e Tornei. La corte sabauda nell'età di Carlo Emanuele I* (Turin: Società Editrice Internazionale, 1991), 8.

[46] Pierpaolo Merlin, *Manuel Filiberto. Duque de Saboya y General de España* (Madrid: Editorial Actas, 2008), 269–70. Merlin cites the report of the Venetian ambassador. On Marguerite of Valois, see Carlo Moriondo, *Testa di Ferro. Vita di Emanuele Filiberto di Savoia* (Turin: UTET, 2007), 79–88; and Merlin, *Manuel Filiberto*, 264–74.

[47] Letter of Cristóbal de Briceño to Juan de Zúñiga, BPG, CEF, MS 23, fol. 405v, January 7, 1586. These men were the marquis d'Este, Carlo Pallavicino, Monsieur Leyní, and Francisco Spínola.

[48] AGS, E1260, fol. 184, May 25, 1585.

So, for instance, the *reposteros de camas* (who in Spanish etiquette had access to the women's bedrooms) also served as guards. Briceño seemed uncomfortable with these adaptations, seeing them as reductions in the *infanta*'s status (and that of her household attendants such as himself). Nevertheless, there was little that he could do about this diminished scale, and, perhaps for this reason, he gave even greater weight to the seclusion and decorum of Catalina's women. As he said,

> given the small household that the *Infanta* my lady has and the manners of the duke's [household] and the small court, there is no other thing of authority nor semblance of a royal household except this estimation of the ladies and how they serve Her Highness with so much authority at meals, in visits and accompaniments and at parties and other public things.[49]

Cultural preconceptions and court etiquette seem even to have led to a few instances of violent confrontation between Italians and Spaniards. One evening at 11 pm, Briceño recounted, six of the *infanta*'s Spanish male attendants were seated on the steps of a church close to a plaza where don Amadeo and his servants were dancing. Amadeo threw a rock at the Spaniards, which hit one of them, prompting the Spaniards to rush over and assault the Italians.[50] Although there were no serious injuries, the duke of Savoy blamed the Spaniards. The duke was no doubt predisposed to believe his half-brother, but he also assumed that Spaniards were prone to take up arms too quickly, leading to problems between his household and that of the *infanta*.

Conflicting court etiquette also seems to have been behind another, much more serious, incident involving an *uger de saleta*, Bernal Madera, nephew of the *infanta*'s physician, Dr. Madera. A Savoyard whom Briceño described as a "gentleman from a place close to Nice" had wanted, the previous winter, to enter the palace in Turin to see a *sarao*. Bernal Madera had denied him entry. Some months later, as Madera was going from Turin to the ducal residence Mirafiori, he was attacked and killed by the Savoyard whom he had affronted by denying him admission to the palace in Turin.[51] This case is interesting because it centered again on the right of entry to court apartments now governed by more restrictive Spanish etiquette. Seemingly, as Briceño regularly reported, courtiers in Turin were accustomed to much freer admittance than

---

[49] Letter of Cristóbal de Briceño to Juan de Zúñiga, BPG, CEF, MS 23, fol. 438, June 11, 1586: "... visto la poca casa que tiene la Infanta mi Señora y el trato de la del duque y poca corte no hay aquí otra cosa de autoridad ni otro rastro de casa Real sino esta estimación de las damas y ver como sirven a su Alteza con tanta autoridad ansí a las comidas, a las visitas y acompañamientos y a las fiestas y a las demás cosas públicas."

[50] Letter of Cristóbal de Briceño to Juan de Zúñiga, BPG, CEF, MS 23, fol. 445–447, June 7, 1586.

[51] Letter of Cristóbal de Briceño to Juan de Zúñiga, BPG, CEF, MS 23, fol. 443v, Mirafiori, June 19, 1586.

Spanish etiquette allowed and were willing to resort to violence when this access was curtailed. The Madera murder is a clear example of cultural shock brought about by the implementation of a new court etiquette in Turin.[52]

Adapting Spanish Etiquette to the Savoyard Court

How did the newly married *infanta* Catalina react to her changed conditions in Turin and to the more open customs of the Turinese court? (See Figures 1.3 and 1.4 for portraits drawn shortly after her arrival in Turin.) Was she—like Briceño—startled by the more relaxed "manners and customs" of Turin, or shocked by the great indecency ("*gran indecencia*") at court performances? Was she disturbed by being served only 10 dishes at the midday meal? Faced with a *mayordomo mayor* who was still learning the rules of etiquette, with female attendants who stood to benefit from more relaxed rules, and with a husband who seemed to treat the Spanish rules lightly, surely Catalina would have to intervene forcefully if the Spanish norms were to be implemented and enforced. But there is little evidence that she felt displeasure with relaxation in court etiquette; rather she seems to have adjusted fairly well. Too well, according to Briceño, who criticized Catalina for failing to conform to Spanish rules of etiquette, noting that she had become lax: "she grows careless."[53] For example, Briceño reported that on several occasions, the *infanta* went off with the duke by herself (or accompanied solely by Sancha de Guzmán), leaving behind all her ladies (almost to fend for themselves) and her *mayordomos*, even though it was growing dark. Briceño complained directly to the *infanta*, telling her that she was disregarding her *damas* and that it was unseemly for her to go off unaccompanied. Catalina responded by telling Briceño that she and the duke would have a better time alone and that even her father, Philip II, had left his attendants behind when he went to visit Barcelona. Catalina thus claimed to be following her father's example and seemed to indicate that she had a right to do so (and that the rules were not gender-specific). Briceño, on the other hand, noted that although Turin was a small city, many foreigners (he mentioned the French specifically) passed through and that it was unseemly for the *infanta* to be seen riding around without a retinue befitting a Spanish princess, because without this retinue she seemed to have so little authority ("*tan poca autoridad*").[54] He also was

[52] For another violent incident at the court in Turin, which resulted in the death of one of the *infanta*'s Spanish cooks, see Martínez Millán, "La casa y los servidores," 404–05, which has a partial transcription of Sfondrato's report to Philip II. This incident does not seem to have been specifically about cultural conflict but certainly indicates the difficulty of managing the *infanta*'s household in Turin.

[53] Letter of Cristóbal de Briceño to Juan de Zúñiga, BPG, CEF, MS 23, fol. 435, June 6, 1586: "Se va descuidando."

[54] Letter of Cristóbal de Briceño to Juan de Zúñiga, BPG, CEF, MS 23, fol. 435, June 6, 1586.

Figure 1.3 Giovanni Caracca, Catalina Micaela, ca. 1585, drawing, phototype by Pietro Carlevaris, 18 × 13 cm. Biblioteca Storica della Provincia, Turin.

Figure 1.4 Giovanni Caracca, Catalina Micaela, ca. 1585, drawing, phototype by Pietro Carlevaris, 18 × 13 cm. Biblioteca Storica della Provincia, Turin.

greatly disturbed that a former mistress of Carlo's was allowed to enter Catalina's private apartments. Far from dismissing the woman from court, Catalina stood and watched as the woman sang and played the clavichord. Briceño reported that everyone in Turin knew of Carlo's relationship with this woman, and that "the Marquis d'Este and Amadeo and all the young men of the chamber, who know well this story and probably laugh at this," had watched as the woman performed in Catalina's bedroom.[55] Such behavior betrayed Catalina's lack of authority at court as well as the lack of respect that the duke and his men had for her—or so Briceño thought.[56]

When she did try to exercise authority, according to Briceño, she blundered publicly in a way unbecoming to a Spanish princess. He recounted that after returning from one of her solitary outings with the duke, the *infanta* was annoyed that her ladies did not come down to the garden to greet her as warmly as she would have liked, suggesting that while she occasionally made light of Spanish court etiquette, she still demanded that her attendants conform to it when it suited her. On this occasion Catalina was so infuriated with her unresponsive ladies that she decided to play a trick on them. A few days later she announced to them that they were going to go on an outing and they should meet her in the courtyard. When they were all gathered there, with the marquis d'Este and other male courtiers present, the *infanta* laughed, got into a carriage, and ordered that, with the exception of Sancha de Guzmán and two servants (*meninas*), all of the ladies should return to their rooms because she had decided not to take them with her. Briceño complained that it was unseemly for an *infanta* to humiliate her ladies in public, especially when they had done their best to conform to Spanish etiquette and had not taken advantage of the extra license given to women at the Turinese court. As Briceño explained, the "ladies have not wanted to take advantage of the license that is found in this land concerning the treatment of ladies. Rather, they have maintained their precision and decorum as if they were in the palace in Madrid."[57] Thus, much to Briceño's dismay, even Catalina failed to follow standards of conduct appropriate for a Spanish *infanta* and did not value sufficiently her ladies-in-waiting, going so far as to make fun of them in front of the duke's Italian courtiers. Briceño suggested that a less rigorous court ethos in Turin allowed the *infanta* to disregard her proper Spanish courtly education. If Briceño is to be believed, Spanish etiquette at the *infanta*'s court was being disregarded and attacked on all fronts, even by the *infanta* herself.

---

[55] Letter of Cristóbal de Briceño to Mateo Vázquez, IVDJ, Envío 5, T. III, fol. 257, September 15, 1585: "… que vieron todo esto el Marqués d'Este y Amadeo y los mozos de cámara que saben bien esta historia y se deben reír bien dello …."

[56] Ibid.: "ven cuan poca autoridad a su Alteza."

[57] Letter of Cristóbal de Briceño to Juan de Zúñiga, BPG, CEF, MS 23, fol. 438, Turin, June 11, 1586: "No han querido aprovecharse de la licencia que en esta tierra ha habido en el trato con las damas sino en todo han guardado su punto y decoro como si estuvieran en palacio en Madrid."

Yet by 1586, both Briceño and Sfondrato reported that the *infanta*'s household was operating along Spanish rules of etiquette.[58] In particular, Catalina followed the rules that insisted that when the duke was absent, several of Catalina's *damas* needed to sleep with her in her bedroom. Within a few years of arriving in Turin, for example, and while anxiously awaiting the duke's return to the court (and to her bed), Catalina wrote telling him which women were sleeping where in her room:

> Chicha has also slept in my room and therefore the beds are [arranged] as I've told you and hers is at the foot of my bed and Doña Beatriz's bed is by the door [*puerta del retrete*] and that of Doña Mariana is by the two windows. I want to tell you everything because of what you ordered me to do but also in case you surprise me, you will know how everything is.[59]

Two days later, when Chicha was sick, Catalina reported temporary personnel changes in her bedroom, noting that a certain Mariana de Tarsis (not the same as the previous Doña Mariana) was now sleeping in the bedroom so that Catalina would not be without a "*vieja*" (an older woman) in her room. Her letters give the impression that she did not want the duke to be surprised—that she thought he needed to be told so he could navigate at night within her room (although presumably the women would have been told to leave)—but her comments suggest both that she was making sure that Spanish court etiquette was implemented in her household and that the duke wanted her to do so. Far from rejecting Spanish etiquette, the duke embraced it, perhaps especially because it protected Catalina's honor while he was absent from court.

Catalina's and the duke's exchange about sleeping arrangements within the *infanta*'s bedroom brings up several factors crucial to understanding the meeting of Spanish and Turinese court culture. Catalina seems to have adjusted quickly and well to life at the court in Turin because she and the duke quickly developed an affectionate—even amorous—bond. This was possible at least in part because the duke knew Spanish; he spoke and wrote the language fluently (with some differences in spelling from Catalina's, and possibly with some Italian expressions), as is evident from his letters to Catalina, which are all in Spanish (except those written by a secretary). Carlo's mother taught him French (and he supposedly knew more French than Italian as a boy), but he had also learned Spanish by the time he arrived in Spain for his marriage to Catalina.[60] Moreover,

---

58 AGS, E1262, fol. 128; Río Barredo, "De Madrid a Turín," 117–18.

59 Letter of Catalina to Carlo, Archivio di Stato Torino, mazzo 35, fol. 44v, October 24, 1588: "Chicha ha dormido también en mi aposento y ansí son las camas como os tengo dicho la suya a los pies de la mía y la de doña Beatriz a la puerta del retrete y la de doña Mariana entre las dos ventantas os quiero dar cuenta de todo por lo que me habéis mandado y también porque si venís a tomarme de sobresalto sepáis como está todo."

60 On Carlo's education, see Stéphane Gal, *Charles-Emmanuel de Savoie. La politique du précipice* (Paris: Payot, 2012), 44–47; Merlin, *Manuel Filiberto*, 275–78.

he had already begun to dress in Spanish style by 1584 (a year before his marriage) and encouraged others at his court to do likewise.[61] The principal courtiers in Turin and those who served the *infanta* all knew Spanish. The *infanta* must have learned some Italian, though the only Italian words that I have found in her letters are *balia* (wet nurse) and *le belle parole* (fine words). No doubt Carlo's willingness to adopt Spanish language and customs—even accepting the rules of etiquette for her household, which entailed greater expenses and more personnel—facilitated Catalina's adaptation to the court in Turin.

Briceño's letters chronicle the first 14 months of Catalina's life at the court in Turin, beginning when she was 18 and Carlo was 23. The incidents recounted by Briceño suggest the gaiety and impetuosity of a young, newly married couple, still unaccustomed to managing a household. Briceño himself ascribed some of the court's disorder to Catalina and Carlo's youth:

> [they] go out hunting every day and return at night racing in carriages, your highnesses on one side and the ladies on the other ... one day they eat early, another very late ... I confess that it is a peaceful life for the young or for strong persons who can take it.[62]

Not so for Briceño, who was 53 in 1586. With time, the birth of numerous children, and Carlo's military engagements, their court in Turin eventually settled down—but by that time, Briceño was dead.

Even as Catalina and the duke saw to the implementation of Spanish etiquette at their court—specifically within the *infanta*'s household—they did so as much as possible on their own terms, and on the whole they seem to have agreed on those terms. While sixteenth-century observers noted and scholars today agree that Catalina and the duke introduced Spanish customs and practices at the court in Turin, the story is (obviously) much more complex. There is evidence of a melding of cultural practices—Catalina's promotion of the Holy Shroud, Our Lady of Mondovi, and the cult of Saint Mauricio, all connected with the House of Savoy, but also of the Virgin of Montserrat (from Catalonia).[63] We might translate

---

61 Pierpaolo Merlin, "Caterina d'Asburgo e l'influsso Spagnolo," in *Assenza del re. Le reggenti dal XIV al XVII secolo (Piemonte ed Europa)*, ed. Franca Varallo (Florence: Olschki, 2008), 212.

62 Letter of Cristóbal de Briceño to Mateo Vázquez, IVDJ, Envío 5, T. III, fol. 258, October 20, 1586: "... como sus altezas son mozos dios los guarde cada día van fuera a las cazas vuelven de noche van corriendo los coches sus altezas por una parte las damas por otra que para seguirlos lomas del camino se anda corriendo un día comen temprano otro muy tarde en fin en todas las cosas hay inquietud confieso es vida apasible para los mozos o personas recias que la pueden llevar."

63 Paolo Cozzo, *La geografia celeste dei duchy di Savoia. Religione, devozioni e sacralità in uno Stato di età moderna (secoli XVI–XVII)* (Bologna: Il Mulino, 2006), 174–76; and by the same author, "'Intus mirabile magis': L'orizzonte devozionale dell'infanta Caterina," in *L'Infanta Caterina d'Austria*, ed. Raviola and Varallo, 213–31.

Briceño's phrase that Catalina was becoming lax—"*se va descuidando*"—in a more positive way, that she was adapting culturally, showing her willingness and ability to modify Spanish practices as they were implemented at the Turinese court. While this was frightening to Briceño, it was no doubt essential for a princess at a foreign court.

Bibliography

Archival Sources

Archivio di Stato, Turin, Italy (AST). Lettere Principe Savoia, Serie Ia, Duchi e Soverani. Mazzo 35.

Archivo General de Palacio, Madrid, Spain (AGP). Sección Histórica, Caja 49, expediente 3.

Archivo General de Simancas, Simancas, Spain (AGS). Sección Estado, legajos 1260 and 1262.

Bibliothèque Publique et Universitaire de Genève, Geneva, Switzerland (BPG). Collection Edouard Favre (CEF), MS 23.

Biblioteca del Palacio Real, Madrid, Spain II/3127.

Biblioteca Francisco de Zabálburu, Madrid, Spain (BFZ). Altamira 85, GD 4/ Altamira, 85, D. 70/1.

Biblioteca Nacional, Madrid, Spain MS 18720, no. 37.

British Library, London, Great Britain, Additional Manuscript 28354.

Instituto Valencia de Don Juan, Madrid, Spain (IVDJ). Envío 5, T III.

Printed and Secondary Sources

Catalina Micaela d'Austria. *Lettere inedite a Carlo Emanuele I*. 3 vols. Edited by Giovanna Altadonna. Messina: Il Grano, 2012.

Cozzo, Paolo. *La geografia celeste dei duchy di Savoia. Religione, devozioni e sacralità in uno Stato di età moderna (secoli XVI–XVII)*. Bologna: Il Mulino, 2006.

Cruz, Anne J., and Maria Galli Stampino, eds. *Early Modern Habsburg Women. Transnational Contexts, Cultural Conflicts, Dynastic Continuities*. Burlington, VT: Ashgate, 2013.

Fórmica, Mercedes. *La infanta Catalina Micaela en la corte alegre de Turín*. Madrid: Fundación Universitaria Española, 1976.

Gal, Stéphane. *Charles-Emmanuel de Savoie. La politique du précipice*. Paris: Payot, 2012.

García Prieto, Elisa. "La infanta Isabel Clara Eugenia de Austria, la formación de una princesa Europea y su entorno cortesano." PhD diss., Universidad Complutense, Madrid, 2012.

Gómez-Centurión Jiménez, Carlo "La herencia de Borgoña: el ceremonial real y las casas reales en la España de los Austrias (1548–1700)." In *Las sociedades ibéricas y el mar a finales del siglo XVI*, vol. 1, *La corte. Centro e imagen del poder*, 11–31. Madrid: Sociedad Estatal para la Conmemoración de los Centenarios de Carlos V y Felipe II, 1998.

Levin, Michael J. *Agents of Empire. Spanish Ambassadors in Sixteenth-Century Italy*. Ithaca NY: Cornell University Press, 2005.

López Álvarez, Alejandro. *Poder, lujo y conflicto en la Corte de los Austrias. Coches, carrozas y sillas de mano, 1550–1700*. Madrid: Polifemo, 2007.

López-Cordon Cortezo, M.V. "Entre damas anda el juego. Las camareras mayores de Palacio en la edad moderna." *Cuadernos de historia moderna*, Anejo [supplement] 2 (2003), 123–52.

Merlin, Pierpaolo. *Tra Guerre e Tornei. La corte sabauda nell'età di Carlo Emanuele I*. Turin: Società Editrice Internazionale, 1991.

_____ . *Manuel Filiberto. Duque de Saboya y General de España*. Madrid: Editorial Actas, 2008.

_____ . "Caterina d'Asburgo e l'influsso Spagnolo." In *Assenza del re. Le reggenti dal XIV al XVII secolo (Piemonte ed Europa)*. Edited by Franca Varallo, 209–34. Florence: Olschki, 2008.

Moriondo, Carlo. *Testa di Ferro. Vita di Emanuele Filiberto di Savoia*. Turin: UTET, 2007.

Pérez de Tudela, Almudena. "La vida festiva de la infanta Catalina en la corte de Turín en la correspondencia del Baron Paolo Sfondrato." *Ars & Renovatio*, no. 1 (2013): 148–66.

Raviola, Blythe Alice, and Franca Varallo, eds. *L'Infanta. Caterina d'Austria, duchessa di Savoia (1567–1597)*. Rome: Carocci, 2013.

Río Barredo, María José del. "De Madrid a Turín: el ceremonial de las reinas españolas en la corte ducal de Catalina Micaela de Saboya." *Cuadernos de historia moderna*, Anejo [supplement] 2 (2003): 97–122.

Sánchez, Magdalena S. "Privacy, Family, and Devotion in the Spain of Philip II." In *The Politics of Space: European Courts, ca. 1500–1750*. Edited by Marcello Fantoni, George Gorse, and Malcolm Smuts, 361–81. Rome: Bulzoni Press, 2009.

Varallo, Franca, ed. *Da Nizza a Torino: I festeggiamenti per il matrimonio di Carlo Emanuele I e Caterina d'Austria: Relatione degli apparati e feste fatte nell'arrivo del serenissimo signor duca di Savoia con la Serenissima Infante sua Consorte in Nizza, nel passaggio del suo Stato, e finalmente nella entrata in Turino 1585*. Turin: Centro Studi Piemontesi, 1992.

Chapter 2
The Queen of France and the Capital of Cultural Heritage

Mark de Vitis

In June of 1660 the Bourbon king of France, Louis XIV, was betrothed to the eldest daughter of King Philip IV of Spain, María Teresa. The marriage formed part of the negotiations for the Treaty of the Pyrenees (1659), which ended the long and bitter conflict known as the Franco-Spanish War (1635–59) and helped resolve the corollaries of the French civil war known as the Fronde (1648–53). Despite the significant political consequences of the marriage, the impact of the new queen's arrival in France remains relatively unexplored.[1] Modern scholarship dedicated to the early reign of Louis XIV generally locates María Teresa (or Marie-Thérèse, as she was known in France), as a marginalized figure at the French court. The justification for her perceived inconsequence within the Bourbon regime is repeated across the literature: she was Spanish. Worse still, she remained attached to the culture and customs of her Spanish homeland even after having become queen of France. With a tenor bordering on condescension, her apparent faults are repeatedly catalogued by scholars.[2] While the claims vary from text to text, their justification inevitably rests with what is presented as the burden of her cultural inheritance. For instance, it is often noted that María Teresa was physically small as a result of the Habsburgs' policy of endogamy.[3] As a visible consequence of

[1] The most important study of the consequences of the marriage of Louis XIV and María Teresa remains Abby Zanger's *Scenes from the Marriage of Louis XIV: Nuptial Fictions and the Making of Absolutist Power* (Stanford, CA: Stanford University Press, 1997). Besides Zanger's study, little research on the effect of the arrival of María Teresa in France is available. While the most recent biography of María Teresa, written by Joëlle Chevé, attempts a reconsideration of the queen's role within the Bourbon state, more focused research is required: Joëlle Chevé, *Marie-Thérèse d'Autriche: épouse de Louis XIV* (Paris: Pygmalion, 2008).

[2] Patricia Cholakian notes a similarly dismissive tone in scholarship addressing the life of the Grande Mademoiselle, Anne Marie Louise d'Orléans, Duchess of Montpensier, the cousin of Louis XIV. Patricia Cholakian, *Women and the Politics of Self-Representation in Seventeenth-Century France* (Newark, DE: University of Delaware Press, 2000), 9–10.

[3] Much of the criticism of María Teresa in modern scholarship originates with Saint-Simon, though it should be noted that he was only eight years old when she died: Louis de Rouvroy, duc de Saint-Simon, *Mémoires 1701–1707*, vol. 2 (Paris: Gallimard, 1983), 422. Writers including Vincent Cronin and Hubert Delpont have followed Saint-Simon's

this program of intermarriage, she had inherited a distinctive Habsburg visage.[4] Furthermore, the near cloistered conditions of her upbringing led to her pronounced timidity, and she was retiring and dutiful and ignorant in all matters other than religion.[5] María Teresa was a poor dancer and an enthusiastic but pitiable card player, who, it is claimed, was fundamentally unable to fulfil her role as queen to the great Sun King.[6]

These accusations of physical gracelessness and mental fatuity belie the fact that María Teresa played a vital role in the development of Bourbon power during the early reign of Louis XIV. I make no claim that the queen was an unacknowledged political strategist of notable genius. She neither sat on councils of state nor operated within any government agency.[7] Yet to assume from this that María Teresa's presence in France had little impact on the nature of Bourbon politics misrepresents the workings of the early modern court system. María Teresa's worth to the Bourbon regime was driven by what has in the past been considered her greatest liability: her Spanish heritage. Upon her arrival in France, manifestations of the new queen's cultural inheritance were utilized by the Bourbon regime to expand its influence within the operations of the state. The meanings embedded within these actions were situational, constructed within the unfolding series of diplomatic exchanges inspired by the Treaty of the Pyrenees, and yet their legitimacy ran deeper still and were supported by the very foundations of French early modern political thought.

While Salic law imposed strict limitations on the power of elite women in France— rendering individual achievement rare in a system geared towards male-led collaborative actions—contemporary political theory offered both men and women access to a form of political agency through and of the crown.[8] In Jean Bodin's highly influential *Les Six Livres de la République* (1576), he maintains that sovereign power was absolute power, ultimately the sole property of the

---

word as law: Vincent Cronin, *Louis XIV* (London: Collins, 1964), 120; Hubert Delpont, *Parade pour une infante: le périple nuptial de Louis XIV à travers le Midi de la France (1659–1660)* (Narrosse: Editions d'Albret, 2007), 160 and 186.

[4] Delpont, *Parade pour une infante*, 161.

[5] Bruno Cortequisse, *Madame Louis XIV: Marie-Thérèse d'Autriche* (Paris: Perrin, 1992), 51, 54, 56–57; Guy Walton, *Louis XIV at Versailles* (London: Viking, 1986), 44–45.

[6] Jean-Christian Petitfils, *Louis XIV* (Paris: Perrin, 1995), 297–98; Simone Bertière, *Les reines de France au temps des Bourbons: les femmes du Roi-Soleil* (Paris: Editions de Fallois, 1998), 51.

[7] The one official role the queen fulfilled during her life in France was to act as regent in 1672. The appointment was presumably made in response to the Franco-Dutch War of the same year, though she performed very few duties. The queen's hereditary rights had been presented as the justification for French military intrusion into Spanish-held territories.

[8] This methodology is presented by Katherine Crawford in her study of regency government in early modern France: Katherine Crawford, *Perilous Performances: Gender and Regency in Early Modern France* (Cambridge, MA: Harvard University Press, 2004), 5.

monarch, but, importantly, divisible if necessary.[9] Accordingly, Bodin understood the operation of power as a form of trusteeship or custodianship, where authority might be allocated by the monarch to others, who were then obliged to act for the good of the monarchy.[10] If power was deindividualized—as, according to Bodin, an individual could act in the name of the state only as a commissioned agent of the sovereign—then instances of power must be understood with reference to the wider concerns of the ruling body whose right it was to distribute and withdraw the ability to wield it.[11]

While Bodin's influential treatise was no doubt championed and ignored in equal measure, it nevertheless identifies a set of conditions at work in early modern France which encourages the assessment of socio-political influence through a collective rather than an individual framework. While is it possible to assert that María Teresa achieved little of political consequence in her own right in France, this conclusion results from the adoption of a particular viewpoint which defines achievement as the result of individual agency.[12] If, instead, Bodin's assessment of the operation of power is applied, and the consequences of Maria Teresa's presence in France are assessed by locating her within the concerns of the Bourbon collective, the magnitude of her political influence is greatly expanded. Ultimately, to reach an understanding of the impact of María Teresa's arrival in France, it is necessary to move beyond a methodology which attempts to catalog her personal achievements, to instead consider what she added to the Bourbon dynasty as a whole. The potential which was unlocked

9 The *Six Livres* influenced a subsequent generation of jurists who wrote in support of increased royal authority, such as Cardin Le Bret and Charles Loyseau. Bodin's theories provided the theoretical basis for the program of centralization undertaken by Louis XIII and Richelieu, and again during the Fronde: Edward Andrew, "Jean Bodin on Sovereignty," *Republics of Letters: A Journal for the Study of Knowledge, Politics, and the Arts*, 2, no. 2 (June 1, 2011): 84.

10 Jean Bodin, *Les Six Livres de la République* (Gabriel Cartier, 1608), 122–24.

11 Later theorists have approached power in similar terms. In "The Subject of Power," Foucault presents power as deindividualized: Michel Foucault, "The Subject and Power," in *Michel Foucault: Beyond Structuralism and Hermeneutics*, 2nd edn., eds. Hubert L. Dreyfus and Paul Rabinow (Chicago: University of Chicago Press, 1982), 220. Foucault also presents the argument that feats of power are inherent in institutions: Michel Foucault, *Discipline and Punish: The Birth of the Prison*, trans. Alan Sheridan (New York: Pantheon, 1977), 202. Current approaches to the seventeenth-century court system, such as William Beik's "common-interest collaboration," demonstrate the legitimacy of this model within the specific context of the seventeenth-century Bourbon court: William Beik, "The Absolutism of Louis XIV as Social Collaboration," *Past & Present*, 188, no. 1 (August 2005): 195–224.

12 Fanny Cosandey reveals the legal restrictions that limit a queen to holding this kind of individual influence, and importantly, her research works to locate queenship in response to dynastic concerns. Fanny Cosandey, *La reine de France: symbole et pouvoir, Xve–XVIIIe siècle* (Paris: Gallimard, 2000).

through her presence in France led to the expansion of Bourbon culture and authority, and her collaboration with her Bourbon kin helped shape a vision for France which saw the Bourbons dominate internal and European politics beyond even the moment of her own death.

Much of this was achieved through the advancement of the queen's cultural heritage, which, rather than a liability, was widely promoted to gain political traction both within France and beyond its borders. Examining state-sponsored representations of the queen which promoted her background, from grand painted portraits to more widely accessible forms of image making (pamphlets and public festivities), affords an opportunity to identify how and why María Teresa's cultural inheritance was deployed during the early period of Louis XIV's majority. Representations of the new queen's Spanish heritage operated to stabilize and invigorate Bourbon France, and while María Teresa herself may not have been responsible for their commission, manufacture, or distribution, the ambitions which saw them produced were born from and sustained by her entry into the Bourbon collective.

Exchange

One of the strongest indicators of the importance of María Teresa's cultural heritage to the development of the Bourbon regime is to be found in the circumstances of the negotiations for the Treaty of the Pyrenees. These negotiations took place on the Île des Faisans or the Isla de los Faisanes, a tiny island in the Bidassoa River bisected by the border between France and Spain. From August to November 1659, both parties came together in this liminal space for a series of 24 conferences headed by Cardinal Jules Mazarin and Luis Méndez de Haro, marquis of Carpio, who acted for the French and Spanish monarchies respectively. A key aim of these negotiations was to draft the marriage agreement between Louis XIV and María Teresa. Indeed there was little to distinguish the discussions concerning the marriage and the wider diplomatic efforts for peace. Haro reveals as much in a letter to Philip IV: "It is the marriage that makes the Peace and is our means for obtaining it."[13] According to one of its own authors then, the marriage agreement not only formed part of the wider negotiations, but was the primary device for securing the longevity of the peace. Additionally, the political significance of the union was emphasized in both the peace treaty and the marriage contract. For instance, article 33 of the peace treaty states: "The said treaty and submission of marriage are of the same strength and vigor, as in being the principal component, the marriage is the most worthy, and the greatest and most precious determinant of

[13] "El casamiento es el que hace la Paz y la prenda que tenemos para ella"; Haro to Philip IV, August 30, 1659, in *Letters from the Pyrenees: Don Luis Mendez de Haro's Correspondence to Philip IV of Spain, July to November 1659*, ed. Lyn Williams (Exeter: University of Exeter Press, 2000), 48.

the security of the peace."[14] While the marriage contract declared that both parties "desire the continued duration of the peace … and tightly renewed their alliance by the good of a marriage,"[15] the tone of the negotiations reveals the belief that the marriage was to act as a diplomatic instrument of the peace and that the handing over of María Teresa was conceived in the hope of leading the states of France and Spain towards a mutually desirable reconciliation.

By no means were these arrangements unusual in an early modern context. In the seventeenth century, royal marriage traditionally functioned to facilitate such cross-cultural exchange. In her innovative study, *Scenes From the Marriage of Louis XIV: Nuptial Fictions and the Making of Absolutist Power*, Abby Zanger presents such unions as an act of transformation, instituted to unite two distinct hereditary monarchies through a process of joining two individual bodies.[16] The opportunity to forge political advantage through kinship associations meant that those engaged in the act of marriage rarely sought to erase traces of cultural difference between the couple. To eliminate difference would have defeated the symbolic purpose of marriage, which was to connect distinct cultural groups.[17] Displaying signs of the queen's Habsburg heritage within the parameters of the marriage was beneficial to the Bourbon regime. The queen represented a connection with the Spanish monarchy and its territories that had not previously existed, and the display of this connection could be used to accumulate significant political advantage.

Such ambitions are in evidence in printed pamphlets produced at the time of the unfolding events of the marriage, which count as some of the first representations of the new queen made for a French audience. Manufactured through the filter of the Bourbon-sponsored press, the pamphlets reveal the monarchy's perspective and were widely distributed for an audience that was eager for an account of the nuptials. Principal among these pamphlets was *La Pompe et Magnificence faite au marriage du Roy et de L'Infante D'Espagne*, produced by Jean Promé. The reporting in *La Pompe* focused on the quotidian minutiae of the occasion and various circumstantial details, which enabled it to draw a mass audience.[18]

---

[14] "Lequel traité à part, et capitulation de mariage, sont de la mesme force et vigueur que le present Traité, comme en estant la partie principale, et la plus digne, aussy bien que le plus grand et le plus precieux gage de la seureté de sa durée." Anonymous, *Traitté de Paix des Pyrénées entre les couronnes de France et d'Espagne fait dans l'île des Faisans, le 7 novembre 1659* (Paris: Imprimeurs & Libraires du Roy, 1660), article 33.

[15] "… desirans que la durée de cette Paix … est de renouer estroitment [*sic*] leurs Alliances, par le bien d'un Mariage." Anonymous, *Contract de Mariage du Roy Tres-Christien, et de la Serenissime Infante Fille aisnée de Roy Catholique. Le septiéme Novembre 1659* (Paris: Imprimeurs & Libraires du Roy, 1660), 295.

[16] Zanger, *Scenes from the Marriage*, 4–12.

[17] Ibid., 8.

[18] *La Pompe* was first published in Toulouse and subsequently in Paris and was so popular that it required a second print run. Anonymous, *La Pompe et Magnificence faite au marriage du Roy et de L'Ifante D'Espagne, Ensemble les entretins qui ont esté faits entre*

For instance, *La Pompe* frequently reports on dress, providing details of what key figures wore on specific days, as well as anecdotes involving dressed bodies as key narrative elements. Through these recurring accounts, *La Pompe* makes it possible to trace the changes in the new queen's dress as she was transferred from her father's court into French territory. Dress in the later seventeenth century was culturally specific and, as a result, held high semiotic value. It was a principal element of courtly ceremony, and individuals could be read, approached, and addressed purely through the information articulated by their dressed bodies.[19] *La Pompe* first refers to the queen's farthingale, or *guardainfante*, a form of hooped skirt stiffened with whalebone.[20] By 1660 it was no longer worn in France, where it was considered inherently Spanish.[21] Unsurprisingly—as it was a ubiquitous garment in the wardrobe of royal Spanish Habsburg women—María Teresa was wearing a farthingale at the climactic moment of her transference to the Bourbon court, which took place on June 7, 1660 on the shores of the Bidassoa, as reported in *La Pompe*: "They were then seated in their beautiful carriage. The Queen occupied the entire front as she did not wish to remove her farthingale. The King and Queen Mother had to sit behind."[22] In relating this key moment in the narrative of the marriage, the pamphlet unambiguously emphasizes the active choice María Teresa made in retaining her farthingale, stating, "she did not wish to remove" it despite the fact that it resulted in the displacement of the king. The reporting of the incident in state-sponsored media amounted to the re-presentation of an event as an instance of the willingness of the French party to negotiate over points of difference. The story acted as a microcosmic retelling of the grander narrative of diplomatic efforts to achieve an accord between the previously warring states, employing acts of dressing to present the Bourbons as culturally aware and prepared to accommodate the needs of the Spanish.

La Pompe's commentary on the farthingale forms part of a wider pattern of narration intent on characterizing Franco-Spanish relations through expressions of

---

les deux Roys, & les deux Reynes, dans l'Isle de la Conference et Relation de ce qui s'est passé mesmes après Consommation (Toulouse: Imprimeurs ordinaires du Roy), 1660.

[19] Daniel Roche, *A History of Everyday Things* (Cambridge: Cambridge University Press, 2000), 194–95.

[20] The term "farthingale" comes from the Spanish word *verdugado*, referring to green rods, for it was originally stiffened with willow shoots: Kimberly Chrisman, "Unhoop the Fair Sex: The Campaign Against the Hoop Petticoat in Eighteenth-Century England," *Eighteenth-Century Studies*, 30, no. 1 (Fall 1996): 7.

[21] Françoise Tétart-Vittu, "À l'espagnole ou à la française: résistances et emprunts dans la mode de cour," in *¿Louis XIV espagnol? Madrid et Versailles, images et modèles*, ed. Gérard Sabatier and Margarita Torrione (Versailles: Centre de recherche du château de Versailles, 2009), 204.

[22] "On la mit en suite dans son beau carrosse [Louis XIV, Anne of Austria and María Teresa], dont Elle [the Queen] occupa tout le devant, á cause de son gard'Infant qu'elle ne voulut pas oster [*sic*: *ôter*; meaning to take off (*se débarrasser de*)] Le Roy & la Reyne Mere estoient au fonds." Anon., *La Pompe*, 8.

María Teresa's cultural heritage. The text repeatedly positions the queen's dressed body as a site of cultural hybridity, presenting it as a quasi-indemnity clause for the peace in order to figure her as channel of communication between the two courts. Importantly, the text traces the changes in María Teresa's dress to incorporate her Habsburg cultural identity visibly into her image as queen of France. For instance, on the day following her transference to the French court, *La Pompe* reports: "This morning the Queen attended Mass around midday, in Spanish dress with her hair half coiffed in the French style. Everyone found her more beautiful and more agreeable than she had previously looked."[23] The usage of "half" is significant in this description, as the reader is presented with an image of María Teresa that positions her as simultaneously connected to the French and Spanish courts. A single feature of her body, her hair, is recorded as displaying traces of the two cultures concurrently. The melding of two styles to produce an "agreeable" situation enacted the queen's value to the Bourbon monarchy, manufacturing a positive and congruous image of a newly forged alliance between former enemies.

La Pompe's reporting on the queen's dress operates to locate her body as a site of assemblage, where signifiers of both French and Spanish sartorial culture are combined to encode her body with political meaning.[24] Acts of dressing which promoted the queen's cultural hybridity, such as her coiffure, assured *La Pompe*'s readership of the ability of the marriage to bring about the desired effects of the peace by locating evidence of Franco-Spanish confederacy within the queen's body. This strategy reoccurs throughout the text of *La Pompe* and continues to the moment of her marriage, two days after her initial transference, on June 9 in the French border town of Saint-Jean-de-Luz, in the church of Saint-Jean-Baptiste. Of the queen's costume on her wedding day, *La Pompe* reports that she had forgone her Spanish farthingale to wear a costume made in the French style but that her hair was still arranged in the Spanish mode: "The pages and valets followed the Queen, who was dressed in the French mode, in a costume of white brocade, coiffed partly in the Spanish style."[25]

---

[23] "Elle a este ce matin a la Messe environ le midi, en habit Espagnol, & coiffèe moitie á la Françoise, chacun l'a trouvée plus belle & plus aimable qu'elle n'avoit encore paru." Ibid., 9.

[24] The concept of assemblage is developed by Gilles Deleuze and Félix Guattari, and defined as a collection of matter organized simultaneously by multiple, often contradictory, processes of stratification, organization, coding, etc. Gilles Deleuze and Félix Guatari, *A Thousand Plateaus: Capitalism and Schizophrenia*, trans. B. Massumi (Minneapolis: University of Minnesota Press, 1987), 406. Interestingly, the theory of assemblage corresponds to seventeenth-century studio practice, as theorists such as de Piles promoted the ideal of forming disparate parts to produce a more perfect whole: W. Gerald Studdert-Kennedy and Michael Davenport, "The Balance of Roger de Piles: A Statistical Analysis," *The Journal of Aesthetics and Art Criticism*, 32, no. 4 (Summer 1974): 493.

[25] "Les Pages et Valets de peid de la Reyne marchoient apres cela devant sa Majesté vestué á la Françoise d'un habit de brocar blanc, coiffée un peu á l'Espagnole." Anon., *La Pompe*, 12.

On the same day as the wedding ceremonies, the marriage was also consummated, a crucial moment in the legitimization of the union.[26] The fact that the queen's body was presented as a Franco-Spanish hybrid during these two important events, and, importantly, was reported as such through publications like *La Pompe*, reinforced the notion that the queen's worth was located in her ability to act as a microcosm of the newly developing relations between the two courts.[27] Other acts of dressing emphasized that María Teresa was an essential component of the union between the Bourbons and Habsburgs on the day of her nuptials. For example, *La Pompe* reported that the queen's maids of honor were dressed in the Spanish manner and were required to hold hands with the *filles* of the queen-mother, who were dressed in the French style.[28] With the hybridity of the queen's body well established, her attendants functioned as an extension of her affiliations, joined as they were with the queen-mother's *filles* to display succinctly the newly instituted solidarity between the states of France and Spain.

The public presentation of the cultural hybridity associated with the queen's body through sources such as *La Pompe* developed her significance beyond simply representing the Spanish half of the peace agreement. As markers of both French and Spanish culture were held within her body, the queen was positioned as a site of exchange, with the ability to facilitate the developing relationship between the two states. *La Pompe* explicitly refers to the queen as a reliable channel of communication between the states:

> … having asked permission from Louis XIV, the Queen wrote to her father the King of Spain on Monday, after which she delivered her letter leaving it open when she gave it to the courier. Louis XIV re-dispatched it without looking at it and was pleased with this willingness to oblige.[29]

By recounting this incident, *La Pompe* reassures its readers of the mutual confidence shared between Louis XIV and María Teresa, her willingness to serve

---

[26] Brucia Witthoft, "Marriage Rituals and Marriage Chests in Quattrocento Florence," *Artibus et historiae*, 3, no. 5 (1982): 46.

[27] French and Spanish courtly hairstyles differed in the period to the degree that it would have been obvious the queen's hair was not dressed in the French style. At the French court women's hair was drawn tight over their heads and bunched in large hanging curls on each side, while Spanish women wore their hair bound up in ribbons, or wore a wig fashioned in the same manner.

[28] "… apres lequel [Mademoiselle] marchoient les Filles de la Reyne Mere toutes vestues fort proprement avec baeucoup de pierreries, chacune d'Elles menant par la main une Filles de la Reyne qui sont encore toutes vestues á l'Espagnole." Anon., *La Pompe*, 13. They wore Spanish dress as they were, indeed, Spanish.

[29] "… la Reyne écrivit Mardy au Roy d'Espagne son Pere, ce fut apres en avoir demandé la permission au Roy, auquel Elle envoya sa Lettre ouverte, avant que de faire partir son Courrier. Le Roy la luy renvoya sans la voir, & luy sceust bon gré de cette complaisance. Anon., *La Pompe*, 10.

the French state (open as she was with her correspondence), and of the link she provided between the Bourbon and Spanish Habsburg dynasties. Combined with other markers of her Spanish heritage, such as the observation that she attended a Spanish play during the return journey from the Île des Faisans, *La Pompe* promoted the queen's Habsburg ancestry as a critical component of the continued life of the Treaty of the Pyrenees.[30]

Entries

Representations of the queen which located her as an agent of exchange extended well beyond the moment of her nuptials, however, and continued to define her role in France as the Bourbon party drew ever closer to the capital on their return voyage from the Bidassoa. Rather than follow the most direct and expedient route, the newly betrothed couple made slow progress back to Paris in order to promote the authority of the monarchy throughout France. This was principally achieved through the staging of entry ceremonies, which were an important political strategy directly related to the rationale for the marriage. Madame de Motteville, an intimate of the queen-mother who traveled with the royal party, noted the effects of the king's presence in the towns they passed through—particularly evocatively in the case of Orléans. Framing the ceremony in relation to the uprising of the citizenry of Orléans during the Fronde, she proclaimed:

> Their past revolt ought to have made them tremble upon seeing their true master, but their repentance and supplications afforded them the effects of his royal virtue, as the king forgot their faults, and as he had just given peace to all Europe he would not leave upon this beautiful city any signs of his indignation.[31]

Madame de Motteville's sentiments at Orléans demonstrate the importance of the king's physical presence in previously unruly regions of France in the early phase of his rule. The pageantry of the entry ceremonies held in celebration of his marriage provided an opportunity to formalize the social contract between ruler and ruled. This occurred through the dramatization of social roles, whereby the populace were required to pay court to the ruler, who was thus able to impose

---

[30] Ibid.

[31] "Leur révolte passée les devoit faire trembler à leur veritable maître, mais leur repentir et leurs supplications attirèrent sur eux les effects de sa royale bonté, par l'oubli de leur faute, et comme il venoit de donner paix à toute l'Europe, il ne voulut pas laisser à cette belle ville acune marquee de son indignation"; Françoise Bertaud, dame de Motteville, *Nouvelle collection des mémoires pour servir à l'histoire de France: Madame de Motteville*, ed. Joseph F. Michaud and Jean J. Poujoulat, vol. 2 (Paris: Guyot Frères, 1853), 499.

the authority of the monarchy through acts of staged homage.[32] Louis XIV's ability to secure peace for his state and ostensibly guarantee its longevity through the display of a Habsburg bride as a permanent fixture of his regime facilitated his image as a potent ruler. His presence in Orléans soon after his marriage further served as a definitive moment in securing his authority, as years earlier the young king had made a similar journey during the Fronde in an attempt to secure allegiances at a time of widespread civil unrest.[33] With a successful peace recently brokered with Spain, Louis XIV was in a position to make a triumphant tour of former centers of disquiet to secure loyalty to his regime. In addition to Orléans, the Bourbon party also travelled through Bayonne and Bordeaux, where some enduring resistance to the king's rule remained after the uprisings of the Fronde or where feudal allegiances to local authorities seemed to challenge the rights of the king. Amboise, Blois, and Chambord—all of which returned to the crown only after the death of the notorious Frondeur Gaston d'Orléans in February 1660—were also visited.[34] Gaston had conspired with the Spanish against the Bourbon crown, and thus the synchronicity of Gaston's death and Louis XIV's tour of the region so soon after obtaining a favorable peace with Spain was purposefully exploited to affirm the king's ability and right to rule in previously disputed regions.

Assertions of Louis XIV's victory over collusions between dissident French nobles and the Spanish monarchy were an explicit feature of the principal entry ceremony arranged to celebrate the marriage, which took place in Paris on August 26, 1660. A great cavalcade of the nobility was organized to mark the occasion. These riders were charged with accompanying the king and queen through the streets of Paris. Importantly, the cavalcade included the Grand Condé, Louis de Bourbon, Prince of Condé, who had only recently been pardoned for his acts of sedition against the French crown during the Fronde. The inclusion of Condé in the festivities as well as the choice of the location of one of the most notorious battles of the Fronde as its first major point—the Faubourg Saint-Antoine—transformed the once hostile city of Paris into a site of Bourbon revitalization. In a single move sites of unrest (such as the Faubourg Saint-Antoine) and daring agitators (Condé) were shown to fall under monarchical authority.[35] While Condé's exoneration was made at the insistence of the Spanish, his attendance on the king and his new bride during the Parisian entry proved valuable for the young king, whose ability

[32] Margit Thøfner, "Marrying the City, Mothering the Country: Gender and Visual Conventions in Johannes Bochius's Account of the Joyous Entry of the Archduke Albert and the Infanta Isabella into Antwerp," *Oxford Art Journal*, 22, no. 1 (1999): 6.

[33] Anthony Levi, *Louis XIV* (London: Constable & Robinson, 2004), 72.

[34] Delpont, *Parade pour une infante*, 65, 71–72.

[35] Alain Thillay, *Le Faubourg Saint-Antoine et ses "faux-ouvriers": liberté du travail à Paris aux XVIIe et XVIIIe siècles* (Seyssel: Champ Vallon; Epoques edn., 2002), 21. The Faubourg Saint-Antoine arch and the bridge of the Porte Saint-Antoine, sites of one of the bloodiest battles of the Fronde, were rebuilt for the event.

to control previously dissident forces within his realm was thus confirmed.[36] The inclusion of the Spanish ambassador to France, who rode beside the queen's carriage, further demonstrated the monarchy's resurgence since the devastating events of the civil war.[37]

The inclusion of former enemies of the Bourbon dynasty in the cavalcade shows the importance of the festivities as a moment of affirmation for the French crown, which, having overcome its recent hardships, re-formed its image in a triumphal mode. Furthermore, the Parisian entry made explicit connections between the presence of María Teresa and improving Bourbon fortunes. As an actualization of both the new political reality (and mounting aspirations) of the Bourbon regime, both Louis XIV and María Teresa were framed as political allegories in the program of festivities and were celebrated as heralds of peace and stability.[38] Witnesses to the entry linked the presence of María Teresa to the rising fortunes of the monarchy, as articulated by Madame de Motteville:

> The grandeur that was seen in his person made him admired by all, and the peace he had just given to France, with this princess he gave France as queen, revived in the hearts of his people their zeal and their fidelity, and all present on this day judged themselves happy in having him for their King and Master.[39]

Madame de Motteville's observation forges a connection between the enthusiastic response offered by the public to their king and the implications of the arrival of his new bride in France. Presumably Motteville's impression was, at least to some extent, informed by the imagery of the entry itself, which presented an analogous notion of the role and status of the king and queen at the time of their marriage.

As with the representation of the events of the exchange and marriage in state-sponsored literature like *La Pompe*, the Parisian entry imagery employed Spanish Habsburg visual motifs to draw them into harmonious engagement with Bourbon heraldry and demonstrate the accord that had been achieved between the two states. The king and queen featured heavily in this visual program and were figured as embodiments of interdynastic cooperation and, ultimately, peace. For instance, the temporary ceremonial arches erected for the occasion displayed the ability of the crown to sustain peace and prosperity, articulated through an intricate program of visual devices specifically related to the bride and bridegroom.

---

36 Anon., *Traitté de Paix des Pyrénées*, article 60.

37 Anon., *La Pompe*, 16.

38 It must be remembered that at this time France was in dire financial circumstances and the pomp of the entries was a projection of the desire for prosperity and economic stability. Levi, *Louis XIV*, 109–10.

39 "La grandeur qu'il faisoit voir en sa personne [Louis XIV] le fit admirer de tous, et la paix qu'il venoit de donner á la France, avec cette princesse qu'il leur donnoit pour reine, renouvela leur zéle et leur fidélité; et tous ceux qui en ce jour purent le regards s'estimèrent heureux de l'avoir pour leur Roi at leur Maître"; Motteville, *Mémoires*, 499–500.

The triumphal arch of the Faubourg Saint-Antoine displayed an even number of French fleurs-de-lis and Spanish (or Castilian) castles arranged in its metopes. Placed on either side of these symbols were the entwined initials of the king and queen, demonstrating the enduring union of previously disengaged forces. The theme of unification was once again taken up on the triumphal arch of the Place de la Dauphine, where the king and queen were shown riding together in a chariot drawn in unison by a cock and a lion (symbols of France and Spain, respectively) with Hymen, the Greek god of marriage ceremonies, conducting their passage. In describing this imagery, the official publication released to mark the event, *L'entrée triomphante de Leurs Majestez Louis XIV Roy de France et de Navarre et Marie Therese D'Austriche*, proclaimed: "Hymen conducts a cock and a lion, who like the marriage represent the reunited states of France and Spain, signified by these courageous animals."[40] *L'entrée* then explicitly states that the marriage should be considered as representative of the peace accord during the festivities. Furthermore, it makes a claim that both the marriage and the peace were understood as unifying forces within the French state itself, stating, "The Peace and the Marriage ... are symbols of mildness and concord, and of the union of a state."[41]

Unity, a recurrent theme of the decorations, also functioned as the message of the visual program that decorated the arch of the Faubourg Saint-Antoine. Its imagery showed the king and queen with comparable weight, pursuing a parallel agenda. Louis XIV was depicted in the company of a personification of peace, who held an olive branch. *L'entrée* reveals that the queen was also shown holding an olive branch and emphasizes the importance of her role by claiming that she wields it as ably as her spouse.[42] The queen's ownership of the olive branch in the triumphal imagery of the Faubourg Saint-Antoine asserted her crucial role in securing the legitimacy of the peace. The symbolic act of her union with Louis XIV was an assurance of the commitment to its very survival. Moreover, the presence of María Teresa in France facilitated an activation of the monarchy's resurgence after years of instability. Through the entry ceremonies in celebration of the marriage, the animosity between the monarchy and its former opponents, Gaston d'Orléans and the Grand Condé, was publicly resolved. As both rebels had relied on Spanish support to agitate

---

40 "L'Hymen qui conduit le Cocq & le Lion, represente comme ce Mariage a reüny La France et l'Espgane signidiées animaux extremement courageux": Anonymous, *L'entrée triomphante de Leurs Majestéz Louis XIV, roi de France et de Navarre, et Marie-Thérèse d'Austriche, son épouse, dans la ville de Paris Capitale de Leurs Royaumes au Retour de la Signature de la Paix Generalle et de leur Hereux Mariages* (Paris: Pierre le Petit, 1662), 26.

41 "La Paix et le Mariage ... sont le symbole de la doucer de la concorde, & de l'union d'un Estat." Anon., *L'entrée triomphante*, 26.

42 "Elle tenoit une branche d'olive á la main aussi bien que le Roy"; Anon., *L'entrée triomphante*, 2.

against the Bourbon crown, incorporating Spanish imagery into the festivities refigured relations between all parties as a collective undertaking for the pursuit of peace.

Portraits

Once installed at court, the image of the queen as a unifying embodiment of peace continued to be promoted. The cousins Charles and Henri Beaubrun, who had long been prominent portraitists at the Bourbon court, were given the commission for the queen's portrait (Figure 2.1).[43] Parallels between the Beaubrun portraits and earlier representations of the queen, such as those offered through the texts of *La Pompe* and *L'entrée triomphante de Leurs Majestez* and in the imagery of the Parisian entry ceremony, demonstrate the rigor with which her image was approached and its value to the state machine.[44] The most significant connection to be made between the earlier imagery and the Beaubrun portraits is that they, too, promoted María Teresa's Spanish ancestry as an essential component of her image as a Bourbon queen.

The system of representation practiced by the Beaubruns has been little understood beyond the early modern period. The few modern scholars who have addressed their work have misrepresented their practice, and with it much of the function and meaning of French seventeenth-century court portraiture. While the Beaubrun oeuvre has been labelled naïve and mediocre, their portraits of the queen served as the basis of her representation in France for much of the duration of her life, and were even taken up and reproduced by other artists, indicating that their work went some way in meeting the expectations of the original commission.[45] Nevertheless, one of the primary objectives in offering the Beaubruns the commission was to connect her image with earlier Beaubrun sitters. As the queen represented the security of the peace for the Bourbons, it was essential that her image locate her firmly within their ranks. No other artist could achieve this with as much credence as the Beaubruns, for they had a history of clientage with the

---

[43] The Beaubruns had helped design the decorations for the Parisian entry festivities and may well have taken inspiration from this body of imagery for their own representation of the queen.

[44] Peter Burke has emphasized the importance of images in the development of Bourbon authority and the way that various forms of image making intersected to create a rich and forceful presentation of Bourbon authority. Peter Burke, *The Fabrication of Louis XIV* (New Haven: Yale University Press, 1992).

[45] While Christopher Wright labels the Beaubrun style as naïve, and Ronald Cohen characterizes the cousins as inferior, it is undeniable that they were long supported by the Bourbons, who must have considered their work successful. Christopher Wright, *The French Painters of the Seventeenth Century* (London: Orbis, 1985), 137; Ronald Cohen, "Sale Room Note: Charles and Henri Beaubrun," *The Burlington Magazine*, 122, no. 933 (December 1980): 872.

Figure 2.1 Charles and Henri Beaubrun, Portrait of María Teresa of Austria, Queen of France, date unknown, oil on canvas, 180 × 140 cm. Palace of Versailles.

Bourbons extending back to the origins of the dynasty in France. They were thus ideally placed to capture the queen's entry into a family whom they themselves had long served.[46] While other painters had begun to build strong relationships with the king during the early part of the 1660s, Charles and Henri Beaubrun had served the Bourbons from the time of Louis XIII through the regency of Anne of Austria.[47] They had painted several generations of the great nobles of the Bourbon court, and their portraits of the new queen provided her a right of entry into this select company.

In addition to the historical association of the Beaubrun and Bourbon families, the highly recognizable style of the cousin artists functioned to build meaning into the queen's image. An early portrait clearly demonstrates the ability of the Beaubruns to objectify the relationship between María Teresa and her Bourbon relatives.[48] The portrait shows the queen wearing a pale gown entering the space of the work from the right and seemingly striding forward into the pictorial field. This striding gesture, and indeed much of the composition of the work, shares its configuration with a number of other Beaubrun portraits. Modern scholars have chided the Beaubruns for their compositional duplications, insisting on originality in art of the past despite the anachronism of this modernist expectation.[49] In fact, the repetition of compositional formulas played a crucial role in imbuing the Beaubrun portraits of the queen with meaning. By connecting her with her compatriots through a shared canon of representation, the Beaubrun works affirmed her location amongst the Bourbon elite. This strategy responded to the conditions of the Treaty of the Pyrenees, as the queen's presence at the Bourbon court acted as an assurance of the peace, which was enacted only upon her arrival in France.[50]

Once established, maintaining the peace was dependent on the continuation of amicable Franco-Spanish relations, and the queen's portrait image was figured to present her role in securing the durability of the agreement. Not only do the Beaubrun portraits of the queen display her within a Bourbon context,

---

[46] The first notable painter of the Beaubrun clan was Mathieu Beaubrun le Vieux (c. 1525–97) who in 1584 was recorded as serving as page to the marquis of Ufré. He later left this post in order to make a career at the royal court, winning the title of painter to Henry IV. Georges Wildenstein, "Les Beaubrun," *Gazette des Beaux-Arts*, 6, no. 56 (November 1960), 262.

[47] Namely Charles Le Brun, the future *Premier peintre du Roi*, who in 1661 painted Louis XIV's portrait. Daniel Wildenstein, *Les oeuvres de Charles Le Brun d'après les gravures de son temps* (Paris: Etablissements Busson, 1965), 38.

[48] Charles and Henri Beaubrun, *Marie Thérèse d'Autriche, Reine de France*, oil on canvas, 134 × 114cm, date unknown, Château de Versailles. Constans catalog number MV3501.

[49] Mérot frames the cousins as "highly conventional" and "contrived": Alain Mérot, *French Painting in the Seventeenth Century* (London: Thames & Hudson, 1995), 193. Grate refers to the Beaubrun process as archaic: Pontus Grate, *French Paintings*, vol. 1 (Stockholm: Swedish National Art Museums, 1988), 85.

[50] Anon., *Contract de Mariage*, 295.

but they also directly reveal her Spanish heritage. This primarily occurs through the representation of her facial features, which are distinctly Habsburg in type, including her large nose which swells at its tip, her small but full lips, and, most tellingly of all, her voluminous cheeks.[51] While the queen presumably possessed these features in reality, the choice to represent her with such naturalism flouted French portraiture convention. French portraiture of the latter seventeenth century relied on classical notions of beauty and was heavily idealized as a result. The eminent seventeenth-century art theorist André Félibien remarked, "Beauty is the result of the proportion of the parts."[52] Félibien no doubt observed that portraitists such as the Beaubruns regularly harmonized the features of their sitter's visage, constructing women's faces on an even oval ground, populated by almond-shaped eyes, a tapering nose, and small mouth. All parts were formed through a systemized program of congruent elements. Another of the great art theorists of the age, Roger de Piles, provides the rationale for this practice: "A nose a little crooked can be rectified … for those who hold some rank in the world, or who are distinguished by the esteem in which they are held, they should not be shown with too much exactitude in the representation of their countenance."[53] According to de Piles, a portrait should not merely map the terrain of the French noble visage but instead reveal the elevated social status of the sitter. In standard Beaubrun portraits, women like the queen's sister-in-law, Henriette d'Angleterre, were revealed as members of the elite expressly through the process of idealization applied to their bodies. In a portrait now held at Gripsholm Castle, Sweden, Henriette is depicted in the same striding position as later applied in the queen's portrait. Yet there is a remarkable difference between their portraits. Henriette's features are typical of the Beaubruns, they are idealized and harmonized, despite the fact that she did not possess such traits in reality.[54] The Beaubrun portraits of María Teresa do not subject her to this process of idealization to the same degree, and she is shown with greater

---

[51] Fernando Checa, "Comment se représente un Habsbourg d'Espagne," in *¿Louis XIV espagnol? Madrid et Versailles, images et modèles*, ed. Gérard Sabatier and Margarita Torrione (Versailles: Centre de recherche du château de Versailles, 2009), 20–27. María Teresa's own son seemingly inherited the same Habsburg features: Charles Seymour Jr., "A Group of Royal Portrait-Busts from the Reign of Louis XIV," *The Art Bulletin*, 34, no. 4 (December 1952): 286.

[52] "La beauté vient de la proportion des parties"; André Félibien, *Entretiens sur les vies et sur les ouvrages des plus excellens peintres anciens et modernes*, vol. 1 (Trévoux: de l'imprimerie de SAS, 1725), 82.

[53] "Un nez un peu de travers peut être redressé … pour ceux qui tiennent quelque rang dans la monde, ou qui se font dinstinguer par leurs dignités … on ne saurait apporter trop d'exactitude dans l'imaitation de leur visagede"; Roger de Piles, *Cours de peintre par principes* (Paris: Gallimard, 1989), 2.

[54] Madame de Motteville wrote a long description of Henriette's physical appearance. It deviates considerably from her features as depicted in her Beaubrun portrait image. Motteville, *Mémoires*, 508.

individualization in her facial characteristics. While the queen's portraits reveal mild evidence of idealization, this remains a peripheral gloss to the main substance of her image, and is applied with considerably less enthusiasm than in the majority of Beaubrun female portraits. Her nose, her lips, and, most importantly, her cheeks, locate her outside of the norm of French portraiture convention.[55] Additionally, by alluding to, though not replicating, the naturalism that distinguished Spanish portraiture in the period, the sign value of the queen's Beaubrun countenance as "Spanish" was reinforced even further beyond the depiction of her Habsburg facial characteristics.[56]

These combined pictorial strategies reveal the early modern portrait as a tool of socio-political organization. In the seventeenth century, portraits of family members would often hang alongside one another in semi-public galleries. Hanging portraits in this manner highlighted the regulation of the social world around familial and dynastic principles which were advanced by the depiction of recognizable familial visages. Visual parallels were often constructed between portraits of family members to form dynastic connections and promote illustrious lineage.[57] Iconographic formulas, including systems of likeness, communicated something significant about sitters, their social connections, and their heritage and status.[58] Such systems enabled those fluent in the visual culture of the age to identify telling familial characteristics easily. Elisabeth Charlotte von der Pfalz, another of the queen's sisters-in-law, demonstrated this ability when she commented of a new arrival at court, "Her mouth is large and thick-lipped. She has, in fact, the real Austrian mouth and chin."[59]

The Beaubruns' inclusion of the queen's Habsburg facial features presents the viewer with more than an opportunity to identify her ancestry, however. The composition of her face, which remains regular across the various portraits, is constructed so as to bring French and Spanish signifiers into communion,

---

55 All four Velázquez portraits of María Teresa depict her with the same features, which are also visible in his portraits of her immediate relatives. John F. Moffitt, "The Theoretical Basis of Velázquez's Court Portraiture," *Zeitschrift für Kunstgeschichte*, 53, no. 2 (1990): 216–25.

56 Stanis Perez, "Quelques polis au bas de la bouche: ou les enjeux du portrait du roi," in *¿Louis XIV espagnol? Madrid et Versailles, images et modèles*, ed. Gérard Sabatier and Margarita Torrione (Versailles: Centre de recherche du château de Versailles, 2009), 61.

57 Dagmar Eichberger and Lisa Beaven, "Family Members and Political Allies: The Portrait Collection of Margaret of Austria," *The Art Bulletin*, 77, no. 2 (June 1995): 225, 233–34.

58 Joanna Woodall, "An Exemplary Consort: Antonius Mor's Portrait of Mary Tudor," *Art History*, 14, no. 2 (June 1991): 204.

59 Madame to Sophia of Hanover, November 8, 1696 in *The Letters of Madame: the Correspondence of Elizabeth-Charlotte of Bavaria, Princess Palatine, Duchess of Orleans*, ed. Gertrude Scott-Stevenson, vol. 2 (London: Chapman & Dodd, 1925), 143–44.

as forcefully registered in another Beaubrun portrait of the queen of the same period, where she is shown seated (Figure 2.1).[60] The queen's hairstyle, jewels, and clothes are all representative of the distinct fashions of the Bourbon court, and the prominent fleur-de-lis motif revealed by the presentation of the outer side of her mantle proclaims her ascent to the throne of France. The queen's dress thus placed her within a Bourbon context, yet these elements are not isolated from other components of the work which operate as cultural signifiers of the queen's Spanish heritage. For instance, as she turns to respond to the imagined presence of the viewer, the bulging mass of her hair which extends to the left of her face is separated from its mate on the right, which remains invisible.[61] The compositional support used to balance the depiction of the queen's voluminous hair thus becomes her rotund face. This gesture aligns the various components of her cultural identity into a consonant whole. With her French hairstyle and her Spanish cheek in perfect balance, the queen is represented as an amalgam of Bourbon and Habsburg parts and thereby figured as a symbol of Franco-Spanish cooperation, much as she was during the events of her marriage.

When considering imagery representing Queen María Teresa of France around the time of her marriage, it is clear that her cultural heritage served as a rich source of political capital for the Bourbon regime and was widely promoted through varying formats, in diverse locations, and to different audiences. At a time of significant change in France, as a young king began to establish the nature and vision of his rule, allusions to the stability and prosperity that the Peace of the Pyrenees would presumably bring to the French state were valuable commodities. María Teresa's personal journey through the splendors and hazards of the Bourbon court largely dominates scholarship dedicated to a study of her status in France, while the implications of her inclusion within the political collective of the Bourbon dynasty are less well understood. Yet from the early moments of her arrival in France, a concerted effort was made to utilize her specific potentials within contemporary political discourse in an effort to ratify the Bourbon regime.

The imagery produced to mark María Teresa's entry into the ranks of the Bourbons is certainly suggestive of a collective, or dynastic, foundation

---

[60] All the Beaubrun portraits of the queen derive from a bust-length drawing now held in the Cabinet des Estampes of the Bibliothèque Nationale de France. The application of the design of the drawing in the paintings reinforces the idea that the queen's image was a concerted and unified effort to present a stable and recognizable visage to an image-viewing public. The decision to repeat the composition was, no doubt, also based on a practical consideration, to save sitters from posing for countless portraits. The unusually high recurrence of the design first established in the drawing, and its longevity, communicates that its meaning lies beyond simple convenience, however.

[61] The queen is depicted coiffed in the fashionable style of the 1660s, when women of the court wore their hair in large bunches at the side of their heads, trained over wire. Richard Corson, *Fashions in Hair: The First Five Thousand Years* (London: Peter Owen, 1971), 256; and Jennifer Jones, *Sexing la Mode: Gender, Fashion and Commercial Culture in Old Regime France* (New York: Berg, 2004), 21.

to identity formation among the early modern elite. Forms of dress, visual devices, artistic style and motifs, and heraldic symbols were potent signs within the queen's image because of their ability to conjure implications beyond her personal history, to connect with the heritage of entire ruling dynasties. The farthingale, the manner of dressing hair, facial characteristics, and even personal ensigns were connected to a wider visual heritage, with the ability to produce meanings across time, space, and cultural boundaries. These values were nevertheless dependent on María Teresa's inclusion within the ranks of the Bourbon regime. Thus, when assessing the contribution she made to the development of Louis XIV's rule, her influence on the collective fortunes of the dynasty form an important component of an understanding of her historical significance in France.

Bibliography

Andrew, Edward. "Jean Bodin on Sovereignty." *Republics of Letters: A Journal for the Study of Knowledge, Politics, and the Arts*, 2, no. 2 (June 1, 2011).

Anonymous. *Contract de Mariage du Roy Tres-Christien, et de la Serenissime Infante Fille aisnée de Roy Catholique. Le septième Novembre 1659*. Paris: Imprimeurs & Libraires du Roy, 1660.

Anonymous. *La Pompe et Magnificence faite au marriage du Roy et de L'Infante D'Espagne, Ensemble les entretins qui ont esté faits entre les deux Roys, & les deux Reynes, dans l'sle de la Conference et Relation de ce qui s'est passé mesmes après Consommation*. Toulouse: Imprimeurs ordinaires du Roy, 1660.

Anonymous. *L'entrée triomphante de Leurs Majestéz Louis XIV, roi de France et de Navarre, et Marie-Thérèse d'Austriche, son épouse, dans la ville de Paris Capitale de Leurs Royaumes au Retour de la Signature de la Paix Generalle et de leur Hereux Mariages*. Paris: Pierre le Petit, 1662.

Beik, William. "The Absolutism of Louis XIV as Social Collaboration." *Past & Present*, 188, no. 1 (August 2005): 195–224.

Bertière, Simone. *Les reines de France au temps des Bourbons: les femmes du Roi-Soleil*. Paris: Editions de Fallois, 1998.

Bodin, Jean. *Les Six Livres de la République*. Gabriel Cartier, 1608.

Burke, Peter. *The Fabrication of Louis XIV*. New Haven: Yale University Press, 1992.

Checa, Fernando. "Comment se représente un Habsbourg d'Espagne." In *¿Louis XIV espagnol? Madrid et Versailles, images et modèles*. Edited by Gérard Sabatier and Margarita Torrione, 17–37. Versailles: Centre de recherche du château de Versailles, 2009.

Chevé, Joëlle. *Marie-Thérèse d'Autriche: épouse de Louis XIV*. Paris: Pygmalion, 2008.

Cholakian, Patricia. *Women and the Politics of Self-Representation in Seventeenth-Century France*. Newark, DE: University of Delaware Press, 2000.

Chrisman, Kimberley. “Unhoop the Fair Sex: The Campaign against the Hoop Petticoat in Eighteenth-Century England.” *Eighteenth-Century Studies*, 30, no. 1 (Fall 1996): 5–23.

Cohen, Ronald. “Sale Room Note: Charles and Henri Beaubrun.” *The Burlington Magazine*, 122, no. 933 (December 1980): 853, 872–73.

Corson, Richard. *Fashions in Hair: The First Five Thousand Years*. London: Peter Owen, 1971.

Cortequisse, Bruno. *Madame Louis XIV: Marie-Thérèse d'Autriche*. Paris: Perrin, 1992.

Cosandey, Fanny. *La reine de France: symbole et pouvoir, Xve–XVIIIe siècle*. Paris: Gallimard, 2000.

Crawford, Katherine. *Perilous Performances: Gender and Regency in Early Modern France*. Cambridge, MA: Harvard University Press, 2004.

Cronin, Vincent. *Louis XIV*. London: Collins, 1964.

Deleuze, Gilles, and Félix Guatari. *A Thousand Plateaus: Capitalism and Schizophrenia*. Translated by Brian Massumi. Minneapolis: University of Minnesota Press, 1987.

Delpont, Hubert. *Parade pour une infante: le périple nuptial de Louis XIV à travers le Midi de la France (1659–1660)*. Narrosse: Editions d'Albret, 2007.

Eichberger, Dagmar, and Lisa Beaven. “Family Members and Political Allies: The Portrait Collection of Margaret of Austria.” *The Art Bulletin*, 77, no. 2 (June 1995): 225–48.

Félibien, André. *Entretiens sur les vies et sur les ouvrages des plus excellens peintres anciens et modernes*, vol. 1. Trévoux: de l'imprimerie de SAS, 1725.

Foucault, Michel. *Discipline and Punish: The Birth of the Prison*. Translated by Alan Sheridan. New York: Pantheon, 1977.

_____. “The Subject and Power.” In *Michel Foucault: Beyond Structuralism and Hermeneutics*, 2nd edn. Edited by Hubert L. Dreyfus and Paul Rabinow, 208–26. Chicago: University of Chicago Press, 1982.

Grate, Pontus. *French Paintings*, vol. 1. Stockholm: Swedish National Art Museums, 1988.

Jones, Jennifer. *Sexing la Mode: Gender, Fashion and Commercial Culture in Old Regime France*. Oxford: Berg, 2004.

Levi, Anthony. *Louis XIV*. London: Constable & Robinson, 2004.

Méndez de Haro, Luis. *Letters from the Pyrenees: Don Luis Mendez de Haro's Correspondence to Philip IV of Spain, July to November 1659*. Edited by Lyn Williams. Exeter: University of Exeter Press, 2000.

Mérot, Alain. *French Painting in the Seventeenth Century*. New Haven: Thames & Hudson, 1995.

Moffitt, John F. “The Theoretical Basis of Velázquez's Court Portraiture.” *Zeitschrift für Kunstgeschichte*, 53, no. 2 (1990): 216–25.

Motteville, Françoise Bertaud, dame de. *Nouvelle collection des mémoires pour servir à l'histoire de France: Madame de Motteville*. Edited by Joseph F. Michaud and Jean J. Poujoulat. 2 vols. Paris and Lyon: Guyot Frères, 1853.

Orléans, Charlotte-Elisabeth. *The Letters of Madame: the Correspondence of Elizabeth-Charlotte of Bavaria, Princess Palatine, Duchess of Orleans*. Edited by Gertrude Scott-Stevenson. 2 vols. London: Chapman & Dodd, 1925.

Perez, Stanis. "Quelques polis au bas de la bouche: ou les enjeux du portrait du roi." In *¿Louis XIV espagnol? Madrid et Versailles, images et modèles*. Edited by Gérard Sabatier and Margarita Torrione, 57–74. Versailles: Centre de recherche du château de Versailles, 2009.

Petitfils, Jean-Christian. *Louis XIV*. Paris: Perrin, 1995.

Piles, Roger de. *Cours de peintre par principes*. Paris: Gallimard, 1989.

Roche, Daniel. *A History of Everyday Things*. Cambridge: Cambridge University Press, 2000.

Saint-Simon, Louis de Rouvroy, duc de. *Mémoires 1701–1707*. Paris: Gallimard, 1983.

Seymour Jr., Charles. "A Group of Royal Portrait-Busts from the Reign of Louis XIV." *The Art Bulletin*, 34, no. 4 (December 1952): 285–96.

Studdert-Kennedy, W. Gerald, and Michael Davenport. "The Balance of Roger de Piles: A Statistical Analysis." *The Journal of Aesthetics and Art Criticism*, 32, no. 4 (Summer 1974): 493–502.

Tétart-Vittu, Françoise. "À l'espagnole ou à la française: résistances et emprunts dans la mode de cour." In *¿Louis XIV espagnol? Madrid et Versailles, images et modèles*. Edited by Gérard Sabatier and Margarita Torrione, 203–20. Versailles: Centre de recherche du château de Versailles, 2009.

Thillay, Alain. *Le Faubourg Saint-Antoine et ses "faux-ouvriers": liberté du travail à Paris aux XVIIe et XVIIIe siècles*. Seyssel: Champ Vallon 2002.

Thøfner, Margit. "Marrying the City, Mothering the Country: Gender and Visual Conventions in Johannes Bochius's Account of the Joyous Entry of the Archduke Albert and the Infanta Isabella into Antwerp." *Oxford Art Journal*, 22, no. 1 (1999): 3–27.

Traitté de Paix des Pyrénées entre les couronnes de France et d'Espagne fait dans l'île des Faisans, le 7 novembre 1659. Paris: Imprimeurs & Libraires du Roy, 1660.

Walton, Guy. *Louis XIV at Versailles*. London: Viking, 1986.

Wildenstein, Daniel. *Les oeuvres de Charles Le Brun d'après les gravures de son temps*. Paris: Etablissements Busson, 1965.

Wildenstein, Georges. "Les Beaubrun." *Gazette des Beaux-Arts*, 56, no. 6 (November 1960): 261–74.

Witthoft, Brucia. "Marriage Rituals and Marriage Chests in Quattrocento Florence."*Artibus et historiae*, 3, no. 5 (1982): 43–59.

Woodall, Joanna. "An Exemplary Consort: Antonius Mor's Portrait of Mary Tudor." *Art History*, 14, no. 2 (June 1991): 192–224.

Wright, Christopher. *The French Painters of the Seventeenth Century*. London: Orbis, 1985.

Zanger, Abby. *Scenes from the Marriage of Louis XIV: Nuptial Fictions and the Making of Absolutist Power*. Stanford, CA: Stanford University Press, 1997.

Chapter 3
A Queen between Three Worlds: Italy, Spain, and France*

María de los Ángeles Pérez Samper

The Princess from Parma

Elisabetta Farnese (1692–1766)—princess of Parma, born and educated in Italy, queen of Spain—lived in Madrid, La Granja de San Ildefonso, El Escorial, Aranjuez, Seville, and Granada for half a century (Figure 3.1). She was queen of Spain for more than 30 years, exercising great influence over her husband, Philip V (r. 1700–46). A skilled political and cultural mediator, her ideas, tastes, and actions had enormous influence in the royal family, at court, and throughout Spanish society. Moreover, her influence extended to her birthplace, Parma, and to other Italian territories, especially Naples and Sicily, where her son Charles reigned. Through marriage she was a member of the Bourbon dynasty and closely linked to France, but her relations with that country were often tense. As an Italian princess who married the Bourbon king of Spain, she lived at the intersection of three worlds—Italy, Spain, and France—and thus she provides an excellent example of how a royal woman adapted to a new setting and helped shape cultural practices.[1]

On her father's side, Elisabetta came from the long line of the Farneses, dating back to the twelfth century. Thanks to their immense patrimony and wealth, the Farnese family was prominent at several points in Italian history, and for two centuries they ruled their duchies as one of Italy's most important families and relatives of Europe's rulers. At the end of the seventeenth century, duke Ranuccio II (1630–94) oversaw the family's decline, though there also were compensations, such as the acquisition of territories from the Landi family in 1682, and some important artistic initiatives, especially the radical transformation of the old Sanseverino castle in Colorno, turning it into a sumptuous summer residence designed by the important architect Ferdinando Bibiena. Ranuccio married Isabella d'Este, and they had several children: Odoardo, Francesco, Antonio, and Elisabetta. The eldest, Odoardo III, born in 1665, was the heir. On April 3, 1690, he married Dorothea Sophie of Neuburg; the wedding was celebrated in a grandiose fashion, with great festivities, which meant the local population was

* This chapter has been translated from the Spanish by Ruth MacKay.

[1] María Ángeles Pérez Samper, *Isabel de Farnesio* (Barcelona: Plaza y Janés, 2003).

Figure 3.1 Louis-Michel van Loo, Portrait of Elisabetta Farnese, ca. 1739, oil on canvas, 150 × 110 cm. Museo Nacional del Prado, Madrid.

heavily taxed at a time of economic hardship. The couple had two children, a boy who died after just a few months and a girl, Elisabetta. Odoardo died before his father, on September 5, 1693.

After Odoardo's death, Francesco Maria (1678–1727) became Ranuccio's heir, and he married his brother's widow, Dorothea Sophie. Francesco and Dorothea governed the duchies of Parma and Piacenza well during the first decades of the eighteenth century, which were difficult, troublesome years. The succession would go next to Ranuccio's second son, Antonio. But both Francesco and Antonio died without male heirs, and the male Farnese line came to an end.[2] The rights would thus pass to Odoardo's daughter, Elisabetta.

There were other inheritances in play as well, as the Farneses had intermarried with many great Italian families. They were particularly close to the Medicis, the dukes who governed Tuscany, lords of the arts, politics, and the economy. Elisabetta could claim rights to the Florentine line through her great-grandmother Margherita de' Medici. The Medicis, whose past had been brilliant for centuries, were by then in clear decline.

On her mother's side, Elisabetta Farnese had German blood. She was the daughter of Dorothea Sophie of Neuburg and the granddaughter of Elector Philipp Wilhelm of Neuburg, duke of Neuburg, and his wife, the duchess Elisabeth Amalie von Hesse-Darmstadt. Her maternal great-grandparents were, on the one side, Wolfgang Wilhelm, Count Palatine of Neuburg, and his wife Magdalena of Bavaria, and on the other side Georg II, Landgrave of Hesse-Darmstadt, and Sophia Eleanore of Saxony. The house of Neuburg ruled both the Upper and Lower Palatinates.

The Neuburgs were both illustrious and fertile; the elector had 24 children, of whom 14 survived past childhood. The Palatinates thus had a male heir, Johann Wilhelm, and could provide princesses throughout Europe. Maria Anna married Charles II and was queen of Spain; Eleonore Magdalena married Leopold I and was Holy Roman empress; Sophie was the second wife of Pedro II of Braganza and queen of Portugal; Dorothea first married Odoardo Farnese and later Francesco Maria Farnese and was grand duchess of Parma; and Eduvigis was princess of Poland. Despite the family's noted fertility, Dorothea managed to have just one daughter, Elisabetta. Through her mother, Elisabetta therefore was related to Europe's principal ruling houses.

But despite these extensive European connections, Elisabetta was raised in Italy, which would have a profound impact on her. Her earliest years were spent in a small world full of natural and artistic beauty. Her first landscapes were those belonging to the Farnese duchies, Parma and Piacenza; in Parma she visited the great Pilotta palace and the beautiful summer house in Colorno, nine miles outside the city, with its large gardens full of orange trees, perfect symmetry, and pleasant avenues decorated with pergolas, fountains, and sculptures. She also stayed in the

---

[2] Gustavo Marchesi, *Dinastia Farnese. Parma e l'Europa tra Rinascimento e Barocco* (Parma: Battei, 1994); Tullio Bazzi and Umberto Benassi, *Storia di Parma* (Parma: L. Battei, 1908); Giovanni Tocci, *Il ducato di Parma e Piacenza* (Turin: UTEC Libreria, 1987).

palace in Piacenza. Hers was a small world in the heart of Italy—a country full of history and political wisdom.

She spent her childhood and adolescence in the Pilotta, by the Parma River, which crosses the city. She grew up in a relatively uncomplicated atmosphere, far away from the luxury and ostentation of the great European courts. It was a fairly free environment, without the severe palace etiquette of Madrid, Vienna, or Versailles, but her mother always maintained tender vigilance over her. Like many aristocratic girls of her age she learned to read, write, sew, embroider, and pray. As a princess she received a good education and learned the usual subjects of philosophy, geography, history, and languages. She learned ancient languages, Latin, her Tuscan mother tongue, German, French (the language of power), and also Spanish, which was still very important, especially in Italy. She also received instruction in the arts, music, dancing, and painting. Her drawing master was the painter Pier Luigi Avanzini. She grew up surrounded by artistic treasures, which helped broaden and refine her artistic taste. She also learned to play the clavichord and was very fond of music, especially opera. She had good manners and was an agreeable and seductive conversationalist. She engaged in physical exercise and became a splendid ballerina, horsewoman, and walker. Dancing and horseback riding were essential skills for life at court. Most observers agreed that even as a child she had a great deal of personality, she was observant and had good intuition, she was active, full of energy, had willpower, and was good at making decisions. It is no surprise, then, that she easily and quickly went beyond the narrow boundaries of her hometown of Parma and became queen of Spain.

Between Italy and Spain

Elisabetta Farnese's arrival in Spain strengthened the Italian presence in the Spanish monarchy. Philip V could not accept the loss of Italy as a result of the War of the Spanish Succession, which ended with the Treaty of Utrecht in 1714. Spain's relations with Italy were centuries old, and there were an infinite number of economic, social, family, cultural, artistic, and religious links between them. Though the political connection may have been severed, the king wished to maintain relations, and he sought a way of strengthening his ties to Italy. Philip V's marriage with Elisabetta Farnese, heir of the Farneses and the Medicis, was a good tactic for the underlying strategy of regaining a presence in Italy. His rights could be used on the international chessboard so as to recover lost territory. From the start, Elisabetta was the symbol of Italy in Spain, especially after she had children and began seeking advantageous marriages for them (see Figure 3.2 for a portrait of the royal family). She used her rights over Parma and Tuscany and encouraged Spain to get involved in a series of European wars so as to obtain Italian thrones or titles for her children. Thus she managed to place her eldest son, Charles, on the throne of Naples and Sicily, and her second son, Philip, became duke of Parma.

Figure 3.2 Jean Ranc, Portrait of Philip V's family, ca. 1723, oil on canvas, 44 × 65 cm. Museo Nacional del Prado, Madrid.

Elisabetta always acted as a bridge between Italy and Spain. There are endless numbers of political examples, not only of the queen's leading role in the strategy of winning territory in Italy for Spain, but also of the protection she provided for Italians at the Spanish court, starting with cardinal Giulio Alberoni, to whom she was indebted for her position, as he was key in choosing her as the king's wife, and she supported him politically during the early years of her reign.

She also had an important cultural and artistic influence at the Spanish court. While Philip was inclined toward French art, Elisabetta preferred that of Italy. The couple agreed, however, on the importance of artistic patronage, and they undertook many important works and projects. After Philip V's marriage to Elisabetta Farnese, the artistic realm in Spain underwent important changes; old styles were rejected as old-fashioned and a new style was created, synthesizing the latest French and Italian fashions. The queen's contribution to and encouragement of these new projects were essential. Thanks to her efforts, Italian artists gradually received commissions in Spain. These included such figures as the architects Filippo Juvara and Giovanni Battista Sachetti, the painters Andrea Procaccini and Francesco Pavona, the stage designer Giuseppe Bibbiena, the poet Ottavio Baiardi, and musicians such as Paolo Antonio Foresi, Domenico Scarlatti, and Carlo Broschi, known as Farinelli. In the arts, as in all else, Philip and Elisabetta acted as one, taking on projects together, each adding to the other's preferences. As art lovers, collectors, and patrons of architects, painters, sculptors, and musicians, both Philip and Elisabetta strove to give the best of themselves in their common enterprise of creating a new Spanish monarchy deserving of its grandeur and in concert with the enlightened times.

An illustrative example is the palace of La Granja de San Ildefonso, a project that was very personal for the king and queen. It was first conceived as a modest retreat, but the complex grew to become an Italianate (more than a French) palace. Inspired by Philip's nostalgia for Versailles and the Chateau de Marly, the palaces where he had spent the first years of his life, La Granja also incorporated elements from the beautiful palace of Colorno in Parma, which Elisabetta remembered from her youth. She recalled the gardens of Colorno in particular, as she explained to her mother in a letter from October 3, 1721: "a house that the king has ordered built, and a garden, which may not be as beautiful as that of Colorno, but at least for this country it will be passable …."[3] From the start, the garden's design owed

[3] Archivio di Stato di Parma (hereafter ASP), Casa e Corte Farnesiana, serie II, busta 41, fascicle (hereafter fasc.) 5, Correspondence of Elisabetta Farnese with her mother Dorothea Sophie of Neuburg. Cited by Laura García and Luigi Pelizzoni, "La construcción del palacio de La Granja a través del epistolario entre Dorothea Sophie de Neoburgo e Isabel de Farnesio. Andrea Procaccini y el modelo parmense de edilicia de jardines," in *El Mediterráneo y el arte español. Actas del XI Congreso del CEHA*, eds. Joaquín Bérchez, Amadeo Serra Desfilis, and Mercedes Gómez-Ferrer (Valencia: Generalitat Valenciana, Conselleria de Cultura, Educació i Ciencia, Direcció General de Patrimoni Artistic, 1998), 182.

a great deal to Colorno. On September 18, 1722, in another letter to her mother, the queen said:

> I send you infinite thanks for the description of the Colorno garden, but as I have not been there for awhile and new things have been added, I did not understand it all. In any case, I think it must be much prettier than ours, if nothing else because of the old statues, which we do not have. The garden there is all flat and ours is on three levels. It is true that everything that could be done was done, given that it is a mountain town. What the garden does have is an abundance of water, and with that you can do anything you want.[4]

The monarchs sought out the advice of trusted artists regarding San Ildefonso. Some enjoyed special favors from the queen, such as Procaccini, a well-known Roman artist who had been director of the Vatican tapestry factory. Summoned to Spain, he arrived in Madrid in 1720 and was appointed the royal painter and put in charge of the new tapestry factory, in which the queen was very interested, so much so that several tapestries were made after her drawings, such as one of St. Cecilia playing the violin. Soon Procaccini was being consulted about San Ildefonso.

In planning the gardens, Elisabetta wanted to obtain a good set of ancient statues as splendid decorations. Searching in Italy, she discovered that Queen Christina of Sweden's collection was for sale, about which she had heard wonderful things already from her grandfather Ranuccio in Parma. Her artistic advisers, especially Procaccini, supported her interest in acquiring it, but the monarchs' own artistic taste was sufficient to judge it properly. As Procaccini said, the statues "had to be the most beautiful, because Their Majesties know how to appreciate them on their own."[5] The queen was determined to buy the collection and, given its high price, she had to persuade her husband to contribute half the money. The purchase was arranged by Cardinal Acquaviva, who managed to obtain Pope Benedict XIII's permission. The queen's efforts were finally satisfied in 1725 when the magnificent statues arrived at the port of Alicante.[6]

---

[4] ASP Casa e Corte Farnesiana, b. 41, s. II, fasc. 5, Correspondence of Elisabetta Farnese with her mother, Dorothea Sophie of Neuburg.

[5] José María Luzón Nogué, "Isabel de Farnesio y la Galería de Esculturas de San Ildefonso," in *El real sitio de La Granja de San Ildefonso. Retrato y escena del Rey*, eds. Delfín Rodríguez Ruiz, Helena Pérez Gallardo, and Mercedes Simal López (Madrid: Patrimonio Nacional, 2000), 203–19.

[6] P.F., "Nota delle casse che gli 2 di marzo de 1725 devono esser imbarcate," *Revista de archivos, bibliotecas y museos* (1876), 163–64 and 180–81; X. de Salas, "Compra para España de la colección de antigüedades de Cristina de Suecia," *Archivo español de arte*, 14 (1940–41), 242–46; Mónica Riaza de los Mozos and Mercedes Simal López, "'La Statua è un prodigio dell'arte': Isabel de Farnesio y la colección de Cristina de Suecia en La Granja de San Ildefonso," *Reales sitios*, no. 144 (2000): 56–67; Mercedes Simal López, "Isabel de Farnesio y la colección real española de escultura. Distintas noticias sobre compras,

The queen also took an interest in decorating the interior of the palace. The marquis Annibale Scotti, who for many years was a servant and advisor to the queen and whose influence increased once Alberoni fell from power, was put in charge of helping the queen with this task. The king contributed to the interior decoration of the palace by purchasing the collection of Carlo Maratti, which Procaccini had suggested buying, and by providing many objects and pieces of furniture from his father, the dauphin of France.[7]

Procaccini's collaboration in designing the interior was considerable. He was put in charge of decorating the ground floor, which had three rooms facing a waterfall. This was where the monarchs planned on living. Procaccini was adept at interpreting the queen's ideas, which involved decorating the walls with various marbles and paintings around an interior fountain and decorating the ceilings with allegorical paintings. Procaccini summoned two of his disciples for help: Sempronio Subisati and Domenico Maria Sani, whom the queen also supported. The work moved ahead quickly. On August 13, 1723, Elisabetta wrote to her mother:

> Later we will return to La Granja, where, after eating, we are going to observe the work, which is well under way. I think if you saw it you would like it, because the garden is different from any other garden. The house is already all furnished; it is not pretty, but it is comfortable and organized. There is one room with marble walls; the marble is from this area, and I assure you it is very beautiful, and there are paintings on those parts of the wall without marble and on the vault, and there will be a fountain and marble floor as well. The design is new, and I am told there is nothing like it anywhere else; it was a caprice I had, and Procaccini drew it for me, I liked it, and thus it will be so, and everyone who has seen it praises it highly.[8]

Philip V, who was always insecure and had an uneasy conscience, wished to abdicate. According to his own confession, he was worried about the salvation of his soul. Like any good Bourbon, according to contemporary witnesses, he thought about the possibility of inheriting the French crown if the young Louis XV should die, but the great European powers (England, Austria, Prussia, and Holland) would not have accepted the union of the French and Spanish crowns. The king was obsessed with renouncing the throne and wished to leave Madrid and move permanently into the palace of La Granja as soon as possible, and so the work was sped up. Elisabetta, who was homesick for Colorno, asked her mother,

---

regalos, restauraciones y el encargo del 'Cuaderno de Aiello'," *Archivo español de arte*, 79, no. 315 (July–September 2006): 263–78.

[7] Manuela B. Mena Marqués, "La colección de pintura de Carlo Maratti," in *El real sitio de La Granja de San Ildefonso*, 194–201.

[8] ASP, Casa e Corte Farnesiana, b. 41, s. II, fasc. 5, Correspondence of Elisabetta Farnese with her mother, Dorothea Sophie of Neuburg.

the duchess Dorothea, for information about the gardens as she kept her informed about the construction work. On August 21 she wrote: "I shall impatiently await the drawings of Colorno and I will order the plans for La Granja, but the drawing will not be complete because the trees, such as the *carpanelle*, are still little, but I will make sure that we do the best we can."[9] The king and queen moved into the palace in September, when it was almost finished.

In addition to the palace of La Granja, Philip and Elisabetta also had the opportunity to rebuild the royal palace in Madrid—the Alcázar, which had served as the royal residence of the Habsburgs in the sixteenth and seventeenth centuries. On Christmas Eve 1734, fire destroyed this royal palace and Philip and Elisabetta were able to build a new one in their own fashion. The new palace was conceived to be a testimony in stone of the ideal Bourbon monarchy, both absolutist and enlightened, that Elisabetta and Philip were building. It would be a new image of the Spanish monarchy, worthy of its renewed grandeur and of the modernity of the Age of Reason and the Enlightenment. It had to be a symbol of the Bourbon dynasty's power and splendor. The king and queen were experienced by now and had defined their artistic taste. As a Bourbon, Philip remembered Versailles, but Elisabetta Farnese wanted to be faithful to her Italian roots, and she chose Italian architects.

Plans for the palace were drawn up in 1735 by one of the most important architects of the time, Filippo Juvara, who was the heir to the great tradition of Bernini and Fontana. Juvara's great opportunity arrived in 1714 when he began working for Vittorio Amedeo II of Savoy, which quickly gave him international renown as he built major palaces, including the Madama in Turin. He also worked in Portugal, England, and France, and in 1735 he was summoned to Madrid to build the royal palace. But his premature death, on January 31, 1736, led to a change in plans, and the work was undertaken by his disciple from Piedmont, Giovanni Battista Sachetti. It was Elisabetta who chose Sachetti, as she wanted Juvara's plans, which he had almost completed, to be closely respected.[10]

The new palace of the Spanish Bourbons would inherit grand traditions. There were many influences: the Versailles of Louis XIV, the Louvre of Bernini, a variety of Italian palaces in Rome, Venice, Parma, and especially Turin, and there also was a Spanish influence, drawing on the Alcázar and the Escorial. The Madrid royal palace was an affirmation of the triumph of the international baroque. Though there were French reminiscences, the dominant tone was that of Italy, especially Rome and the work of Bernini. But the palace combined all these influences and acquired enormous personality, clarity, and majesty.

Elisabetta's passion for art crossed many time periods and styles. Classical art fascinated her, as shown by her interest in obtaining Queen Christina of Sweden's collection of antiquities. The continual discovery of Roman ruins in Italy drew her

---

[9] Ibid.

[10] Carlos Martínez Shaw and Marina Alfonso Mola, *Felipe V* (Madrid: Arlanza Ediciones, 2001), 103.

interest, and she liked being well informed about those matters. Her son Charles gave her books about the excavations of Herculaneum and Pompeii, near Naples, as he wrote to Bernardo Tanucci, his chief minister in October 1762: "I gave the other copy you sent me of the third volume of *Herculano* to my mother."[11]

Elisabetta was a great art collector, preferring Italian artists and adding the great baroque Italians to the royal collection: Luca Giordano, of whom Elisabetta bought 19 paintings; Francesco Solimena, 10; and Mariano Nani, 24. Thanks to the queen these painters were much more appreciated in Spain. The royal collection also featured paintings by Tintoretto, including *Esther Before Ahasuerus*, *Moses Saved from the Waters of the Nile*, *Solomon and the Queen of Sheba*, *Joseph and Potiphar's Wife*, *Susanna and the Elders*, and *Archbishop Peter*. She also acquired *Earthly Paradise* by Jacopo Bassano; *Virgin and Child with the Young Saint John the Baptist* by Corregio; *Lucrecia* by Guido Reni; *Virgin and Child with Saint John the Baptist* by Andrea del Sarto; *The Virgin and St Joseph Adoring the Child*, by Gian Francesco Maineri da Parma; *Flagellation*, attributed to a disciple of Michelangelo; and several anonymous works including *Portrait of a Young Violinist, or the Viola Player*, at the time attributed to Bronzino; and *Mystical Betrothal of St Catherine*, attributed to Palma il Giovane.[12]

Patron of Italian Music in Spain

The queen had enormous influence as a patron of music. The king also had been a music lover ever since he was very young and living in Versailles, and after his accession to the Spanish throne he encouraged musical activities, especially at court. Elisabetta's arrival augmented and refined royal enthusiasm for music and opera. She loved Italian music, had herself studied music, and was quite an accomplished keyboardist. The queen wanted Madrid to have a resident Italian opera company, and so the Trufaldines company was revived in 1715. To achieve her goal she counted on the assistance of Alberoni and his friend, the count of Rocca, who hired actors who would spend years serving the Spanish monarchs. Later these actors were replaced by others, ensuring that there would always be performances and that Spanish society and the court could continue enjoying music, especially bel canto. The Trufaldines eventually dissolved, and it would not be until Farinelli's arrival in 1737 that opera was revived, but this time it was not light opera.

---

[11] Archivo General de Simancas (hereafter AGS), Estado, libro 324, San Ildefonso, October 5, 1762.

[12] Gonzalo Anes, *Las colecciones reales y el Museo del Prado* (Madrid: Amigos del Museo del Prado, 1996), 33–37; Juan José Luna, "Inventario y almoneda de algunas pinturas de la colección de Isabel de Farnesio," *Boletín del Seminario de Arte y Arqueología de la Universidad de Valladolid*, 39 (1973): 359–69.

During his years as the monarchs' favorite, Alberoni took charge of everything, including the opera, both at the palace and outside the court, as protector of the Italian comic companies and theatrical performances. After he fell from power, Elisabetta Farnese gave the job of musical promoter to one of her friends, Annibale Scotti di Castelboco, marquis of Scotti. In a decree on December 25 of 1719 he was appointed director of the Caños del Peral theater.

There were a variety of musical activities at court, especially focused on chamber music and religious music. Music also played a major role in the great public spectacles organized for festivals and celebrations. Opera became one of the principal forms of entertainment at court, where there was a cosmopolitan atmosphere and a noteworthy presence of French and Italian musicians, as in other arts. Elisabetta's taste definitely was inclined toward Italian music, and in 1729 she brought another Italian, Dominico Scarlatti, to join the other Italians, Frenchmen, and Spaniards who played for the queen and king. Scarlatti arrived from the Portuguese court in the entourage of princess Barbara of Braganza, yet another music lover. Scarlatti, an important composer and excellent clavichordist, had considerable influence on Spanish music during these years.

Foreign music reached Madrid through many means. Charles, king of Naples, sent his mother sheet music and *libretti* of the operas performed at the old San Bartolomeo theater and, beginning in 1737, at the new royal theater of San Carlo, which he ordered built though he himself was not much of an opera fan.[13] Although he did not share his parents' enthusiasm for bel canto, he always tried to please his mother, and he knew music was one of her great passions. He was always thoughtful toward her; in December 1737 he sent her volumes containing the operas of Pietro Antonio Domenico Trapassi, known as Metastasio.[14] The queen's correspondence with friends and family always contained commentaries on music and opera. Her friend the duchess of Saint Pierre wrote from Paris in the 1730s about the musical performances in the French capital, and the queen's daughter María Antonia would do the same after she moved to Turin in 1750 to marry.

Elisabetta Farnese was enormously worried about her husband's declining health and wanted to find a musician who could pull the king out of his doldrums. She chose the best singer of the age, Carlo Broschi, known as Farinelli or Farinello, who at the time was at the peak of his career. Born in Andria, in the kingdom of Naples, in 1705, he was a castrato who had had a brilliant musical career and was extremely well connected with important figures of the day, thanks to having been Nicola Porpora's student and a close friend of Metastasio. Quickly he triumphed in opera houses throughout Europe, in Naples, Bologna,

[13] AGS, Estado, Kingdom of the Two Sicilies, legajos (hereafter leg.) 5717, 5808–11 and 5836.

[14] Ibid., leg. 5811, Correspondence of Count of Santisteban and D. Joseph de Montealegre, fol. 113.

Vienna, and London. Starting in 1734 he sang in London for Opera of the Nobility, a company there, and was hugely popular, becoming a superstar among aficionados of bel canto.[15]

Queen Elisabetta, hoping that Farinelli's beautiful voice might cheer up the king, summoned him through Sir Thomas Fitzgerald, also known as Tomás Geraldino, who was then secretary at the Spanish embassy in London. As a result of these efforts, Farinelli left for Spain in 1737, planning to return soon to London, where he had several commitments for the coming season. On his way to Madrid he stopped off in Paris to give several recitals, one of them on July 9 in Versailles for Louis XV and his court.

Once he arrived in Spain the singer went to meet the monarchs at La Granja, and the miracle Elisabetta was hoping for came to pass. The king heard Farinelli sing, was enchanted with his sublime voice, and wanted him to stay forever. On August 25, 1737, he was appointed "Chamber musician of Their Majesties, who will no longer sing in public theaters." On August 30 the title of family servant was bestowed upon him, making him answerable exclusively to the sovereigns. He had an annual salary of 135,000 *reales de vellón*, an enormous amount, lived at the palace, and was given the use of a carriage and horses from the royal stables. Other members of the royal family gave him presents; the prince and princess of Asturias gave him valuable jewels, and the *infantes* Felipe and Luis gave him 800 *doblones*. The monarchs used their diplomatic corps in London to explain the change of plans that meant Farinelli would not return to England. Indeed, he would leave Spain only in 1759, after the death of King Ferdinand VI.

Farinelli never performed in public in Spain; his art was reserved exclusively for the royal family, whom he accompanied both in Madrid and on their visits to the nearby palaces. He gave daily recitals, and was not only a brilliant singer but also an intelligent, cultured, and friendly man as well as an excellent event organizer. As a result, he was an agreeable, trustworthy presence, additional reasons why he became so friendly with the royal family. Farinelli's day began at midnight when the king, after his "lunch," summoned him to his room to hear him, generally accompanied by the king's favorite string trio, whose players were Domenico Porreti, Gabrielle Terri, and Domenico Ciani. The "Farinelli entertainment," as it was called in the palace, lasted until dawn.

For the rest of Philip V's life, music at the palace consisted primarily of Farinelli's daily recitals, hundreds of arias and sonatas sung or played by Pergolesi, Leonardo Leo, Johann Adolph Hasse, and Scarlatti. Though the king had his favorites, which he often requested, the repertory was broad. In addition, Farinelli also organized what they called "domestic theater," which the royal family enjoyed on many an afternoon and which was an important part of court festivities.

A few months after Farinelli's arrival, on the king's fifty-fourth birthday, December 19, 1737, the singer organized an ambitious celebration that cost

[15] Patrick Barbier, *Farinelli. Le castrat des Lumières* (Paris: Bernard Grasset, 1994).

hundreds of thousands of *reales*. Giacomo Bonavia was put in charge of building a magnificent stage in the Casón del Buen Retiro. Aside from overseeing the music, Farinelli was responsible for the costumes, upon orders from the queen, who wanted this occasion to be the most magnificent ever. Luxurious fabrics had been ordered from Venice and Milan seven months earlier, and the costumes glittered with thousands of real diamonds, creating a fantastic effect. The set was imaginative and baroque. The orchestra had nineteen musicians, there were two choruses, and the four *infantes* sang solos. The work they performed was *Ceder honor por honor, nunca deslustra el valor*.[16]

Though Farinelli sang only before the royal family, his influence extended beyond court. Soon he took charge of musical performances outside the palace, and he was very successful.[17] His presence led to a shift in musical taste toward serious opera, productions with heroic themes, which were popular throughout Europe, codified and adapted to the style of the court in accordance with the great Metastasio's aesthetic and theoretical principles. From that point on, enthusiasm for musical drama spread throughout Spanish society.[18]

Farinelli's influence inspired the royal family and had an impact as well on Scotti, who undertook the job of remodelling and enlarging the small public theater of Caños de Peral. He was assisted in this task by Vigilio Rabaglio, a young architect whom Scotti had brought from Italy. The renovated theater, which drew Farinelli's praise, opened on February 16, 1738, Carnival Sunday, with a work by Metastasio called *Demetrio*. A group of actors from Italy participated in Madrid's new opera season, among them Annibale Pio Fabri, or Annibalino, an internationally famed tenor from Bologna who had been discovered by Vivaldi. Several members of the group—the bass Tommaso Garofalini and the sopranos Santa Marchesini and Elisabetta Uttini—were contracted by Farinelli to stay on with the monarchs. The Caños del Peral opera program was a great success and turned a profit, but a series of disputes among singers, musicians, and landlords dashed the venture, and the theater closed at the end of 1739. But a passion for musical theater was alive and well at court, and so the Coliseo del Buen Retiro was remodeled so that its stage could accommodate the large operas being prepared. Caños del Peral remained closed for many years, and the Coliseo del Buen Retiro thus became Madrid's only musical theater.[19]

---

[16] Margarita Torrione, "Fiesta y teatro musical en el reinado de Felipe V e Isabel Farnesio: Farinelli, artífice de una resurrección," in *El real sitio de La Granja de San Ildefonso*, 226–27.

[17] Francesca Boris, "Vado al teatro per disporre festa. Farinelli: Cartas desde España al Conde Sicinio Pépoli," in *España festejante. El siglo XVIII*, ed. Margarita Torrione (Málaga: Centro de Ediciones de la Diputación de Málaga, 2000), 349–63.

[18] José Luis Morales Marín, "La escenografía durante el reinado de Felipe V," in *España festejante*, 287–93.

[19] Margarita Torrione, "El Real Coliseo del Buen Retiro: Memoria de una arquitectura desaparecida," in *España festejante*, 295–322.

The queen was so interested in music that she took charge of everything, supervising all the details. The festivities around royal weddings involved premieres of new compositions; one such case was the opera *Alexander in the Indies* by Metastasio, with music by Francesco Corselli (or Francisco Coursellé), written on the occasion of the wedding in Naples of Charles and Maria Amalia of Saxony in 1737. In 1739 the wedding of the *infante* Felipe and the daughter of Louis XV, princess Louise Elisabeth, was the perfect opportunity to celebrate lyric opera at the Spanish court, and there were several important performances, all organized by Farinelli under the queen's supervision. On October 29, in the Salón de Reinos, a special stage was built for a serenade called *Los dioses vencios*, with music composed by the baron of Astorga, a well-known Sicilian composer and a friend of Scarlatti's. With the entire royal family in attendance, the singers included Annibale Pio Fabri, Ana Peruzzi ("la Peruchiera"), Gaetano Majorano ("Caffarelli"), and Lucia Fachinelli, all of them famous. On November 4, the festivities ended with the most important of the musical events, the premiere in the Coliseo del Buen Retiro of the opera *Farnace*, written by Courcelle, master of Philip V's chamber, with set designs by Bonavia. No efforts were spared (nor money saved) in making this a spectacular event. Along with the court singers, a group of Italian singers were contracted by Farinelli, including the castrato Caffarelli, who had studied with Farinelli in Bologna and took his place in London when Farinelli stayed in Spain. The soprano Vittoria Tesi also sang. For the orchestra, the Parma violinist Mauro Alai was there, having arrived from Naples; in 1714 he had come to Spain accompanying Elisabetta Farnese. The monarchs were so impressed by him that they paid him 200 *doblones* and gave him presents, clocks, and gold boxes, as well as a contract to remain in their service, which he did until 1747, earning an excellent salary. *Farnace* was so successful that it was performed several times. Another occasion for bel canto was the wedding of *infanta* María Teresa with the dauphin of France. On December 8, 1744, to celebrate the engagement, Metastasio's drama *Achilles in Sciro* was performed at the Real Coliseo del Buen Retiro; the music was by Courcelle and the sets by Bonavia. In this case, Farinelli, the producer, wanted to use only singers in the monarchs' service, such as Peruzzi and Uttini.[20]

Family ties increased the Italian influence even further. In 1750 the queen's youngest daughter, María Antonia, married Vittorio Amedeo, heir to the House of Savoy, and thus gained a throne. She would be a queen in Italy, which filled her mother with pride and satisfaction. Mother and daughter would never see each other again, but they corresponded week after week until Elisabetta died. Their letters were intimate, affectionate, and sincere, mostly about family news but also about cultural affairs, especially music.[21]

---

20 Archivo General del Palacio, DGR, Inventario 25, leg. 8.

21 Archivo Histórico Nacional (hereafter AHN), Estado, leg. 2693, letters from María Antonia de Borbón to her mother, Elisabetta de Farnesio.

Between Spain and France

The queen's life would always be marked by Italy, but there were many more influences. The princess of Parma became queen of Spain in 1714, and she lived in that country until her death in 1766. She was as Spanish, or more, as she was Italian. When she arrived, Elisabetta Farnese found herself in a complex situation in which French culture was predominant at the Spanish court. Philip V, a Bourbon prince, grandson of Louis XIV, born and raised in Versailles, brought about a rapid and intense influx of French influences throughout the crown, government, culture, and arts, and the gradual transformation of society and customs. French culture triumphed in Europe, and the court of Versailles became the model for all European courts, but especially in Spain. Philip V would symbolize France; the queen would symbolize Italy.

Elisabetta maintained a complicated relationship with France and all things French. She valued French culture, but the political and diplomatic rivalry made her pull back, and she tried to balance her husband's strong inclination toward his country of birth. Despite the fact that both Spain and France were ruled by branches of the Bourbon family, harmony did not always reign, and there were many conflicts, such as the war of 1718 after Spain's entry into Italy, the rupture of diplomatic relations in 1725 after the broken engagement between Louis XV and the *infanta* María Ana Victoria, and especially as a result of France's role in the War of the Austrian Succession (1740–48).

But beyond these conflicts, Elisabetta was very much drawn to French fashions. She bought French works of art, including books, jewels, miniature boxes, fabrics, and clothes. French fashion became the rule at the Spanish court, and the queen sought the most luxurious fabrics and the most exquisite lace and embroidery, along with the best-known stylists and tailors to make the royal family's wardrobes.[22] The queen's correspondence with the duchess of Saint Pierre includes many references to French clothing and hairstyles and the queen's purchases from afar, such as "one of the most beautiful silk cloths in Paris, [whose] background is straw yellow with subtle flowers that look as if they were embroidered."[23]

The *infante* Philip's marriage in 1739 to the princess Louise Élisabeth of France, known as Babet, the eldest daughter of Louis XV and Marie Leszczyńska, drew the queen much closer to the French court.[24] During the years that she and her daughter-in-law spent together at the Spanish court they became very close, and through their relationship the French influence at court expanded. After the wedding in 1744 of her daughter María Teresa with Louis, the dauphin of France, who would one day be king, the ties were further strengthened, and the marriage marked the consolidation of the two branches of the dynasty, one of

---

22 Amalia Descalzo Lorenzo, "El arte de vestir en el ceremonial cortesano. Felipe V," in *España festejante*, 197–204.

23 AHN Estado, leg. 2720.

24 Michel Antoine, *Louis XV* (Paris: Fayard, 1989), 470–72.

the so-called *Pactos de Familia* (family agreements) between Spain and France. The wedding was especially important for Elisabetta Farnese because it meant her daughter would inherit the French throne. What had not been possible with María Ana Victoria was going to come true for María Teresa. The queen and her daughter exchanged hundreds of letters about family, politics, and culture; but the premature death of María Teresa put an end to that means of cultural exchange.

Although Elisabetta Farnese never forgot Italy and always was drawn to France, her husband's great love, she also discovered Spain. She was especially interested in Spanish painting, and particularly admired Murillo, whose work she first saw when she was in Seville.[25] His sensitive, delicate paintings suited her taste exactly, and she took advantage of the time she spent in Andalusia to buy with her own money several of Murillo's works and add them to her own collection. Many religious works joined the royal collection, among them portraits of children such as *The Good Shepherd* and *Children with Shell*, and representations of the Virgin including an *Annunciation*, *St. Anne Teaching the Virgin to Read*, the *Appearance of the Virgin to St. Bernard*, and several *Immaculate Conceptions*.[26] There also was a *Christ on the Cross*, biblical scenes such as *Rebecca and Eliezer*, paintings of saints (*St. Jerome* and the *Chasuble of St. Ildefonso*), and of churchmen, such as the portrait of Father Cavanillas. It was more difficult for the queen to obtain scenes of popular customs, of which very few were available, but she managed to find some, such as *The Girl with a Coin*. She would always keep these Murillos, first in La Granja and later in Madrid, and for the rest of her life she followed his career. When Cardinal de Molina, president of the Council of Castile, died in 1744, the queen bought several more Murillos from his estate, among them the *Holy Family with the Little Bird*, which was always with her.

Her criteria for choosing paintings were varied, and she favored not only certain painters, such as Murillo, but also certain themes, especially family scenes, children, depictions of everyday life (*costumbrismo*), popular customs, and scenes of courtship.[27] She bought many and she also received gifts and inherited art, for example from her aunt, Maria Anna of Neuburg, widow of Charles II. When Marianne died in Guadalajara in 1740 she had named her niece Elisabetta as sole heir, and thus the latter received many jewels, more than 80 paintings (including several by Luca Giordano), and sculptures (including several works by Luisa Roldán), which would add to the decoration at La Granja.

At the same time, the traditional Habsburg enthusiasm for Flemish and Dutch painters continued, including Rubens, Dürer, Van Dyck, and Teniers. Elisabetta commissioned Annibale Scotti to go to Holland to buy a good collection of

---

[25] Ángel Aterido Fernández, "Las colecciones reales y el lustro andaluz de Felipe V," in *Sevilla y corte: las artes y el lustro real (1729–1733)*, eds. Nicolá Morales and Fernando Quiles García (Madrid: Casa de Velásquez, 2010), 205–18.

[26] One *Concepción* is in the Escorial; two (nos. 971 and 973) are in the Prado Museum.

[27] Teresa Lavalle Cobo Uriburu, "El mecenazgo de Isabel de Farnesio, reina de España," (PhD diss., Universidad Autónoma de Madrid, 1993).

paintings, given how much she liked Flemish and Dutch *costumbrismo*. She was especially drawn to Van Dyck's elegant portraits and bought eight of his paintings, among them *Self-Portrait with Sir Endymion Porter* and the *Portrait of Mary Ruthwen*, the artist's wife. Elisabetta and Philip also liked Poussin, the great seventeenth-century French classical painter, who spent much of his career in Rome.

Elisabetta loved beauty and she surrounded herself with beautiful objects to use or simply to gaze upon. In accordance with eighteenth-century fashion, she collected fans, buying some and receiving others as gifts. The count of Fuenclara, who was Spain's ambassador to Venice, in late 1735 sent her 12 beautiful fans painted by the best Roman artists.[28] Throughout her life, she collected many more, using them, taking care of them, and looking at them. A few painted by Batoni, which had suffered from use, were framed, and they decorated her boudoir.

She also liked miniature boxes and tobacco cases, luxurious objects that were very fashionable then and which she particularly liked because she was fond of tobacco. In her correspondence with the duchess of Saint Pierre there are many references to the lovely tobacco cases that the duchess sent from France, one of jasper and another of carnelian. The obsequious count of Fuenclara, now ambassador in Dresden to arrange Charles's marriage to Maria Amalia, sent Elisabetta six little porcelain boxes and two of amethyst. The messenger who brought the present also brought a letter from the count in which he said he knew "the queen, our lady, likes different sorts of boxes, and also likes porcelain, so I decided to place at her royal feet six of this material with two of amethyst." The package arrived on April 27, and on May 8 a reply stated that the queen appreciated and valued the delicate gift.[29]

Elisabetta was very fond of books, and since childhood had spent hours reading, a custom she would retain throughout her life. As queen, most of the books she read were religious, and the same was true of her husband, but she liked other things as well. Both read works of history. Elisabetta acquired books to add to her collection at the palace, which was considerable.

She often bought books from Paris, and she corresponded regularly with diplomats, friends, and agents about books. For example, Monsieur de Coulange and the duchess of Saint Pierre frequently gave her advice and sent her things to read. The queen's letters with Saint Pierre in the 1730s contain many references to books, both things the queen wanted to read and asked her friend to buy, and recommendations by the duchess.[30] Sometimes they were recently published, other times they were old, hard to find, and very expensive.

---

[28] Eugenio Sarrablo Aguareles, *El conde de Fuenclara (1687–1752)* (Seville: GEHA, 1955), 92.

[29] AHN Estado, leg. 2773, Fuenclara to Quadra, Dresden, April 2, 1738, and draft of reply.

[30] AHN Estado, leg. 2720, Saint Pierre to Isabel Farnesio (1730–32).

Elisabetta's tastes were unusual, and they revealed her thoughts. She was very drawn to chivalric novels, which were old (from the sixteenth century) but still circulated so both kings and commoners could enjoy them. *Amadís de Gaula* was in Elisabetta's library, of course, along with all his descendants, his wife Oriana, his son *Esplandián*, along with *Florisando*, *Lisuarte de Grecia*, *Amadís de Grecia*, *Florisel de Niquea*, *Rogel de Grecia*, and *Silves de la Selva*. In order to complete the cycle, the queen ordered the 15 volumes of Amadís, published in six well-bound books. She also ordered the saga of the Palmerines, including *Palmerín de Oliva*, *Primaleón de Grecia*, and *Palmerín de Inglaterra*, along with similar novels such as *Jean de Saintré*, also a chivalric novel but more realistic, and *Gerard de Euphrate*.

Several historical works are mentioned in her letters. For example, the duchess of Saint Pierre told Elisabetta about "a serious history by Mr Rollin … which was very well written and is very popular in France." The duchess was referring to Charles Rollin's *De la manière d'enseigner et d'étudier les Belles-Lettres, par rapport a l'ésprit et au coeur*, first published in 1726, which proved very popular.[31] Both Elisabetta and the duchess were keenly interested in ancient history, and the duchess recommended that Elisabetta read a three-volume history of Shapur I, king of the Sasanian empire (Persia) who ruled from 241 to 272 CE. The duchess also sent Elisabetta books on Greek history. But Elisabetta also was interested in more recent events, and in one letter mentioned a three-volume history of the regency of the duke of Orléans.

The two women also discussed novels. One of the favorites was apparently *Clélie*, a sentimental court novel by Madeleine de Scudéry, published in installments from 1654 to 1660 in 10 volumes. Other novels mentioned included the first volume of *Mariane*, a book referred to in Spanish as *Los desesperados*, *Antiope*, *Byon*, *Gerard duque de Nevers*, *Aristée et Télasie*, *Les veillées de Thessalie*, and *Mr. de Cleveland*, which the duchess said was "interesting." Elisabetta had a good library.[32] It included many books in French, most by French writers but also some translated from English or German. Some were recent, some were old. They indicate the many cultural influences on the queen, especially from France.

Some had been first published in the seventeenth century and were republished in the eighteenth century. She owned the multivolume memoirs of Omer Talon (1595–1652), *Memoires de feu de M. Omer Talon avocat general en la cour de parlement de Paris*. She owned Guillaume Girard's *Histoire de la vie du duc d'Espernon*, first published in 1655, about the life of Jean Louis de Nogaret de la Valette (1554–1642), a French noblemen, politician, military officer, lord of La Valette, and first duke of Epernon, one of Henry III's minions; the queen owned the edition published in 1763 in Rouen.

---

31 Charles Rollin, *Oeuvres complètes* (Paris: Didot, 1816–20), vols. 23–26.

32 Elena Santiago Páez, "La biblioteca de Isabel de Farnesio," in *La Real Biblioteca Pública, 1711–1760. De Felipe V a Fernando VI*, ed. Elena Santiago Páez (Madrid: Biblioteca Nacional, 2004), 269–84.

Among the seventeenth-century translations from English, and indicative of the queen's curiosity, were Sir Thomas Brown's works on medicine, religion, science, and esoterica. She owned a French translation of Brown's *Pseudodoxia Epidemica, or Enquiries into Very Many Received Tenets and Commonly Presumed Truths*, published from 1646 to 1672. The translation was published in Paris in 1733 as *Essai sur les erreurs populaires: ou examen de plusieurs opinions reçues comme vrayes, qui sont fausses et douteuses. Traduit de l'anglois*.

Most of her books were published in the eighteenth century. Some were on history and politics. She owned *Parallele des romains et des françois par rapport au gouvernement: premiere partie* (Paris, 1740) by Gabriel Bonnot de Mably (1709–85), a French *philosophe* from one of France's oldest noble families, son of the viscount of Mably and half-brother of Etienne Bonnot de Condillac.

She also liked reading biographies, and it is very significant that in her library was a biography of Queen Christina of Sweden along with three volumes of Queen Christina's correspondence. Elisabetta also owned *Les vies des hommes illustres de la France: depuis le commencement de la monarchie jusqu'à présent* (Amsterdam, 1745) by Jean du Castre d'Auvigny (1712–43), a French military officer and writer; when he died, his work was continued by Gabriel-Louis Calabre Pérau (1700–67), some of whose other writings the queen also possessed, for example, *Les vies des hommes illustres de la France continuées par M. L'Abbé Pérau* (Amsterdam, 1751). She also read historical novels, such as *Le doyen de Killerine: histoire morale composée sur les mémoires d'une illustre famille d'Irlanda*, by Antoine François Prevost, who also wrote the famous *Histoire du chevalier des Grieux et de Manon Lescaut*.

Her library contained important books on antiquity, some of them published at her initiative, such as *Stampe degli avanzi dell'antica Roma*, by Bonaventura van Overbeke. Republished by Jacopo Amiconi in London in 1739, it is dedicated to Elisabetta, probably to please her and also to facilitate his move to the Spanish court, which finally took place in 1747. She also owned the fourth volume of Giuseppe Vasi's *Delle magnificenze di Roma antica e moderna*. She also kept up to date on the latest archeological discoveries in 1725 at the Orti Farnesiani excavations, and later at the ruins of Herculaneum.

The queen also was interested in military matters, given her involvement in the monarchy's war efforts, and she owned P.P.A. Bardet de Villeneuve's *Cours de la science militaire: a l'usage de l'Infanterie, de la Cavalerie, de l'Artillerie, du Genie [et] de la Marine*, published in The Hague in 1739–40.

She was as interested in letters as in science, and she possessed many books about literature. She had several volumes of *Observations sur les ecrits modernes* (Paris, 1736), and *Raison, ou, idée de la poésie, ouvrage traduit de l'italien de Gravina par Réquier*, by Giovanni Vincenzo Gravina (1664–1718), an Italian writer and jurist and one of the founders of the Arcadia Academy.

Like others of her time, she was curious about science. She had several volumes of the *Memoires de l'Academie royale des sciences* (Paris, 1718). She also owned *Pyritologie ou Histoire naturelle de la pyrite: ouvrage dans lequel on examine l'origine, la nature, les propriétés et les usages de ce minéral important et de la plûpart des autres substances du même regne: on y a joint le Flora saturnisans où l'auteur démontre l'alliance qui se trouve entre les végétaux et les minéraux et les opuscules minéralogiques*, by Johann Friedrich Henckel (1678–1744), a German doctor who also was an expert on minerals, metallurgy, and chemistry.

Even the queen's culinary tastes reflected this blend of Italian, French, and Italian culture that would mark her life. She enjoyed eating and liked to eat well. The duke of Saint-Aignan, Paul-Hippolyte de Beauvilliers, who met her shortly after her wedding, commented on the young queen's predilection for good cooking, and in one of his letters he wrote, "She said that the late queen [María Luisa Gabriela of Savoy], who was Piedmontese, didn't eat a thing, but she [Elisabetta] is from Lombardy, where people eat twice as much and twice as well."[33]

Food at court was opulent, refined, and cosmopolitan, corresponding to high gastronomic ideals and entirely at odds with popular cooking. The arrival of the Bourbons in 1700 brought with it radical changes in many areas, which included eating habits. Philip V wished to reorganize the Spanish monarchy along the lines of Louis XIV's France. Accustomed to high French cuisine, he refused to alter his eating habits and brought with him French cooks from Versailles who introduced Spain to French cooking, which at the time was fashionable and prestigious throughout Europe. During Elisabetta's reign, French cuisine continued to dominate, according to the king's taste, but Italian influences were added, in accordance with the new queen's taste. Elisabetta Farnese had a significant impact on the menus at the royal table.[34]

Alberoni, who knew her well, also knew how much Italian cooking could please her. He wrote to the count La Rocca on January 1, 1715, "The queen has admitted me and does not hesitate to put her trust in me. She has repeatedly asked that I provide her with succulent Italian sausages and good Parma wine. Just yesterday she asked me to send her a dish of macaroni, which she loves."[35]

As a woman and as a queen, Elisabetta was a political and cultural mediator of the highest order. Her ideas, tastes, and behavior had enormous influence within the royal family, at court, and throughout Spanish society, as well as in her birthplace, Parma, and in other Italian kingdoms, especially Naples and

[33] Alfred Baudrillart, *Felipe V y la corte de France*, ed. Carmen Cremades, trans. Inés Martínez Cuenca and María del Pino Mendoza Lorente (Murcia: Universidad de Murcia, 2004), 481.

[34] María de los Ángeles Pérez Samper, "La alimentación en la Corte de Felipe V," in *Felipe V y su tiempo* (Zaragoza, Spain: Institución "Fernando el Católico," 2004), 529–83.

[35] Emile Bourgeois, ed. *Lettres intimes de J.M. Alberoni adressées au Comte J. Rocca, ministre des finances du Duc de Parme et publiées d'après le manuscrit du Collège de S. Lazaro Alberoni* (Paris: G. Masson, 1893), vol. 13, 372, 404, 548, 634.

Sicily, where her son Charles reigned. Though to a lesser degree, her influence also was felt in France. The impact of Elisabetta Farnese crossed borders. As a woman and a queen, she lived at the intersection of three worlds—Spain, Italy, and France—but her influence extended even further, reaching all of eighteenth-century Europe.

Bibliography

Archival Sources

Archivio di Stato di Parma (ASP). Casa e Corte Farnesiana.
Archivo General de Palacio, Madrid (AGP), DGR, Inventario 25, Legajo 8.
Archivo General de Simancas, Simancas, Spain (AGS). Sección Estado, Reino de las Dos Sicilias, legajos 5717, 5808–11, and 5836; libro 324.
Archivo Histórico Nacional, Madrid (AHN), Estado, legajos 2693, 2720, and 2773.

Secondary Sources

Anes, Gonzalo. *Las colecciones reales y el museo del Prado*. Madrid: Amigos del Museo del Prado, 1996.
Antoine, Michel. *Louis XV*. Paris: Fayard, 1989.
Aterido Fernández, Ángel. "Las colecciones reales y el lustro andaluz de Felipe V." In *Sevilla y corte. Las artes y el lustro real (1729–1733)*. Edited by Nicolás Morales and Fernando Quiles García, 205–18. Madrid: Casa de Velázquez, 2010.
Barbier, Patrick. *Farinelli. Le castrat des Lumières*. Paris: Bernard Grasset, 1994.
Baudrillart, Alfred. *Felipe V y la corte de Francia*. Edited by Carmen Cremades. Translated by Inés Martínez Cuenca and María del Pino Mendoza Lorente. Murcia: Universidad de Murcia, 2004.
Bazzi, Tullio and Umberto Benassi. *Storia di Parma*. Parma: L. Battei, 1908.
Bourgeois, Emile, ed. *Lettres intimes de J.M. Alberoni adressées au Comte J. Rocca, ministre des finances du Duc de Parme et publiées d'après le manuscrit du Collège de S. Lazaro Alberoni*. Paris: G. Masson, 1893.
García, Laura and Luigi Pelizzoni. "La construcción del palacio de La Granja a través del epistolario entre Dorothea Sophie de Neoburgo e Isabel de Farnesio. Andrea Procaccini y el modelo parmense de edilicia de jardines." In *El Mediterráneo y el arte español. Actas del XI Congreso del CEHA*. Edited by Joaquín Bérchez, Amadeo Serra Desfilis, and Mercedes Gómez-Ferrer, 180-84. Valencia: Generalitat Valenciana, Conselleria de Cultura, Educació i Ciencia, Direcció General de Patrimoni Artistic, 1998.
Lavalle Cobo Uriburu, Teresa. "El mecenazgo de Isabel de Farnesio, reina de España." PhD diss., Universidad Autónoma de Madrid, 1993

Luna, Juan José. "Inventario y almoneda de algunas pinturas de la colección de Isabel de Farnesio." *Boletín del Seminario de Arte y Arqueología de la Universidad de Valladolid*, 39 (1973): 359–69.

Marchesi, Gustavo. *Dinastia Farnese. Parma e l'Europa tra Rinascimento e Barocco*. Parma: Battei, 1994.

Martínez Shaw, Carlos, and Marina Alfonos Mola. *Felipe V*. Madrid: Arlanza Ediciones, 2001.

Morales Marín, José Luis. "La escenografía durante el reinado de Felipe V." In *España festejante. El siglo xviii*, edited by Margarita Torrione, 287–93. Málaga: Centro de Ediciones de la Diputación de Málaga, 2000.

Pérez Samper, María Ángeles. *Isabel de Farnesio*. Barcelona: Plaza y Janés, 2003.

Pérez Samper, María de los Ángeles. "La alimentación en la Corte de Felipe V." In *Felipe V y su tiempo*. Edited by Eliseo Serrano, 529–83. Zaragoza, Spain: Institutión 'Fernando el Católico, 2004.

P.F. "Nota delle casse che gli 2 di marzo de 1725 devono esser imbarcate." *Revista de archivos, bibliotecas y museos* (1876): 163–64; 180–81.

Riaza de los Mozos, Mónica, and Mercedes Simal López. "La statua è un prodigio dell'arte: Isabel de Farnesio y la colección de Cristina de Suecia en la Granja de San Idelfonso." *Reales sitios*, 144 (2000): 56–67.

Rodríguez Ruiz, Delfín, Helena Pérez Gallardo, and Mercedes Simal López, eds. *El real sitio de la Granja de San Idelfonso. Retrato y escena del rey*. Madrid: Patrimonio Nacional, 2000

Rollin, Charles. *Oeuvres complètes*. Paris: Didot, 1816–20.

Salas, X. de. "Compra para España de la colección de antigüedades de Cristina de Suecia." *Archivo español de arte*, 14 (1940–41): 240–46.

Santiago Páez, Elena. "La biblioteca de Isabel de Farnesio." In *La real biblioteca pública, 1711–1760. De Felipe V a Fernando VI*. Edited by Elena Santiago Páez, 269–84. Madrid: Biblioteca Nacional, 2004.

Sarrablo Aguareles, Eugenio. *El conde de Fuenclara (1687–1752)*. Seville: GEHA, 1955.

Simal López, Mercedes. "Isabel de Farnesio y la colección real española de escultura. Distintas noticias sobre compras, regalos, restauraciones y el encargo del 'Cuaderno de Aiello.'" *Archivo español de arte*, 315 (2006): 263–78.

Tocci, Giovanni. *Il ducato di Parma e Piacenza*. Turin: UTEC Librería, 1987.

Torrione, Margarita, ed. *España festejante. El siglo xviii*. Malaga: Centro de Ediciones de la Diputación de Málaga, 2000.

PART II
Male Consorts

PHILIP THE HANDSOME (1478–1506),
DUKE OF BURGUNDY AND KING OF CASTILE

PHILIP II (1527–98),
KING OF SPAIN AND ENGLAND

JOÃO SOARES DE ALARCÃO (D. 1546)
AND HIS FAMILY

Chapter 4
Voyages from Burgundy to Castile: Cultural Conflict and Dynastic Transitions, 1502–06*

Bethany Aram

The political strategy expressed in the motto "Let others wage war. Thou, happy Austria, marry" entailed geographic displacements and cultural discomfort for male as well as female protagonists. Wars and weddings constituted alternative, yet related, instruments for pursuing dynastic strategies. They also, almost inevitably, provoked cultural conflicts and transformations. Under such circumstances, recourse to peace rather than war exposed the young people involved to underlying contradictions and, often, conflicted loyalties.

On the threshold of the early modern period, female displacements and male inheritance/succession were the norm, whether sanctioned by custom or by the Salic law (which allegedly prohibited women from inheriting kingdoms and transmitting the rights to them), or by both. Nevertheless, dynastic accidents could happen. The imperatives of inheritance and demands of dynastic politics, which typically sent princesses to foreign courts, also could push young princes beyond their patrimonial estates and into unfamiliar cultural contexts. As Bartolomé Yun Casalilla has recently noted, such alliances could entail trauma, and cultural exchange was far from easy or automatic.[1] Displaced princes faced particular affronts to established gender roles. The short-lived King Philip I

* Preparation of this chapter has been supported by the research project P09-HUM 5330, New Atlantic Products, Science, War, Economy and Consumption in the Old Regime, financed by the Junta de Andalucía and directed by Bartolomé Yun Casalilla. An Erasmus grant for teaching mobility also facilitated part of the research.

[1] Bartolomé Yun Casalilla, "Introducción. Entre el imperio colonial y la monarquía compuesta. Élites y territorios en la Monarquía Hispánica (ss. XVI y XVII)," in *Las redes del Imperio. Elites sociales en la articulación de la monarquía hispánica* (Madrid: Marcial Pons Historia, 2009), 11–35. Another recent article has focused on the ties that local elites developed and maintained to royal courts through marriage alliances, along with their possibilities for social ascent. See Enrique Soria Mesa, "Family, Bureaucracy and the Crown. The Wedding Market as a Form of Integration among Spanish Elites in the Early Modern Period," in *Polycentric Monarchies. How did Early Modern Spain and Portugal Achieve and Maintain a Global Hegemony?* eds. Pedro Cardim, Tamar Herzog, José Javier Ruiz Ibáñez, and Gaetano Sabatini (Eastbourne,

Figure 4.1 Master of the Legend of the Magdalen, Portrait of Philip I of Castile, 1501, oil on canvas, 65 × 44 cm. Louvre Museum, Paris.

of Castile (see Figure 4.1), analyzed in this chapter, and the future Philip II, discussed in the following one, reluctantly accepted mobility derived from marriage rather than war.[2]

The vicissitudes of dynastic succession forced Philip of Burgundy (1478–1506) to travel to Castile and Aragon in 1501–02, and to return to Castile in 1505–06. These voyages threatened the prince's political and gender identities, upset his health, and, ultimately, claimed his life. The following case study traces the interdependence of love and war for young people with destinies tied to specific territories yet forced beyond them. Contemporary chronicles and archival documents suggest that cultural conflict and resistance numbered among the obstacles to Philip's and, subsequently, his son Charles's accession to the throne of Castile. How did princes raised in the Low Countries come to claim such distant and different realms? After examining this process in the case of Philip I, the discussion will turn to the impact of Philip's inheritance and succession on his equally, if not more, mobile descendants, whose multicultural inheritance and servants may have facilitated a shift from cultural conflict to cultural exchange.

A Fatal Alliance: The Failure of the Catholic Monarchs' Dynastic Strategy

A marriage accord established in 1495–96 had fateful consequences for European history as well as for the adolescents involved. By this accord Philip married Juana of Castile and Philip's sister Margaret of Austria married Juan of Castile, the two marriages laying the groundwork for the unexpected and unlikely ascendance of the Habsburg dynasty on the Iberian Peninsula. (See Figure 4.2 for joint portraits of Philip and Juana.) Philip and Mary were the children of Mary of Burgundy and Maximilian of Austria, and Juan and Juana were the children of the Catholic Monarchs, Isabel and Ferdinand, rulers of Castile and Aragon. Ferdinand and Isabel had negotiated the marriages of their four daughters and only son so as to circumscribe France politically, diplomatically, and geographically, although that design clashed with the francophile preferences that Philip and many of his closest advisors would manifest.

Prince Juan, the heir to the crowns of Aragon and Castile, was supposed to transmit his parents' kingdoms to his offspring with Margaret of Austria, but he died in 1497, shortly before Margaret delivered a stillborn child. To ensure dynastic continuity even in the case of Juan's demise or failure to produce an

UK: Sussex Academic Press, 2012), 73–89. Cultural tensions impeding integration, and the possibilities for social descent (as opposed to ascent), remain relatively unexplored.

[2] The most recent biographies of Philip I are those of Jean-Marie Cauchies, *Philip le beau. Le dernier duc de Bourgogne* (Turnhout, Belgium: Brepols, 2003) and José Manuel Calderón Ortega, *Felipe el hermoso* (Madrid: Espasa Calpe, 2001), although neither addresses the question of cultural transfer.

Figure 4.2 Unknown artist, South Netherlandish School, Philip the Fair and Juana the Mad of Castile in the gardens of the castle of Brussels, Triptych of Zierikzee, oil on canvas, each panel 125 × 48 cm. © Musées Royaux des Beaux-Arts de Belgique, Brussels.

heir, Isabel and Ferdinand had already married their eldest daughter, Isabel, to the heir of the Portuguese throne, who was closely related to Castile's ruling family. When the groom died in a riding accident, Isabel's parents obliged her to marry his brother, King Manuel of Portugal. Two years later, young Isabel died giving birth to a son, who survived only a few years. Any of these candidates—Juan, his elder sister Isabel, or either of their offspring—would have inherited the Spanish realms before Juana, Philip, and their descendants. No one had expected Philip of Burgundy to become king of Castile.

The marriage agreements his father negotiated placed the Burgundian prince and his consort in a difficult position. Among other conditions, Maximilian insisted on the obligation of mutual alliance against common enemies (at the time, France), and Isabel and Ferdinand argued that Maximilian should assign Juana a greater dowry for the sake of his son, as they would provide for Margaret of Austria.[3] The decision to situate each bride's expenses in her husband's territories would accentuate the dependence of both princesses and their retinues upon foreign lands and rents. This provision, moreover, would strengthen the control of Isabel and Ferdinand over Margaret's household on the one hand, and that of Philip's councilors over Juana's entourage on the other. Hence the double marriage agreement of 1495–96 reinforced the husbands' identification with territories obliged to adopt their spouses. In theory, women could inherit, exercise, and transmit sovereign authority to their heirs in Burgundy and Castile, whereas cultural norms described as the Salic law were cited to bar women from the throne in France and, more debatably, Aragon. Female inheritance, while possible in some territories, was considered undesirable and pernicious due to the risk of foreign domination that it could entail.[4] For greater security, upon contracting marriage to Prince Juan of Castile, Margaret of Austria renounced her claim to her mother's inheritance in favor of her brother in exchange for 200,000 gold ducats.[5] No one requested any such renunciation from Juana, perhaps considered too distant from the throne of Castile to be in any danger of inheriting it. Outside of France, dynastic alliances attempted to offset, or, alternatively, to exploit, the risks of female succession.

---

3 Instructions to the archdeacon of Seville for his negotiations with Maximilian of Austria, c. 1495, Archivo General de Simancas (hereafter AGS), Patronato Real (hereafter PR) 56–1; and minute of instructions from Ferdinand and Isabel to Francisco de Rojas to ratify accords, c. 1495, AGS, Estado I–ii, no. 360. For the mutual renunciation of the obligation to provide dowries for the brides, see the agreements of November 18, 1495, in AGS PR 56, 3 and 4.

4 On Salic law and the disadvantages of female succession, see Claude de Seyssel, *The Monarchy of France*, trans. J.H. Hexter (New Haven: Yale University Press, 1981), 48–49.

5 Renunciation of Margaret, the Archduchess of Austria, in favor of her brother, Philip, March 22, 1495, Archives du Département du Nord à Lille (hereafter ADN Lille), B 432, N. 17.810b.

The marriage accords of 1495–96, informed by hostilities toward France and the possibility of imminent warfare, were ratified by the 13-year-old prince, Philip, and his 15-year-old sister, Margaret, in Mechelen and in the imperial city of Nördlingen, more firmly under their father's influence, in November of 1495 and January of 1496. The notary's mark on the parchment that Philip and Margaret signed featured a cannon, its bang crowned by the cross and accompanied by trumpets: a collection of instruments for war celebrating the peace. The symbol, repeated three times throughout the capitulations, alluded to festivities that could not conceal tensions at the heart of the double alliance.[6]

Although Maximilian of Austria had a list of grievances against the French Valois (including their repudiation of Margaret as the Dauphin's future spouse after she had spent years residing at the French court), many of his son Philip's closest councilors considered themselves friends and vassals of Louis XI. These advisors, eager to maintain good relations with France, shunned the diplomatic and commercial alliance that came with a Spanish bride. Against the will of some of his closest advisors, Philip had acceded to that of others who supported his father. The prince's malleability—or at least his willingness to trust his councilors—was reflected in the epithet "*croit conseil*" (believer of council) recorded by Olivier de la March long before Philip became known as "the Handsome."[7] His dependence on councilors with diverse political and cultural agenda would lead to seemingly contradictory behavior; Prince Philip would claim, yet neglect, his bride and her unanticipated inheritance.

Whatever the political views of Philip's councilors, the marriage agreements forged in 1495–96 required the successive displacement of both female consorts. Prevailing hostilities between Spain and France made sea voyages the only option. Setting sail, both brides embarked upon what they envisioned as permanent separations from the lands and cultures that they had known. Facing rough weather at sea, Juana sought comfort from a confessor who assured her that childbirth would be worse, and Margaret allegedly joked that, having been "married" three times (most recently to the French dauphin), she could still die a virgin.[8] Only a series of twists of fate would oblige Philip himself to travel twice to Castile: the first time by land in 1501–02 to be recognized as the legitimate consort of the kingdom's heiress and reluctantly a second time by sea in 1506 as king consort. Festivities and celebrations hardly concealed the cultural discomfort or perils and the gender reversal

---

[6] For the cannon illustration on the notary's mark on the ratification of marriage alliances by Maximilian, Margaret, and Philip, 1495–96, see AGS PR 56–5, fols. 52, 54v, 57.

[7] Olivier de la Marche, *Mémoires* (Paris: Librairie Renouard, 1888), vol. 3, 315.

[8] Fray Andrés de Miranda to the Archduchess Juana, September 1, 1498, AGS, Estado I–ii, no. 366. The marriage contracted between Margaret and the French dauphin in 1482 is preserved in the Archives Général du Royaume à Bruxelles (hereafter AGRB), Audience 1082, fols. 117–35v.

that such displacements entailed. Dynastic marriages that marked the end of international conflicts could prove the harbingers of new ones.

Ideally, dynastic marriages facilitated exchanges between courts that would lead to further alliances, fostering, in turn, greater cultural and political integration. The Catholic Monarchs and the Emperor Maximilian had attempted to set a trend by sponsoring the marriage of Queen Isabel's attendant, María Manuela de la Cerda, to Maximilian's ambassador, Baudoin of Burgundy, an illegitimate son of Duke Philip "the Good." Expecting such miscegenation to continue, Isabel assigned 12 noble damsels from families attached to her court to accompany Juana to the Low Countries, with the idea that they would marry into Philip's ruling elite. Yet Juana and Philip failed (or refused) to allow their servants to intermarry.[9] The lack of alliances between Juana's Spanish maids and Philip's Burgundian nobles offended the ladies' families.[10] It also reflected—and may have perpetuated—Juana's lack of political and economic influence at her husband's court, pointing to deeper cultural prejudices. Indeed, evidence of rejection and conflict appears more readily than that of cultural exchange. In the absence of further intermarriage among servants, eventually the veterans of Juana and Philip's travels and the offspring of their endogamous elites born in each other's lands would prove better equipped to serve their lords' mobile successors. The seductive danger of a foreign alliance became epitomized in the fate of Juana's brother, Prince Juan, whose conjugal passion allegedly precipitated his death in 1498. The idea that the prince died of sexual over-indulgence became part of family lore, recorded in Charles V's 1543 instructions to his own successor, the future Philip II. Once Philip consummated his marriage, his father advised him, he should guard against excessive intercourse with his bride in order to protect his health, ensure successful procreation, and avoid the fate of Prince Juan.[11] Allegedly refusing to separate Juan from his bride ("what God had joined with the conjugal yoke"),[12] Queen Isabel lost her son, Juan, followed by her eldest daughter Isabel, and then her grandchild Miguel.

---

9 Bethany Aram, *Juana the Mad, Sovereignty and Dynasty in Renaissance Europe* (Baltimore: Johns Hopkins University Press, 2005), 34–63. For another example of a princess deemed "unsuccessful" for failing to marry her female attendants locally, see M.J. Rodríguez Salgado, "'Una perfecta princesa'. Casa y vida de la reina Isabel de Valois (1559–1568)," *Cuadernos de historia moderna*, 28 (2003): 71–98, Anejo [supplement] 2, 39–96.

10 Gutierre Gómez de Fuensalida, *Correspondencia de Gutierre Gomez de Fuensalida ... publicada por el Duque de Berwick y de Alba* (Madrid: Duque de Berwick y de Alba, 1907), 143–44.

11 "Instrucciónes de Carlos V a Felipe II" (May 4, 1543), in *Corpus Documental de Carlos V*, ed. Manuel Fernández Álvarez (Salamanca: Universidad de Salamanca, 2000), II: 100.

12 Pedro Mártir de Anglería to the Cardinal of Santa Cruz, June 13, 1497, in *Documentos inéditos para la historia de España* (Madrid: Imprenta Góngora, 1953), vol. 9, Epist. 176, 334–35.

Hence Juana's succession and that of her husband as consort crowned the failure of her parents' dynastic policies. Contrary to the Catholic Monarchs' political and cultural interests, the "conjugal yoke" that joined their heiress, Juana, to Philip also joined the kingdoms of Castile and Aragon to the Habsburg family's territories.

A Restless Prince: The Voyage of 1502

The possibility and, indeed, inevitability of cultural exchange on the Burgundians' travels through Castile and Aragon produced tension and hostility. Even before Philip's departure from Burgundy, the ambassador representing Isabel and Ferdinand at the court in Brussels, Gutierre Gómez de Fuensalida, warned: "The gentlemen abhor this journey because their customs in all things are as different from Castilian customs as is good from evil."[13] On the other hand, in a later panegyric for Philip I, Desiderius Erasmus wrote that many of Philip's northern subjects had feared that the journey to Spain would render him less cosmopolitan, more rustic, and more tyrannical if the "bad example of other kingdoms" corrupted him.[14] More than literary tropes, Gómez de Fuensalida and Erasmus expressed popular prejudices.

The Burgundian court, while itinerant, like that of Castile, also featured rotating terms of service, which bound the ruler to his lands and provided a potential escape valve for tensions at court. Customarily, Burgundian servants would alternate bi- or tri-annual periods of service in their home districts with terms of residence at court. Hence Philip's voyage to Castile and Aragon disrupted the mechanics of a household government that featured its members' periodic presence in the prince's territories. Burgundians and Flemings who accompanied Philip to Iberia could not return to their home towns and provinces during the habitual terms that enabled them to reinforce those regions' ties to the prince. Moreover, to win acceptance as future king or even king consort of Castile and Aragon, Philip needed to forge relationships with the elites of those kingdoms and their lands. No wonder, then, that his gentlemen and territories felt threatened.

Far from frivolous or inconsequential, courtly entertainments enabled elites to enact, transcend, or displace the tensions exacerbated by mobility and expressed in the binary oppositions that Gómez de Fuensalida and Erasmus evoked. French chronicles recording the voyage of 1502 highlight means of competition and cultural conflict alongside potential exchange in court entertainments, religious services, and sporting events. An emphasis on display, revelry, and disguise could not conceal tensions: as Philip's company neared the city of Burgos, municipal guards mistook his entourage of over 2,000 for an invading army and closed the

---

[13] Gómez de Fuensalida, *Correspondencia*, 181.

[14] Desiderius Erasmus, *Obras Escogidas*, trans. and ed. Lorenzo Ribera (Madrid: Aguilar, 1956), 266.

city gates until the *comendador mayor* of León interceded with city officials to solve the "misunderstanding."[15] Philip's position as the future Prince of Asturias at the head of a Burgundian invasion appeared ambiguous as well as threatening. Similarly, a Burgundian chronicler recorded that the Admiral of Castile, one of the highest-ranking Castilian nobles, later appeared accompanied by 400 to 500 men in red robes on horseback carrying javelins, producing the impression of a "great army," galloping one after another, "each with his javelin poised, crying out as the Turks do, with the trumpets sounding as if it were an assault in war."[16] The interdependence of love and war, attraction and hostility, inherent in marriages that bound distant kingdoms may have led to a heightened interest in representing a common opponent or "enemy" within a festive, courtly context.

For a combination of reasons, the voyage of 1502 intensified a "Moorish" craze at the Burgundian court. Reveling in the exotic fashion, Philip enjoyed dressing as a "Turk" to stage battles against the Christians, and mock warfare figured prominently in his honeymoon with the Castilian nobility.[17] On June 24, 1502, the day of Saint John the Baptist, Philip and the Admiral of Castile appeared dressed "in Moorish fashion, quite gorgeously," with "sashes of crimson and blue velour, all bordered in Moorish style" and "the bottom of their sleeves in crimson satin, with great scimitars beneath them, as well as scarlet cloaks and turbans on their heads." Outside the city of Toledo, they were ambushed by the duke of Bejar and his company, also in Moorish dress, skirmishing and throwing their spears "Castilian style" before Prince Philip and King Ferdinand.[18] Mock battles, in this case to commemorate the Christian takeover of Toledo from Islamic rulers in 1085, enabled Christian knights to show off rich attire, even circumventing sumptuary laws.[19] Appearing to enjoy such entertainments, in July Philip switched sides to dress as a "Moor" with the Constable of Castile and the duke of Alba.[20]

Judging from the chronicles, Philip dressed as a Turk more often than as a Spaniard, although the styles among elites tended to overlap.[21] Of two recorded

---

[15] "Relation du premier voyage que Philippe le Beau fit en Espagne," in *Collection des voyages des souverains des Pays-Bas*, ed. L.P. Gachard (Brussels: F. Hayez, 1876), vol. 1, 152. For a different interpretation, see Miguel Ángel Zalama, "Felipe I el Hermoso y las artes," in *Felipe I el Hermoso: la belleza y la locura*, eds. Miguel Ángel Zalama and Paul Vandenbroeck (Madrid: Centro de Estudios Europa Hispánica, 2006), 17–48, 23.

[16] "Reise des Erzherzogs Philipp nach Spanien 1501," in *Die Handschriften der K.K. Hofbibliothek in Wien, im Interesse der Geschichte, besonders der österreichische, verzeichnet und excerpirt*, ed. Joseph Chmel (Vienna, 1841), vol. 2, 622.

[17] Gachard, "Relation du premier voyage," 185, 193–94; Chmel, "Reise des Erzherzogs," 637.

[18] Barbara Fuchs, *Exotic Nation: Maurophilia and the Construction of Early Modern Spain* (Philadelphia: University of Pennsylvania Press, 2009), 185, 196.

[19] Chmel, "Reise des Erzherzogs," 612.

[20] Gachard, "Relation du premier voyage," 193.

[21] The archduke donned "Castilian fashions" on two recorded occasions: once to watch horse races and once to disguise himself in a crowd. Chmel, "Reise des Erzherzogs," 638.

occasions on which he donned garb identified as Castilian, one took place during the fair of Medina del Campo, which Philip visited incognito wearing a wig in addition to "Spanish" dress, and was observed at a distance by three or four of his chief officials.[22] The fashion for "Turkish" or "Moorish" attire—popular among the Castilian nobility since the thirteenth century—facilitated a flamboyant display of rich cloth. Yet the play of identities and costumes could disguise neither tensions among nobles vying for favor nor deeper cultural and historical divides. The Burgundians' festive appropriation of luxuries associated with Islamic Spain accompanied their vehement, and ultimately violent, rejection of Islamic persons and beliefs.[23]

The Burgundians, who delighted in fantastic Turks, rejected real Muslims. Their chroniclers frowned upon the large number of "Saracens" in Castile and Aragon, identified from afar not by crimson robes but rather by pieces of yellow cloth that they were obliged to wear. Nor did chroniclers fail to note these Muslims' social and economic roles; specialized in hanging tapestries and building houses and furniture, each of these "Saracens" reportedly paid one gold ducat in annual tribute.[24] The Easter holidays enabled Philip and Juana to sponsor a number of public baptisms and to bestow their own names upon the converts.[25] Increasingly determined to eradicate religious "pollution," pressured by Burgundian as well as Castilian ecclesiastics, Queen Isabel ordered the Muslims in her realms to convert to Christianity or to abandon them within four months.[26] Real or imaginary Muslims could unite Christian princes in their shared faith.

Religious services, another prominent backdrop to political events, emphasized a common heritage and, therefore, the possibility of cultural exchange between courts. Before potential cultural transfers, however, chroniclers often recorded reactions of marvel and astonishment, even rejection, among courtiers. In ceremonial efforts to sacralize the prince, the chapel figured as prominently as the banquet hall. On one occasion in Toledo, an ornate gallery used for the mass was subsequently converted into a room where the sovereigns dined beneath a gold canopy.[27] Each court aimed to awe the other: the Castilians displayed many tiers of gold and silver dishes during banquets and entertainments in order to amaze observers. In Toledo, the highest-ranking Burgundians astonished the Castilians by serving Isabel and Ferdinand in complete silence, which the Catholic monarchs admired greatly, being unable to replicate the Burgundian

22 Gachard, "Relation du premier voyage," 169.

23 This paradoxical attitude is further explained in Fuchs, *Exotic Nation*, esp. chs. 3 and 4.

24 Chmel, "Reise des Erzherzogs," 611; Gachard, "Relation du premier voyage," 225.

25 Chmel, "Reise des Erzherzogs," 640–41; Gachard, "Relation du premier voyage," 172.

26 Gachard, "Relation du premier voyage," 225.

27 Chmel, "Reise des Erzherzogs," 654.

ceremonial.[28] In Toledo, the Burgundian and Castilian households struggled to distinguish and to flaunt their own characteristic identities.

Along the same lines, each party's trumpeters competed to out-play the other's to the point that the Burgundians complained about the Spaniards' noise.[29] More harmonious collaborations ensued between the cantors in the Castilian, Aragonese, and Burgundian chapels, who accompanied their respective sovereigns. After competing in separate masses, these groups of musicians joined forces in the cathedrals of Burgos and Toledo.[30] On the first occasion, Burgundian cantors sang with the Castilian chapel. On the second, Castilians sang the first half of the mass and Burgundians the other.[31]

Sporting events, which Philip adored, also facilitated cultural display and competition. When the bishop of Cambray joined the court in Madrid after a visit to Santiago de Compostela, Philip astonished his Castilian hosts by jumping and bounding from one horse to another in an ostentatious display of skill, ordering his squires to follow suit. Castilian observers appeared caught between fear for the prince's life and horror at his rash revelry and unprecedented breach of decorum.[32] In the midst of ubiquitous jousts and tournaments, Spaniards noticed that Philip admired their riding style with short stirrups and bent knees "*a la jineta*," a style inspired by the Muslims. Seeking to oblige the prince, the master of King Ferdinand's stables, Ramón de Cardona, presented Philip with horses and riding gear and supposedly taught him the technique in only a few days.[33] Indeed, Philip's penchant for this riding style suggests a possible origin for the epithet "the Handsome" later applied to the prince. According to a 1611 dictionary,

---

[28] Gachard, "Relation du premier voyage," 188. On rivalries from the royal chapels to the banquet halls, see Álvaro Fernández de Córdova, "L'impact de la Bourgogne sur la cour castillane des Trastamare," in *La cour de Bourgogne et l'Europe. Le rayonnement et les limites d'un modèle culturel*, ed. Werner Paravicini, Beihefte der Francia 73 (Ostfilden: Thorbecke, 2013), 593–630, esp. 627.

[29] Chmel, "Reise des Erzherzogs," 612.

[30] The possibility of musical exchange among the chapels before and during their four-month convergence in Toledo are considered in Tess Knighton, "Una confluencia de capillas. El caso de Toledo, 1502," in *La Capilla Real de los Austrias. Música y ritual de corte en la Europa moderna*, eds. Juan José Carreras and Bernardo García García (Madrid: Fundación Carlos Amberes, 2001), 127–49. For the argument that relatively little musical exchange took place, see Alejandro Masso, "La corte y la música," in *Felipe I el Hermoso: la belleza y la locura*, ed. Miguel Ángel Zalama and Paul Vandenbroeck (Madrid: Centro de Estudios Europa Hispánica, 2006), 183–93.

[31] Chmel, "Reise des Erzherzogs," 612–13, 616; Gachard, "Relation du premier voyage," 177.

[32] Chmel, "Reise des Erzherzogs," 637.

[33] Lorenzo de Padilla, "Crónica de Felipe I llamado el Hermoso," in *Colección de Documentos Inéditos para la Historia de España*, eds. Miguel Salvá and Pedro Sainz de Baranda (Madrid: Imprenta de la Viuda de Calero, 1846), vol. 8, 86, 142.

> … jinete [rider] might come from cinete, which is *cinetum* in Arabic, and means ornament, from the word *ceyene*, to beautify or make beautiful ["*hermosear o ser hermoso*"], from the gallantry of riders when they rally to festivities with their turbans and feathers, fitted Moorish dresses and boots and the harnesses of their rich horses.[34]

This tenuous etymology suggests that Philip engaged in very handsome behavior, indeed. He also became adept at playing handball ("*la grosse pelotte a la palme*") with different nobles.[35] According to a Castilian chronicler, Lorenzo de Padilla, the prince "played all sports as a pastime, and was fonder of *la pelota* than any other."[36]

Bullfights and bull runs, while prominent festivities, inspired mixed reactions among the Burgundians. One chronicler described the spectacles as "a lovely pastime until the animals were killed" or "killed and martyred."[37] Following such events, Philip found it most entertaining to watch the crowds scramble for morsels of spices that he enjoyed hurling to them, in yet another transgression of Castilian norms reflecting social status.[38] Philip's largesse with edible spices, usually consumed only in the most elite banquets, created a public spectacle.[39]

While delighting in such activities, the prince became increasingly restless. As if fearing entrapment in Castile, he refused to be lodged in the castle of Segovia (or any other stronghold, for that matter), hunted whenever possible, and frequently escaped to the countryside to watch hares run or falcons flown.[40] Catering to such interests, King Ferdinand sent 150 falconers to accompany Philip from outside the town of Olias, where he had fallen ill with smallpox, to the city of Toledo.[41]

Following a series of festive triumphs, the sojourn in Toledo, where the Cortes, Castile's representative assembly, confirmed Juana as heiress to her mother's realms and her husband as her consort, marked the beginning of the end of Philip's forbearance. Two illustrations in a manuscript prepared for Juana

---

34 Covarrubias cites the Arabic translator Diego de Urrea on this point: Sebastián de Covarrubias Orozco, *Tesoro de la lengua castellana o española* (Madrid: Castalia, 1996 [1611]), 683.

35 Chmel, "Reise des Erzherzogs," 638, 641; Gachard, "Relation du premier voyage," 183.

36 Padilla, "Crónica de Felipe I," 149.

37 Chmel, "Reise des Erzherzogs," 627, 637.

38 Chmel, "Reise des Erzherzogs," 627, 629, 633, 637.

39 On the symbolic importance of spice ceremonies, see Bethany Aram, "Taste Transformed. Spice, Sugar and the Sixteenth-Century Hispano-Burgundian Court," in *Global Goods and the Spanish Empire, 1492–1824. Circulation, Resistance and Diversity*, eds. Bethany Aram and Bartolomé Yun-Casalilla (Basingstoke: Palgrave Macmillan, 2014).

40 Chmel, "Reise des Erzherzogs," 614, 616, 620, 626, 631, 635, 637, 639, 640.

41 According to another version, only 120 falconers were sent. Gachard, "Relation du premier voyage," 174.

depicted her seated above Philip in Toledo.[42] Juana, not Philip, appeared as Queen Isabel's successor in Castile. Although chroniclers phrased the matter discretely, Juana's superior status in Castile clashed with and may have exacerbated Philip's insistent recourse to masculine prerogatives such as hunting, sportsmanship, and, ultimately, marital infidelity. As Philip began to rebel against his situation as prince consort, conflict and illness pervaded his party.

In Toledo, a dispute erupted between Philip's top-ranking courtiers: his childhood caretaker (*ayo*), Henry de Berghes, bishop of Cambray and leader of the pro-Spanish faction; and the prince's former tutor, François de Busleyden, archbishop of Besançon. The disagreement culminated in Philip's expulsion of de Berghes and five other gentlemen sympathetic to the bishop from his entourage.[43] Despite the intercession of the queen and the princess on their behalf and the Catholic Monarchs' efforts to pacify, gratify, and compensate all parties, Philip restructured his own household and insisted that his pro-Spanish servants return to the Low Countries.[44] Yet their dramatic expulsion only appeared to exacerbate tensions in Toledo. First, a violent confrontation between the captain of Philip's archers, Rodich, "the bastard of Lalaing," and Philip's carver, Jean de Martigny, led the prince to order both of them placed in chains and subsequently expelled from the court and deprived of their property. On this occasion, however, the prince apparently heeded Queen Isabel's pleas to readmit the offenders to his presence.[45]

In another outbreak of violence, 20 or more armed Castilians assailed one of Philip's cantors, monsieur de Boussut, "the bastard of Trazegnies and Lourdault," and other Burgundians on August 16.[46] The Flemish fled to the monasteries of Saint Bernard and Saint Jerome, where Juana's soup-maker, Francequin, later died from the wounds received. Rather than placating her successors, Queen Isabel pardoned the aggressors in an attempt to pacify a local population increasingly hostile toward the Burgundians.[47]

The ensuing distrust may have intensified Philip's reaction to the death of the archbishop of Besançon, the leader of the anti-Spanish faction, in Toledo on August 23. In reference to Besançon, Erasmus would declare that the prince "treasured his health and well-being more than the possession of the Spanish kingdoms."[48] Apparently unsatisfied with the bishopric of Coria, which Isabel

---

42 Pedro Marcuello, *Cancionero*, ed. José Manuel Blecua (Zaragoza: Institución Fernando el Católico, 1987 [1502]), 64, 167.

43 Padilla, "Crónica de Felipe I," 87–88.

44 Gachard, "Relation du premier voyage," 190.

45 Ibid., 217.

46 Months earlier Boussut had attracted attention by forcing his carriage through the mountain pass of St. Adrian in northern Spain, despite the insistence of local Vizcayans that St. Adrian could be crossed only on mules. Boussut also managed to secure membership in a military order from King Ferdinand before leaving Castile. Ibid., 150, 244.

47 Ibid., 195–96. Erasmus, *Obras Escogidas*, 227 n1.

48 "Panegírico Gratulatorio a Felipe … acerca de su triunfal viaje a España y su feliz regreso." Erasmus, *Obras Escogidas*, 239–40.

and Ferdinand granted him, Besançon had solicited that of Segovia and even a cardinal's hat.[49] Had opponents poisoned the covetous archbishop? Suspicions persisted, despite the recorded deaths of six other Burgundians in the same city and the illnesses that many of them attributed to its "bad air."[50] Whatever their causes, these deaths, and especially that of Bensançon, increased Philip's desperation. The destruction of part of his lodging by fire in September, whether accidental or deliberate, ensured the Burgundians' much-awaited departure for the kingdom of Aragon.[51]

Upon leaving Toledo, the Burgundians received news of the death of companions who had opted to travel to the Holy Land rather than enter the Spanish kingdoms. The courtiers, enraged at this loss, which compounded others, expressed their fury by sacking a mosque on the way to Aragon, breaking lamps and everything in sight, to celebrate the day of Saint Luke.[52] Anti-Islamic rage in Philip's entourage did not prevent him from entering Zaragoza "gorgeously dressed in Castilian style" on October 26 or retreating in Burgundian attire on November 5, 1502, after the representatives of Aragon, Catalonia, and Valencia confirmed his succession in their realms as Juana's consort while stipulating that any legitimate male heir born to King Ferdinand would take precedence over Juana's rights (and his).[53] In a final, violent incident, some 25 servants of Diego Ramírez de Villaescusa—Juana's confessor, the bishop of Málaga, and a future rebel against Habsburg rule—left his household and were attacked by men affiliated with Englebert, the count of Nassau.[54] While difficult to interpret, such hostile encounters had become increasingly frequent.

The francophilic stance of Philip and his remaining councilors became completely untenable at the Spanish court when French and Spanish troops led by the *Gran Capitán* Gonzalo Fernández de Córdoba fought to control the Kingdom of Naples. Political and cultural conflicts, exacerbated by warfare, marked the end of Philip's first Spanish sojourn and the limits of his endurance. Abandoning Juana in the midst of her third pregnancy and fleeing his in-laws, Philip reentered French territory on the pretext of negotiating a truce between them and Louis XII. Ultimately, Philip may have attempted to use negotiations for the marriage between his own heir, the future Charles V, and Claude, the daughter of Louis XII, in order to wrest the Kingdom of Naples from Aragonese control. The prince of Castile apparently hoped to attain by marriage the same end that the Valois

49 Gachard, "Relation du premier voyage," 176; Padilla, "Crónica de Felipe I," 88; Chmel, "Reise des Erzherzogs," 631.

50 Philippe Haneton to the Chambre de Comptes à Lille, March 28, 1502, ADN (Lille), B 17795 (voyage de Philippe …); Gachard, "Relation du premier voyage," 166, 193–94, 216–17; Chmel, "Reise des Erzherzogs," 642.

51 Gachard, "Relation du premier voyage," 218.

52 Ibid., 238.

53 Ibid., 239–40.

54 Ibid., 243.

pursued by force. Such negotiations, while favoring French interests, clearly contravened those of Castile and Aragon. Once relieved of his son-in-law's increasingly unwelcome presence, King Ferdinand would deny having granted Philip the power to represent him in any such capacity.

Events surrounding Juana's confirmation as heiress to her parents' kingdoms highlighted the cultural and political interests, as well as hostility and misunderstanding, that accompanied her marriage to Philip and unintended succession. In addition to the cultural divide, these events foregrounded conflicting gender roles: Juana's obedience to Philip as his wife yet assertion of her own rights as heiress, and Philip's dominance as a husband yet subordination to his wife as prince consort.

The Voyage of 1506: King Consort or Regent?

Having become well acquainted with Philip and his entourage, Queen Isabel dictated her last will and testament one year after their departure, reaffirming Juana's rights as her successor and proprietary heiress. The queen also added a clause to her testament stating that if Juana were absent from Castile at the moment of her mother's death or otherwise unable or unwilling to rule, King Ferdinand should govern on her behalf. Hence Isabel attempted to ensure that Philip could not rule without Juana, while recognizing, simultaneously, that Juana would need her father's authority, experience, resources, and military capacity to rule without Philip.[55] Isabel died on November 26, 1504.

Philip's flirtation with the Castilian nobility in 1502 served him exceedingly well in 1506. Whether offended by Ferdinand's swift remarriage to a French princess, Germaine de Foix, or simply hoping to obtain more favors from Philip, most of the Castilian nobility rushed to please the Burgundian when he returned to Spain. Almost unanimously, Castilian elites turned their backs on Ferdinand and rallied in support of Philip and Juana. Although the duke of Medina Sidonia had invited them to disembark in Andalusia and Ferdinand expected them to arrive close to Vizcaya, the Burgundians chose to come ashore at La Coruña in late April of 1506, with Juana and others reportedly weary of the sea. Some 2,000 mariners and 1,400 unpaid German pikemen added additional, volatile elements into the cultural mix.[56] As if securing familiar ground after one month in La Coruña, Philip returned to the house of the Constable of Castile in Burgos, where he set about appointing his own men to strategic fortresses and posts, including the Royal Council and financial offices.

Philip's generous inclinations, on the one hand, contrasted with a practical inability to pay his escort and entourage, on the other. His financial situation

[55] AGS PR 56–18, "La carta patente de la reyna …," November 23, 1504.

[56] Gachard, "Relation du premier voyage," 450.

only became worse upon granting King Ferdinand handsome rents and control over the military orders to hasten Ferdinand's departure from Castile. Whereas in 1502 Philip had avoided entrapment and steered far from the castle of Segovia, in 1506 he granted the fortress to Juan Manuel, his favorite after the death of the archbishop of Besançon, and attempted to confine Juana there in order to prevent her from allying with her father or attempting to rule in her own right.[57] In addition to cultural differences, the Burgundians' main source of "desperation and discomfort" in 1506 was the fact that they went unpaid. Meanwhile, Philip alienated crown rents and patrimony in a paradoxical attempt to obtain (short-term) authority over the kingdom and its queen.[58]

The many embassies exchanged and two meetings that ensued between Philip and Ferdinand highlight the role of specific cultural intermediaries. Initially, Ferdinand chose his master horseman, Ramón de Cardona, as an ambassador to the prince whose affection Cardona had won by demonstrating equestrian techniques in 1502. In fact, Cardona and the accountant Juan Velázquez were among the only servants of Ferdinand who would retain Philip's favor.[59] Meanwhile, Don Diego de Guevara, a Castilian nobleman attached to the Burgundian court, who had accompanied Margaret of Austria to Castile in 1497,[60] and "La Mouche" de Veyre, Philip's ambassador to King Ferdinand, negotiated the principal accords between Philip and Ferdinand—accords which they subsequently renounced.[61] Another of these interstitial mediators, Philip's forementioned favorite Juan Manuel, the brother of María Manuela de la Cerda and a member of Philip's private council, guided Philip's attempt to exclude Juana and her father from the government of Castile.[62] In return, Philip

57 Ibid., 447.

58 Ibid., 452.

59 Diego de Guevara to Philip I, July 1506, ADN (Lille) B 18.826 (24463).

60 Payment of 800 *livres* to Diego de Guevara, squire, who would accompany Margaret of Austria to Castile, November 23, 1496, ADN (Lille), B 2.157 (70.901); Philip's orders to pay Diego de Guevara 400,000 *maravedíes*, January 15, 1504, ADN (Lille), B 2192 (73.953). Philip referred to Guevara as his "councilor" in 1504. Payment to Don Diego de Guevara, January 16, 1504, AGRB, 2191, fol. 277–277v.

61 Following Philip's death, de Veyre received safe conduct to return to Flanders with up to 50 horses and mules and some 25 donkeys, along with all of the jewels, gold, silver, coin, and cloth that they could carry within 30 days. Safe conduct for de Veryre, his entourage, and their goods, December 16, 1506, AGS, Registro General de Sello (RGS)1506, 12. King Ferdinand to Don Juan de Ribera, general captain on the frontier with Navarre, March 15, 1508, AGS, Cámara de Castilla Cédulas vol. 7, 239; minutes of letters of Ferdinand of Aragon to the King of England and the Princess of Wales, November 17, 1507, AGS PR 54:84(i).

62 The Venetian ambassador, Vicenzio Quirini, recorded the roles of de Verye, Juan Manuel, and Diego de Guevara as cultural (and political) intermediaries: see "Die Depeschen des Venetianischen Botschafters Vicenzo Quirino," ed. Constantin von Höfler, *Archiv für Österreichische Geschichte*, 66 (1885): 204–35.

appointed him one of the kingdom's chief accountants and governor of Asturias, entrusting him with the fortresses of Segovia, Burgos, Plasencia, and Jaén, as well as a captaincy of 100 lances and other revenues.[63] De Veyre and Guevara, like many of Philip's former servants with experience in Castile, would return to the service of his heir, Prince Charles, in Mechelen.

To increase Philip's authority, his advisors popularized the idea that the Kingdom of Castile had been conquered by love. After the death of Queen Isabel, de Veyre circulated a letter allegedly signed by Juana but really a forgery stating her great love for Philip and consequent unwillingness to confer the kingdom on anyone but Philip and his offspring.[64] In this sense, Juana's "great love" for Philip justified and legitimized the Burgundian takeover of Castile. Juana's supposed conjugal passion, like that of her brother, Prince Juan, had devastating consequences. Burgundian chroniclers depicted the queen as enraged with jealousy and slavishly attached to Philip even after he died on September 25, 1506.[65] Ambassadors echoed such accounts, which, in addition to their political utility, made attractive gossip. According to the Venetian ambassador, Vicenzo Quirini, King Ferdinand had urged Philip to endure Juana's jealousy "just as he had endured that of Queen Isabel, her mother, who, when overcome by jealousy, found herself in a much worse situation than that of his daughter."[66] Juana herself fed rumors of her dangerous jealousy by refusing to accept a female entourage, "knowing the nature of her husband." She did, however, appease the Cortes by agreeing to dress in Castilian rather than Burgundian style to identify her person visibly with that kingdom rather than that of her husband.[67]

Juana's great love for Philip became a political tool for avoiding war, securing the succession of Philip I as well as that of Charles V in Castile. Traveling to Castile in 1518, Charles drew upon crucial precedents that his parents had established. He, his siblings, and their heirs would also benefit from a network of increasingly cosmopolitan and experienced, if not always intermarried, servants at the service of the Habsburg dynasty.

---

63 Don Juan Manuel, declaring the receipt of one half of his annual pension of 4,000 L, October 15, 1505, ADN (Lille), B 2194 (74.278); AGS, RGS 1506, 12, royal decree regarding the appointment of Don Pedro Manuel, son of Don Juan Manuel "mi contador mayor" as regidor of Palencia. King Ferdinand, on the other hand, labeled Juan Manuel a traitor who had tried to "place divisions between parents and their children." Minutes of letters from King Ferdinand to Juana and Philip, undated [1504], AGS, Estado I–ii, N. 242; Petitions in favor of Philip's former servants, December 12, 1510, AGS, PR, 56:43.

64 Bethany Aram, "Juana 'the Mad's' Signature: The Problem of Invoking Royal Authority, 1505–1507," *Sixteenth Century Journal* 29, no. 2 (1998): 333–61.

65 Gachard, "La relation du premier voyage."

66 Von Höfler, "Die Depeschen," 239.

67 Ibid., 242.

Second-Generation Displacements and Cultural Baggage

Just as the voyage of 1502 provided training for that of 1506, Philip I's entourage (and Juana's position) in 1506 laid the political and cultural groundwork for the succession of Charles in 1518. Although they did not marry Spaniards, the servants who returned to Flanders after Philip's death in 1506 formed a nucleus of courtiers with experience in Spain. They may also have established a precedent for the alleged later plunder of Castile by Burgundians. In 1518, according to the chronicler Prudencio de Sandoval,

> the Flemings were enflamed with the fine gold and virgin silver that come from the Indies, which the poor Spaniards blindly gave them for their pretensions, so that it was a common proverb for the Burgundian to call the Spaniard "my Indian," which was to say the truth, for the Indians gave the Spaniards less gold than the Spaniards gave the Flemish .... The Burgundians, moreover, valued the Spaniards so little that they treated them like slaves and ordered them as if they were beasts, entering their houses, taking their women, and robbing their estates, without there being any justice for them.[68]

Burgundian rule of Castile, and the asymmetrical relationship that it implied, provoked resistance in 1518, when Charles traveled to Spain. Sandoval's analogy explained that Spaniards balked and eventually rebelled at the possibility of being subjected to a Burgundian "conquest."

Another chronicler of Charles's 1518–19 visit to Spain, Laurent Vital, recorded cultural tensions as well as Burgundian strategies to overcome them. Ecclesiastics in Valladolid refused to house the courtiers and excommunicated the marshal who attempted to force them to provide lodgings. They even refused to say mass in the presence of Flemings.[69] According to Vital, a Burgundian eyewitness, many robberies and "other crimes" were committed during Charles's residence in Valladolid.[70] The churches of Valladolid, moreover, had posters on their doors condemning the Kingdom of Castile "for permitting and allowing your sons, friends, and neighbors to be killed and assassinated by foreigners every day, without any justice being done." Castile, "very disgraced and cowardly," had failed to resist the Burgundian takeover. The document also lamented that Juana's second son, Ferdinand, born and bred in Castile, would be sent away to rule distant kingdoms.[71]

---

68 Prudencio de Sandoval, *Historia de la vida y hechos del Emperador Carlos V* (Madrid: Biblioteca de Autores Españoles, 1955 [1604 and 1606]), vol. 1, book V, fol. 193.

69 Laurent Vital, *Relación del primer viaje de Carlos V a España* (Madrid: Ministerio de Educación Nacional, Junta Nacional del IV Centenario de Carlos V, 1958), 259.

70 Ibid., 262.

71 Ibid., 327–28.

In an attempt to gain his subjects' affection, Charles sponsored jousts, tournaments, and other entertainments marked by varying degrees of violence.[72] He capitalized, moreover, on dynastic ties by visiting his mother (who resided in the royal palace of Tordesillas after 1509), holding memorial services for his father, and parading his siblings, Leonor, Catalina, and, of course, Ferdinand, before the populace.[73] By 1518 the turbaned "Turkish or Jewish fashion" celebrated in 1502 had become identified with older elites, and Charles entered Valladolid in a more Roman style: accompanied by some 6,000 horsemen and clad in armor, he wore a helmet adorned by an ostrich feather bearing an enormous ruby and pear-shaped oriental pearl.[74] Like his father, Charles dressed to conquer Castilian hearts.

In 1518–19, as in 1502, the Burgundians would visit Castile, demand resources, and depart: due to death, in the case of Philip I, and following election to the Holy Roman Empire, in the case of Charles. The anti-Burgundian reaction, which first surfaced in 1502, would find fuller expression in the Comunero rebellion against Habsburg rule in 1520–21. The effort to claim, rule, and defend the vast territories bequeathed though dynastic marriage and allegedly conquered by love, committed Charles I of Spain and V of the Holy Roman Empire to continual war and itinerancy. The inheritance secured on the voyages of 1502 and 1506 would subject its beneficiaries to further displacements.

Men Displaced, Rulers Replaced

While claiming his inheritance in Castile and Aragon, Charles oversaw the displacement and marriage of his siblings. The new king of Castile escorted his elder sister, Leonor, to marry King Manuel of Portugal, and also dispatched his younger brother, Ferdinand, born and bred in Castile, to Flanders. The attitude of these displaced siblings remains difficult to decipher. The populace and even the Cortes protested Ferdinand's exile. But what about the young prince himself? Geographical mobility and the requisite cultural flexibility may have been more "natural" for the second- and (especially) third-generation offspring of dynastic alliances who were trained to uphold and perpetuate them.

Charles V's dynastic strategy replicated that of his grandparents, Ferdinand and Isabel, which had proven as devastating for them as fortunate for the Habsburgs. The Portuguese alliance, reinforced by the emperor's own marriage to Isabel of Portugal (d. 1539) remained a priority: their heir, Philip, married María Manuela of Portugal before wedding Mary Tudor, and their younger daughter, Juana of Austria, married Prince João of Portugal when Philip was sent to England. The emperor's oldest daughter, María, would wed Maximilian, the offspring of Charles's brother, Ferdinand, and Anne, the rulers of Hungary and Bohemia.

---

[72] Ibid., 253, 267, 271, 337, 346.

[73] Ibid., 201–16.

[74] Ibid., 220, 223.

The marriages Charles V negotiated for his offspring maintained the dynastic capital that he needed to govern far-flung territories. With the departure of his heir, Philip, for England, María and Maximilian of Austria would exercise the regency in Castile.[75] In letters to Maximilian's father, the chaplain and licentiate Juan Alonso de Gamiz reported that Maximilian conducted himself perfectly during his Castilian sojourn, easily adapting to lands that had caused his grandfather Philip I such discomfort. Having traveled to meet his bride, Maximilian reportedly found his place in Castile with relative ease. Gamiz even claimed that Maximilian had conquered Castile by love.

The cultural and political attitude that Gamiz celebrated in Maximilian began with conduct that would perpetuate the dynasty. Gamiz assured Ferdinand that, after a reluctant start, his son performed as a "good husband" and visited María of Austria every night.[76] When María gave birth to a first child in Benavente, Gamiz informed Queen Juana that Maximilian remained with his wife during the labor. Based on such information, he reported, the queen declared her grandson "a good man, son of a good man."[77] Gamiz presented Maximilian as an Austrian model of conjugal and filial excellence. Although Juana suggested that the newborn could be named after her, when Gamiz reminded her that the child had two grandmothers, the queen reportedly understood that the House of Austria would commemorate the baby's paternal grandmother by naming her Anne. Based on his conversations with Juana, Gamiz assured Ferdinand of her great affection for the king of Hungary and his descendants. Following one conversation with the queen, Gamiz informed King Ferdinand that she had "called him [Ferdinand] 'my son' three times," yet never used the expression to refer to Charles.[78] Along the same lines, Gamiz claimed that the queen expressed greater affection for Maximilian than she had ever shown for the emperor or his offspring.[79] Different branches of the family vied for affection from the queen and, by extension, her people.

The queen welcomed her grandchildren, María and Maximilian, to Tordesillas in 1550, much as she had received her offspring, Leonor and Charles, in 1518. After expressing great "joy and contentment" at their arrival and asking them about the journey, she granted them leave to rest. The following day, according

---

[75] On this appointment see M.J. Rodríguez Salgado, *The Changing Face of Empire. Charles V, Philip II and Habsburg Authority, 1551–1559* (Cambridge: Cambridge University Press, 1988), 37–38.

[76] Lic. Gamiz to Ferdinand I, January 17 and February 18, 1549, Haus-, Hof- und Staatsarchiv, Vienna (hereafter HHSA), Spanien, Diplomatische Korresponden (hereafter DK), 2–13 and 2–14.

[77] Lic. Gamiz to Ferdinand I, November 7, 1549, HHSA, Spanien, DK, 2–14, fol. 48.

[78] Lic. Gamiz to Ferdinand, August 4, 1550, HHSA, Spanien, DK, 2–14, fol. 76–77. A nineteenth-century transcription of this letter can be found in the AGRB, Fonds Gachard, 615.

[79] Lic. Gamiz to Ferdinand, July 2, 1549, HHSA, Spanien, DK, 2–14, fol. 32–33.

to Gamiz, the queen engaged in long conversations with both of the regents, as María shared family portraits and Maximilian gave her a cross from his father that had belonged to the archduke of Austria Frederick III.[80]

In addition to visiting the queen, Gamiz reported, Maximilian delighted the court by continually engaging in "virtuous deeds." Without being obsessed with sports, the prince jousted one Sunday and won a prize, which he sent to his wife.[81] While planning to visit Santiago de Compostela, Maximilian allowed his gentlemen to travel six days ahead of him in order to spend more time with his spouse.[82] According to Gamiz, the prince even enjoyed the right reading:

> In addition to certain spiritual books that I have sought in Latin so that His Highness will read them and keep them in his chambers, as he does, I have now purchased the *Siete Partidas*, which is a legend that no prince should be without. His Highness has them now and delights in reading the first book, which touches on our Holy Catholic Faith and Church, and the second, which discusses emperors, kings, princes, and knights, as well as their obligations and how they should live, govern peoples, etc. They please him so much that he always wants to take them with him.[83]

Maximilian appeared to acquire the requisite cultural baggage effortlessly at the hand of Gamiz. Having been raised to rule the Low Countries and the Holy Roman Empire, the young prince adapted himself to other roles. He had traveled, guided by Gamiz, to wed María of Austria and to assume the co-regency of Castile.

The cultural adaptability demonstrated by Ferdinand and Maximilian of Austria suggests that men may have accepted displacement to marry or to claim distant kingdoms more easily when there existed a clear dynastic (and gender) precedent for such mobility. In this sense, Habsburg marriages and displacements across Europe facilitated still others. Philip I was received better in 1506 than in 1502, and his son, Charles, still better in 1518, even if his departure would provoke an uprising. While Ferdinand I appeared resigned to his own exile from Castile, his son, Maximilian, accepted displacement without complaint. The cultural clashes of 1502, while traumatic for the princes involved, appear less significant from the perspective of subsequent generations, which overcame their predecessors' cultural limitations.

A perspective spanning voyages through Castile examined from 1502 through 1550 points to displaced princes' growing cultural initiative and adaptability.

80 Lic. Gamiz to Ferdinand, August 4, 1550, cited from HHSA, Spanien, DK, Karton 2 (alt. Fasz. 2) by José Luis Cano de Gardoqui García in *Tordesillas 1494* (Valladolid: Electa, 1994), 226.

81 Lic. Gamiz to Ferdinand, January 17, 1549, HHSA, Spanien, DK, 2–13.

82 Lic. Gamiz to Ferdinand, February 18, 1549, HHSA, Spanien, DK, 2–14, fol. 12.

83 Lic. Gamiz to Ferdinand, February 26, 1549, HHSA, Spanien, DK, 2–14, fol. 13.

Philip's successors largely overcame the cultural and gender discomfort that he experienced in 1502 and 1506. Meanwhile, the servants who accompanied these mobile princes acquired reservoirs of indispensable, multigenerational experience, whether or not they married and established roots in foreign lands. The success of dynastic marriage and cultural transfer, real or perceived, required their mediation.

Bibliography

Aram, Bethany. "Juana 'the Mad's' Signature: The Problem of Invoking Royal Authority, 1505–1507." *The Sixteenth Century Journal*, 29, no. 2 (1998): 333–61.

_____. "Juana 'the Mad,' The Clares, and the Carthusians: Revising a Necrophilic Legend in Early Habsburg Spain." *Archiv für Reformationsgeschichte*, 93 (2002): 172–91.

_____ . *Juana the Mad: Sovereignty and Dynasty in Renaissance Europe*. Baltimore: Johns Hopkins University Press, 2005.

_____ . "Taste Transformed. Spice, Sugar and the Sixteenth-Century Hispano-Burgundian Court." In *Global Goods and the Spanish Empire, 1492–1824. Circulation, Resistance and Diversity*. Edited by Bethany Aram and Bartolomé Yun-Casalilla, 119–136. Basingstoke: Palgrave Macmillan, 2014.

Calderón Ortega, José Manuel. *Felipe el hermoso*. Madrid: Espasa Calpe, 2001.

Cano de Gardoqui García, José Luis. *Tordesillas 1494*. Valladolid: Electa, 1994.

Cauchies, Jean-Marie. *Philip le beau. Le dernier duc de Bourgogne*. Turnhout, Belgium: Brepols, 2003.

Chmel, Joseph, ed. *Die Handschriften der K.K. Hofbibliothek in Wien*. Vienna: Carl Gerold, 1841.

Covarrubias Orozco, Sebastián de. *Tesoro de la lengua castellana o española*. Madrid: Castalia, 1996 [1611].

Erasmus, Desiderius. *Obras Escogidas*. Translated and edited by Lorenzo Ribera. Madrid: Aguilar, 1956.

Fernández Álvarez, Manuel, ed. *Corpus Documental de Carlos V.* Salamanca: Universidad de Salamanca, 2000.

Fernández de Córdova, Álvaro. "L'impact de la Bourgogne sur la cour castillane des Trastamare." In *La cour de Bourgogne et l'Europe. Le rayonnement et les limites d'un modèle culturel*. Edited by Werner Paravicini, 593–630. Beihefte der Francia 73. Ostfilden: Thorbecke, 2013.

Fuchs, Barbara. *Exotic Nation: Maurophilia and the Construction of Early Modern Spain*. Philadelphia: University of Pennsylvania Press, 2009.

Gachard, Louis Prosper, ed. *Collection des voyages des souverains des Pays-Bas*. Brussels: F. Hayez, 1876.

Gómez de Fuensalida, Gutierre. *Correspondencia de Gutierre Gómez de Fuensalida ... publicada Por el Duque de Berwick y de Alba.* Madrid: Duque de Berwick y de Alba, 1907.

Höfler, Constantin von, ed. "Die Depeschen des Venetianischen Botschafters Vincenzo Quirino." *Archiv für Österreichische Geschichte*, 66 (1885): 45–256.

Knighton, Tess. "Una confluencia de capillas. El caso de Toledo, 1502." In *La Capilla Real de los Austrias. Música y ritual de corte en la Europa moderna.* Edited by Juan José Carreras and Bernardo García García, 127–49. Madrid: Fundación Carlos Amberes, 2001.

Marche, Olivier de la. *Mémoires.* Paris: Librairie Renouard, 1888.

Marcuello, Pedro. *Cancionero.* Ed. José Manuel Blecua. Zaragoza: Institución Fernando el Católico, 1987 [1502].

Mártir de Anglería, Pedro. *Epistolario.* Ed. and trans. José López de Toro. Madrid: Imprenta Góngora, 1953.

Masso, Alejandro. "La Corte y la Música." In *Felipe I el Hermoso: la belleza y la locura.* Edited by Miguel Ángel Zalama and Paul Vandenbroeck, 185–94. Madrid: Centro de Estudios Europa Hispánica, 2006.

Padilla, Lorenzo de. "Crónica de Felipe I llamado el Hermoso." In *Colección de Documentos Inéditos para la Historia de España.* Vol. 8. Edited by Miguel Salvá and Pedro Sainz de Baranda. Madrid: Imprenta de la Viuda de Calero, 1846.

Rodríguez Salgado, M.J. *The Changing Face of Empire. Charles V, Philip II and Habsburg Authority, 1551–1559.* Cambridge: Cambridge University Press, 1988.

———. "'Una perfecta princesa'. Casa y vida de la reina Isabel de Valois (1559–1568)." *Cuadernos de historia moderna*, 28 (2003): 71–98, Anejo [supplement] 2, 39–96.

Rodríguez Villa, Antonio. *Bosquejo Biográfico de la Reina Doña Juana.* Madrid: Aribau, 1874.

———. *La Reina Doña Juana la Loca: estudio histórico.* Madrid: Librería de M. Murillo, 1892.

Sánchez, Magdalena S. "Melancholy and Female Illness: Habsburg Women and Politics at the Court of Philip III." *Journal of Women's History*, 8, no. 2 (1996): 81–102.

———. *The Empress, the Queen, and the Nun: Women and Power at the Court of Philip III of Spain.* Baltimore: Johns Hopkins University Press, 1998.

Sandoval, Prudencio de. *Historia de la vida y hechos del Emperador Carlos V.* Madrid: Biblioteca de Autores Españoles, 1955.

Seyssel, Claude de. *The Monarchy of France.* Trans. J.H. Hexter. New Haven: Yale University Press, 1981.

Soria Mesa, Enrique. "Family, Bureaucracy and the Crown. The Wedding Market as a Form of Integration among Spanish Elites in the Early Modern Period." In *Polycentric Monarchies. How did Early Modern Spain and Portugal Achieve and Maintain a Global Hegemony?* Edited by Pedro Cardim, Tamar Herzog, José Javier Ruiz Ibáñez, and Gaetano Sabatini, 73–89. Eastbourne, UK: Sussex Academic Press, 2012.

Vital, Laurent. *Relación del primer viaje de Carlos V a España*. Madrid: Ministerio de Educación Nacional, Junta Nacional del IV Centenario de Carlos V, 1958.

Yun Casalilla, Bartolomé, ed. *Las redes del Imperio. Elites sociales en la articulación de la monarquía hispánica*. Madrid: Marcial Pons Historia, 2009.

Zalama, Miguel Ángel, and Vandenbroeck, Paul, eds. *Felipe I el Hermoso: la belleza y la locura*. Madrid: Centro de Estudios Europa Hispánica, 2006.

Chapter 5

"Great Faith is Necessary to Drink from this Chalice": Philip II in the Court of Mary Tudor, 1554–58*

Anna Santamaría López

The inhabitants of Puerto de La Herradura awoke one freezing morning in February 1593 to find that the icy storm that had raged all night in the southern Spanish bay had churned the waters and left all sorts of relics that the sea had swallowed over the years. A small crowd gathered on the beach and saw how the wind and the tides had dragged part of a wrecked ship onto the sand, the remains of a *galera* that had sunk off the coast in 1563. One person wandered away from the group, drawn to the wreckage; he was Pedro de Castro (1534–1623), the archbishop of Granada, and the objects that caught his attention were a pile of coins. "Amid the salt and the sand,"[1] he could see an image of the young Philip II of Spain, identified by the inscription "Rex Angliae."[2] Days later, Castro sent his discovery to the monarch along with a letter in which, perhaps with melancholy, he remembered those far-off times when England and the Hispanic Monarchy had been closely aligned.[3]

By the time Castro found the coins, however, England had become Philip II's principal enemy, and the king was used as the "bogeyman to frighten English children in their cradles."[4] Castro had practically forgotten the

* This chapter has been translated from the Spanish by Ruth MacKay. This study would not have been possible without the support and guidance of Professor Joan-Lluís Palos, whom I thank sincerely for asking me to contribute to this volume. I also would like to mention the valuable guidance provided by Maria José Rodriguez-Salgado (London School of Economics and Political Science) and Miles Pattenden (University of Oxford) during moments of doubt, and to thank Judith Loades for her kind words and interest in my research.

1 Instituto de Valencia de Don Juan, envío 43, caja 56, doc. 392 (Granada, February 22, 1593). Cited in José Luis González Sánchez-Molero, "Philippus, rex Hispaniae & Angliae. La biblioteca inglesa de Felipe II," *Reales sitios. Revista del Patrimonio Nacional*, 160 (2004): 31.

2 González Sánchez-Molero, "Philippus, rex Hispaniae," 30.

3 Ibid., 30–31.

4 David Loades, *The Reign of Philip and Mary* (Burford: Davenant Press, 2011), 32. Philip of Spain used the title "Prince of Spain" from birth until 1556, the year when he

Figure 5.1 Antonis Mor, Portrait of Philip II, 1555–58, oil on panel, 41 × 35 cm. Museo Nacional del Prado, Madrid.

days when the Spanish king also was king consort of England thanks to his marriage with Mary Tudor. More than four centuries later, the friendship that this dynastic connection meant for Anglo-Spanish relations continues to be overshadowed by the aggression, decades later, of the Spanish king toward Elizabeth I of England. While Spanish historians have studied Philip's attitude toward England almost entirely from the perspective of these confrontations, the reign of the young man who would be Philip I of England from 1554 to 1558 is practically unknown in the British historical memory. As a result, our knowledge of Philip's experience in England and his marriage to Mary is still fragmentary. (See Figure 5.1 for a contemporary portrait of Philip.)

It is thus necessary to study this phase of his life carefully, interpreting it through new analytical perspectives. To that end, his strategies of cultural communication as king consort in a country that always remained strange to him can be especially revealing. What was life like for the young Habsburg in the Tudor court? Was his marriage a channel for cultural exchange between Spain and England in the mid-sixteenth century? What were the constitutional and symbolic implications of a marriage in which, in contrast to most other dynastic marriages in early modern Europe, the husband was the one who moved to a foreign court? This chapter aims to answer some of these questions so as to contribute, thanks also to others' research, toward an understanding of a key episode in the configuration of political and cultural relations in Europe.

The Construction of a Dynastic Marriage: Philip and Mary in Mid-Sixteenth-Century Europe

The wedding of Philip of Spain (1527–98) and Mary I of England (1516–58) was, like all royal weddings in the early modern era, a largely political affair. Though their marriage had an enormous impact on the lives of the bride and groom and their respective courts, the union of the Spanish and English royal houses was the direct result of new diplomatic challenges that faced both countries during the 1550s.

Philip was the first son of Emperor Charles V and therefore heir to an immense collection of European and American territories that later on would transform him into the ruler of the first global empire.[5] Nevertheless,

was crowned king of those territories which made up the Hispanic Monarchy after the abdication of this father, Charles V. In this chapter I refer to Philip as "prince" when I am referring to those actions in which he functioned primarily in the service of the Hispanic Monarchy, whereas I refer to him as "king" only to refer to that time when he held the English throne thanks to his marriage with Mary.

[5] Geoffrey Parker, *Felipe II. La biografía definitiva* (Barcelona: Planeta, 2010), 15.

during his youth, his life was entirely conditioned by his father's struggles to achieve European political hegemony. Indeed, it was the search for resources to finance these efforts that most affected Philip's adolescence, leading to his marriage with the princess María Manuela of Portugal (1527–45), who died shortly after giving birth to a son, the *infante* don Carlos. Imperial politics thus transformed Philip into a husband, father, and widower when he had barely turned 18.[6]

In the years following his first marriage, his life would continue being defined by imperial designs, as he was the center of intense diplomatic activity aimed at preparing him to succeed his father. But in 1553 something happened that would interrupt this process: King Edward VI of England (1516–53) died with no heir, and for the first time in English history there was a female ruler, his unmarried half-sister, Mary Tudor. Charles V, still involved in a struggle with France for European hegemony, saw his son, by this time 27 years old, as the most effective instrument for taking advantage of the new situation in England for the benefit of the empire. For Charles, it was the right time to forge an alliance between the Habsburg and Tudor dynasties, and as soon as the new English queen had been crowned, he proposed that she marry his son.

Mary had always trusted Charles. As the daughter of Henry VIII of England (1491–1547) and Catherine of Aragon (1485–1536), throughout her life she had regarded the emperor as something more than the first cousin he was, seeking in him protection and even paternal attention. Though she spent her early childhood surrounded by luxury and attention as the first-born daughter of the English king, her life quickly became an obstacle course full of insecurities. As a result of her parents' divorce when she was still a child, she was sent far away from court, separated from all those who were close to her, and she was deprived of her right of succession.[7] As the years passed, Mary grew aware of the hostilities surrounding her, while anguish and fear for her own life turned her into an introvert, with physical problems that were probably the principal cause of her infertility.[8]

The princess thus grew up completely traumatized and without anyone whom she could trust. When her half-brother Edward VI died prematurely in 1553, she became the direct heir to the English throne and was subsequently the object of multiple conspiracies and rebellions aimed at removing her from the throne. Taking this turbulent background into consideration, it is no surprise that the queen sought the emperor's protection; he had defended her mother against Henry VIII and, like her, had remained a loyal Catholic in the face of the spread of Protestantism. These were the circumstances, then,

6 Antonio Martínez Llamas, *Felipe II, el hombre* (León: Lobo Sapiens, 2009), 179.

7 Loades, *Reign of Philip*, 4–8.

8 María Pilar Queralt del Hierro, *Las mujeres de Felipe II. Deber y pasión en la casa del rey* (Madrid: EDAF, 2011), 94.

when Mary was 37 years old and she listened to Charles as he proposed that she marry his son Philip.[9]

Works by Judith M. Richards and Glyn Redworth have made it clear that Mary at first rejected the idea of marrying, probably because she was worried about holding on to power amid such fierce competition. But the queen's obsession with the survival of the Tudor dynasty and her wish to conceive a Catholic heir outweighed her hesitation. As soon as the queen's—and, especially, her advisors'—intention was made public, candidates to share the English throne with her began making their desire known in London.[10] The Privy Council was quite keen on the proposal of Edward Courtenay (1527–56), son of the marquess of Exeter, and Maximilian of Habsburg (1527–76), son of Archduke Ferdinand of Austria. But Mary argued that Philip was the best candidate for her; he was the son of her principal international protector, he had shown he was capable of fathering a child and, above all, he was strongly Catholic. And, though the union of the English and Spanish crowns would allow the Habsburgs to acquire a base in northern Europe and ensure control over the Low Countries, it also would help England strengthen its commercial ties to Dutch ports and gain a powerful ally with which to combat the traditional anti-English alliance of Scotland and France.[11]

It would appear that Mary's choice of the emperor's heir was so clear that, by September 1553, there were rumors at court that either she would marry Philip or she would remain single for the rest of her life. Ignoring suggestions by her advisors, led by Lord Chancellor Stephen Gardiner (1483–1555), to consider proposals from English candidates, Mary prevailed for the first time ever and announced her irrevocable acceptance of the emperor's proposal, made months earlier. From then on, the sealed agreement was simply a matter of time. In January 1554 Pope Julius III (1487–1555) issued the necessary dispensation for Philip to marry his first cousin once removed, and soon the terms of the marriage were made public.[12]

What role did Philip play in these negotiations? The proxy wedding in London on March 6, 1554, clearly showed that he had no involvement. It was the count of Egmont, a servant of Charles V with whom the prince had no contact, who signed the marriage agreement in Philip's stead. While Mary, as queen, was the principal protagonist of the negotiations over her future, Philip played only a supporting rule, subject to his father's actions.

---

[9] Loades, *Reign of Philip*, 15.

[10] Judith M. Richards, "Mary Tudor as 'Sole Quene'? Gendering Tudor Monarchy," *The Historical Journal*, 40, no. 4 (December 1997): 895–924; Glyn Redworth, "'Matters Impertinent to Women': Male and Female Monarchy under Philip and Mary," *The English Historical Review*, 112, no. 447 (1997): 597–613.

[11] Loades, *Reign of Philip*, 15–16.

[12] John Edwards, *Mary I: England's Catholic Queen* (New Haven: Yale University Press, 2011), 144–57.

Hopes and Disappointments: Philip and Mary at the Tudor Court

"If you wish to arrange a marriage for me, know that I am an obedient son who has no other wish than yours."[13] These words, which Philip wrote to his father in a letter, have led most historians to say that Philip willingly accepted Charles V's decision to marry him to Mary. But a more careful look at the prince's activities during the first half of 1554 seems to show quite a different picture and provides a more complex and complete portrayal of his reaction.

Indeed, during the months prior to his move to England, he communicated little or not at all with Mary. At that point he probably did not have much reason to be optimistic about the English venture, which involved marrying a woman nearly 12 years older than himself and who, in the opinion of many observers, was sterile, had lost her beauty many years earlier, and now was the cause of constant political instability. Portraits of the queen he had seen showed her to be overly thin, excessively pale, and with wispy hair, and she was said to be capricious and not fond of men.[14] One can safely say, then, that Philip's feelings about marrying and living with Mary of England were not enthusiastic.

But were these the main reasons for Philip's reticence? There are indications that the emotional distance he showed toward the woman who was already his wife by proxy was in part motivated by the secrecy with which Charles V had carried out the marriage negotiations. That is the opinion of the historian María José Rodríguez-Salgado, who has hypothesized that father and son had a more problematic relationship than historians have believed. According to Rodríguez-Salgado, starting in late 1553 Philip was deeply hurt that his father had quashed the marriage negotiations that he himself had undertaken to marry another Portuguese princess and had agreed upon contractual clauses with Mary that, as will be shown, limited his authority as consort of England.[15] It is very possible, therefore, that his unhappiness on that count led the prince to remain silent regarding the next phase of his life.

Mary, however, made no effort to hide her impatience. For her, Philip was the compensation for all the humiliations and lack of affection she had suffered.[16] According to contemporary chroniclers, she fell in love with Philip upon seeing the portrait of him painted by Titian a few years earlier, and secretly, as she confessed to the imperial ambassador Simon Renard

[13] "Si deseáis arreglar este matrimonio para mí, sabed que soy tan obediente hijo que no tengo más voluntad que la vuestra." Josep Tomàs Cabot, *La vida y la época de Felipe II* (Barcelona: Planeta, 1998), 100.

[14] Martínez Llamas, *Felipe II*, 182.

[15] See Maria José Rodríguez-Salgado, *Un Imperio en transición. Carlos V, Felipe II y su mundo, 1551–1559* (Barcelona: Editorial Crítica, SA, 1992).

[16] Edwards, *Mary I*, 206.

(1523–73), she thought "the model was attractive, but she would be even more attracted to the image in real life."[17]

Even so, Mary began to get nervous at the lack of communication from her husband. He had not sent any presents, not even an official letter to the English court. Mary, quite disturbed, subtly reproached this behavior; she wrote, despite "my desire and duty to correspond with Your Highness ... you have not written directly to me since our union was decided."[18] Her nervousness was felt at court, and soon there was fear that the prince would never arrive. As a result of this pressure, Philip found himself obliged to break his silence, and in early June 1554 he sent the marquis of Las Navas (1492–1567) to England to give the queen, among other things, a beautiful piece of jewelry as a sign of his affection. It was a pendant made of two diamonds; the smaller of the two had belonged to his mother, Empress Isabel (1503–39), and the larger was cut in the shape of a rose, with a teardrop pearl. Greatly relieved at the arrival of this confirmation of Philip's affection, the English court began to mobilize in anticipation of the royal consort's arrival.

How did they react when they first were face to face? Prince Philip, heading an entourage of the highest Castilian nobility, landed in Southampton on July 20, 1554 in the midst of torrential rain and quickly went to Winchester to meet Mary.[19] According to several observers, the queen's impatience got the better of her when she learned that her husband had entered the city, and despite the fact that an official presentation was prepared for the following day, she told her servants to bring the prince to her room that night.[20] There, accompanied by the queen's ladies in waiting, Philip and Mary conversed a little over an hour—he in Spanish, which she remembered from when she lived with her mother, and she in French, which Philip understood but did not speak. At this meeting, the queen

17 "Veía muy bien al modelo, pero que aún vería con mejores ojos la imagen viva del mismo." Tomás Cabot, *La vida*, 40.

18 "La voluntad y deber que tengo de corresponder a Vuestra Alteza para siempre, ... no me habéis escrito en particular después de que nuestra unión a sido tratado." British Library, Department of Manuscripts, Cotton MS Vespasian F III, fol. 26 (London, April 20, 1554). Cited in Parker, *Felipe II. La biografía*, 119–20.

19 José Miguel Morales Folguera, "El arte al servicio del poder y de la propaganda imperial. La boda del príncipe Felipe con María Tudor en la Catedral de Winchester y la solemne entrada de la pareja real en Londres," *POTESTAS. Revista del Grupo Europeo de Investigación Histórica*, 2 (2009): 165–89.

20 Andrés Muñoz, "Sumario y verdadera relación del buen viaje que el invictissimo Príncipe de las Españas don Felipe hizo á Inglaterra, y recebimiento en Vincestre donde caso y salio para Londres. en el cual se contiene grandes y maravillosas cosas que en este tiempo pasaron ... (Zaragoza: E. Nagera, 1554)," in *Viaje de Felipe Segundo á Inglaterra, por Andrés Muñoz (impreso en Zaragoza en 1554), y relaciones varias relativas al mismo suceso*, ed. Pascual de Gayangos (Madrid: Sociedad de Bibliófilos Españoles, 1877), 1–84; Juan de Baraonda, *Relación del viaje del Príncipe Don Felipe a Inglaterra*, Archivo del Monasterio de El Escorial, vol. 2.4.

must have understood that communication with her husband would not be fluid, as he could barely say "Good night," the first words in the language of his new subjects pronounced by the king consort of England.[21] Philip, for his part, must have seen that Mary's small figure and physique were not at all tempting. Even so, he knew the rules of court and was warm toward the woman whom he would always refer to, in private, as "my aunt."[22]

The first time the couple appeared in public was at the official blessing of their marriage, held in Winchester Cathedral on July 25. The ceremony was entirely symbolic of early modern cosmopolitanism. Present were not only the leading figures of the English and Spanish courts but also Flemings, Germans, Hungarians, Bohemians, Italians, and others, all of whom must have taken note of the intense downpour that accompanied the newlyweds as they entered the cathedral that morning and that totally soaked the sumptuous ornaments decorating the church's exterior.[23] Nevertheless, the decorations inside the cathedral were admired and commented upon in the following days. There were carpets and many tapestries, and in the middle of the nave there was a raised wooden platform leading to the high altar, which allowed everyone there to see the entire ceremony.

At around noon, Philip and Mary entered the cathedral, both wearing magnificent clothing in shades of gold decorated with precious stones they had exchanged as wedding gifts.[24] While Stephen Gardiner celebrated the wedding, the Castilian nobleman Gómez Suárez de Figueroa (1523–71) made a grand entrance into the cathedral carrying several sheets of paper from the emperor announcing that Charles V had given the kingdom of Naples to Philip. Thus his son would have a title of king and would be ranked equally with his wife.[25]

The wedding festivities lasted for days and the couple then went to London, where they made a splendid and triumphant entry. The new English monarchs paraded through the streets of the city from London Bridge to Temple Bar, accompanied by all manner of celebration. The city was exultant, the streets were decorated, and everywhere there were enormous statues of mythical figures, triumphant arches, and other ephemeral constructions praising the king, welcoming him, and comparing him to other great Philips such as Philip of Macedonia, the Roman Philip the Arab, or the dukes of Burgundy, Philip the Good and Philip the Bold. All the city's church bells rang, and the Tower

[21] Mariano González-Arnao, "La boda inglesa de Felipe II," *Historia*, 16, no. 97: 36.

[22] Loades, *Reign of Philip*, 19; González Sánchez-Molero, "Philippus, rex Hispaniae," 16.

[23] Alexander Samson, *The Marriage of Philip of Habsburg and Mary Tudor and Anti-Spanish Sentiment in England: Political Economies and Culture, 1553–1557* (London: University of London, 1999), 230.

[24] González Sánchez-Molero, "Philippus, rex Hispaniae," 180.

[25] Rodríguez-Salgado, *Un Imperio en transición*, 141–42.

artillery fired salutes. According to members of his entourage, Philip was absolutely amazed by such joy at his arrival.[26]

But one cannot say that Mary of England and Philip of Spain's marriage was passionate or that it satisfied their personal and political expectations. Officially it lasted for four years, until the queen's death in 1558, but the couple lived together, intermittently, for barely a year and a half. Philip's time in England was one of great uncertainty, and from the start his father was not candid with him about how long he would have to remain in England before going to the Continent to help the imperial army. There was constant discussion at court regarding Mary's ability to get pregnant, and important sectors of the English people were slowly but surely showing hostility toward Philip.[27]

Mary, on the other hand, was a happy bride during the first months of their marriage. As queen she could stay in her court, and her husband apparently paid her the attention she had lacked during her youth. Ruy Gómez de Silva (1516–73), one of Philip's chief aides, went so far as to say that the prince "made her so happy that when they were alone the other day she nearly spoke of love, and he responded in a similar fashion."[28] But all indications are that Mary's optimism was ill-placed. Whether on account of her character or, especially, her looks, Philip never reciprocated her feelings. Gómez de Silva himself said, perhaps repeating the words that the king of England had confessed to him, "may the queen have children so he can go back to where he came from … To tell the truth … great faith is necessary to drink from this chalice."[29]

It was clear that Philip was not happy. Soon people at court were saying he no longer visited his wife's apartments, though he did frequently find his way to the rooms of various of her ladies.[30] Even so, a few months after the wedding the queen announced she was pregnant. Doubts about her ability to conceive diminished as her belly grew and she suffered ailments typical of pregnancy. It was announced with great celebration that the desired heir would be born in April 1555. But the days passed, and by late June Mary had not given birth. It

---

[26] See Kevin Sharpe, *Selling the Tudor Monarchy: Authority and Image in Sixteenth-Century England* (New Haven: Yale University Press, 2009).

[27] Rodríguez-Salgado, *Un Imperio en transición*, 156.

[28] "Tiénela tan contenta que cierto, estando el otro día ellos dos a solas, casi le decía ella amores, y él respondía por los consonantes." See Martín Fernández Navarrete, Miguel Salvá, and Pedro Sainz de Baranda, *Colección de documentos inéditos para la historia de España* [hereafter CODOIN] (Vaduz: Kraus Reprint, 1964–75), vol. 3, 531–36, August 12, 1554; cited in Parker, *Felipe II. La biografía*, 123. The Spanish version literally says Philip responded "by consonants," which refers to consonant rhyme. Gómez de Silva was indicating that Philip responded to Mary's expression of love with similar intensity.

[29] "Tenga la reina hijos y pueda él volverse por donde vino … Para hablar verdad …, mucho Dios es menester para tragar este cáliz." Fernández de Navarrete, Salvá, and Sainz de Baranda, CODOIN, vol. 3, 526–29, July 26/29, 1554. Cited in González-Arnao, "La boda inglesa," 41.

[30] Queralt del Hierro, *Las mujeres de Felipe II*, 104–05.

became clear that her physical transformation was not the result of pregnancy but rather the symptom of an advanced and serious disease, and the queen fell into a deep depression.

In these circumstances, Philip decided to put an end to his stay on the island, and, in September 1555, he left for the Continent. His departure greatly affected Mary, who probably was convinced he would never return.[31] In fact, he did return to England in March 1557, but only to ask her for financial support for the imperial troops fighting France. Once he got the answer he wanted, he left again. Mary and Philip would never see each other again, and Mary's time was running out. Physically and mentally defeated, she took to her bed after the king's definitive departure, and she would never rise again. She died at the dawn of November 17, 1558, just after dictating a last request that her husband keep the diamond and pearl jewel he had given her for their engagement and not give it to anyone else. Shortly after the queen's death, in violation of Mary's last request, Philip ordered that all her jewels, including the diamond and pearl one, be given to the new queen, Elizabeth I (1533–1603).[32]

Learning to be English: Cultural Transfers and Contradictions at the Anglo-Spanish Court

With Mary's death, Philip put an end to his English venture. Thus ended Philip's four years of living at the Tudor court during which he was head of two households, the Spanish and the English, which most historians of the sixteenth and seventeenth centuries have described as incompatible. Did he ever adapt to the customs of his English subjects? What were his symbolic communication or cultural immersion strategies to solidify his position as king of England?

As soon as he landed on the English coast in July 1554, Philip was aware that he would have to undergo a complex and intense process of cultural adaptation. From the timid and uninspiring "Good night" he bade to Mary Tudor after their first private meeting, the consort slowly integrated himself into the culture of his new subjects.[33] From the start, he encouraged his entourage to adopt English customs so as to make themselves more popular. For example, he ordered his courtiers to cease drinking wine and switch to beer, which was not at all agreeable to the Iberian taste,[34] and to dress following French fashions—though

---

31 Santiago Nadal, *Las cuatro mujeres de Felipe II* (Barcelona: Juventud, 1960), 146.

32 David Loades, "Philip II and the Government of England," in *Law and Government under the Tudors. Essays presented to Sir Geoffrey Elton, Regius Professor of Modern History in the University of Cambridge on the Occasion of his Retirement*, eds. Claire Cross, David Loades, and J.J. Scarisbrick (Cambridge: Cambridge University Press, 1988), 194.

33 González Sánchez-Molero, "Philippus, rex Hispaniae," 16.

34 González-Arnao, "La boda inglesa," 36.

France was the Hispanic Monarchy's principal political and cultural enemy—because that was the general tendency among the English.[35]

Aside from these anecdotal examples, however, Philip developed a complex strategy to overcome the main obstacle between him and England, which was that he did not know English history or about its system of government. To correct this shortcoming, he acquired an important collection of books and manuscripts, most of which today are at the Escorial library. It is likely that the first item was the original manuscript of *Crónica de Inglaterra, llamada Fructo de los tiempos*, written in 1509 by Rodrigo de Cuero at the request of Catherine of Aragon. This is a compendium of various English, French, and Latin chronicles about English history from its origins to the Tudor era. All indications are that Mary, having received it from her mother, gave it to her husband when he arrived at her court. Philip's English library grew to include works by English, Spanish, and Flemish writers. Though access was very limited, it created an artistic and literary nexus between Spain and Tudor England.[36]

Philip's true intention, however, was to present himself as an authentic English sovereign, so his strategy could not remain private but had to make itself felt at court; he understood that he urgently needed to become the center of court life. Until then, Mary's court had been dominated by music, games, and masked balls. But as a woman, the queen could not lead the jousts and noble tournaments that had been so important for strengthening the image of the early Tudor kings. So Philip's arrival was the occasion of a pronounced change in English court life. The esplanade in front of Westminster became the site of jousts and boxing matches that, according to an anonymous Londoner, were the most prestigious and commented-upon events one could remember.[37] Though he was unsuccessful in introducing the Castilian *juego de cañas* (a game of lances played by cavalry) the king nonetheless was remarkably successful in his efforts to integrate himself into English court culture.

Following the advice of his aides, he also tried to win the support of important political sectors in England. To that end, he deployed an intense patronage campaign among the nobility, distributing favors (*mercedes*) and pensions that David Loades estimates cost him between 22,600 and 27,000 crowns a year.[38] Little by little, he managed to create what we might call a pro-Philip party at the English court, which included such prominent figures as Lord Paget and the earls of Arundel, Derby, Shrewsbury, and Pembroke.

Given this success, why is Philip II regarded in the English historical memory as having been an extremely unpopular monarch? Why did Loades himself affirm,

---

35 Alexander Samson, "Changing Places: The Marriage and Royal Entry of Philip, Prince of Austria, and Mary Tudor, July–August 1554," *Sixteenth Century Journal*, 36, no. 3 (2005): 764–65.

36 González Sánchez-Molero, "Philippus, rex Hispaniae," 14–33.

37 Sharpe, *Selling the Tudor Monarchy*, 285.

38 Loades, "Philip II and the Government," 183.

"as a King of England there is no doubt that Philip was a failure"?[39] The answer to these questions might well lie in the relations between English courtiers and the Spanish nobility. Indeed, there was considerable competition between these two groups, who from the beginning struggled over preeminence and prestige.[40] But the rivalry was not limited to protocol or etiquette. Soon after the wedding there were acts of vandalism in London against the ephemeral architecture erected to celebrate the monarchs' entry in the city, and rumors spread about conspiracies to expel all the Spaniards who had come to the city for the wedding. Philip was deeply bothered by all this, particularly upon discovering that the rivalries were spurred on by courtiers. Thus, as one Spanish nobleman put it, "every day in the palace there are knife fights between the English and the Spaniards. And there have been deaths on both sides."[41]

What was behind this hostility? Whig historiography traditionally pointed to two main causes, both of which are regarded today as invalid.[42] First, most of these historians believed that hostilities between the courts were the result of historical incompatibility between English and Spanish culture. That also is the reason they gave for the aggressiveness of Anglo-Spanish relations during the last decades of Philip II's reign and into the following centuries. This argument is both anachronistic and teleological, based on events that, though known to historians today, occurred after Philip and Mary's marriage. On the contrary, when the marriage was announced, Spain and England had enjoyed a long tradition of commercial and dynastic friendship going back to the twelfth century.

Since the Middle Ages, intense material and commercial exchange between the two territories had been reinforced through numerous royal marriages.[43] The marriages of Alfonso VIII of Castile and Eleanor Plantagenet (1170), Edward I of England and Leonor of Castile (1254), and Henry III of Castile and Catherine of Lancaster (1388) are examples of this strategy of dynastic alliances between Spain and England that began centuries before Philip II and Mary Tudor were born.[44] When their marriage was arranged, therefore, there was no historic hostility in

[39] Ibid., 194.

[40] *The Chronicle of Queen Jane*, 170 (Edward Underhill's account). Cited in David Loades, *Mary Tudor. The Tragical History of the First Queen of England* (Richmond: National Archives of England, 2006), 126.

[41] "Hay cada día en palacio cuchilladas entre ingleses y españoles. Y ansí ha habido algunas muertes de una parte y de otra." Gayangos, *Viaje de Felipe Segundo*, Third Letter, 118; cited in Samson, *The Marriage of Philip*, 225.

[42] For Whig historiography, see James Anthony Froude, *The Reign of Mary Tudor* (London: J.M. Dent & Sons, 1913); Albert Frederick Pollard, *The Political History of England* (London: Longmans, Green, and Co., 1915).

[43] See William D. Phillips, "The Frustrated Unity of Atlantic Europe: The Roles of Spain and England," in *Material and Symbolic Circulation between Spain and England, 1554–1604*, ed. Anne J. Cruz (Aldershot: Ashgate, 2008), 3–12.

[44] See Rose Walker, "Leonor of England and Eleanor of Castile: Anglo-Iberian Marriage and Cultural Exchange in the Twelfth and Thirteenth Centuries," in *England*

England regarding things Castilian or Spanish. On the contrary, the most recent royal marriage between the two countries—that of Henry VIII and Catherine of Aragon in 1509, which produced Mary I—was very popular and heightened the English people's feeling of friendship with Castile. In this context, when Philip landed in England, he registered no sign of distrust or dislike on the part of his new subjects. In fact, the prince himself said he had been received "with universal signs of love and joy."[45] So Philip and Mary's marriage, far from being the starting point of confrontation between England and Spain, represented simply the latest manifestation of a long tradition of dynastic collaboration.

Nor did the Spanish noblemen who accompanied the king show any signs of dislike toward England. On the contrary, most members of the prince's entourage arrived with romantic and idealized notions of England learned from books of chivalry, which were read widely on the Iberian Peninsula. Enthusiasts believed England was a mythical land where epic heroes and knights such as Amadis of Gaul had waged their daring deeds. The Spanish nobility, therefore, had the highest hopes, and many of the first reports by the Spanish party regarding beautiful landscapes, exuberant scenes of nature, and the sublime charms of the young Englishwomen at court were described in a manner fitting any chivalric novel.[46] With this in mind, then, arguments for cultural incompatibility between Spain and England or the existence of historic hostilities between them would appear to lack any basis.

However, another argument has been used to explain why Philip gradually became unpopular as king consort of England. According to that thesis, Mary's principal error was precisely to marry him, because the English people, by then presumably Protestant, did not accept the idea of being ruled by a deeply Catholic king. Furthermore, Whig historiography, dipping into the black legend that accompanies Philip in the collective memory, affirms that the king had a negative influence on Mary, inspiring her to burn more than 300 Protestants, thus becoming known as Bloody Mary. This tradition argues that there was a popular feeling of Hispanophobia by Protestants who rejected Catholicism. But recent research has shown that England in the 1550s was still mostly Catholic and that Philip, far from spurring on Protestant repression, used his men of the church, such as Alonso de Castro (1495–1558), to try to halt persecution by Mary and her council.[47] Philip,

---

and Iberia in the Middle Ages, Twelfth–Fifteenth Century. Cultural, Literary, and Political Exchanges, ed. María Bullón-Fernández (New York: Palgrave, 2007), 67–87.

[45] Royall Tyler, *Calendar of Letters, Dispatches, and State Papers, Relating to the Negotiations between England and Spain* (London: HMSO, 1916–54), vol. 13, 53; cited in Samson, "Changing Places," 767.

[46] See Glyn Redworth, "¿Nuevo mundo u otro mundo?: Conquistadores, cortesanos, libros de caballerías y el reinado de Felipe el Breve de Inglaterra," in *Actas del Primer Congreso Anglo-Hispano*, eds. Ralph Penny, Alan Deyermond, and Richard Hitchock (Barcelona: Castalia, 1993–94), vol. 3, 113–25.

[47] Loades, *Mary Tudor*, 140.

then, did not introduce repression and the black legend into England; rather, the latter was used on the island as a pretext for political, not religious, opposition to Philip.

Nevertheless, the question remains of what the causes were of this opposition to the king and all things Spanish. What was the reason behind saying, as did an anonymous nobleman who accompanied Philip, "were that we had stayed in [Spain] or its court and had never seen the sea, much less England, and we are anxious to leave this kingdom, which we understood was paradise, and go to Flanders"?[48] It is likely that an answer may be found in the anomalous limitations placed on Philip and his court during the marriage negotiations, the result of the anomalous and unprecedented accession to the throne of a woman. Given these circumstances, it is plausible that the rejection of Philip was simply the result of growing opposition to Mary and female rule.

A Queen, Her Consort, and Female Rule: Representations of Power

Historians often focus on the reign of Elizabeth I of England when analyzing the mechanisms through which female sovereignty was legitimized in that country. But we often forget that it was her stepsister, Mary I, who was the first woman to be crowned as a monarch in her own right. When she assumed power there was no reference to define the limits and legitimacy of female sovereignty. This legal vacuum, along with scant confidence in the capacity of a government led by a woman, led to uncertainty among the nobility and Parliament regarding England's future. That uncertainty soon led to open rejection of Mary's rule, not because she was a Catholic but because she was a woman.

Quickly the queen's council responded, and as soon as she was crowned its members developed a strategy aimed at legally strengthening her position at the head of the English monarchy. From the start, Mary was presented as both king and queen, as both man and woman, in a process that Alexander Samson described as "constitutional hermaphroditism."[49] In the words of Judith M. Richards, "if monarchy could not be always simply male, at least the difference should be as understated as possible."[50] The chief architect of Mary's government, Gardiner, appears to have accepted this notion, taking advantage of the powers that previous monarchs had attributed to Parliament to obtain legislation protecting the queen's authority. In spring 1554 Parliament passed the famous "Woman's State," according to which

---

[48] "Harto más nos valiera estar en esa tierra o corte [de España] que no haber visto [a] la mar, ni menos a Inglaterra, y ansí deseamos ya salir deste reino que teníamos por paraíso ir a Flandes." Redworth, "¿Nuevo mundo," 123.

[49] Samson, *The Marriage of Philip*, 15.

[50] Richards, "Mary Tudor," 895.

> the lawe of thys realme is, and ever hath bene … that the kingely or regal offyce of the realme … being invested eyther in male or female, are, and be, and ought to be, as fullye, wholye, absolutelye and enteerlye deemed, judged, accepted, invested and taken in throne as in throthe.[51]

Thus Mary used Parliament's legitimacy to attain power equal to that of her predecessors.

Even so, considerations of gender continued outweighing constitutional law, which became quite clear when Mary announced her impending marriage. Until then, her sovereignty had been based on the assumption that she was both king and queen of England. Her wedding and the king's arrival, however, undid this logic and raised a new question, given that a king consort also was an anomaly in England. The only relevant legal provision, in accordance with *jure uxoris* and the formula of "tenancy by courtesy of the realm," was that if Mary married, all her rights and properties would be transferred to her husband. As queen, these properties also affected the crown.[52]

Fears regarding the loss of sovereignty that this would entail for England reached their height when Mary announced that if she were to marry she would do so with a foreign prince of the Habsburg family. By the mid-sixteenth century the Habsburgs were well-known for having expanded their dominions through the strategy of "conquest by marriage." In this framework, if Mary married and transferred her rights and properties, England ran the risk of becoming a mere Habsburg satellite, losing her sovereign independence and becoming subject to the interests of the empire.[53] This prospect engendered fierce opposition; the diminishment of England's power could be avoided only if the throne were once again occupied by a king or, at the very least, an unmarried queen who retained full powers. Mary and Philip therefore had to be rejected.

The queen's advisors during the marriage negotiations were well aware of this opposition. Indeed, their proposal to Charles V was aimed at limiting to the utmost Philip's freedom of movement in England, ensuring he would pose no threat to the queen's sovereignty or to the survival of the Tudor dynasty. The marriage agreement therefore was structured around three main points: first, Philip would hold the title of king of England only as long as Mary lived, thus blocking any aspiration on his part to control the kingdom beyond the queen's wishes; second, England could not be governed in the interests of European imperial interests; and, finally, the king had obstacles placed in the way of any potential complicity with English courtiers. This last clause stipulated that Philip must be attended exclusively by the English household, removing members of the Spanish entourage from the center of power. When Castilian

---

51 Cited in ibid., 904.

52 Samson, *The Marriage of Philip*, 14–15.

53 Loades, "Reign of Philip," 16.

noblemen began arriving in England, they saw how they were marginalized at court by the English, and that was the principal reason for the rivalry between two courts battling for sovereignty.

Each clause of the marriage agreement was aimed at constitutionally limiting Philip's authority in England. While Mary's position was protected, Philip, heir to the throne of Spain, Europe's most powerful monarchy, was in England legally a mere queen consort. As David Loades has noted: "England was not to become just another Habsburg matrimonial conquest."[54] In the opinion of Glyn Redworth, the marriage agreement was a direct insult to the king's masculinity, denying him his rights as Mary's husband.[55] That must have been how Philip saw things, judging from his indignation when he discovered the conditions to which his father had agreed. Surely he believed that, in the exceptional case of a woman being invested with sovereignty, her husband must be able to wield more authority than a queen consort. Otherwise, his prestige and authority throughout Europe would be reduced once he inherited his father's possessions. That is probably what moved the prince to tell Charles V shortly after the wedding that "the queen and her council will be at my disposal" because "being that I am her husband, she and all her kingdom must follow my will." Philip could envision only the possibility of being the dominant half of this married couple.[56]

The marriage of Philip and Mary, then, was marked by a serious and extraordinary problem entailing a direct confrontation between their respective political interests. While she needed to impose her preeminence over her husband so as to quash attempts by her opponents to use the alleged alienation of the Tudor dynasty as a pretext for deposing her, he needed to proclaim his authority in England so as to maintain his international prestige. In this situation, both used one of the most effective tools of early modern monarchs—visual imagery—to symbolize their power.

Kevin Sharpe, one of the leading scholars of Tudor symbolic propaganda, has written of the "theatre of power" to describe Mary's representations of monarchical authority.[57] Though she had not been raised as a future queen, Mary was, after all, Henry VIII's daughter, and therefore heir to the visual revolution of monarchical representation that her father had undertaken. As a girl she grew familiar with the use of ceremony and symbolism to transmit messages of authority, and, after her marriage to Philip, she and her advisors employed symbolic means both to proclaim her sovereignty as queen in her own right and her preeminence in the marriage.

---

[54] Ibid.

[55] Glyn Redworth, "Felipe y las soberanas de Inglaterra," *Torre de los Lujanes*, 33 (1997): 108.

[56] "La reyna y los del consejo estarán a mi disposición," "ella, siendo yo su marido, ha de seguir mi voluntad con todo su reyno," November 16, 1554; cited in Manuel Fernández Álvarez, *Corpus Documental Carlos V* (Salamanca: Gráf. Europa, 1973–81), vol. 4, 130.

[57] Sharpe, *Selling the Tudor Monarchy*, 63.

The principal expression of this symbolic battle took place during the nuptial blessing of their union. The large wooden platform on which the service took place allowed complete visibility of the couple throughout the rite. It had been built precisely because Mary's advisors wanted to make sure that everyone there could see that, on a symbolic level, it was the queen who was marrying a man of lesser status and that she would retain her superiority. To that end, once they were standing before the high altar, Mary placed Philip to her left so that she could stand to the right of the altar. As Alexander Samson has argued, this spatial arrangement harbored major symbolic meaning. Traditionally, royal weddings embodied a gender hierarchy; it was always the man/king who stood on the right, while the woman/consort stood on the left. With her extraordinary gesture, then, Mary took the dominant or masculine position and turned Philip into a queen consort in the presence of everyone, displacing both his physical and his symbolic authority.[58]

The queen repeated the strategy during the wedding banquet and the entrance into London. Nobody living in a society that understood the use of symbolic messages by those in power could fail to capture the political meaning of the ritual. But that was not the only means by which the queen communicated her message of preeminence. During the wedding ceremony and the entry into London, she asked her husband not to wear the purple velvet outfit he had brought from Spain—which, according to the rules of etiquette, corresponded to a monarch—and that instead he wear white and gold, colors traditionally reserved for queens.[59] So ceremony, etiquette, and even attire also turned Philip into a queen consort subject to Mary.

But the queen was suffering great internal conflict. On the one hand she needed to transmit a message of power in order to debilitate any conspirators; on the other, she believed that, as a married woman, she must cede some of her authority to her husband. This internal battle led to considerable ambiguity in the symbolic communication she deployed during the first months of their marriage. The queen never ceased publicizing her status as a married woman and, perhaps weakening her own position, she made the royal marriage the center of her representations. She wanted to turn Philip into a true English monarch who was committed to his new subjects, and so throughout the kingdom she spread genealogical messages stressing her husband's blood ties to Henry III of England (1207–72). Already during the wedding ceremony and, especially, during the London parade, elaborate family trees were visible showing the royal couple beneath the English crown, descending directly from Henry III.[60]

But this genealogical campaign directly contradicted the initial messages defending the queen's preeminence. By placing both of them beneath one single

[58] Samson, *The Marriage of Philip*, 230.

[59] Samson, "Changing Places," 764–65.

[60] Ibid., 766.

Figure 5.2 Hans Eworth (or Ewoutsz), Philip II and Mary I, 1558, oil on panel. Trustees of the Bedford Estate, Woburn Abbey, United Kingdom. Bridgeman Art Library.

crown, Mary paradoxically transmitted the idea that she shared equal sovereignty with her husband; a "co-monarchy" had symbolically been established in England.[61] Trapped between her interests as queen and her wishes as a wife, Mary found herself in a serious quandary. Even so, she used two objects of political representation to proclaim widely to her subjects the principle of shared sovereignty: coins and stamps. Starting in September 1554, Mary replaced coins and stamps that had only her image with those containing Philip's face with hers, beneath the protection of one crown.[62] Such actions and representations could certainly give the impression that Mary shared power with her husband.

Reception of these inconsistent symbolic messages confused not only the English people but also the political elites, who debated Mary's paradoxical situation. Courtiers and noblemen, in fact, were the targets of the message of power by Mary that has triggered the most historiographic discussion: the joint portrait of her and Philip that she commissioned in 1558, at the end of her reign, and which today forms part of the duke of Bedford's collection at Woburn Abbey (Figure 5.2). This portrait is one of the principal examples of the contradictory representations of Mary, as it contains both messages of primacy and of collaboration. Despite showing her enthroned on the right-hand (preeminent) side of the painting, the main object was to display the couple's equal sovereignty through the union of their titles and heraldic emblems and to evoke mutual loyalty, represented by the dogs who lie placidly at Mary's feet.[63]

Now that we have examined some of Mary's strategies of symbolic communication, what were Philip's representational reactions to his constitutional limitations? We have seen that Charles V's heir suffered political humiliation at the conditions of his marriage agreement. He could not present himself on the European diplomatic stage as a mere consort to a queen. So Philip undertook a counter-offensive, based largely on visual effects and painting. The unusual characteristic of his strategy was that he did not use his own image to advertise his power, but rather that of Mary, which he symbolically subordinated to his authority as husband. In a way, one could speak of Philip's strategy as having symbolically "kidnapped" the queen's image. The best example of this can be seen in the portrait that Philip ordered from the Dutch painter Antonis Mor (1517–77) in 1554, after his arrival in England. In this well-known painting, today in the Prado Museum, Mor captured the king's aspirations and painted the queen of England as if she were a Habsburg consort (Figure 5.3). In other words, Mor ignored the iconographic canons associated with Tudor portraits and replaced them with all the elements identifying Habsburg rulers and their wives.

---

[61] Samson, *The Marriage of Philip*, 225.

[62] Sharpe, *Selling the Tudor Monarchy*, 276–77.

[63] See P.G. Matthews, "Portraits of Philip of Spain as King of England," *The Burlington Magazine*, 142, no. 1162 (2000): 13–19.

Figure 5.3 Antonis Mor, Portrait of Mary Tudor, 1554, oil on panel, 109 × 84 cm. Museo Nacional del Prado, Madrid.

First, while Tudor monarchs were traditionally depicted standing, so as to display their regal position, Mor painted Mary seated, like other artists who painted Habsburg consorts. Mor's portrait of Mary is notably similar to the one Titian had painted of the last Habsburg queen consort, Philip's mother, the empress Isabel of Portugal. Similarities include the placement of the hands and the pyramidal structure of the paintings. There has been speculation regarding the red rose Mary holds in her right hand, which could be an emblem of the English dynasty or a reference to Venus's flower, a metaphor for love and conjugal loyalty. But there is no doubt about the pillar in the background, alluding to the mythical pillars of Hercules, one of the supreme Habsburg symbols, or the emphasis on the diamonds and pearl jewelry that Philip had given her for their wedding, which clearly signals Mary's connection to the Habsburg dynasty.

In all its symbolic complexity, Mor's portrait of Mary Tudor turned the English queen into a Hispanic consort by using Habsburg iconographic traditions. Philip, with great intelligence, used Mary's image to transmit a message of authority that suited his European interests. Joanna Woodall has written that this propagandistic strategy becomes even more important when one considers that while Mor was painting, the English court commissioned Hans Eworth (1520–74) to paint another portrait of Mary. Eworth followed Tudor iconography, showing Mary standing, regal, and sovereign. It was a portrait that satisfied the expectations of the English court, and probably the queen as well.[64]

These two, parallel portraits, which transmitted diametrically opposing messages, clearly indicate the divergent interests at the Tudor court in the late 1550s. The origin of this divergence was the fact that a woman was on the English throne, resulting in conflicting interpretations on the part of her contemporaries. Mary Tudor's arrival on the throne was exceptional and anomalous and it affected her marriage to Philip of Habsburg. As a result of these circumstances, Philip underwent a political and personal process that traditionally corresponded to the women of his dynasty; not participating actively in the construction of his future, he had to travel to a faraway land to which he would never adapt and integrate himself in a cultural system very different than the one he knew. Any aristocratic princess of the mid-sixteenth century would have regarded marriage to an English monarch as a substantial gain in terms of prestige and dignity, but for Philip the marriage was synonymous with diminished political authority, which he tried to overcome by using representational strategies that directly opposed the interests of his wife. These efforts placed him in an intermediate position in terms both of sovereign power and power over his own image, making him somewhat more than a consort but somewhat less than a monarch in his own right.

No analysis of Philip's English experience could deny that during his relatively short stay at the English court, he acclimatized himself to some small

---

[64] Joanna Woodall, "An Exemplary Consort. Antonis Mor's Portrait of Mary Tudor," *Art History*, 14, no. 2 (1991): 192–224.

degree, enough to build a bridge between things English and things Spanish. Thus the material and cultural transfers that had characterized Anglo-Spanish relations since the Middle Ages did not disappear with Mary Tudor's marriage contract. But her subjects' rejection of female sovereignty also led them to reject Philip and everything he represented. From then on, and into the following centuries, English-Spanish political and cultural relations were more aggressive and hostile.

From our privileged position, looking back and knowing how things turned out, we cannot continue denying a more intermediate position. Endings are often unexpected, and they do not properly reflect what came before. This is most certainly the case with Philip II's relations with England. Historiography and the historical discourse continue interpreting the Spanish monarch's relationship to England in terms of his ultimate confrontation with Elizabeth I. But in fact it is possible to understand the true nature of this relationship only if we take another look at his marriage with Mary Tudor. Philip's English experience became a tale of conflict, but it was, from the start, a family tale.

Bibliography

Baraonda, Juan de. *Relación del viaje del Príncipe Don Felipe a Inglaterra.* Archivo del Monasterio de El Escorial. Vol. 2.4.

Cruz, Anne J., ed. *Material and Symbolic Circulation between Spain and England, 1554–1604.* Aldershot: Ashgate, 2008.

Duncan, Sarah. *Mary I. Gender, Power, and Ceremony in the Reign of England's First Queen.* Basingstoke: Palgrave Macmillan, 2012.

Edwards, John. *Mary I. England's Catholic Queen.* New Haven: Yale University Press, 2011.

Fernández Álvarez, Manuel. *Corpus Documental Carlos V.* Vol. 4. Salamanca: Ediciones Universidad de Salamanca, 1979.

Froude, James Anthony. *The Reign of Mary Tudor.* London: J.M. Dent & Sons, 1913.

Gayangos, Pascual de, ed. *Viaje de Felipe Segundo á Inglaterra, por Andrés Muñoz (impreso en Zaragoza en 1554), y relaciones varias relativas al mismo suceso.* Madrid: Sociedad de Bibliófilos Españoles, 1877.

González-Arnao, Mariano. "La boda inglesa de Felipe II." *Historia,* 16, no. 97 (May 1984): 34–42.

González Sánchez-Molero, José Luís. "Philippus, rex Hispaniae & Angliae. La biblioteca inglesa de Felipe II." *Reales sitios. Revista del Patrimonio Nacional,* no. 160 (2004): 14–33.

Loades, David. "Philip II and the Government of England." In *Law and Government under the Tudors. Essays Presented to Sir Geoffrey Elton, Regius Professor of Modern History in the University of Cambridge on the Occasion of His Retirement.* Edited by Claire Cross, David Loades and J.J. Scarisbrick, 177–94. Cambridge: Cambridge University Press, 1988.

_____ . *The Reign of Philip and Mary*. Burford: Davenant Press, 2001.

_____ . *Mary Tudor. The Tragical History of the first Queen of England*. Kew: National Archives, 2006.

_____ . *Mary Tudor*. Stroud: Amberley, 2011.

Martínez Llamas, Antonio. *Felipe II, el hombre*. León: Lobo Sapiens, 2009.

Matthews, P.G. "Portraits of Philip of Spain as King of England." *The Burlington Magazine* 142, no. 1162 (2000): 13–19.

Morales Folguera, José Miguel. "El arte al servicio del poder y de la propaganda imperial. La boda del príncipe Felipe con María Tudor en la Catedral de Winchester y la solemne entrada de la pareja real en Londres." *POTESTAS. Revista del Grupo Europeo de Investigación Histórica*, no. 2 (2009): 165–89.

Nadal, Santiago. *Las cuatro mujeres de Felipe II*. Barcelona: Juventud, 1960.

Queralt del Hierro, María Pilar. *Las mujeres de Felipe II. Deber y pasión en la casa del rey*. Madrid: EDAF, 2011.

Parker, Geoffrey. *Felipe II. La biografía definitiva*. Translated by Victoria E. Gordo del Rey. Barcelona: Planeta, 2010.

Pollard, Albert Frederick. *The Political History of England*. London: Longmans, Green, and Co., 1915.

Redworth, Glyn. "¿Nuevo mundo u otro mundo? Conquistadores, cortesanos, libros de caballerías y el reinado de Felipe el Breve de Inglaterra." In *Actas del Primer Congreso Anglo-Hispano*. Vol. 3. Edited by Ralph Penny, Alan Deyermond and Richard Hitchock, 113–25. Barcelona: Castalia, 1993–94.

_____ . "Felipe y las soberanas de Inglaterra." *Torre de los Lujanes*, 33 (1997): 103–12.

_____ . "'Matters Impertinent to Women'. Male and Female Monarchy under Philip and Mary." *The English Historical Review*, 112, no. 447 (1997): 597–613.

Richards, Judith M. "Mary Tudor as 'Sole Quene'? Gendering Tudor Monarchy." *The Historical Journal*, 40, no. 4 (December 1997): 895–924.

_____ . *Mary Tudor*. London: Routledge, 2008.

Rodríguez-Salgado, María José. *Un Imperio en transición. Carlos V, Felipe II y su mundo, 1551–1559*. Barcelona: Editorial Crítica, SA, 1992.

Samson, Alexander. *The Marriage of Philip of Habsburg and Mary Tudor and Anti-Spanish Sentiment in England. Political Economies and Culture, 1553–1557*. London: University of London, 1999.

_____ . "Changing Places. The Marriage and Royal Entry of Philip, Prince of Austria, and Mary Tudor, July–August 1554." *Sixteenth Century Journal*, 36, no. 3 (2005): 761–84.

Sharpe, Kevin. *Selling the Tudor Monarchy. Authority and Image in Sixteenth-Century England*. New Haven: Yale University Press, 2009.

Tomàs Cabot, Josep. *La vida y la época de Felipe II*. Barcelona: Planeta, 1998.

Walker, Rose. "Leonor of England and Eleanor of Castile: Anglo-Iberian Marriage and Cultural Exchange in the Twelfth and Thirteenth Centuries." In

England and Iberia in the Middle Ages, Twelfth–Fifteenth Century. Cultural, Literary, and Political Exchanges. Edited by María Bullón-Fernández, 67–87. New York: Palgrave, 2007.

Woodall, Joanna. "An Exemplary Consort. Antonis Mor's Portrait of Mary Tudor." *Art History*, 14, no. 2 (1991): 192–224.

Chapter 6

The Marriage of João de Alarcão and Margarida Soares and the Creation of a Transnational Portuguese–Spanish Nobility*

Mafalda Soares da Cunha

Introduction

The main aim of this chapter is to analyze the social and political effects of dynastic marriages between the Portuguese and Castilian-Aragonese crowns on the configuration of transnational, aristocratic families during the sixteenth and seventeenth centuries. To illustrate these questions I have chosen to follow the Soares de Alarcão family (known in Spain as Suárez de Alarcón) and the paths it took between the royal houses of Portugal and Castile for seven generations. (See Table 6.1 for a genealogy of the Soares de Alarcão family.)

The working hypothesis of the chapter is that the identity of the Iberian nobility during this era was characterized by a shared noble culture rather than by any particular features derived from the family's land of origin. That assumption allows us to discuss whether the use of a particular language or culture indicates ties or political loyalties based on criteria of nationality, or, at the very least, place of birth.

Therefore, this chapter discusses the miscegenation of Iberian nobilities derived from dynastic marriages. It articulates the structural characteristics of this group and its political impact with the individual trajectories and historical contexts in which they developed. While these topics can be of interest for the comprehension of Portuguese early modern history, they can also help us to reflect more broadly on processes of identity construction. When discussing identity construction, I consider both what we would designate today as national—language and cultural production—and social, related with the identity of the nobility.

The Soares de Alarcão Family in Portugal

The marriage of João de Alarcão [?–1546] with Margarida Soares de Melo [dates unknown] represents the beginning of a transnational family trajectory

* This chapter was translated from the Portuguese by Stewart Lloyd-Jones, CPHRC Editorial Services.

Table 6.1 Genealogical Chart of the Soares de Alarcão Family (Fifteenth to Seventeenth Centuries)

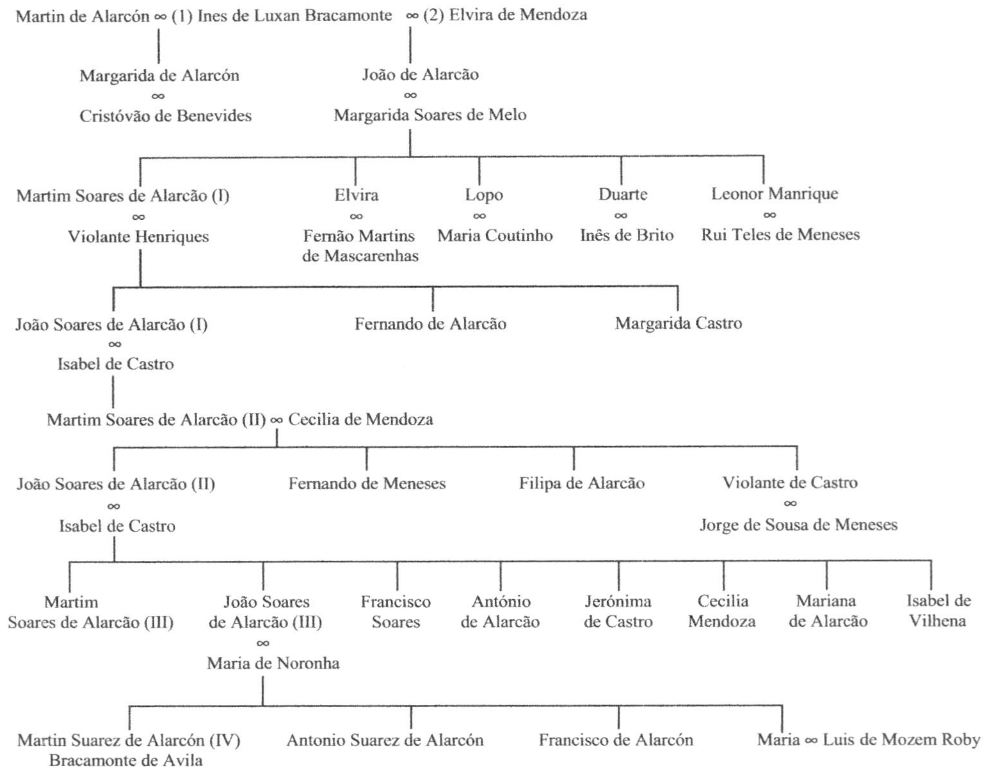

between families from Castile and Portugal structured in the shadow of the royal court.

João de Alarcão was the only son of the second marriage of Martín de Alarcón with Elvira de Mendoza. Martín, in turn, was the fourth son of Lope Ruiz de Alarcón, the lord of Valverde, Talayuelas, Veguillas, and Hontecillas in the region of Cuenca. Peerage books identify Martín de Alarcón as a servant of the Catholic Monarchs and as a participant in the conquest of Granada. Maybe as a result of this military service, he received the offices of captain of the guard (*capitão da guarda*) of the Monarchs and governor (*alcaide*) of the fortresses of Porcuña and Moclin (in Andalusia), and also was named commander of the Order of Santiago. João de Alarcão's mother was Elvira de Mendoza, daughter of Juan Furtado de Mendoza, the king of Spain's chief forester (*monteiro-mor*). She became a widow in the late 1490s and went to Portugal in 1500 in the entourage of Princess María, daughter of the Catholic Monarchs and the second wife of the Portuguese king Manoel I. João de Alarcão was still a child, and he accompanied his mother.

Elvira served as Queen María's lady-in-waiting. Due to her close relationship with the queen, in 1508 she received a pension of 200,000 *reis*.[1] Shortly after the queen's death she was given the position of nurse (*aia*) to princesses Isabel and Beatriz because she was thought to have the virtues and knowledge required to educate them in accordance with the high dignity of their station.[2] This close relationship continued after Manoel I married for the third time, with Elvira serving as Queen Eleanor's lady-in-waiting. Lady Elvira accompanied her on her return to Castile in 1523 and died that same year in Vitoria, in the Basque Country, while in the service of Queen Eleanor, who had been sent to France as a consort to King Francis I.[3] Elvira's destiny was intimately linked to her personal relationship with the princesses of Castile and queens of Portugal, and this explains why her roots in Portugal remained shallow. Her instructions to her son, calling on him to expand the chapel in Granada in which her husband was buried, confirms that her main family references continued within the crown of Castile.

The same was not true of João de Alarcão, her only son. He was raised in the same palace as the successor to the Portuguese crown, the future João III. Because of the trust Queen Maria had in Lady Elvira, along with the lady-in-waiting's closeness to the young princesses, she was able to obtain royal permission to pass her pension on to her son and for him to be granted the position of grand master of the hunt (*caçador-mor*) at the royal court in 1521.[4] Unlike his mother, João

---

1 Arquivo Nacional da Torre do Tombo (hereafter ANTT), Chancelaria de D. Manuel, L. 24, fol. 178v.

2 ANTT, Chancelaria de D. Manuel, L. 25, fols. 172–172v, November 6, 1517.

3 Antonio Suárez de Alarcón, *Relaciones genealogicas de la casa de los marqueses de Torcifal, condes de Torresvedras, su varonia Zevallos de Alarcon y por la casa y primer apellido Suarez* (Madrid: Diego Diaz de la Carrera, 1656), 321.

4 ANTT, Chancelaria de D. Manuel, L. 24, fol. 99v; ANTT, Chancelaria de D. Manuel, L. 10, fols. 72–72v; ANTT Chancelaria de D. Manuel, L. 10, fols. 71v–72.; Suárez de Alarcón, *Relaciones genealógicas*, 325–26.

de Alarcão remained in Portugal. One reason for this was his agreement in 1515 to marry Margarida Soares de Melo, who was also a lady in the court of Queen Maria, although of Portuguese birth.

Margarida was daughter of Gomes Soares de Melo, a member of a medieval *fidalgo* family that belonged to the highest rank of the Portuguese nobility. As a result of inheritances and his loyal service to the Portuguese kings, Gomes Soares de Melo had accumulated land and estates. He was governor-general (*alcaide-mor*) of the town of Torres Vedras and lord of Vila de Rei, as well as master of the royal cushion (*reposteiro-mor*) and councilor to Kings Alphonse V, João II, and Manoel I. Margarida was his only heir. Her high social status was proof of the rapid rise of the young Alarcão into the highest levels of the Portuguese nobility and of the active protection Queen Maria extended to her lady-in-waiting's son. João de Alarcão's relative lack of familial roots helps to explain why Gomes Soares de Melo chose João as his son-in-law. In fact João, though favored by the queen, had no family background in Portugal. He was, therefore, more ready to adopt the symbols of his wife's lineage, as demonstrated by the fact that his descendants used the name Soares and adopted Torres Vedras for their home and final resting place. Gomes Soares de Melo had ordered the construction of a sumptuous tomb in the Franciscan monastery in Varatojo, near Torres Vedras, in which the remains of João de Alarcão, who died in 1546, rest. This tomb became a pantheon for successive generations of the family. In a move that signaled both the existence of a new male line and the wish to keep the connection to his wife's estates and family identity, João de Alarcão had a stately home built within the castle of Torres Vedras, separate from that of his father-in-law, who lived in the lower part of the town.[5] His intentions to settle in Portugal can be confirmed by the sale of his part of his father's inheritance in Granada, retaining only the chapel, which was enlarged in 1532 in accordance with his mother's last wishes.

The consolidation of Soares de Alarcão's integration into Portugal's top nobility can be seen in the social distinction of subsequent family alliances. Marriages were arranged only with descendants of titled nobles or with heirs and daughters of *fidalgos* with senior positions within the royal household. João de Alarcão's second marriage was to a daughter of the third count of Abrantes and granddaughter of the first count of Tarouca.[6]

Succeeding generations maintained this standard, seeking matrimony at the top levels of the Portuguese nobility. João's successor, Martim Soares de Alarcão (I), married into the house of Mascarenhas and became brother-in-law of Fernão Martins de Mascarenhas. (See Table 6.2 for a genealogy of the Mascarenhas family.)

[5] Suárez de Alarcón, *Relaciones genealógicas*, 96, and Manoel Agostinho Madeira Torres, "Descripção Histórica e Economica da Villa e Termo de Torres Vedras" in *História e Memórias da Academia Real das Sciencias de Lisboa*, vol. 6, part 1 (Lisbon: Typografia da Mesma Academia, 1819), 96.

[6] Suárez de Alarcón, *Relaciones genealógicas*, 330–31.

Table 6.2 Genealogical Chart of the Mascarenhas Family (Mid-Sixteenth Century)

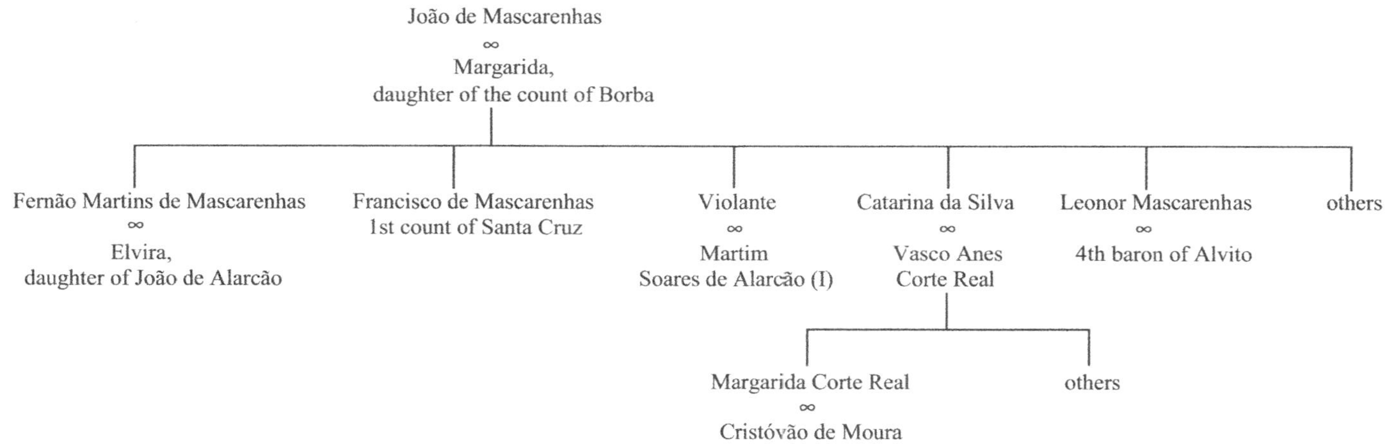

The Mascarenhas family included Francisco de Mascarenhas, first count of Santa Cruz, viceroy of India and future governor of Portugal. The wife of the fourth baron of Alvito also came from the Mascarenhas family, as did the wife of Vasco Eanes Corte-Real. The latter and his wife would be the parents of the future wife of Cristóvão de Moura, first marquis of Castelo Rodrigo, whose central role in the negotiations for the annexation of Portugal to the Hispanic Monarchy in 1580 is well known. It was a kinship network of huge political weight and recognized importance. João de Alarcão's grandson, the second generation to be born in Portugal, who was also called João, married the daughter of the third baron of Alvito. By then, the middle of the sixteenth century, the Soares de Alarcão family was thoroughly incorporated into the highest Portuguese noble elite.

In the following generation, the sixth lord of the house, Martim Soares de Alarcão (II), who was orphaned at a young age, was raised by Fernão Martins de Mascarenhas, head of the Mascarenhas family at that time. As a result, Martim reinforced the family links with the Mascarenhases and inherited part of the estates of Fernão Martins de Mascarenhas and his wife, thereby increasing his house's economic strength. Through the intervention of Queen Catherine, wife of João III, marriage was arranged between him and the heiress of a court *fidalgo*, Filipe de Aguilar, who shared the queen's Castilian origins.

This description of the integration of the Soares de Alarcão family in Portugal now merits a brief pause to allow us to underline the importance of the queen's retinues. While Filipe de Aguilar had been born in Portugal, he was the son of the Castilian Francisco Velázquez de Aguilar, who had arrived in Portugal with his grandmother, María de Velasco. She was married to the Castilian king's treasurer (*contador-mor*), who had lands and title in Extremadura (Castile). The parallels between María de Velasco's life and that of Elvira de Mendoza, insofar as family migration is concerned, are further strengthened by the fact that María de Velasco had also been an important person in queens' households. Before her death in 1539 she was lady-in-waiting to Queen Germana and then to Queen Catherine. As was the case with Elvira, it was María de Velasco's loyalty and service that secured her descendants' integration into the court of the kings of Portugal. Francisco Velázquez was appointed carver (*trinchante*) to the Portuguese Prince João Manoel by royal warrant in 1554[7] and was married to Cecilia de Mendoza e Bocanegra, also a Castilian in Queen Catherine's retinue and later the queen's maid.[8] Underlining the importance of the queen's patronage in integrating families of Castilian birth in Portugal, one of the daughters of this marriage was one of Queen Catherine's ladies, who went on to marry António de Lima, a member of Prince Duarte's retinue.

As the oldest son, Filipe de Aguilar inherited his father's estate. His early adult life included time in the royal court and in the Portuguese army in Morocco, more particularly in Ceuta, where he had been since the 1540s and where his

[7] Ibid., 366 and in appendix, 117.

[8] Ibid., 367ss.

military activities were acknowledged.[9] He also served on missions throughout the Mediterranean, receiving orders to return to Portugal in 1558.[10] He was afterwards appointed herald (*mestre-sala*) to the royal house, a position he held under Kings Sebastian, Henry, and Philip II. His experience in North Africa resulted in Cardinal King Henry appointing him captain of Mazagão. He also was named commander of St. Peter of the Order of Christ in Torres Vedras and founded a *morgado* (entailed property).[11]

Through the good offices of Queen Catherine, after 1554 Filipe de Aguilar married Ana de Lugo, the only daughter of Fernando de Lugo, a Galician exiled in Portugal who was also governor of the Cape Verde Islands.[12] Showing he wished to firmly establish his house in Portugal, Fernando de Lugo founded a *morgado* and chapel within the Convent of Santo Agostinho in Lisbon.[13] There was only one child from this marriage, Cecilia de Mendoza, who inherited both the Aguilar and Lugo *morgados*. As an example of the patrimonial nature of positions and offices within the court, she inherited the position of herald and the commander of St. Peter of the Order of Christ in Torres Vedras. It was with this wealthy heiress that Martim Soares de Alarcão (II), the sixth lord of the house, married before 1580.

Both father-in-law and son-in-law took Philip II's side in the dynastic dispute in Portugal between 1578 and 1581. Martim commanded forces opposing Anthony, the Prior of Crato, the boisterous son of Prince Luis who was challenging Philip II for the throne. Martim's military effectiveness earned him the animosity of the Prior of Crato, who, "angry with Lord Martim, several times referred to Torres Vedras [Old Towers] as traitors' towers, declaring Martim lost and his house confiscated."[14] Regarding Filipe de Aguilar's participation, we know that he represented his son-in-law in presenting the keys of Lisbon to Philip II in 1581, and that the new king rewarded him with the position of state councilor, which he held until 1586.

Cultural Transfer

Martim's successor to these many estates was João Soares de Alarcão (II), who died in 1618. He married Isabel de Castro, who belonged to a branch of the

---

[9] Letter of D. Afonso de Noronha to João III, from Ceuta, October 7, 1545 in Robert Ricard, *Les sources inédites de l'Histoire du Maroc*, vol. 4 (January 1542–December 1550) (Paris: P. Geuthner, 1951), 170–77.

[10] Letter of Queen Catherine to Filipe de Aguilar, from Lisboa, August 28, 1558, in *Catálogo de um seleccionado leilão de manuscritos, autógrafos, fotografias e efémera* (Lisbon: Livraria Luís Burnay: 2010), 27.

[11] Suárez de Alarcón, *Relaciones genealógicas*, 367.

[12] He was asked to return to Portugal in 1554 by the queen: see ibid., in appendix, 117–18.

[13] Ibid., 368.

[14] Ibid., 345.

Mascarenhas family, thereby strengthening once more the relationships within the family group. While this endogamous tendency was common at the time, in this case it was to have important implications for the future, as we shall see. Perhaps because he was sickly, João's life was quieter and without military action. However, other actions in his life were to prove important for the argument being developed in this chapter.

The first of these was associated with a complaint against Philip III's policy of favors. The motive was related to the monarch's wish to recover Cascais, a town of little importance but located strategically on the banks of the Tagus and, consequently, crucial to the defense of Lisbon. In order to do so the king had to recompense the counts of Monsanto, to whom Cascais belonged. The count of Monsanto asked for the governorship of Torres Vedras as compensation. However, that post had belonged to the Soares de Alarcão family for generations. In return for this loss, Philip III offered João Soares de Alarcão (II) the title of count of Trocifal (today Turcifal). As that was an insignificant place within the district of Torres Vedras, the seventh head of the Soares de Alarcão family thought the honor in no way made up for the loss of the governorship. His reaction took the form of a judicial claim against the crown, pursuit of which took him to the court in Madrid. The arguments he presented were enough to stop the plan and prevent the deal from being made.

In 1607 he was called to the succession of the estate of Valverde, close to Cuenca, in Castile, as Diego Ruiz de Alarcón, the first count of Valverde and head of the house of Alarcón in Castile, was dying. The Castilian origins of the Portuguese Alarcão family had re-emerged as a consequence of the laws of succession. The matter, however, was problematic. When the count recovered from his illness, it seemed to the count and the other lords of the houses of Alarcón that João's right to inherit might be at risk because he lived in a different kingdom. In order to prevent future juridical doubts they established an instrument of justification, signed by all interested parties, in which João and the house of Alarcão's right of immediate succession by primogeniture was recognized.[15]

However, the information here is rather inconsistent, with other documents stating the date of 1624 for the concession of the title of count of Valverde to Diego Ruiz de Alarcón, and declaring that he had a son. Whatever the case, it is important to stress the persistence of kinship relations with the Alarcóns on both sides of the border and the seemingly natural status of blood succession rights in overcoming any difficulty caused as a result of a foreigner enjoying land and title in another kingdom.

The final important fact in the life of João Soares de Alarcão (II) is associated with his becoming an author. It was said that he "composed some poems, some of which were published."[16] One of these was *La Iffanta coronada por El Rey Don Pedro, Doña Ines de Castro: en octava rima* (The princess crowned by His

[15] Ibid., 371–72, in appendix, 118.

[16] Torres, "Descripção Histórica e Economica," 97.

Majesty King Peter, Lady Ines de Castro: in ottava rima),[17] which was printed in Lisbon in 1606 by Pedro Crasbeeck, a member of a famous line of printers. It is a very rare work of which there are few known copies. Adrien Roig discussed it,[18] as did Leonor Machado de Sousa more recently.[19] It is an epic in which the heroine is Ines de Castro, a lady who became famous for her disastrous affair with the Portuguese King Peter I. As Roig notes, this work is interesting on many levels. First, it was written in Castilian by a Portuguese *fidalgo*. If the language choice cannot be considered anything other than a "demonstration of the bilingualism that prevailed on the Peninsula in that era," the fact that the dedication, addressed to Francisco de Mascarenhas, first count of Santa Cruz, was written in Portuguese reveals the ability for both languages to be understood on either side of the border.[20]

It is also worth emphasizing to whom the book was dedicated. As João Soares de Alarcão (II) wrote, the links between the Alarcão and Mascarenhas families were many and lasting. This "close consanguinity" was renewed with his marriage.[21] His wife, Isabel de Castro, was the sister of Jorge de Mascarenhas, the future count of Castelo Novo and marquis of Montalvão. Therefore, the first count of Santa Cruz was his father-in-law's cousin. The reason for the dedication could have been the mutual adherence of the Alarcão family and the count of Santa Cruz to the cause of Philip II. Although the count was a faithful servant of Philip II in Portugal, what the author highlights with this dedication is his kinship with Ines de Castro and the "rare happiness" with which he "administered government posts in the East and the West, defending one and the other area from the greatest of dangers."[22] Thus while the Portuguese empire was not part of João Soares de Alarcão's political trajectory, it seems to have occupied a central place in his value framework.

In terms of theme and literary genre, Roig notes the choice of a Castilian heroine to support a Portuguese epic with the intention of calling attention to the poet's position regarding Spanish and Portuguese values. In Roig's words, this work "appears as a symbol of peninsular duality under the rule of the Philips."[23] In effect, João Soares de Alarcão chose examples that present Spain as a "common mother" and is fulsome in his praise for the Habsburg monarchs while not seeing

[17] Juan Soares de Alarcão, *La Iffanta coronada por El Rey Don Pedro, Doña Ines de Castro: en octava rima* (Lisbon: Pedro Crasbeeck, 1606).

[18] Adrien Roig, "La Infanta coronada de Juan Soares de Alarcón (1606)," in *Actas del séptimo Congreso de la Asociación Internacional de Hispanistas, celebrado en Venecia del 25 al 30 de agosto de 1980*, ed. Giuseppe Bellini (Rome: Bulzoni, 1982), 893–901.

[19] Maria Leonor Machado de Sousa, introduction to João Soares de Alarcão, *La Iffanta coronada por El Rey Don Pedro, Doña Ines de Castro* (Torres Vedras: Livro do Dia, 2009).

[20] Roig, "La Infanta coronada," 894. On bilingualism, see Pilar Vásquez Cuesta, *A língua e a cultura portuguesas no tempo dos Filipes* (Lisbon: Publicações Europa América, 1988).

[21] Soares de Alarcão, *La Iffanta coronada*, Dedication.

[22] Ibid.

[23] Roig, "La Infanta coronada," 901.

any contradiction with the historical appreciation of the actions of the Portuguese and of the "Lusitanian nation." The same can also be seen with the use of a combined Portuguese and Castilian heraldry in the book's frontispiece. Even more expressive of this merger is that his name is printed in a mixture of Castilian (Don Juan) and Portuguese (Soares de Alarcão).

Roig's analysis of the influence of this poem on Spanish literature, particularly the circulation of the theme of Ines de Castro, is also interesting. At that time this tragic love tale had been little touched upon in Spain; hence, its incorporation into the patrimony of literary references on an Iberian scale was very limited. It is worth considering, therefore, that *La Iffanta coronada* had a significant impact on the spread of this literary theme in Spain and on Luis Vélez de Guevara's work, *Reinar después de morir* (To reign after death), which many consider a baroque masterpiece.

The case we must now follow, and which is also the climax of this narrative, is that of the poet's second son who, because of the premature death of his older brother, became head of the house of Soares de Alarcão. Like his father, he was named João Soares de Alarcão (III). From his succession until 1640 he did not distinguish himself from other *fidalgos* of his rank living in Portugal. He served in the king's army at Cascais, where he led companies of men from his estates while preparing to defend against the disembarkation of English troops in 1625–26. He also played an important role in putting down the tax riots that spread throughout the Portuguese kingdom at the end of the 1630s. Along with other nobles he raised men from his estates to support royal troops in this task. In 1639 he responded to a new appeal by the monarch for military support to confront the threat of a French armada approaching Lisbon. This time he was asked to be part of the army from around Lisbon which included 1,200 men from his lands at Torres Vedras. On the eve of December 1, 1640, Philip IV appointed him governor and captain of Ceuta, one of Portugal's fortresses in Morocco.

Competing Loyalties: Between João IV and Philip IV

The rupture between Portugal and the Spanish kingdom took place on, precisely, December 1, 1640. The secessionist movement advanced smoothly, seemingly responding to an expectation felt throughout society. The coronation of the new king took place in Lisbon on January 28, 1641 in the presence of representatives of the three estates united in the Cortes, the representative assembly. Thus the eighth duke of Braganza ascended to the throne with the name João IV. His reign over this new political entity, which had recovered the independence lost at the hands of Philip II in 1580, lasted until 1656.[24]

---

[24] Leonor Freire Costa and Mafalda Soares da Cunha, *D. João IV, 1604–1656*, rev. edn. (Lisbon: Temas e Debates, 2008).

The social background to this political change is not, even today, sufficiently explained in the historiography. Is it possible, as the publicists and historians of the Restoration claim, that there was a social consensus? Is it possible that the loyalties and the convergence of interests demonstrated by the majority of the social elite towards the Habsburgs during these 60 years just melted away? The flight of Portuguese *fidalgos*, including João Soares de Alarcão and his family, to Castile during the first months of 1641 challenges the more simplistic explanations and demands more complex answers that involve further examination of dynastic loyalty and strategic questions present in the consolidation of the newly sovereign Portugal.

The following is the narrative of the events in which João Soares de Alarcão (III) played a central role.[25] On February 7, 1641 two ships left the Tagus River and set sail. One of the ships (*bergantim*) carried some *fidalgos* and their families. Among them were Pedro and Jerónimo Mascarenhas, sons of the viceroy of Brazil, the first marquis of Montalvão; Lopo da Cunha, lord proprietor of Assentar, and his son Pedro; and Luís da Cunha the only son of Lourenço da Silva, the well-known retired president of the Portuguese high court (*regedor da Casa da Suplicação*). On the other ship, from Hamburg (although some say it was English), were the governors of Ceuta and Tangier—João Soares de Alarcão and Duarte de Meneses, third count of Tarouca—along with their families and servants. Days later it was reported the passengers had disembarked in Andalusia with the intention of seeking refuge in Castile as a sign of their loyalty to Philip IV, whom they considered the legitimate king of Portugal. A few days later there was another defection of *fidalgos*. While fewer in number, their reasons for leaving Portugal were the same. Fearing the marquis of Montalvão's sympathy towards Castile, in February a new ship was ordered to set sail for Brazil, on which embarked the Jesuit Francisco de Vilhena with express orders to determine the viceroy's loyalty to the new king of Portugal. Should it prove necessary, he was given the authority to remove Montalvão and appoint a new governor of Brazil.

The departure of the *fidalgos* for Castile during February caused concern in Lisbon. They were all well-known nobles with land, knighthoods, commanderships in military orders, and governorships granted by the king. Some, such as Duarte de Meneses, third count of Tarouca, even had titles or, such as Pedro Mascarenhas, João Soares de Alarcão, and Luís da Silva, were heirs to well-established noble houses. It became clear to all that the apparent unanimity of December 1 was wide of the mark. João IV and his supporters discovered that their hope that Portuguese *fidalgos* and dignitaries in Madrid would rally to the Braganza cause could not be assured and that the oaths sworn at the January coronation were no guarantee of loyalty. Moreover, the dispensation of favors and positions by João IV could not ensure either the gratitude or allegiance of those appointed. Therefore, this was the beginning of a period of distrust and suspicion.

[25] Ibid., 128ff.

In fact, many of the fugitives kept the positions within the royal household they had held before December 1. For example, Pedro Mascarenhas was comptroller (*vedor*) of the royal household, in which role he participated in the Cortes; João Soares de Alarcão was herald; and Jerónimo Mascarenhas was a deputy to the Mesa da Consciência e Ordens.

They served disingenuously, as they themselves later confessed, since they had immediately decided not to accept the new political situation. Margarita of Savoy, duchess of Mantua, who was at that time vicereine of Portugal, later confirmed to Philip IV that on the very day of the uprising, João Soares de Alarcão, after trying unsuccessfully to take control of one of Lisbon's fortresses, came to warn her of the fact and to ask her for orders. He was undecided as to whether to stay and wondered how he could best serve the Habsburgs in Portugal. The duchess two years later conveyed to Philip IV João's dilemma: he was unsure

> whether he should seek to leave that kingdom immediately and establish order in Ceuta, to which Your Majesty had appointed him captain general, and in which he had already been sworn by me; and I, after having given him much deserved thanks, recognized that the most important royal service would be to secure the fortress at Ceuta, which was key to the Straits and the preservation of the Andalusian coast as well as the swiftest way to subdue the Portuguese kingdom.[26]

João Soares de Alarcão (III), Pedro Mascarenhas, Duarte de Meneses (count of Tarouca), Luís da Silva, and Lopo da Cunha even presented Philip IV with a letter written on December 5 by the marquis of La Pueblas—who was in prison at Lisbon—recommending them to Philip IV and noting

> that they are Your Majesty's loyal subjects and know no better thing than to live or die in your service. They cannot declare this loudly, in order to protect their persons and their lives for the greater service of Your Majesty … they protest that any action contradicting this truth is violent and untrue and that as soon as they are able they will leave this kingdom to throw themselves at Your Majesty's feet.[27]

As a result, and supported by the knowledge stemming from their close kinship—João Soares de Alarcão was cousin to the two Mascarenhas brothers, while Lopo da Cunha was the brother-in-law of the third count of Tarouca—they jointly prepared their flight. Given the steps taken by João IV in a document of December 19, 1640 designed to prevent the unauthorized departure of Portuguese over the border, the *fidalgos* had to wait for the right time. Their chance came with the

---

26 Suárez de Alarcón, *Relaciones genealógicas*, 389–90.

27 "Conspiração contra D. João 4o," *Archivo bibliographico* (Coimbra: Imprensa da Universidade, 1877), vol. 1, 317.

order to take up their posts as governors of Ceuta and Tangier, to which they had been appointed during the time of Philip IV. As king, João IV confirmed these appointments, demanding only that they restate their oath of loyalty—which is what they clearly did, though João Soares de Alarcão later claimed he did so under duress. After this proof of loyalty to the new king, those two *fidalgos* received royal authorization to leave Lisbon in haste as well as financial support to help with the arrangements they needed to make for their departure. Speed was crucial because the fortresses in Ceuta and Tangiers had not yet declared support for the new Portuguese king.

The secrecy surrounding this departure was remarkable. The governors of the Moroccan fortresses chose not to impart the escape plan to those family members traveling with them, let alone to those who were staying behind in Portugal. Their mediator in Castile was Father Manuel de Macedo, a Dominican who was later arrested and tortured in Portugal for information. Outside the group of fugitives only the archbishop of Braga knew of the plan. With less certainty, it is also claimed that the marquis of Vila Real had been warned of their intention to leave Portugal.

The hastiness of the *fidalgos*' departure may have prevented the archbishop of Braga from joining them. He remained in Lisbon to assess the possibility of, or even to prepare, a counter-coup. The archbishop took the opportunity, through João Soares de Alarcão, to send letters to Philip IV, the count-duke of Olivares, Diogo Soares, and to royal councilors stating his loyalty. João Soares de Alarcão also carried missives from the duchess of Mantua and lists of *fidalgo*s loyal to João IV and those who were for Castile. With this they sought to pass on as much information as possible about the condition of the kingdom with the aim of organizing a successful counter-offensive. Consequently, the papers with all this information were hidden in a box containing pieces of quince cheese, although Maria de Noronha, wife of the newly appointed governor of Ceuta, often spoke of them while in her chamber. The countess of Tarouca, wife of the governor of Tangiers, would later declare that she was astounded by Maria de Noronha's careless conversation as her husband had told her nothing prior to their departure and spoke of the matter only once they had arrived in Gibraltar.[28]

They longed to serve the king to whom they had sworn an oath, take up arms against the Braganza traitor, and make Portugal obey, and through such words and deeds ensure honor and royal favor. In a long letter to his father, the marquis of Montalvão, written in Niebla on February 12, Pedro Marcarenhas did not disguise his intentions. He expected a sizeable reward for his service and that Philip IV would raise him "higher than the duke of Braganza," even making his the greatest house in all Spain. As for João Soares de Alarcão it was loyalty that was important:

---

[28] Biblioteca Nacional de Portugal (BNP), *Coleccção Pombalina*, 476, fols. 38–40. *Diligência feita com dois criados de D. João Soares de Alarcão e de sua mulher que vieram de Madrid*, s/d [1641].

> I see it as my duty not to part from those with whom I stood, and in my conscience I have not found enough reasons to break my oath and homage to a king who preserves the Catholic faith and as long as it is so and I am alive, I will not stop bowing to him no matter how lost he may be, nor will I ever abandon my king whom I followed in better days, and with my sword I shall follow him unto death, and if ever I would see him beaten, I will stand at his feet and weep at his misfortune.[29]

Their motivation for leaving Portugal indicates both their refusal to accept the legitimacy of the duke of Braganza's ascendancy to the Portuguese throne, which they did not hesitate to describe as treachery, and their belief that the usurper's reign would be brief and that Portugal would soon be restored to Philip. They wished, therefore, to take part in this restoration and sought to ensure they were not compromised by the situation in Portugal. Moreover, it was in the power of the two new governors to prevent the delivery of the two strategic outposts of Ceuta and Tangier to the new king in Lisbon, which was a matter of some significance.

João Soares de Alarcão clearly understood the situation. In support of his material disinterest, and reinforcing the honor that motivated him, he wrote to his brother, stating that as soon as he arrived in Castile he would hand over his credentials as governor of Ceuta and declare, "I want nothing from Ceuta, neither from Portugal nor from Castile." He added:

> I can give up Ceuta, since I have not yet taken possession of it. I do not wish that what was entrusted to me be lost to Portugal by my hand; I seek only to save my honor by following unto death the king to whom I have sworn an oath of loyalty.[30]

The prevailing view was that support or opposition by Brazil for the Braganza cause depended upon the speed with which the marquis of Montalvão was informed and of the persuasiveness of the letters from his sons. Pedro Mascarenhas wrote to his father explaining that his position had never altered and that it was only circumstances that obliged him to feign support for the duke of Braganza. He also warned that the marquis of Montalvão should send ships to Castile rather than to Portugal, for in that way "Portugal would lose power in all ways." He also suggested that Lisbon had neither the desire nor the ability to help Brazil and that he, Pedro, had heard no further discussion on this subject, "as if it had never existed and had never been necessary."[31]

---

[29] António Gomes da Rocha Madahil, *Cartas da restauração* (Coimbra: n.p., 1940), 41.

[30] Madahil, *Cartas da restauração*, 42–43.

[31] Ibid., 52.

As we can see, the departure of these *fidalgos* had an effect that went beyond a simple declaration of loyalty to a king they considered legitimate. It implied a defined strategy that sought to halt the process of Portuguese independence through the appropriation of its sources of overseas revenues, of which Brazil was the most important contributor. If we add to this the matter of the North African settlements, then their tactics are even clearer.

Although João de Alarcão had declared his disinterest in Ceuta, the geostrategic analyses of that settlement being made at the time in the Spanish court took a different view. As the duchess of Mantua recognized, Ceuta was the "key to Africa and to Spain"[32] and was essential for the protection of the Andalusian coast and the security of the ocean fleets to Seville. This was in addition to the military advantage for the subjugation of the kingdom of Portugal. The neighboring settlement of Tangier reinforced these offensive and defensive possibilities. From this viewpoint, the opportunity to retain Ceuta and Tangier under Castilian control was not a negligible advantage. However, the Catalonian uprising, France's aggressive policies, and constant Muslim piracy placed Castile's Mediterranean strategy in peril and, more importantly, created potential risks for the Castilian coast.

The arrival of the governors appointed to the two Portuguese fortresses in Ceuta and Tangier was, therefore, important to Philip IV. In fact, the gratitude of the Castilian monarch, who felt indebted to João Soares de Alarcão for the retention of Ceuta as part of his kingdom, was significant to promote Alarcão's career. So much so that he made specific mention of it in the letter granting him Castilian nationality (*naturaleza*), which he signed in 1645, following the reference to Alarcão's departure from Portugal, "and in so doing you have secured the fortress of Ceuta, the only one owned by that crown, which remains under my orders."[33]

Quite surprisingly, in Lisbon there was no significant mention of the loss of these two fortresses. The same cannot be said in relation to the judgment of the acts committed, for which the punishment was severe. There was no room for complacency or for delay. On February 26, a royal warrant was issued ordering summary judgment of the fugitive rebels, who were declared guilty of *lèse-majesté* and of rebellion against the state and the royal person. Issuing sentence on May 4, the Mesa da Consciência e Ordens expelled the fugitives from the military orders to which they belonged. They were afterwards condemned to death and their land and titles confiscated.

However, time was to show that the matter of North Africa had not yet been resolved. Subsequent events prolonged the restlessness relating to those frontiers

[32] Francisco Manuel de Melo, *Tácito Português. Vida, Morte, Dittos e Feitos de El Rey Dom João IV de Portugal*, pref. and transcription by Raul Rêgo (Lisbon: Livraria Sá da Costa Editora, 1995 [1650]), 105.

[33] Suárez de Alarcón, *Relaciones genealógicas*, 115 appendix.

that were to have important repercussions in the 1641 conspiracy against João IV and in the political destiny of Ceuta.[34]

In Spain Once More

These *fidalgos* left behind rich estates. They also left memories and some symbols of their family identity. Returning to the Soares de Alarcão family, João said, "I left my parents, my friends, and above all the bones of my grandfathers. To sustain their blood and pride I have left their ashes." He asked his brother, "if at any time, my brother, you pass Torres Vedras, I ask that you go to the chapel in Varatojo, or to the grave of our grandfathers, and ask for their blessing in my name."[35] With a clear understanding of his composite origin he added, "from today on my children will only keep their Alarcão surname. The Soareses, being from Portugal, shall remain there."[36] However this did not happen, as in all subsequent documents concerning the identity of his children, the composite surname was retained. In fact, the genealogy written by one of his descendants is credited using both surnames.[37]

The fugitive *fidalgos* remained confident Philip IV would reward them generously and enable them to re-establish houses matching those they had left behind. The king did not do this for all of them, despite his initial generous reception, in which he offered a whole series of noble titles and funds to enable them to remain in Castile. The count of Tarouca was made marquis of Tarouca (although some authors say marquis of Penalva), Pedro de Mascarenhas was made count of Castelo Novo, João Soares de Alarcão was made count of Torres Vedras, Lopo da Cunha was named count of Assentar, and Luís da Silva, count of Vagos. They were all Portuguese titles, and the grateful king in this way insisted on representing himself as the king of Portugal. However, the titles came with neither land nor the political and taxation rights with which they were customarily associated.

João Soares de Alarcão (III) remained firm in his refusal to govern Ceuta, despite Philip IV's insistence on sending him there. However, he gave immediate proof of his loyalty when, in April 1642, he fought bravely on the border, across from the Portuguese province of Beira. Later he found his place among the institutions of Spain. In April 1642 he was appointed councilor of war, and in May chief steward (*mordomo-mor*) to the queen. The following year, recognition of his role in consolidating Castilian control of Tangier led Philip IV to appoint him governor of the fortress. However, before he was

---

34 Costa and Cunha, *D. João IV*; Mafalda de Noronha Wagner, *A Casa de Vila Real e a conspiração de 1641 contra D. João IV* (Lisbon: Edições Colibri, 2007).

35 Madahil, *Cartas da restauração*, 41.

36 Ibid., 43.

37 Suárez de Alarcón, *Relaciones genealógicas*, frontispiece.

able to take office, the residents of Tangier declared themselves for King João IV, and the troops under Soares de Alarcão's command were unable to reduce them. Nevertheless, his military advance continued. It is said that he excelled in the arts of war and that he wrote about them, although the writings were never published. Diogo Barbosa Machado, a well-known Portuguese bibliographer from the seventeenth century, said its title was *Arte militar, e do que deve obrar qualquer soldado e cabo em governar e menear as arenas.*[38] In 1644 he fought at Lérida and later took part in the Portuguese intelligence committees (*Juntas de Inteligencias*). In 1645 he was granted the privilege of Castilian *naturaleza*. Finally, in 1646, he agreed to govern Ceuta, a post he held for the next eight years, despite his asking to return immediately after the usual three years.[39]

He was reunited with his sons in Spain, where they served with him in the war, being trained in the use of arms in his company in Ceuta. The elder, Martim Soares de Alarcão (IV), who was seeking to make his name, enlisted in the royal navies and served during the revolts of Naples before returning to Ceuta and then to Catalonia. He died during an assault on the fort of San Juan de los Reyes in Barcelona in 1652. At the time of this painful loss the house was granted the royal favor of 2,000 escudos in a Castilian command and the title marquis of Trocifal, the small place close to Torres Vedras that Philip III had wanted to turn into a county and which Martim (II), João Soares de Alarcão's father, had refused to do.[40]

Antonio Suárez de Alarcón, the second son, became heir to the estate. The prestige of the Alarcão lineage lacked visibility in the years that followed. The size of the Hispanic monarchy and the opulence of the Spanish aristocracy made competition for positions of prominence very difficult, especially in view of the mistrust hanging over the Portuguese exiles. Matching the revenues and prestige they enjoyed in Portugal would be almost impossible. This could be one of the justifications for the book *Corona Sepulcral. Elogios à morte de D. Martin Suarez de Alarcón*, which was dedicated to console the youth's father, the recently appointed marquis of Trocifal and count of Torres Vedras.[41] This book is a collection of writings, mainly poems, written by several famous contemporary authors, including Alonso de Alarcón, the canon of Ciudad Rodrigo and secretary to the bishop of Pamplona, Francisco de Alarcón. The coming together of so many individuals from the same family group to

[38] Diogo Barbosa Machado, *Biblioteca Lusitana: histórica, crítica e cronológica*, vol. 4, 2nd edn. (Lisbon: Bertrand, 1935), 700. This book was originally published in 1759.

[39] Suárez de Alarcón, *Relaciones genealógicas*, 114–15ff.

[40] Ibid., 395.

[41] *Corona Sepulcral. Elogios à morte de D. Martin Suarez de Alarcón escritos por diferentes plumas sacados a luz por Don Alonso de Alarcon, canonigo de la Santa Iglesia de Ciudad Rodrigo e secretario de D. Francisco de Alarcon …* (Madrid: Petrus de Villafranca, 1652).

publicly praise the virtues of the young relative is significant. The poems eulogize the bravery and qualities of Martim, composing a funerary crown in a "monument worthy of his noble ashes."[42] If "with mysterious propriety the Ancients considered parents responsible for all glories of their sons, even more so if both of them were heroes."[43] Such offspring could only be explained through the qualities of their predecessors. Another way of comforting the grieving father was "to show how the life of Martin was lost while serving his king."[44]

The genealogical work Antonio developed through the publication of three books from 1656 to 1665 is evidence of his perception for the need to enhance the Alarcón lineage in Spain.[45] The books were written in Castilian and tell of the military achievements, the antiquity, and the glorious past of the heads of this family. The first to be published, in 1656, was a long and well-researched genealogical investigation of both the Alarcão and the Soares families. It was dedicated to the king and contained a detailed notice of the merits of the progenitors of the family's male line and of the Soares family from remote times. It also describes in minute detail the matrimonial alliances and the attributes of their ancestors, highlighting that many of them had royal blood.

In 1661 *Arbol genealógico* was published. It gave form to the desire of one of his cousins, Fernando Teles de Faro, the count of Arade, who wanted "an account of my male line, for since all the documents pertaining to my house were left in Portugal, I find myself with no such documentation." He hesitated in his request, but since he "saw in the chamber some books in which everything about the Silva family was written," he gained courage. The genealogist agreed immediately, and even thanked him for the opportunity because he had several predecessors in the Silva family," and because of this he was interested in their glories."[46] Like Antonio, Fernando Teles was Portuguese, but he had only recently been exiled. His defection created a political scandal in Lisbon, since he had been one of the first supporters of the duke of Braganza and had rendered him loyal service for almost 20 years.

The *Commentarios de los hechos del señor Alarcon, Marques de la Valle Siciliana y de Renda*, which was published in 1665, had been written in 1663,

---

42 Ibid., 2.

43 Ibid., 3.

44 Ibid., 11.

45 Suárez de Alarcón, *Relaciones genealógicas*; Antonio Suárez de Alarcón, *Arbol genealogico y resumen breve de la varonia de Don Fernando Tellez de Faro y Silva, Conde de Arada* (Madrid: Diego Diaz de la Carrera, 1661); and Antonio Suárez de Alarcón, *Commentarios de los hechos del señor Alarcon, Marques de la Valle Siciliana y de Renda, y de las guerras en que se halló por espacio de cinquenta y ocho años* (Madrid: Diego Diaz de la Carrera, 1665).

46 Suárez de Alarcón, *Arbol genealógico*, 2–3.

a short time before the author's death. The book was dedicated to the king as a pledge of his commitment to continue serving him, though he had to leave army life because of ill health. He was only 27. In a letter to the king printed with the book, he said that the book

> should be of great service to Your Majesty for the glory it brings his vassals by referring to the invincible bravery and feats particular to the Spanish ... and those of the present, seeing the example of those past, can become enflamed in generous emulation to try to imitate them, because the occasions that have led to wars caused by rebellion in Spain are no fewer than the ones caused by ambition in Italy.[47]

It was therefore the military exploits of his ancestor, Fernando de Alarcón, in the wars of Granada and of Italy from 1482 to 1540, that Antonio Suárez de Alarcón bequeathed to the Spaniards as a remedy for the revolts of the present.

Tying up Loose Ends

The case of the Soares de Alarcão family confirms the importance of the houses of Portuguese queens both in the circulation of nobility between the two kingdoms and in their patronage in support of integration of newcomers within the receiving society. However, if it is clear that the queens' favor facilitated these processes, the truth is that their patronage does not seem to have met with great resistance from among Portuguese courtiers.

Similarly, the replacement of a Portuguese male line (Soares) with one of Castilian origin (Alarcón) does not seem to have caused any upset. Nor were any doubts raised about this new male Castilian line becoming the head of a well-established house of Portuguese origin. The formulas used in the inheritance of wealth replicated those that were usual in such circumstances, and the later reproductive strategies followed a standard common among *fidalgos* in Portugal who were on the fringes of the titled nobility. Some of the more apparent factors included concentrating the transmission of wealth and the establishment of *morgados*; and also arranging marriages that were either economically advantageous—to heiresses belonging to the houses of Soares de Melo first, and then of Aguilar, with the incorporation of estates, distinctions such as military orders, governorships, and senior court positions—or socially advantageous, such as with descendants from houses with a noble title. I also ought to highlight that the relatively endogamous marriage trends of the Soares de Alarcão family—conducted within the orbit of the Mascarenhas family—also agree with the propensity to exclusivity in matrimonial choices within the upper echelons of the Portuguese nobility. Equally similar to that

---

[47] Suárez de Alarcón, *Commentarios*, n.p.

of their Portuguese peers was their attention to overseas military service, although not in just any territory. It was traditional at that time for the heirs to *fidalgo* houses to engage in military service in North Africa, a tradition the Soares de Alarcão family kept.

It is also important to point out that family roots in Portugal did not prevent the retention of links, property, and family memories across the border. These were operational and capable of activation, as was demonstrated by the ability of the Portuguese Soares de Alarcão branch to inherit from the Castilian Alarcóns despite possible contradictions between the legal systems of the two kingdoms. As the genealogical treaties of the last title-holder of the house state, it was the illustrious quality of forebears that mattered and should be remembered. Also in this respect, there were no ideological differences between the Iberian nobilities.

Nor did language present an obstacle to group identity—either in the specific case of this family or among the nobility as a whole. Within court circles and among gentlemen of culture, both Portuguese and Castilian were spoken and written. The topic is well known.[48] What is worthy of note in the 1606 epic poem is the appreciation of the moral qualities of the several characters that were in no way altered by mentioning their country of origin. Nor did this present any contradiction with their belonging to the political space that was the Spanish monarchy. The epithets—Portuguese, Luso and Lusitano, or Spanish or Castilian—were simply employed as attributes to describe certain characteristics, and not as denunciatory categories suggesting political opposition. The linguistic mix existing within these circles was proof of the intermingling of families and of the expectations of an Iberian public. The same is not true, however, in relation to the genealogical texts produced in Spain after the 1640 restoration.

It is for this reason that the kingdom of birth is perhaps not the best category for justifying the political choices of members of the nobility (or of any other social group), although historians still hotly debate this question. There is currently a consensus regarding its complexity and that its analysis demands careful attention to the contextualization of behavior. It is therefore important to make clear that the labels "Portuguese" and "Castilian" existed and that in certain contexts they could be used to indicate differentiated, and even conflicting, political spaces.[49] The Portuguese knew their own spaces, rights, and privileges and believed it was absolutely clear they did not wish to be Castilian, nor did they wish the kingdom to be assimilated by Castile or any other crown.

---

[48] Vásquez Cuesta, *A língua e a cultura portuguesas*; Diogo Ramada Curto, "A língua e a literatura ao longo do século XVI," in *Cultura escrita. Séculos XVI a XVIII* (Lisbon: ICS, 2007), 57–90. See also the bibliographies in both of these books.

[49] Pedro Cardim, "De la nación a la lealtad al rey. Lorenço de Mendonça y el estatuto de los portugueses en la Monarquía española de la década de 1630," in *Extranjeros y enemigos en Iberoamérica: la visión del otro. Del imperio español a la Guerra de la Independencia*, ed. David González Cruz (Madrid: Sílex, 2010), 57–88.

The dynastic question that had hung over Portugal since the third quarter of the sixteenth century paved the way for suspicions and the appearance of parties that some politicians in those days classified as being specifically pro- or anti-Castilian. However, historical literature has already proven that this "black and white" labeling of political oppositions is difficult to apply to the choices that were made in 1580 and in 1640, either within the kingdom or, as we have seen, among the nobility. The decision process was far more complicated than that. In any case, these Manichaean perceptions serve as a reminder of the growing social understanding of Spain as a potential political threat and, therefore, of the need that was felt to define more precisely (and then monitor) the rights of the Portuguese. Frontiers and divisions were established in order to identify more rigorously this universe of private rights and privileges. It was in this sense that the Letters Patent of Tomar (*Carta Patente*) and conviviality with other kings of the Spanish monarchy contributed more towards a Portuguese reflection on identity and the creation of mechanisms of exclusion than to encouraging the vassals of both kingdoms to integrate. Nevertheless, there were coexisting ambivalent plans.[50] The example analyzed here demonstrates that.

The Soares de Alarcão family (and perhaps others who did not support the new king of Portugal in 1640) struggled with this set of questions. For the first time they were confronted with contradictory loyalties and bonds. Loyalty to the king, reverence for the memory of their ancestors, regard for their honor, and love of their land were until then sentiments that had coexisted naturally. However, the 1640 succession introduced an external and disruptive element, and with it the need to prioritize these different bonds, leaving no margin for doubt that the political space no longer coincided with social and cultural spaces.

João Soares de Alarcão's 1641 letter to his brother reflects this difficulty. Juridical legitimacy and links to the monarch were of prime importance in coming to a decision. Perhaps a lack of confidence in the Braganza enterprise's chances of success was also a consideration. Whatever the case, we see from the subsequent actions of João Soares de Alarcão and his sons that they sought to capitalize on their assets in order to ensure their integration into Spain. This forced them to significantly alter their discourse. They tried to link the retention of the Ceuta fortress in the hands of Philip IV with the struggle to maintain the integrity of the territories within the Spanish monarchy and with their Spanish family's deeds and service. Within this framework the contents of the genealogical writings are a very good indication of the need for the Soares de Alarcão family to adapt to the new political reality in Spain and to their exile from Portugal. By remaining loyal to the king, they became Spaniards.

---

50 Cardim, "De la nación a la lealtad al rey."

Bibliography

Buescu, Ana Isabel. *Catarina de Áustria. Infanta de Tordesilhas, Rainha de Portugal*. Lisbon: Esfera dos Livros, 2007.

Cardim, Pedro. "'Todos los que no son de Castilla son yguales'. El estatuto de Portugal en la Monarquía española en el tiempo de Olivares." *Pedralbes*, no. 28 (2008): 521–52.

______. "De la nación a la lealtad al rey. Lorenço de Mendonça y el estatuto de los portugueses en la Monarquía española de la década de 1630." In *Extranjeros y enemigos en Iberoamérica: la visión del otro. Del imperio español a la Guerra de la Independencia*. Edited by David González Cruz, 57–88. Madrid: Sílex, 2010.

Catálogo de um seleccionado leilão de manuscritos, autógrafos, fotografias e efémera. Lisbon: Livraria Luís Burnay, 2010.

"Conspiração contra D. João 4o." *Archivo bibliographico*. Coimbra, Imprensa da Universidade, 1877.

Corona Sepulcral. Elogios à morte de D. Martin Suarez de Alarcón escritos por diferentes plumas sacados a luz por Don Alonso de Alarcon, canonigo de la Santa Iglesia de Ciudad Rodrigo e secretario de D. Francisco de Alarcon. Madrid, Petrus de Villafranca, 1652.

Costa, Leonor Freire, and Mafalda Soares da Cunha. *D. João IV, 1604–1656*. Rev. edn. Lisbon: Temas e Debates, 2008.

Cunha, Mafalda Soares da. "Títulos portugueses y matrimonios mixtos en la Monarquía Católica." In *Las redes del Imperio. Élites sociales en la articulación de la monarquía hispánica, 1492–1714*. Edited by Bartolomé Yun Casalilla, 205–32. Madrid: Marcial Pons, 2009.

Curto, Diogo Ramada. "A língua e a literatura ao longo do século XVI." In *Cultura escrita. Séculos XVI a XVIII*. Edited by Diogo Ramada Curto, 57–90. Lisbon: Imprensa de Ciências Sociais, 2007.

Labrador Arroyo, Félix. "Las dimensiones del servicio de la emperatriz Isabel." In *La corte de Carlos V*, ed. José Martínez Millán. Vol. 1, book 2, *Corte y gobierno*. Edited by José Martínez Millán and Carlos Javier de Carlos Morales, 93–97. Madrid: Sociedad Estatal para la Conmemoración de los Centenarios de Felipe II y Carlos, 2000.

______. "Los servidores de la princesa María Manuela de Portugal." In *La corte de Carlos V*. Edited by José Martínez Millán. Vol. 1, book 2, *Corte y gobierno*. Edited by José Martínez Millán and Carlos Javier de Carlos Morales, 121–25. Madrid: Sociedad Estatal para la Conmemoración de los Centenarios de Felipe II y Carlos, 2000.

______. "La casa de la reina Catalina de Portugal: estructuras y facciones políticas (1550–1560)." *Miscelánea Comillas*, no. 61 (2003): 203–52.

Machado, Diogo Barbosa. *Biblioteca Lusitana: histórica, crítica e cronológica*. Vol. 4, 2nd edn. Lisbon: Bertrand, 1935.

Madahil, António Gomes da Rocha. *Cartas da restauração*. Coimbra, 1940.

Magalhães, J. Romero. "A sociedade." In *História de Portugal*, ed. José Mattoso. Vol. 3, *O Alvorecer da Modernidade (1480–1620)*. Edited by J. Romero Magalhães. Lisbon: Editorial Estampa, 1993.

Martínez Millán, José. "Élites de poder en las Cortes de las Monarquías española y portuguesa en el siglo XV: los servidores de Juana de Austria." *Miscelánea comillas*, no. 61 (2003): 169–202.

Melo, Francisco Manuel de. *Tácito Português. Vida, Morte, Dittos e Feitos de El Rey Dom João IV de Portugal*. Preface and transcription by Raul Rêgo. Lisbon: Livraria Sá da Costa Editora, 1995.

Ricard, Robert. *Les sources inédites de l'Histoire du Maroc*. Vol. 4 (January 1542–December 1550). Paris: P. Geuthner, 1951.

Roig, Adrien. "La Infanta coronada de Juan Soares de Alarcón (1606)." In *Actas del VII Congreso de la Asociación Internacional de Hispanistas*, held in Venice, August 25–30, 1980. Edited by Giuseppe Bellini, 893–901. Rome: Bulzoni, 1982.

Sá, Isabel dos Guimarães and Michel Combet. *Rainhas-Consortes de D. Manuel I. Isabel de Castela. Maria de Castela. Leonor de Áustria*. Lisbon: Círculo de Leitores, 2012.

Soares de Alarcão, Juan. *La Iffanta coronada por El Rey Don Pedro, Doña Ines de Castro: en octava rima*. Lisbon: Pedro Crasbeeck, 1606.

Suárez de Alarcón, Antonio. *Relaciones genealogicas de la casa de los marqueses de Torcifal, condes de Torresvedras, su varonia Zevallos de Alarcon y por la casa y primer apellido Suarez*. Madrid: Diego Diaz de la Carrera, 1656.

———. *Arbol genealogico y resumen breve de la varonia de Don Fernando Tellez de Faro y Silva, Conde de Arada*. Madrid: Diego Diaz de la Carrera, 1661.

———. *Commentarios de los hechos del señor Alarcon, Marques de la Valle Siciliana y de Renda, y de las guerras en que se halló por espacio de cinquenta y ocho años*. Madrid: Diego Diaz de la Carrera, 1665.

Torres, Manoel Agostinho Madeira. "Descripção Histórica e Economica da Villa e Termo de Torres Vedras." In *História e Memórias da Academia Real das Sciencias de Lisboa*. Vol. 6, part 1. Lisbon: Typografia da Mesma Academia, 1819.

Vásquez Cuesta, Pilar. *A língua e a cultura portuguesas no tempo dos Filipes*. Lisbon: Publicações Europa América, 1988.

Wagner, Mafalda de Noronha. *A Casa de Vila Real e a conspiração de 1641 contra D. João IV*. Lisbon: Edições Colibri, 2007.

PART III
Women's Contribution to a Cosmopolitan Nobility

ELEONORA ÁLVAREZ DE TOLEDO
(1522–62)

MARIA MANCINI
(1639–1715)

JOHANNA THERESIA LAMBERG
(1639–1716)

Chapter 7
"A Spanish Barbarian and an Enemy of Her Husband's Homeland": The Duchess of Florence and Her Spanish Entourage*

Joan-Lluís Palos

A Wife for the Duke of Florence

She entered Florence for the first time in the late afternoon of Sunday, June 29, 1539, accompanied by a large entourage of Spaniards. Her name was Leonor Álvarez de Toledo (Figure 7.1), and she was the daughter of Pedro de Toledo, marquis of Villafranca, Spain's viceroy in Naples and Emperor Charles V's principal agent in Italy. Three months earlier, on March 29, she had been married by proxy to Cosimo I de' Medici, duke of Florence (Figure 7.2.) She was probably 17, three years younger than her husband.[1]

Negotiation of the union had commenced a year earlier, in June 1538, when the emperor and Pope Paul III, a member of the Farnese family, met in Nice. The duke of Florence's marriage had become a key problem in Italian politics, a question of balance, as his rise to power had been entirely unexpected. He belonged to a secondary branch of the Medici family but the assassination of his cousin, Duke Alessandro, on January 6, 1537, left him as the most direct heir. Three days later the members of the Florentine Senate chose him as "chief and head of the government and the city of Florence," thinking that his inexperience and scant

---

* This chapter has been translated from the Spanish by Ruth MacKay and forms part of the research project *Poder y Representaciones en la Edad Moderna: la Monarquía Hispánica como campo cultural (1500–1800)* (HAR12-39516-C02-01) financed by the Spanish government.

[1] For the year of her birth see Janet Cox-Rearick, "Bronzino's Chapel of Eleonora in the Palazzo Vecchio," *California Studies in the History of Art*, 29 (Berkeley: University of California Press, 1993); Claudia Rousseau, "The Pageant of the Muses at the Medici Wedding of 1539 and the Decoration of the Salone del Cinquecento," in *Art and Pageantry in the Renaissance and Baroque*, ed. Barbara Wisch and Susan Scott Munshower (University Park: Pennsylvania State University Press, 1990), vol. 2, 423; Bruce L. Edelstein, "The Early Patronage of Eleonora di Toledo: The Camera Verde and Its Dependencies in the Palazzo Vecchio" (PhD diss., Harvard University, 1995), 20–21 and 47–8. While the first two authors say Eleonora probably was born in 1519, the third proposes 1522, though the evidence suggests this assessment is mistaken.

Figure 7.1 Agnolo Bronzino, Portrait of Eleonora of Toledo, ca. 1543, oil on panel, 59 × 46 cm. Národní Gallery, Prague.

Figure 7.2 Giacomo Pontormo, Portrait of Cosimo I de' Medici, 1538, tempera on panel, 100.9 × 77 cm. Private collection. Sotheby's.

preparation would allow them to bend him to their will. They could not have been more mistaken.

The first marriage plan for Cosimo involved Alessandro's widow, Margaret of Austria, the illegitimate daughter of the emperor himself. That plan was opposed by the Farnese family, bitter rivals of the Medicis, who utilized the influence afforded them by having one of their own in the Holy See. Margaret was thus betrothed to Ottavio, the pope's nephew and the duke of Parma; Cosimo would have to cast his net in other waters, though there was no lack of candidates. A great many names were considered, among others, Christina of Denmark, who was Charles V's niece, an English princess (though we do not know which), and a sister of the duke of Alba.

The viceroy of Naples took advantage of the indecision to play his cards, audaciously offering his daughter Isabel. The Farneses adamantly protested, as a new alliance between the Medicis and the empire, even through a relative of an imperial representative, was the last thing they wanted. The Farnese pope tried to pull some strings to prevent the marriage, seeking the help of the imperial ambassador in Rome, the marquis of Aguilar, and other influential ministers of Charles V who agreed that it was not a good idea to strengthen the Medicis, who in the past had proven themselves to be unreliable allies. Cosimo, who had shown how he treated his adversaries when defeating the Florentine republicans on August 2, 1537 in the battle of Montemurlo, clearly would be a dangerous opponent. To win their point, they looked to the future, pointing out to the Medici agent in Rome, Agnolo di Matteo Niccolini, that marrying the viceroy's daughter was out of the question because of the match's "inequality and scarce utility" being that the viceroy "could be removed at any time and the marriage would end up a private matter."[2] As an alternative, the pope offered his niece Vittoria.[3]

But by then Cosimo had already reached a decision. He badly needed the emperor's support. After being expelled twice from Florence, the Medicis had been restored to power in 1531 thanks to Charles V, who had occupied Florence the previous year, and in April 1532 had made Alessandro duke. But the emperor's support was tutelary, as imperial troops held the principal Tuscan strongholds in Livorno and Florence and Cosimo himself did not become duke until September 30, 1537. Thus any decision that did not have Charles's support was unthinkable. And so he married the daughter of the viceroy, one of the few imperial ministers who had favored his cause. However Cosimo imposed a condition: he would not marry Isabel, the eldest daughter, but rather Leonor, her younger sister, who would henceforth be known as Eleonora di Toledo.

Some scholars have argued that the couple had met in 1535 when Cosimo was in Naples to attend the betrothal of Duke Alessandro and Margaret, and Cosimo

---

[2] Cited in Carlos José Hernando, *Castilla y Nápoles en el siglo XVI. El virrey Pedro de Toledo* (Valladolid: Junta de Castilla y León, 1994), 121.

[3] The particulars of the union are in Giorgio Spini, *Cosimo I e l'indipendenza del principato mediceo*, 2nd ed. (Florence: Vallechi, 1980), 52.

had been impressed. It is impossible to know if this is true, and it is likely he never even saw her, as the women did not participate in the celebration, watching the public festivities from the palace balconies.[4] But as his rivals and servants would learn, it was always better to pay attention to Cosimo's actions rather than to his words.[5] Time would show how beneficial the marriage would be for him.

On February 26, 1539 his representatives in Naples and the viceroy's delegates signed the marriage agreement. A month later, on March 29, the proxy wedding took place in the Castelnuovo fortress, where Pedro de Toledo lived. Two more months were needed to prepare the bride's journey. Eleonora left Naples on June 11, 1539 and reached Livorno on June 22. After visiting Pisa, where the bride met the groom, the entourage reached the Medici villa of Poggio a Caiano on the 25th. There they waited for the final arrangements before making their solemn entry into Florence.

Cosimo, always calculating, knew that what he needed right then was not a loving wife but someone to guarantee the continuation of his line, which had never been especially prolific. Therefore the inscription on the ephemeral architecture installed in the Prato gateway the day that Eleonora arrived in Florence was more than a mere welcome: "Enter, enter your city with auspicious fortunes. Oh Eleonora, fertile and from the best lineage! May you bring forth progeny similar to your father in your native land and your grandfather abroad and thus ensure the eternal survival of the Medici name and their most devoted citizens." In case the bride had difficulty reading the Latin text, a 24-voice choir at the top of the arch sang the words, put to music by Francesco Corteccia. And if even then she did not get the message, a 3-meter-high allegorical figure representing fertility hung from the front of the arch accompanied by five playful cherubs, symbolizing her future children.[6]

From the moment she arrived in Florence, the city's political stability and the consolidation of the Medicis' authority were associated with the new duchess's fertility. Even the most optimistic observers could not have expected that she would so completely fulfill the hopes placed in her. In the following 15 years Eleonora was almost always pregnant, giving birth to 11 living children: the first was Maria, born on April 3, 1540, and the second and heir to the title was Francesco, born on March 25, 1541. One could not have asked for more, nor could one blame her for the fact that when she died, on December 17, 1562, six of her children had predeceased her.

---

[4] Bruce L. Edelstein, "Eleonora di Toledo," in *Encyclopedia of Women in the Renaissance: Italy, France and England*, eds. Diana Robin, Anne Larsen, and Carole Levin (Santa Barbara, CA: ABC-Clio, 2007), 362–67.

[5] On Cosimo's preference for Eleonora and the economic aspects of the arrangement see Hernando, *Castilla y Nápoles*, 122.

[6] Pier Francesco Giambullari, *Apparato et feste nelle nozze dello Illustrissimo signor duca di Firenze et de la duchessa sua consorte, con le sue stanze, madrigali, comedia, et intermedi in quella recitati* (Florence: Benedetto Giunta, 1539).

Despite Cosimo's efforts to present his wife as a symbol of life and renewal, not all Florentines agreed. Was it really necessary, they asked, that she always be surrounded by Spaniards?

The Spanish Entourage of the New Duchess of Florence

Eleonora had traveled to Florence in the company of a large entourage of her countrymen whom her father had carefully chosen. They included diplomats, secretaries, scribes, soldiers, ladies-in-waiting, maids, slaves, chaplains, butlers, cooks, drivers, singers, and pages, along with some of her closest relatives.[7]

Pedro de Toledo had planned that some of these people would return to Naples after making sure his daughter's new surroundings were in accordance with his instructions. But many others were to remain in Florence at her service, including some of the viceroy's own servants such as secretary Cristóbal de Herrera and the theologian Francisco de Astudillo. The leader of this group was Pedro de Solís, another longtime aide of Eleonora's father, who would be her *mayordomo mayor* (chief steward). The women would be under the leadership of the *camarera mayor* (chief lady-in-waiting), María de Contreras. February 1540, when Eleonora was pregnant for the first time, saw the arrival of an additional group of female attendants, trusted by her father for having raised her. Among them was María Pimentel, who had served Eleonora's mother, and Isabel Reinoso, both of whom in later years would form part of the close circle surrounding the duchess.[8] All told, according to a 1553 account, of the 136 servants in the duke's household, at least 28 were Spaniards, which does not include the large colony of merchants, diplomats, soldiers, and adventurers who lived in Florence in the duchess's shadow and prayed together in the Spanish chapel in the Santa Maria Novella convent.[9]

Those closest to her were her own relatives, who were frequently seen in Florence, where they resided with full honors at the Palazzo della Signoria.[10] They included her brothers García, who had led the wedding procession from Naples, and Luis, who had a magnificent home next to the Servi convent; uncles including Cardinal Juan de Toledo, Pedro's brother, who was the duchess's source at the papal court; cousins including Pedro and Gutierre de Toledo; members of

[7] Archivio di Stato di Firenze (hereafter ASF), Mediceo del Principato, 5922/A. Eleonora di Toledo, Ultime Volontà.

[8] Hernando, *Castilla y Nápoles*, 139 and 470.

[9] Blanca González Talavera, "Presencia y mecenazgo español en la Florencia medicea. De Cosme I a Fernando I" (PhD diss., University of Granada and University of Florence, 2011), 132–35.

[10] A 1553 account of the palace shows that Luis de Toledo and Francisco de Toledo lived in the mezzanine rooms where Cosimo's mother, Maria Salviati, had lived until her death in 1543.

secondary branches of the family including Francisco de Toledo, who lived there for long periods of time as imperial ambassador, and the viceroy's namesake, Pedro de Toledo, whom Eleonora called "uncle" though in fact he was not. He was married to another Leonor, and together they formed part of the closest family circle. The duchess's father took advantage of his frequent trips to Geneva and Siena to visit his daughter and control his son-in-law; indeed, Pedro de Toledo died in Florence, on February 22, 1552.

Should anyone have doubted Eleonora's attachment to her origins, such doubt would have vanished by looking at the names she chose for her children, which included Isabel and Fernando (in honor of the Catholic Monarchs) along with Pedro and García (in honor of her father and brother). Some of her children not only had Spanish names but a Spanish upbringing, which was particularly intense in the case of the heir, Francesco, who spent almost two years at the court of Philip II of Spain.

So it was not surprising that many Florentines reached the conclusion that Eleonora was being held captive by her Spanish retinue. They had good reasons to think that. Even writers working for Cosimo, such as Bernardo Segni, complained of the "incomparable costs spent on the upkeep of colonels, spies, Spaniards, and women who serve the lady."[11] The will she wrote years later confirmed the truth of this, as the main beneficiaries of her generosity were her Spanish ladies.[12]

Naturally there were those who took advantage of these circumstances, and not only her relatives, who seemed to multiply at an astonishing rate. When the first members of the Company of Jesus, the recently founded religious order that was perceived by many Italians to be truly Spanish, arrived in Florence after having been received with open arms by the viceroy in Naples, there was no doubt in the Jesuits' minds that their best way of reaching the rest of Florence was the duchess; this was assuming, of course, that they could reach her and, even more difficult, know how to treat her.[13]

Thus immediately after arriving in Florence in 1547, Diego Laínez, who later would replace Ignatius of Loyola as the Company's general, knew where to go. "Leave everything in the duchess's hands, directly or through friends."[14] It was clear that the friends in question were all Spaniards. So Laínez began by cultivating the friendship of Pedro de Toledo, Eleonora's uncle, and then moved on to "the

---

11 Bernardo Segni, *Storie Fiorentine* (Livorno, 1830), vol. 2, book 11, 301.

12 ASF, Mediceo del Principato, 5922/A. Eleonora de Toledo, Ultime Volontà.

13 Carolyn Smyth, "An Instance of Feminine Patronage in the Medici Court of Sixteenth-Century Florence: The Chapel of Eleonora da Toledo in the Palazzo Vecchio," in *Women and Art in Early Modern Europe. Patrons, Collectors and Connoisseurs*, ed. Cynthia Lawrence (University Park: Pennsylvania State University Press, 1997), 89.

14 Cited in Chiara Franceschini, "Los scholares son cosa de su excelentia como lo es toda la Compañia: Eleonora di Toledo and the Jesuits," in *The Cultural World of Eleonora di Toledo, Duchess of Florence and Siena*, ed. Konrad Eisenbichler (Aldershot: Ashgate, 2004), 191n46.

leading lady of the ladies at her court" (perhaps Isabel de Reinoso) and Astudillo.[15] With those credentials it was not difficult for him to inspire the duchess, to the point that she told him she would be a Jesuit if she were a man. As Father Diego de Guzmán, another Jesuit who traveled to Florence during these years, wrote shortly thereafter, it was clear that the duchess "felt no affection for any other nation nor does she wish to speak to any of us who are not Spanish."[16]

One of the reasons that many people judged Eleonora to be Spanish was, clearly, her clothing. As soon as he met her, shortly after her arrival in Livorno, the duke's chief steward, Pierfrancesco Riccio, was surprised by the new duchess's appearance: "She entered Pisa wearing a black silk dress speckled with gold, including her headdress and collar, and a few hours later changed into a peacock-colored (*veste pavonada*) velvet dress trimmed with gold with a gold bonnet and a necklace given to her by the duke."[17] Years later people were still struck by her manner of dressing; in 1550 the bishop of Vaison, Jacopo Cortesi da Prato, a papal legate who participated in the baptism of Eleonora's son García, could not help but note that "the illustrious duchess was dressed in white velvet and a Spanish-style vest of silver cloth, very beautiful."[18] Her style certainly was different from that of the Florentine ladies, and it ultimately would have quite an impact on local fashion.[19]

Many of the portraits Bronzino painted of her show her dressed in a broad vest, or *zimarra*, worn over a long tunic with a low neckline, her hair in a bun in a hairnet, sometimes wearing a man's hat with a feather, and adorned with many jewels including strands of pearls, often with a jewel pendant, and her characteristic teardrop earrings.[20]

For many Florentines, the most familiar element was the *zimarra*, which some, such as the bishop of Vaison, called a "Spanish vest," or sometimes a "Neapolitan vest." It was derived from Spain and had become typical of feminine court attire, used even by the wife of Charles V, Empress Isabel. Eleonora already owned several when she arrived in Florence in 1539 and she continued collecting them, placing frequent orders with her tailor, Agostino d'Agobio.[21] A total of 80 appear in inventories from 1544 to 1559, featuring the 30 obligatory "Hungarian-style" clasps. Along with the *zimarra*, the hairnet, which she wears in all her portraits,

---

15 Astudillo to Ignatius of Loyola, October 6, 1554, cited in Franceschini, "Los scholares," 190.

16 Guzmán to Laínez, August 17, 1560, cited in Franceschini, "Los scholares," 185.

17 Cited in Anna Baia, *Leonora di Toledo, Duchesa di Firenze e di Siena* (Todi: Foglietti, 1907), 20–21.

18 Janet Cox-Rearick and Mary Westerman Bulgarella, "Public and Private Portraits of Cosimo de' Medici and Eleonora di Toledo: Bronzino's Paintings of His Ducal Patrons in Ottawa and Turin," *Artibus et historiae*, 25, no. 49 (2004): 101–59, 157n118.

19 Roberta Orsi Landini and Bruna Niccoli, *Moda a Firenze 1540–1580. Lo stile di Eleonora di Toledo e la sua influenza* (Florence: Polistampa, 2005), 29.

20 Ibid., 33–35.

21 Cox-Rearick and Bulgarella, "Public and Private Portraits," 132.

was another of her favorite items of clothing, so much so that a workshop was set aside in the Palazzo Della Signoria to weave them.[22]

Eleonora's Critics

It is not at all surprising that someone whose very presence was aimed at strengthening her husband's autocratic rule should be the subject of sharp attacks from several fronts, particularly from those who defended the old republican traditions. The surprise in Eleonora's case was that some of the criticism came from within the Medici camp and was almost always associated with the fact that she was Spanish.

The best-known of these critics was the goldsmith and sculptor Benvenuto Cellini, who never liked her whims regarding jewels and even less her intercession with Cosimo that the great Neptune sculpture (which today still graces the Piazza Della Signoria) was first assigned to Baccio Bandinelli, Eleonora's preferred sculptor.[23] Many of her critics perceived her as distant and aloof, typical of Spaniards' attachment to form and ceremony. As the Florentine cleric Giovanni della Casa wrote, "I believe these ceremonies were imported from Spain to Italy, but they were not well received here and few people have accepted them, as they dislike these distinctions of nobility."[24]

These criticisms, however, were mild compared to the fierce language used by the anonymous author of the *Cronaca fiorentina*. The author believed Eleonora was "a Spanish barbarian and an enemy of her husband's homeland [*patria*]," and a "haughty woman and de facto enemy of the Florentines." During a famine in summer 1554, she was so insensitive to city dwellers' needs that

> Eleonora, a Spaniard, caring little about anyone, would say that anyone who could not eat twice a day should eat just once. She is a truly cruel woman to the Florentines, and when she heard that there was no bread in Florence, it did not disturb her in the least.

All of these remarks led the author to conclude that "the Florentine Republic hated the wife."[25]

This hatred, naturally, extended to the Medicis. According to the author of the *Cronaca*, Cosimo had "gone from being a sheep to a snake, and no one could

---

22 Ibid., 133.

23 Benvenuto Cellini, *Vida*, ed. and trans. Santiago R. Santerbás (Madrid: Cátedra, 2007), 516–22.

24 Giovanni della Casa, *Il Galateo*, ed. Emanuela Scarpa (Modena: Einaudi, 1990), 30.

25 Anonymous, *Cronaca Fiorentina, 1537–1555*, ed. Enrico Coppi (Florence: Olschki, 2000), 128, 25, 65, 93, 166, and 118.

recognize him, and the reason was said to be his wife, who was Spanish." This hatred toward Spaniards and, in general, toward all the foreigners who occupied Italy was comparable only to the author's sympathy for the *piagnoni*, the remaining partisans in Florence of the Dominican friar Girolamo Savonarola, who had called on people to repent and had denounced the scandalous lifestyle of the rich, now epitomized by the duke and duchess.[26]

Regardless of their veracity, the *Cronaca*'s judgments had a powerful impact on later opinions of Eleonora by many Italian historians. Her redemption would come thanks only to art historians, awed by Bronzino's portraits of her and her patronage of artists including Bandinelli and Ammanati, Niccolò Tribolo, Francesco Ubertini il Bachiacca, Giulio Clovio, Ridolfo del Ghirlandaio, Michele Tosini (di Ridolfi), Giampaolo and Domenico Poggini, Francesco Salviati, Giovanni Stradano, and Giorgio Vasari.[27]

In his huge and well-documented study of the Medicis, the doctor and Florentine historian Gaetano Pieraccini called Eleonora "an uncultured woman of mediocre intelligence with hardly any altruistic inclinations" who was incapable of "making the people even like her, much less feel fondness toward her."[28] Despite all her efforts to be fair-minded, Anna Baia, author of the only monograph on Eleonora to date (published in 1907) could only lament "the extravagant spending on extraordinary luxuries with which she, a true Spaniard, always loved to surround herself."[29] More recently, in a description of Eleonora that vastly improved upon older clichés, Arnaldo D'Addario wrote:

> The Florentines did not understand her or love her. They saw her walk down the street surrounded by guards and servants, always luxuriously dressed, with jewels, enclosed in her carriage or her litter that she ordered lined with green silk and covered with velvet of the same color. They did not even understand her language, because the duchess spoke little Italian and preferred to speak and write in Spanish.[30]

It is difficult to assess the impact of these criticisms on Eleonora's spirits or, more generally, on her husband's regime. If we are to believe the author of the *Cronaca*, the Medici response was the imposition of censorship so strict that "nobody dared speak of it unless they wanted to be handcuffed and find themselves in jail."[31] A government that wished to use persuasion could not settle for simple repression.

---

26 Ibid., 175.

27 Smyth, "An Instance of Feminine Patronage," 72–98.

28 Gaetano Pieraccini, *La stirpe de' Medici di Cafaggiolo: saggio di ricerche sulla trasmissione ereditaria dei caratteri biologici* (Florence: Vallecchi, 1925), vol. 2, 64.

29 Baia, *Leonora di Toledo*, 64.

30 Arnaldo D'Addario, "Eleonora di Toledo duchessa di Firenze e Siena," in *Donne di Casa Medici*, 2nd edn. (Florence: Arnaud, 1993), 33–62, 40.

31 Anonymous *Cronaca Fiorentina*, 118.

The paintings in Eleonora's palace apartments in the Palazzo Vecchio can be seen as an attempt to respond to criticism that she was Spanish and to connect with Florentine traditions. After long discussions coordinated by Vasari, it was decided that the vaulted ceilings should depict the lives of various remarkable women (*mullieres illustribus*) to whom the duchess wished to compare herself. The figures chosen were Penelope (a Greek), Esther (a Jew), the Sabine women (Romans), and Gualdrada (a Florentine). The message was especially clear with the story of Gualdrada, which Boccaccio included in *On Famous Women* and had been recounted by a contemporary of Dante, the local chronicler Giovanni Villani, whose manuscript was not published until 1559. According to the story, when Emperor Otto IV visited Florence around 1180, he was so struck by the young Gualdrada's beauty that he asked her to kiss him. She refused, saying she would only kiss he who would be her husband. Admiring her virtue, Otto offered to marry her to one of the men of his court, Guido Guidi, who until then had been a firm opponent of the Florentines but from then on became one of their principal allies. The children of Gualdrada and Guido would play important roles in the course of the city's history. Anyone who entered Eleonora's rooms and who knew the story would immediately see the suggested parallel between Gualdrada and Eleonora: the duchess's beauty that had so struck Cosimo, the emperor's role in the marriage, the celebration of chastity, and the role that their children would play in Florentine history.[32] Though Vasari let it be known that he had spoken more with Eleonora about the paintings than with the duke, art historians have not agreed on the degree to which she participated in this and in other artistic commissions.[33]

The debate concerning Eleonora's abilities as a patron of the arts with her own personal vision has focused on the greatest artistic creation during her years as duchess of Florence: her private chapel in the Palazzo Vecchio, which established Bronzino as her favorite painter.[34] The enormous visual complexity of Bronzino's work in scenes such as the Crossing of the Red Sea fresco, the miracle of the serpent in the desert, the exaltation of the Holy Trinity that covers the vault, and the Lamentation Altarpiece, along with the absence of any of his instructions, have led to great differences of opinion regarding this small space. Some have

---

[32] Pamela J. Benson, "Eleonora di Toledo among the Famous Women: Iconographic Innovation after the Conquest of Siena," in *The Cultural World*, ed. Eisenbichler, 150–55.

[33] Andrea M. Gáldy, "L'appartamento di Eleonora di Toledo in Palazzo Vecchio: la scena della nuova Isabella la Cattolica," in *Le donne Medici nel sistema europeo delle corti XVI–XVIII secolo* (Florence: Polistampa, 2008), 618; Illaria Hoppe, "A Duchess's Palace at Court: The Quartiere di Eleonora in the Palazzo della Signoria in Florence," in *The Cultural World*, ed. Eisenbichler, 98–118.

[34] Bruce L. Edelstein, "Bronzino in the Service of Eleonora di Toledo and Cosimo I de' Medici: Conjugal Patronage and the Painter-Courtier," in *Beyond Isabella: Secular Women Patrons of Art in Renaissance Italy*, eds. Sheryl E. Reiss and David G. Wilkins (Kirksville, MO: Truman State University Press, 2001), 232–3.

seen the work as the outcome of a program worked out within the framework of the Florentine Academy to present Cosimo as the father and savior of his *patria*. Others have disagreed, saying the chapel reflects Eleonora's religious inclinations, which could be deduced from Cosimo's remark when Riccio asked for instructions: "Ask the duchess, it's her affair."[35] In any case, Bronzino's paintings take on distinct meaning when viewed through the lens of the late fifteenth-century spiritual literature of the court of Isabel of Castile, which is certainly how Eleonora would have seen them because her mother had grown up at Isabel's court.[36]

Aside from the debates regarding Eleonora's participation in the remodeling of the palace, there is no doubt that she could exercise considerable artistic patronage and had a considerable budget to do so. Her spending was not only independent from that of her husband but sometimes openly opposed to his, as Cellini and Vasari knew firsthand. Though they were favored by Cosimo for various projects, over time the duchess's preference for Bandinelli won out.[37]

Cosimo's Interests

This did not mean that Cosimo could not at times blatantly use his wife's image to favor his own interests. At least during the early years of their marriage, he was the one most interested in accentuating her Spanish background as a way of emphasizing his loyalty to Charles V and his firm support for Spain's policies in Italy. The fact that the duchy was in the hands of the Medici depended on Charles's approval, and after the assassination of Alessandro, it was not at all clear that the emperor's approval was guaranteed. Indeed, there were those in the circles closest to Charles who argued in favor of revoking the ducal title and ordering Spanish troops to take back direct control of Florence and Tuscany. Cosimo not only needed the emperor to confirm his status as a duke but also as an ally against those who, for various reasons, did not want the Medicis to rule. These opponents comprised three groups: the *ottimati*, the Florentine patricians who favored an oligarchy which they would control; the *fuoriusciti*, the exiled republicans; and the *piagnoni*, Savonarola's followers, who wanted a theocracy.[38] Cosimo, probably feeling like Daniel in the lion's den, used Eleonora as a shield

35 Cox-Rearick, *Bronzino's Chapel*, 254–55, considers the chapel to be a celebration of Cosimo, while Edelstein, "Bronzino in the Service," 245–61, sees it as reflecting Eleonora's religiosity.

36 Robert W. Gaston, "Eleonora di Toledo's Chapel: Lineage, Salvation and the War Against the Turks," in *The Cultural World*, ed. Eisenbichler, 157–80.

37 Giuseppina Carla Romby and Emmanuela Ferretti, "Aggiornamenti e novità documentarie su palazzo Pitti," *Mitteilungen des Kunsthistorischen Institutes in Florenz*, 46 (2002–1): 169.

38 Cox-Rearick, *Bronzino's Chapel*, 256.

against his many adversaries. In so doing he made political gains but at the price of damaging his wife's image in Florence.

Cosimo's utter dependence on Charles V lasted at least until 1543, when he managed to get back two of Tuscany's most important military installations, in Livorno and in Florence itself at the cost of 150,000 *scudi*, which came out of Eleonora's pocket. Though Cosimo as a result felt somewhat more free to act as he wished, he quickly discovered that Spain's shadow was longer than he had thought. If he wished to consolidate his authority and be a true member of the select club of Italian and European princes, he would have to create a princely court, something entirely foreign to Florence. But he knew where to look for examples: in a letter on March 13, 1540, his agent in Naples, Pirro Musefilo, provided him with details of the remodeling of the main rooms in the Castelnuovo, where his father-in-law lived.[39] Two months later, on May 14, barely a year after his marriage, the duke decided to move out of the Medici palace on the Via Larga and move into the Palazzo in Piazza, also known as the Palazzo della Signoria, the former headquarters of the Florentine communal government. That same day he told his father-in-law that in Florence Eleonora would live in regal apartments (*stanze regali*), as she had in Naples.[40] It was basically a statement of his intention to transform the republican palace into a true *reggia* (royal palace) and turn Florence into a princely capital. Of course, Cosimo was very well informed about Pedro de Toledo's reform of his residence of Castelnuovo and his ambitious plans for urban transformation in Naples, which included hiring the architect Ferdinando Manlio to build him a new palace.[41] Cosimo's own plans would not be outshone. His decision to undertake a redesign of Florence with dynastic objectives would lead to a fundamental change in the appearance of the city, which in 1540 still looked medieval. His ancestors had been great patrons of the arts but they had never involved themselves in city planning. He would be the first, and he began with his palace and its surroundings.[42]

The project to transform the public Signoria palace into a private residence began with a very particular goal, which was to make it suitable for the demands of ceremonial practices inspired in large part by those used in Spain and Naples. This was, naturally, not the first time such a large-scale project had been undertaken

[39] Andrea M. Gáldy, "Tuscan Concerns and Spanish Heritage in the Decoration of Duchess Eleonora's Apartment in the Palazzo Vecchio," *Renaissance Studies*, 20, no. 3 (2006): 302.

[40] ASF, Mediceo del Principato, vol. 10, doc. 5378, fol. 113.

[41] Andrea M. Gáldy and Robert La France, "Golden Chambers for Eleonora of Toledo: Duchess and Collector in Palazzo Vecchio," in *Women Patrons and Collectors*, eds. Susan Bracken, Andrea M. Gáldy, and Adriana Turpin (Newcastle upon Tyne: Cambridge Scholars Publishing, 2012), 17–21; Franco Strazzullo, *Edilizia e urbanistica a Napoli dal '500 al '700* (Naples: Arte Tipografica, 1995), 3027; Gáldy, "Tuscan Concerns," 302.

[42] Vega De Martini and José M. Morillas Alcázar, "Eleonora da Toledo: un modello artistico tra Napoli e Firenze," *Rivista storica del Sannio*, 3 (2005): 194–95.

in Florence, a city full of magnificent buildings. Both in the classical and in the Christian era, great buildings were a sign of magnificence. But the approach taken during the republican era was quite different from that of the monarchies. While during the republican regimes private citizens financed buildings to glorify family, the city, and God, in the later regimes they glorified rulers. That is what Cosimo wished to do.[43]

Remodeling an old building like the Signoria palace with very little space for expansion was a difficult task. No one who witnessed the process had the slightest doubt that Eleonora, who was used to participating in public audiences with her father in Naples, played a key role in adopting new court practices.[44] The anonymous author of the *Cronaca Fiorentina* wrote that "she was so haughty that she never, or rarely, walked or rode horseback; mostly she was carried in a litter," and "in public she appeared as if in a reliquary; half the litter was visible, and in the other half she sat. It was truly amazing to see a woman of such arrogance." Thus Medici residences that had been domestic spaces became sites of Spanish pomp, wrote Domenico Mellini, a member of the Florence Academy and a faithful aide to Cosimo, who also noted that the redesign of the Palazzo della Signoria had begun with what would become Eleonora's third-floor apartments. Never before had the rooms of the lady of the house been in such a prominent location.[45]

But it would not be right to think that the influences ran in only one direction, from Naples to Florence. Despite the Spaniards' pride, which many Florentines found hard to take, many Spaniards in the Tuscan capital, including the family of the duchess herself, were favorably impressed by the artistic environment there. When Pedro de Toledo in 1548 decided to build a chapel in the old palace of Castel Capuano, which he had turned into a court of justice, he looked to Florence, probably through his son-in-law, and contracted the painter Pedro Rubiales, who had worked in Rome under Francesco Salviati and Giorgio Vasari, who later would paint Eleonora's rooms. Rubiales surely was familiar with the work that his Florentine colleagues were doing for Cosimo and Eleonora, and he was a member of the artistic circle that linked Castile, Naples, and Florence. Though his work for Pedro de Toledo was inferior to that of Bronzino in Eleonora's chapel, he tried to emulate the latter, especially in the altarpiece, which also depicted Christ's descent from the Cross.[46]

Rubiales was not the only painter to bring Florentine ideas to Naples. The list of Tuscan artists who worked in the viceroy's court includes Salviati and Vasari,

---

[43] Natalie R. Tomas, *The Medici Women. Gender and Power in Renaissance Florence* (Aldershot: Ashgate, 2003), 91.

[44] Gabrielle Langdon, *Medici Women. Portraits of Power, Love and Betrayal from the Court of Duke Cosimo I* (Toronto: University of Toronto Press, 2007), 7; De Martini and Morillas Alcázar, "Eleonora da Toledo," 193.

[45] Domenico Mellini, *Ricordi intorno ai costumi, azioni e governo del sereniss. gran duca Cosimo I* (Florence: Magheri, 1820).

[46] Hernando, *Castilla y Nápoles*, 531–32.

along with Marco Pino and Leonardo da Pistoia.[47] Eleonora herself encouraged this relationship, regularly sending paintings (several by Bronzino) to her family and friends in Naples and Spain and sculptures, such as those that were later placed in the villa that her brother García had in the Chiaia area in Naples.[48] Other examples of this circulation included marble that Cosimo sent from Florence so that Giovanni da Nola could sculpt Pedro de Toledo's funerary monument, today in the San Giacomo degli Spagnoli church in Naples; and the fountain that Eleonora's younger brother Luis hired Francesco Camillani to sculpt, with the help of the Neapolitan Michelangelo Naccherino, for his gardens in Florence and which would end up in the Piazza Pretoria in Palermo, where it stands today, having been taken there when Eleonora's brother García was appointed viceroy of Sicily.[49] Thus Eleonora's presence in Florence led to considerable cultural exchange.

Being a Woman in Florence

Both the duchess's behavior and her husband's use of her image served to introduce new ideas regarding women in the public sphere that marked a sharp contrast with the role of wives in the past, both in patrician families in general and the Medicis in particular. Florentine republican traditions were very masculine. While Cosimo gave Eleonora the best rooms in the Palazzo della Signoria and made more and more copies of Eleonora's portraits to use as diplomatic gifts, he ordered that the small rooms adjacent to the Salone del Cinquecento be decorated with pictures of his lineage, among which there was not a single painting of a woman. Of course this was not because women played no decisive roles in the rise of the Medicis—indeed they often filled in for their men and exerted influence informally—but because they lacked formal avenues to political power.[50]

---

[47] De Martini and Morillas Alcázar, "Eleonora da Toledo," 194.

[48] On April 18, 1550, from Livorno, she asked Bronzino to make "a sketch of an altarpiece like the one in her chapel, with the same figures and a handsome frame, to be sent to Spain," cited in Baia, *Leonora di Toledo*, 75. On January 1, 1551, she turned once again to Bronzino, urgently requesting a painting of the Virgin which she wished to send immediately to Naples: Victoria Kirkham, "Cosimo and Eleonora in Shepherdland: A Lost Eclogue by Laura Battiferra degli Ammannati," in *The Cultural Politics*, ed. Eisenbichler, 159.

[49] De Martini and Morillas Alcázar, "Eleonora da Toledo," 191n13.

[50] The literature concerning the role of women in the Italian Renaissance in general, and in the Medici family in particular, has been abundant in recent years. Titles worthy of mention include Letizia Arcangeli and Susanna Peyronel Rambaldi, eds., *Donne di potere nel Rinascimento* (Rome: Viella, 2008); Judith C. Brown and Robert C. Davis, eds., *Gender and Society in Renaissance Italy* (London: Longman, 1998); Giulia Calvi and Ricardo Spinelli, eds., *Le donne Medici nel sistema europeo delle corti XVI–XVIII secolo, Atti del convegno internazionale* (Florence: Polistampa, 2008); Letizia Panizza, ed., *Women in Italian Renaissance Culture and Society* (Oxford: European Humanities Research Centre,

It is no surprise that upon her arrival in Florence, Eleonora was constantly compared to other Medici women, particularly Cosimo's mother, Maria Salviati, who was always, despite her key role in her son's career, presented as the incarnation of domestic virtue.[51] In fact, it would have been very surprising had Eleonora's conduct not caused displeasure. Was it because she was a Spaniard? Yes, but also because she was a woman. Despite the image projected by its unmatched artistic treasures, Florence was one of the worst places in Italy to be a woman, though it was not the only bad place.[52] Women had far more opportunities for independence in the northern seigneurial states, in the kingdom of Naples, or even in the Papal States than they did in republics such as Genoa, Venice, and Florence. There, until Eleonora's arrival, there would have been no space for women such as the duchess of Ferrara, Eleonora d'Aragona, and her two daughters, Isabella d'Este, marquise of Mantua, and Beatrice d'Este, duchess of Milan. Likewise republics had little room for other politically powerful women such as Bianca Maria Visconti Sforza; Lucrezia Borgia, duchess of Ferrara; Caterina Sforza, governess of Imola; Battista de Montefeltro; or Ippolita Maria Sforza, duchess of Calabria. All of these women contributed substantially to changing the role of women in the public sphere of their husbands' states. In this environment, it was difficult for Eleonora to find a model to follow, so she sought it elsewhere. And she found it in her homeland: none other than Queen Isabel of Castile.[53]

The relationship between Eleonora and the Catholic Queen was highlighted by Domenico Bruni da Pistoia in his *Difese delle donne*, published in Florence in 1552. After stating that Isabel had possessed even greater feminine virtue than mythical and Biblical heroines, Bruni went on to say that after Isabel it was Eleonora, thanks to her imitation of the Castilian queen, who most gloriously possessed these same qualities.[54] Some of the attributes he pointed to were commonplaces but others, such as caring for the education of one's children, or intimacy with one's ladies of honor, were much more specific.

The publication of Bruni's book coincided with the decoration of Eleonora's apartments in the Palazzo della Signoria, suggesting a direct link between the

2000); and Paola Tinaglia, *Women in Italian Renaissance Art: Gender, Representation, Identity* (Manchester: Manchester University Press, 1997).

[51] "[Eleonora's] manner of thinking was quite distinct from that of the duke's mother, Maria Salviati, a simple and humble housewife who was always attentive to the kitchen, the laundry, and the smallest housekeeping tasks." Baia, *Leonora di Toledo*, 24–25.

[52] Samuel K. Cohn, Jr., "The Social History of Women in the Renaissance," in Samuel K. Cohn, Jr., *Women in the Streets: Essays on Sex and Power in Renaissance Italy* (Baltimore: Johns Hopkins University Press, 1996), 15.

[53] Gáldy, "Tuscan Concerns," 293–319; and Gáldy, "L'appartamento di Eleonora di Toledo," 621–24.

[54] *Opera di M. Domenico Bruni da Pistoia intitolata Difese delle donne, nella quale si contengono le difese loro, dalle calumnie dategli per gli scrittori e insieme le lodi di quelle* (Florence, 1552); see fols. 25–25v for Bruni's list of virtues that Eleonora shared with Isabel.

two. Even as the decoration of Eleonora's rooms—with the story of the Florentine heroine Gualdrada—sought to downplay Eleonora's Spanish lineage and make her acceptable to a Florentine audience, the majority of the paintings presented a model of feminine virtue embodied by Queen Isabel of Castile. In fact, except for Gualdrada, the heroines depicted in her rooms had no direct relationship with Florentine traditions, but they did fit nicely into the Castilian custom of educating girls through *exempla* of illustrious predecessors; one such treatise was *El jardín de las nobles doncellas*, by Fray Martín de Córdoba, dedicated to Queen Isabel, which praised female rulers who, like the Sabines, had freed their peoples from oppression thanks to their piety, which saved them and their husbands from evil.[55]

Neapolitan Women

Though Isabel of Castile had a powerful influence on Eleonora, one must not forget that she was later educated in Naples. Most of the women who played leading roles in Italian Renaissance courts, who were praised for their beauty and celebrated for their merits, were either Neapolitan or directly related to the Neapolitan court, especially the Aragon, Colonna, and Ávalos families.[56] This was not a simple coincidence, of course. While in the rest of Italy women encountered obstacles to their development, in Naples they had a direct route to the throne. Three women had been queen of Naples: Giovanna I, from the Anjou family, ruled from 1344 to 1381; Giovanna II, also an Anjou, ruled from 1414 to 1435; and Juana de Castilla, obviously much closer to Eleonora, as she was Isabel's daughter, queen of Naples from 1516 to 1519, when she gave the title to her son, Charles V.[57] Juana never visited southern Italy, but Giovanna I and II built palaces, castles, churches, and hospitals, along with monumental tombs for their husbands.

When she was growing up in Naples, Eleonora surely also heard about Isabella d'Aragona (1470–1524), the daughter of King Alfonso II of Naples and Ippolita Maria Sforza. Isabella married the duke of Milan, Gian Galeazzo Sforza, and after she was widowed she returned to Naples, where she became the center of a bustling court. Her daughter, Bona, was made immortal as the object of courtly love in *Question de amor de dos enamorados*, an anonymous tale published by a Spanish nobleman in Valencia in 1513. Eleonora also would have heard the love poems that Luigi Tansillo, a soldier and Pedro de Toledo's official court historian, dedicated to Maria d'Aragona, the marquis of Vasto's wife.[58]

---

[55] Gáldy, "Tuscan Concerns," 297 and 308–09; and Gáldy, "L'appartamento di Eleonora di Toledo," 621–24.

[56] Bruce L. Edelstein, "Nobildonne napoletane e committenza: Eleonora d'Aragona ed Eleonora di Toledo a confronto," *Quaderni storici*, 35, no. 2 (2000): 295–329.

[57] Tomas, *The Medici Women*, 90–91.

[58] Edelstein, "Nobildonne napoletane," 295–329.

The Naples of Eleonora's childhood was also a Parnassus of female poets: Laura Terracina, Isabella di Morra, and, above all, Vittoria Colonna, the sister of Cardinal Pompeo, Pedro de Toledo's predecessor as viceroy of Naples. Along with Constanza d'Ávalos (the cultured duchess of Francavilla) and Giulia Gonzaga, Vittoria Colonna established a refuge for erudite women who admired the reformist doctrines of Juan de Valdés. They went to the island of Ischia, which they defended during the struggles between the imperial and French forces after the Sack of Rome. In December 1560, when Eleonora read a letter from a friar encouraging her to model herself on Vittoria Colonna, surely she regarded it as good advice.[59] All these examples were close to her, not only because she was raised in Naples but because of family connections; one of Vittoria Colonna's nieces, the poet's namesake, married Eleonora's brother, García de Toledo.

But the woman whose trajectory was most similar to her own was Eleonora d'Aragona (1450–93), daughter of King Ferrante I of Naples, who married the duke of Ferrara, Ercole I d'Este.[60] Beyond having the same name, the similarities are such that it is hard not to think there was deliberate emulation, especially when one considers the close relationship between the Medicis and the d'Este family when Eleonora was duchess of Florence. Her daughter Lucrezia married Eleonora d'Aragona's great-grandson, Alfonso II d'Este.

Both Eleonoras helped their husbands during serious political difficulties. Both collected similarly luxurious objects, protected convents, and commissioned many portraits, relying mostly on one artist: Bronzino in the case of Eleonora de Toledo and Cosmè Tura in the case of Eleonora d'Aragona. Both remodeled their main palaces and acquired villas outside the city.

If we were to seek a Florentine model for Eleonora de Toledo, the closest one would be Alfonsina Orsini, the wife of Piero de' Medici, who in her day had been the brunt of criticisms just like Eleonora. As one might expect, Alfonsina was born in Naples, in 1472. She was the daughter of Roberto Orsini, count of Tagliacozzo, and Catalina de Sanseverino. In 1488, when she was 17, she married Piero lo Sfortunato, the eldest son of Lorenzo the Magnificent and Clarice Orsini. The marriage was part of a larger plan by Lorenzo and Ferrante to draw Naples and Florence closer together.[61]

As soon as she arrived in her new city, Alfonsina showed signs of her typically Neapolitan independence, commissioning paintings directly from Mariotto Albertinelli, some of which she sent to her Orsini relatives. This was a type of patronage that may have been normal in the south but was completely unknown to Florentine women, even in the Medici family. When her husband was expelled from Florence in 1494, Alfonsina, who was allowed to remain, interceded on his behalf with Charles VIII of France to obtain a pardon. She did not succeed, and

59 Benson, "Eleonora di Toledo among the Famous Women," 136.

60 Edelstein, "Nobildonne napoletane," 297.

61 Natalie R. Tomas, "Alfonsina Orsini de' Medici and the Problem of a Female Ruler in Early Sixteenth-Century Florence," *Renaissance Studies*, 4, no. 1 (2000): 76–77.

Piero died in exile in 1503. But the return of the Medicis in 1512 and the election the following year of her brother-in-law Giovanni as Pope Leo X allowed her to spread her influence as far as Rome, where she agitated on behalf of her son Lorenzo and her son-in-law Filippo Strozzi, married to her daughter Clarice. Lorenzo became captain general of Florence, and Filippo became the pope's banker.

When Lorenzo had to leave the city in 1515 to fight the French in Milan, Alfonsina, who had settled in the pontifical court, returned to Florence to take over the government, though she never received a formal title because she was a woman. Eleonora would have had no better example to follow when she herself had to oversee the governance of Florence during Cosimo's absences. As Filippo Strozzi wrote to his brother-in-law Lorenzo: "Her ladyship [Alfonsina] is always busy, writing to Rome or to you or receiving people in audience, and the house is always full, which honors the state, encourages friends, and frightens enemies. In short, she carries out her duties as no other woman, and few men, could do."[62] As those who lived under her power could attest, Alfonsina's government was far from being merely symbolic; she commuted punishments and death penalties, assigned jobs, and gave orders regarding tax collection. The expression "ex commissione Domine Alphonsine" (by order of the Lady Alfonsina) appears on many government documents issued during these months.[63] What she did best, however, were face-to-face meetings, especially to retain the loyalty of Medici family allies.

Her many governmental obligations did not stop Alfonsina from patronizing the arts, and she did so in a manner quite different from the traditional republican style, clearly adopting models more typical of monarchies and seigneurs. At the urging of Leo X she directly oversaw the conclusion of construction at the Poggio a Caiano villa, near Prato in Tuscany, which Lorenzo the Magnificent had begun.[64] She knew exactly what had to be done. Before traveling to Florence she personally took charge of acquiring the land in Rome where a new residential palace for her family (today known as Medici-Lante) would sit, and hired architect Giuliano de Sangallo to design it. It was a project that surely she could not have undertaken in Florence where, as Eleonora would discover later when she bought and tried to remodel the Palazzo Pitti, it was believed that that sort of building project was suitable only for men. Women, at most, could sponsor convents.

Both then and later, Alfonsina was harshly criticized, mostly owing to what some believed was greedy acquisition and use of Tuscan lands, which also would be one of Eleonora's specialties.[65] What would have been considered an admirable

---

[62] Tomas, *The Medici Women*, 187n18.

[63] Ibid., 169n39.

[64] Ibid., 92.

[65] D'Addario, "Eleonora di Toledo," 54, compares Eleonora to Alfonsina based on her interest in acquiring uncultivated lands in Pisa, Barbaricina, and Campalto that turned out to be very fertile.

quality in a man—managing his wealth and making it grow—in a woman was still seen as a sign of inappropriate ambition.[66]

A New Identity

Like many other European women who were obliged to move from one place to another due to marriages arranged for political reasons, Eleonora was seen by her subjects not only as a consort but as an ally of a foreign power, in her case of the hated Spaniards, who in 1530, after a long siege, had conquered Florence and suppressed the latter's ancient freedoms.

When Cosimo went to Genoa in May 1543 to negotiate with Charles V for the return of the fortresses of Livorno and Florence, Eleonora remained at the head of the government. On May 26 she wrote him a letter that clearly reflected her fears regarding the withdrawal of Spanish troops from the city: "I lament my fortune, as I see that I am in danger without you in a city that regards the Spanish name and this manner of government as its enemy, and I do not know how I can remain in this state with my children."[67] Judging from her words, it is clear that four years after she arrived in Florence she did not at all identify with the city or its inhabitants.[68] Like future female members of the Medici family, most notably the queens of France, Catherine and Marie, she was condemned as a "double agent," something she could not help but be, despite her best wishes.[69]

Whether or not the criticisms were justified, her behavior made it clear that she had no intention of becoming a Florentine. And why should she? Despite what the pope's agents had told Agnolo Niccolini, Cosimo's ambassador in Rome, neither she nor her family showed any sign that they regarded the marriage as a step up that would require her to adapt. Over time, her husband laid the foundation for a firm state that would astonish the world with its cultural and artistic creations, but when he married Eleonora he was simply a ruler walking a tightrope. During the bride's journey from Naples to Florence there was nothing even approaching the ritual known as the "*ceremonia de la entrega*." In this ceremony, which would become typical of many dynastic marriages, the bride was formally handed over to the groom's family and obliged to cast off, even physically, her former identity.[70]

---

66 Tomas, *The Medici Women*, 178–85.

67 Cox-Rearick, *Bronzino's Chapel*, 35.

68 On Eleonora's fears and the tense political situation created by the Medici's enemies, see Guglielmo Enrico Saltini, *Tragedie Medicee Domestiche (1557–1587)* (Florence: G. Barbera, 1898), 71; and Baia, *Leonora di Toledo*, 91.

69 Christina Strunk, ed., *Medici Women as Cultural Mediators (1533–1743). Le donne di casa Medici e il loro ruolo di mediatrice culturali fra le corti d'Europa* (Milan: Silvana Editoriale, 2011), 9.

70 María José del Rio Barredo, "Imágenes para una ceremonia de frontera. El intercambio de las princesas entre las cortes de Francia y España en 1615," in *La historia*

We can imagine the feelings of someone like Eleonora, who not only was surrounded by her countrymen but knew she was protected by the ruling Spanish-imperial powers, embodied by her father, who ruled from a city just a few days away from where he kept a close eye on her husband's activities. Unlike other women who traveled similar itineraries, Eleonora fortunately never had to undergo the traumatic experience of seeing her father or her brothers go to war against her husband.

And in any case, which identity would Eleonora have cast off in order to become a Florentine? Her detractors were far off the mark in seeing her as, above all, a Spaniard. It was an error her admirers would also make; her way of dressing, for example, was in fact a mixture of elements from Flanders, Germany, Castile, and Naples.[71] Indeed, her identity was far more complex than people grasped, a blend of superimposed layers of influences combining the local with the global.

Furthermore, in her case the complex identity was accentuated by the fact that her move to Florence was not her first move. Years earlier she had left Castile for Naples, where her education was in the hands of a cultured and extremely intelligent Jewish woman named Bienvenida Abravanel, with whom she probably kept in close touch for the rest of her life.[72] In short, before reaching Florence, Eleonora di Toledo had undergone at least two processes of cultural hybridization. She might be a barbarian, as the unpleasant author of the *Cronaca fiorentina* wrote, but it was less clear that she was a Spaniard.

Bibliography

Archival Sources

Archivio di Stato, Florence, Italy, Mediceo del Principato, 5922/A.

Printed and Secondary Sources

Anonymous. *Cronaca Fiorentina 1537–1555*, ed. Enrico Coppi. Florence: Olschki, 2000.

Arcangeli, Letizia, and Susanna Peyronel Rambaldi, eds. *Donne di potere nel Rinascimento*. Roma: Viella, 2008.

Baia, Anna. *Leonora di Toledo, Duchesa di Firenze e di Siena*. Todi: Foglietti, 1907.

---

imaginada. Construcciones visuales del pasado en la Edad Moderna, eds. Joan-Lluís Palos and Diana Carrió-Invernizzi (Madrid: Centro de Estudios Europa Hispánica, 2008), 153–84.

71 Orsi Landini and Niccoli, *Moda a Firenze*.

72 Edelstein, "Nobildonne napoletane," 299–300.

Bruni, Domenico. *Opera di M. Domenico Bruni da Pistoia intitolata Difese delle donne, nella quale si contengono le difese loro, dalle calumnie dategli per gli scrittori e insieme le lodi di quelle.* Florence: Appresso i Giunti, 1552.

Calvi, Giulia, and Ricardo Spinelli, eds. *Le donne Medici nel sistema europeo delle corti XVI–XVIII secolo, Atti del convegno internazionale.* Florence: Polistampa, 2008.

Casa, Giovanna della. *Il Galateo.* Edited by Emanuela Scarpa. Modena: Einaudi, 1990.

Cellini, Benvenuto. *Vida.* Ed. and trans. Santiago R. Santerbás. Madrid: Cátedra, 2007.

Cox-Rearick, Janet. *Bronzino's Chapel of Eleonora in the Palazzo Vecchio.* Berkeley, CA: University of California Press, 1993.

_____, and Mary Westerman Bulgarella. "Public and Private Portraits of Cosimo de' Medici and Eleonora di Toledo: Bronzino's Paintings of His Ducal Patrons in Ottawa and Turin." *Artibus et historiae*, 25, no. 49 (2004): 101–59.

D'Addario, Arnaldo. "Eleonora di Toledo duchessa di Firenze e Siena." In *Donne di Casa Medici*, ed. Franco Cardini. 2nd edn. Florence: Arnaud, 1993.

De Martini, Vega, and José M. Morillas Alcázar. "Eleonora da Toledo: un modello artístico tra Napoli e Firenze." *Rivista storica del Sannio*, 3 (2005): 181–97.

Edelstein, Bruce L. "Nobildonne napoletane e committenza: Eleonora d'Aragona ed Eleonora di Toledo a confronto." In *Quaderni storici*, 35, no. 2 (August 2000): 295–329.

_____. "Eleonora di Toledo." In *Encyclopedia of Women in the Renaissance: Italy, France and England.* Edited by Diana Robin, Anne Larsen, and Carole Levin, 362–67. Santa Barbara, CA: ABC-Clio, 2007.

Eisenbichler, Konrad, ed. *The Cultural World of Eleonora di Toledo, Duchess of Florence and Siena.* Aldershot: Ashgate, 2004.

Gáldy, Andrea M., and Robert La France. "Golden Chambers for Eleonora of Toledo: Duchess and Collector in Palazzo Vecchio." In *Women Patrons and Collectors.* Edited by Susan Bracken, Andrea M. Gáldy, and Adriana Turpin, 17–21. Newcastle upon Tyne: Cambridge Scholars Publishing, 2012.

Giambullari, Pier Francesco. *Apparato et feste nelle nozze dello Illustrissimo signor duca di Firenze et de la duchessa sua consorte, con le sue stanze, madrigali, comedia, et intermedi in quella recitati.* Florence: Benedetto Giunta, 1539.

González Talavera, Blanca. "Presencia y mecenazgo español en la Florencia medicea. De Cosme I a Fernando I." PhD diss., University of Granada and University of Florence, 2011.

Hernando, Carlos José. *Castilla y Nápoles en el siglo XVI. El virrey Pedro de Toledo.* Valladolid: Junta de Castilla y León, 1994.

Langdon, Gabrielle. *Medici Women. Portraits of Power, Love and Betrayal from the Court of Duke Cosimo I.* Toronto: University of Toronto Press, 2007.

Mellini, Domenico. *Ricordi intorno ai costumi, azioni e governo del sereniss. gran duca Cosimo I.* Florence: Magheri, 1820.

Orsi Landini, Roberta, and Bruna Niccoli. *Moda a Firenze 1540–1580. Lo stile di Eleonora di Toledo e la sua influenza*. Florence: Polistampa, 2005.

Panizza, Letizia, ed. *Women in Italian Renaissance Culture and Society*. Oxford: European Humanities Research Centre, 2000.

Pieraccini, Gaetano. *La stirpe de' Medici di Cafaggiolo: saggio di ricerche sulla trasmissione ereditaria dei caratteri biologici*. 3 vols. Florence: Vallecchi, 1924–25.

Reiss, Sheryl E., and David G. Wilkins, eds. *Beyond Isabella: Secular Women Patrons of Art in Renaissance Italy*. Kirksville, MO: Truman State University Press, 2001.

Río Barredo, María José del. "Imágenes para una ceremonia de frontera. El intercambio de princesas entre las cortes de Francia y España en 1615." In *La historia imaginada. Construcciones visuales del pasado en la Edad Moderna*. Edited by Joan-Lluís Palos and Diana Carrió-Ivernizzi, 153–84. Madrid: Fernando Villaverde Ediciones, 2008.

Romby, Giuseppina Carla, and Emmanuela Ferretti. "Aggiornamenti e novità documentarie su palazzo Pitti." *Mitteilungen des Kunsthistorischen Institutes in Florenz*, 46 (2002–1): 152–96.

Rousseau, Claudia. "The Pageant of the Muses at the Medici Wedding of 1539 and the Decoration of the Salone del Cinquecento." In *Art and Pageantry in the Renaissance and Baroque*. Edited by Barbara Wisch and Susan Scott Munshower, vol. 2, 416–57. University Park: Pennsylvania State University Press, 1990.

Saltini, Guglielmo Enrico. *Tragedie Medicee Domestiche (1557–1587)*. Florence: G. Barbera, 1898.

Segni, Bernardo. *Storie Fiorentine* (Livorno, 1830), vol. 2.

Smyth, Carolyn. "An Instance of Feminine Patronage in the Medici Court of Sixteenth-Century Florence: The Chapel of Eleonora da Toledo in the Palazzo Vecchio." In *Women and Art in Early Modern Europe. Patrons, Collectors and Connoisseurs*. Edited by Cynthia Lawrence, 72–110. University Park: Pennsylvania State University Press, 1997.

Spini, Giorgio. *Cosimo I e l'indipendenza del principato mediceo*, 2nd edn. Florence: Vallechi, 1980.

Strazzullo, Franco. *Edilizia e urbanistica a Napoli dal '500 al '700*. Naples: Arte Tipografica, 1995.

Strunk, Christina, ed. *Medici Women as Cultural Mediators (1533–1743). Le donne di casa Medici e il loro ruolo di mediatrice culturali fra le corti d'Europa*. Milan: Silvana Editoriale, 2011.

Tinaglia, Paola. *Women in Italian Renaissance Art: Gender, Representation, Identity*. Manchester: Manchester University Press, 1997.

Tomas, Natalie R. "Alfonsina Orsini de' Medici and the Problem of a Female Ruler in Early Sixteenth-Century Florence." *Renaissance Studies*, 4, no. 1 (2000): 70–90.

———. *The Medici Women. Gender and Power in Renaissance Florence*. Aldershot: Ashgate, 2003.

Chapter 8
Paintings, Fans, and Scented Gloves: A Witness to Cultural Exchange at the Courts of Paris, Rome, and Madrid*

Leticia de Frutos[1]

> I write you by special courier to let you know I have received the portraits [of her children Filippo, Marcantonio, and Carlo] and the scented gloves, and I am pleased with all of them, which are perfect gifts for this country. The crowns and medallions were especially pleasing; one of them, of agate, is beautiful enough to give to the queen. I have distributed the relics and medallions to the nuns, and gloves to the ladies and their relatives. If you could send me coconut crowns and ordinary medallions to give to people of lower standing, with other crowns of rose-scented wood, I would be very grateful, and above all the gloves and the fans from Naples, which people have loved. The last gloves were simply perfect … I also would like fans scented with orange blossom oil.[2]
>
> Maria Mancini Colonna
> Madrid, December 26, 1674

---

* This chapter has been translated from the Spanish by Ruth MacKay. Davide van Vlijmen translated the quotes in Italian. This contribution forms part of the research project *Poder y Representaciones en la Edad Moderna: Redes diplomáticas y encuentros culturales en la monarquía hispánica (1500–1700)* (HAR2012-39516-C02-02), financed by the Spanish government. I would like to thank Elia Mariano and the Benedictine Father Romano, of the Colonna archive, without whom it would have been impossible for me to conduct this research. I also thank Cristina Bravo and Roberto Quirós for their comments. This chapter is dedicated to Elia and Romano.

[1] This study is based on María Mancini's extensive correspondence with her husband, Lorenzo Onofrio Colonna, and with her children and agents. This correspondence, which is in large part unedited, is found in the Archivo de Subiaco, Rome, where I consulted it. Maria Mancini's correspondence is not catalogued in the archive, and therefore I refer to the letters by date and recipient. I have modernized spelling and punctuation. This article is part of a larger study I am undertaking about Maria Mancini's presence in Spain from 1674 to 1702.

[2] "Gia vi scrissi per un straordinario come avevo ricevuto i ritratti, li guanti con palle (?) d'odore, è tutto di mia sodisfatione ed a propósito per regalare in questo paese. Tra l'altra le corone, e le medaglie mi hanno gustato in estremo; ve ne una, quella d'agata, che si puol [*sic*] dare alla Regina, tanto è bella; le reliquie e le medaglie, la è spartite alle monaque

Maria Mancini (1639–1715) wrote this letter to her husband, Lorenzo Onofrio Colonna (1637–89), from a house adjacent to the Convent of Santo Domingo el Real in Madrid. She was practically cloistered, and despite having petitioned the queen regent and the nuncio for permission to leave at least once a week, as she had done previously at the Visitation convent in Turin, she had not been successful.[3] It was just after Christmas, and these letters and the obligatory gifts she offered to the few visitors she received—many of them relatives of her husband—allowed her to continue the social life she had led before. Maria was not accustomed to this sort of life. Though her mother had planned a religious life for her, and she had lived in various convents, her character and her personality were not a good fit for enclosure.

Maria Mancini (see Figure 8.1), one of the so-called Mazarinette, nieces of the powerful Cardinal Giulio Mazarin (1602–61), was born in Rome in 1639. She was the daughter of Michele Lorenzo Mancini, a Roman baron, and Gerolama Mazarini, the cardinal's sister, and she was the third of five sisters.[4] Her mother had wished, Maria wrote in her memoirs, that Maria enter a Benedictine convent and choose a religious life.[5] Ill health saved her from that life, which would not

e li guanti a queste dame e parenti. Del resto quando potete inviarmi ancor guanti e corone de cocco con medaglie ordinarie per dare a persone più inferiori con delle altre di legno di rose odorose mi farete grande piacere, è sopra tutto de guanti e ventaglie di Napoli che ne hanno impazite, li ultimi guanti sono perfettissimi, e anche le palle; vorrei anche qualque ventaglio alla nevola." Archivio Colonna, María Mancini to Lorenzo Onofrio Colonna (hereafter AC, MMC-LOC), Madrid, December 26, 1674.

[3] The queen regent was Mariana de Austria (1634–96), Philip IV's second wife and mother of Charles II. The papal nuncio was Cardinal Galeazzo Marescotti (1670–75).

[4] There is ample bibliography on Maria Mancini, ranging from biographies to monographs on gender studies that have emphasized her role as a woman in the early modern age. See for example: Marie Mancini, *La Vérité dans Son Jour, ou les Véritables Mémoires de M. Mancini, Connétable Colonne*, eds. Patricia Frances Cholakian and Elizabeth Goldsmith (New York: Scholars' Facsimiles and Reprints, 1998); Elizabeth Goldsmith and Abby Zanger, "The Politics and Poetics of the Mancini Romance: Visions and Revisions of Louis XIV," in *The Rhetorics of Life-Writing in Early Modern Europe: Forms of Biography from Cassandra Fedele to Louis XIV*, eds. Thomas F. Mayer and D.R. Woolf (Ann Arbor: University of Michigan Press, 1995), 341–72; Elizabeth Goldsmith, *Publishing Women's Life Stories in France, 1647–1720: From Voice to Print* (Aldershot and Burlington, VT: Ashgate, 2001); Elizabeth Goldsmith, "Publishing the Lives of Hortense and Marie Mancini," in *Going Public: Women and Publishing in Early Modern France*, eds. Elizabeth Goldsmith and Dena Goodman (Ithaca, NY: Cornell University Press, 1995), 31–45. Elizabeth Goldsmith recently published a book about Maria and Hortensia Mancini that includes some of the letters I have used: Elizabeth Goldsmith, *The Kings' Mistresses. The Liberated Lives of Marie Mancini, Princess Colonna, and her Sister Hortense, Duchess Mazarin* (New York: Public Affairs, 2012).

[5] She published her memoirs in 1677: *La Vérité dans Son Jour, ou les Véritables Mémoires de M. Mancini, Connétable Colonne*, responding to apocryphal memoirs titled *Mémoires de M.L.P.M.M. Colonne*, which had appeared the previous year. She addressed her book to her husband, Lorenzo Onofrio Colonna. Her memoirs were translated into

Figure 8.1 Jacob Ferdinand Voet, Portrait of Maria Mancini, 1660–80, oil on canvas, 73 × 63 cm. Rikjsmuseum, Amsterdam.

have suited her. In 1653, a letter from her uncle the cardinal to her mother and her aunt, Madame Martiniozzi, inviting them to France along with their eldest daughters, would change Maria's life.

Life at the Parisian court called for preparation. One of the sisters, Laura Vittoria Mancini, who was married to the duke of Mercu, could help prepare them during the eight months they spent with her in Aix. But that was not enough; Maria's bad health and, above all, the fact that she still could not speak French, led her uncle to send her to the Visitation convent in the district of Saint-Jacques in Paris, where soon she would be joined by her sister Hortensia.[6] Parisian convents—or at least this one—were not like those she had known in Rome, nor were they like Santo Domingo el Real in Madrid, from where she wrote the letter above. In the Visitation, there were no grilles separating the religious and secular realms.[7]

The convent had been founded in 1619 by Francis de Sales and Madame de Chantal, and it quickly became a leader in female education in France. Francis de Sales wrote a book on the vocational life justifying the life of devout women who were actively involved in the secular world.[8] Their dwellings, far from being cells for spiritual reclusion, were often places of sociability quite similar to worldly sites such as the Parisian salons and hotels. It is safe to say that the education that Maria and her sister received there was not limited to religious matters. Maria indeed wrote in her memoirs that they had been "handed over to Mother Soror de la Moñón, sister of the first president of Paris, who oversaw our education and taught us French and other things that she thought necessary for people of our age and milieu."[9]

There was nothing odd about the girls preparing for a life in society while they were in a religious space.[10] Even among the circle of women who later were known as the Precious Ones (*Précieuses*), led by Catherine de Vivone (Madame de Rambouillet), we find testimonies of women who, while in the convent,

---

Spanish in a more complete version, which is what I have used: Maria Mancini, *La verdad en su luz o verdaderas memorias de María Mancini Colonna ...* (Zaragoza, 1677). On her memoirs, see Patricia Frances Cholakian, *Women and the Politics of Self-Representation in Seventeenth-Century France* (Newark, DE: University of Delaware Press, 2009), 101–21.

[6] Mancini, *La verdad en su luz*, 11–14.

[7] Benedetta Craveri, *La civiltà della conversazione* (Milan: Adelphi Edizioni, 2001); I used the Spanish translation: *La cultura de la conversación*, trans. César Palma (Madrid: Siruela, 2007), esp. 31–51.

[8] François de Sales, *Introduzione alla vita devota*, ed. Benedetta Papàsogli (Milan: Rizzoli, 1986); René Bady, "François de Sales maître d'honnêteté," *XVIIe siècle*, 78 (1968): 3–20.

[9] This was Marie Elizabeth de Lamoignon, sister of the president of the Parlement of Paris. Maria Mancini remained her student for a year and a half. See Mancini, *La verdad en su luz*, 18.

[10] On the education of young noblewomen see Roger Chartier et al., *L'éducation en France du XVIe au XVIIIe siècle* (Paris: Sedes, 1976).

lived almost a literary life in which reality became fiction, everything appeared designed, and nothing was improvised.[11] That was the case, for example, of Maria Eléanore de Rohan-Montbazon, the eldest daughter of Madame de Montbazon, one of the *Précieuses*, who was abbess first of the Trinity convent in Caen and then in Malnoue; her writings show her to be an assiduous and knowledgeable member of Madame Rambouillet's circle.[12]

The space these *Précieuses* inhabited was a sort of Arcadia. Not only did they try to live their lives in a theatrical fashion, which remained distinctively noble, but they also created a utopia of a happy place where they could dream of moral and aesthetic perfection. Maria may have been one of these *Précieuses* (Somaize includes her in his dictionary), enjoying that distinctive and obligatory relationship that only the few could attain, not by virtue of their social class but rather of their common interests.[13] In the circle of *Précieuses* at the Visitation convent she learned to love music, literature, astrology, and the arts and, above all, to gain consciousness of her own individuality. It is possible that without that apprenticeship she never would have dared to leave her husband and Rome in 1672. In 1677, when she was in Madrid, she reminded her husband how much she disliked Rome:

> If I could overcome the aversion I feel for Rome, I could overcome everything else, but you know well what people are like there and how little loyalty there is among families, everyone wanting the other to be like them. And I'm not even mentioning the illnesses and ailments that the climate causes me. Though it is true that I have had occasional indispositions here, they have been due to the enclosure and the little exercise one gets here. Without a doubt, it is the best and healthiest place one could be.[14]

---

[11] On the *Précieuses*, see Victor Cousin, *La société française au XVIIe siècle d'après le Grand Cyrus de Mlle. de Scudéry* (Paris: Didier, 1852); Charles-Louis Livet, *Précieux et précieuses, caractères et moeurs littéraires du XVIIe siècle* (Paris: Didier, 1859); on Madame de Rambouillet, see her biography by Nicole Aronson, *Madame de Rambouillet ou la magicienne de la Chambre bleue* (Paris: Fayard, 1988).

[12] Benedetta Borello, *Trame sovrapposte: la socialità aristocratica e le reti di relazioni femminili a Roma (XVII–XVIII secolo)* (Naples: Edizione scientifiche Italiane, 2003), 41n74; Mary Rowan, "Between Salon and Convent: Madame de Rohan, a Precious Abbess," *Papers on French Seventeenth-Century Literature*, 22 (1985): 191–207.

[13] Antoine Baudeau de Somaize, *Le Grand Dictionnaire des prétieuses, historique, poétique, géographique* (Paris: Jean Ribou, 1661).

[14] "Si pudiera vencer la aversión que tengo a Roma, lo demás fuera vencible, pero bien sabéis cuál es el humor de la gente y la poca unión que hay entre las familias queriendo cada uno ser tanto como vos; dejo a parte los achaques y la poca salud que me causa el clima, que, si bien, a veces he tenido acá alguna indisposición, más ha sido ocasionada de la clausura y del poco ejercicio que del temple del lugar, que sin contradicción alguna es el mejor y más sano que sea posible hallarse." AC, MMC-LOC, Madrid, April 29, 1677.

During the year and a half Maria was in the Visitation convent in Paris, she was exposed to a new model of life that seemed to place her closer to the court. She would complete this education alongside Madame de Gaillard, one of her sister Vittoria's former ladies-in-waiting, with whom she began to read the classics and write poetry.

Shortly thereafter, ready for social life, she was in La Fère (Picardy), where she was supposed to marry the son of the marshal Milleray. It was then, in her own words, that Maria began discovering the pleasures of life at court:

> Since then I never left court. My age and the care of my teachers had instructed me well, and I found things there that had been hidden from me before. I did not enjoy them with liberty, however, as my mother, seeing how lively I was and not so tender with me as she was with my sisters (as I have already said), took care to keep me confined, and she protected me so firmly that I could go nowhere without her, and the rest of the time I remained alone at home.[15]

This was Maria's life during these years, between the convent and the pleasures of the court, and this duality between the habit and the corset, prayer and gallantry, would be repeated for the rest of her life.

In 1656 Maria's mother died and she immediately went to the court of Louis XIV, where she received the attention of the king himself.

> All we did was have fun. Every day, every minute, we devoted to pleasure, and I can say that I was never more entertained. As His Majesty wished for our pastimes to continue, he ordered our group to alternate banquets and parties, so they were both endless. And though we did all this out in the country, it was all nevertheless splendid. As proof, the noblest of gentlemen partook in these pleasures.[16]

This peace was interrupted in 1659 when Louis XIV signed the Peace of the Pyrenees, which entailed his engagement to María Teresa of Spain. Maria Mancini, who had been Louis's lover, could no longer stay in Paris and Cardinal

---

15 "Desde aquella jornada no me aparté de la corte, y como la edad y los cuidados ajenos en enseñarme habíanme infundido algunas noticias, hallaba en ella atractivos hasta entonces ocultos, aunque con libertad no gozase sus deleites, mi madre, a vista de mi viveza, y menos cariñosa conmigo, que con mis hermanas (como ya lo tengo advertido), desvelándose cuanto podía en tenerme recogida y guardándome con tan singular recato, que nunca salía sino en su compañía y las más veces me dejaba sola en casa [*sic*]." Mancini, *La verdad en su luz*, 21–22.

16 "Solo atendimos a divertirnos; no había día, poco decir es, no había instante que no estuviese destinado a las holguras, y puedo decir que jamás hubo tiempo más entretenido. Queriendo su majestad asegurar la continuación de nuestros pasatiempos, mandó a todos de nuestro correo alternasen los convites y saraos; eran, pues, perennes unos y otros." Ibid., 37–38.

Mazarin arranged for her to leave the court and marry the eldest son of one of Rome's greatest families, the Colonna, who also had long-standing relations with Spain.[17]

Her apprenticeship at the French court would be critical as Maria returned to Italy. Despite the rigid limitations of Roman society, she would have a powerful impact in Rome, so much so that she influenced how women presented themselves.

A Lady *alla francese* in Rome

Maria was married by proxy to *condestable* (constable) Lorenzo Onofrio Colonna in 1661 in the royal chapel of the Louvre.[18] After a long and painful journey, during which she fell ill several times, she arrived in Rome, a far cry from Paris. Indeed, women there lacked the freedom she had known in France. They could not even manage their own wealth and were considered as simple instruments at court, which was dominated by a strong masculine hierarchy.[19] The Rome that Maria lived in was that of Pope Alexander VII (1655–67); it was a city of great artistic development but also one marked by a series of measures imposing rules on Roman society that clearly clashed with the liberal notions to which Maria was accustomed.[20]

Fortunately for her, Lorenzo liked music and art.[21] Perhaps there they would find common ground. But Maria was suffocating in Rome. She found relief only

---

[17] On the Colonna, see Antonio Coppi, *Memorie colonnesi* (Rome: Salviucci, 1855); P. Colonna, *I Colonna dagli origini agli inizi del secolo XIX* (Rome, 1927); Pio Paschini, *I Colonna* (Rome: Istituto di Studi Romani, 1955); Vincenzo Celletti, *I Colonna principi di Paliano* (Milan: Ceschina, 1960).

[18] It is possible that Maria's marriage was a maneuver by Cardinal Mazarin to strengthen the French faction at the Vatican. After all, Pope Chigi was elected over the opposition of Mazarin and Louis XIV. When Mazarin died in 1661, the French king seized the papal territory in Avignon, which he kept until the Peace of Pisa in 1664. I do not know if Maria played any role in the resolution of the conflict. On Franco-Spanish relations during those years see Isabel Yetano Laguna, *Relaciones entre España y Francia desde la paz de los Pirineos (1659) hasta la Guerra de devolución (1667): la embajada del Marqués de La Fuente* (Madrid: Fundación Universitaria Española, 2009).

[19] Simona Feci, *Pesci fuor d'acqua: donne a Roma in età Moderna: diritti e patrimoni* (Rome: Viella, 2004).

[20] "Vueltos a Roma (de donde el papa Alejandro, por una aversión que tenía a cualquier género de entretenimiento, había desterrado hasta las comedias) el condestable desvelándose como siempre en nuestras holguras, y atento a suplir la falta de ellas, discurrió en hacer una máscara." Mancini, *La verdad en su luz*, 83–84.

[21] On his collections see Natalia Gozzano, *La quadreria di Lorenzo Onofrio Colonna* (Rome: Bulzoni, 2004); on his interest in theater and music see Elena Tamburini, *Due teatri per il Principe. Studi sulla commitenza teatrale di Lorenzo Onofrio Colonna* (Rome: Bulzoni, 1997).

when she celebrated Carnival in Venice, where she could live more freely, use her French ways, and find relief from the oppressive atmosphere in Rome.[22] She knew she was not well-liked in Rome and that her manner of dressing—décolletage and off-the-shoulder—and her show of liberty were criticized.[23] But perhaps it was criticized only by some; others appeared to fetishize women who dressed in this fashion, going so far as to make such women into precious and necessary props (*atrezzo*) at court. Women such as Maria were invited to parties or gatherings, lavished with gifts, fed sweets, given gloves and fans, and serenaded in the evenings. They were portrayed in portraits following a model that Maria herself made fashionable. The Flemish painter Jacob Ferdinand Voet, who lived in the Piazza di Spagna, was the one to "invent" these galleries of beautiful women (*gallerie di belle donne*) when he painted the portraits of Maria and her sister Hortensia for Cardinal Flavio Chigi, just before the sisters' flight from Rome.[24] It became fashionable to display these series, featuring the faces of the leading women of Roman society, in spaces which were analogous to Madame de Rambouillet's blue salon in Paris.[25] The women in the portraits wore simple, low-cut dresses, adorned with delicate flowers or pearls in their hair that looked natural and improvised. The *condestable* himself had one of these galleries and admitted that Madama Mancini had become the stage manager of his life.[26]

Maria convinced him that they should travel to Venice where she loved the opera. Later she played a key role in making it possible for the opera to come to Rome.[27] She continued writing, and maintained her interest in astrology, as in

---

22 "A vista de estas holguras, mucho temía dejar lugar tan divertido, y volver a Roma, cuando el condestable me dijo, era preciso absolutamente resolverme a partir … confieso fue para mí esta orden de mucho sentimiento (aunque no inesperada) y así para obedecerla, obliguele a que me diese palabra de que volveríamos a pasar otras Carnestolendas en este deleitoso lugar [Venecia]." Mancini, *La verdad en su luz*, 94–95.

23 In her memoirs she refers to the contrast between her style of dressing and what she calls the Italians' "decent" dress: "empecé a ir al paseo, y a donde quiera que hubiese algún entretenimiento, y esto en traje decente (quiero decir italiano) en el cual uso había entrado por la sola novedad." Ibid., 77.

24 See Lada Nikolenko, "The Beauties' Galleries," *Gazette des Beaux-Arts*, 67 (1966): 19–24, fig. 5; Lada Nikolenko, "The Source of the Mancini-Mazarini Iconography. Catalogue of Portraits in the Chigi d'Ariccia Collection," *Gazette des Beaux-Arts*, 76 (1970): 145–58, image 17, p. 153; Francesco Petrucci, *Ferdinand Voet (1639–1689), detto Ferdinando de' ritratti* (Rome: Ugo Bozzi, 2005).

25 Among these series was one commissioned by the duke of Savoy, Charles Emanuele II (1634–75), a fervent admirer of Maria and Hortensia Mancini who hosted them in Turin.

26 There was possibly only one other woman in Rome who could match or supersede Maria's influence, and that was Queen Christina of Sweden (1626–89).

27 Valeria De Lucca, "'Dalle sponde del Tebro alle rive dell'Adria': Maria Mancini and Lorenzo Onofrio Colonna's Patronage of Music and Theater between Rome and Venice (1659–1675)" (PhD diss., Princeton University, 2009).

Paris.[28] In Rome she socialized with Giuseppe Terzi, the author of various treatises including *De Curiositatibus physicis tractatus* (1686) and *De gradu horoscopante* (1690), and it is possible that she went to Queen Christina of Sweden's palace.[29] Her fascination with the stars and palmistry was manifest in the publication of two treatises which she wrote: *Discorso astrofisico delle mutazioni de' tempi e di altri accidenti mondani dell'anno 1670*, and a similar one in 1672. After all, Maria was the granddaughter of Paolo Mancini, founder of the Accademia degli Umoristi and someone who was specifically interested in astrophysics.

Her first child, Filippo, was born in 1663, and the Austrian artist Giovanni Paolo Schor, who had worked alongside Bernini, was commissioned by the *condestable* to design a spectacular bed for her to give her son:[30]

> It was a sort of shell that appeared to float in a sea that was depicted so well that it did not appear as such, and the waves served as a baseboard. It was held aloft by four seahorses ridden by sirens, all of them beautifully sculpted of a substance that shone like gold, and anyone who saw it would say it was a precious metal. Ten or twelve little Cupids formed lovely clasps for luxurious gold brocade curtains, which were artfully draped so that everything worth seeing of this magnificent display could be seen, though the cupids were adornments and were not necessarily seen.[31]

News gazettes enjoyed describing Maria, a new Venus. A year later Marcantonio was born, and Carlo followed in 1665.

Despite having tried to adapt to life in Rome, the differences she found with France, which she continued to miss, were too much for her. The stressful competition among families, the hypocrisy, and the false adulation were unbearable for her, reflecting a narrowness that was also evident in the way women presented themselves. When her sister Hortensia arrived in Rome from Paris in 1668, fleeing her husband, the duke of Mazarino, and leaving behind a life that, in comparison to hers in Italy, was the height of liberty, Maria wrote:

> Being that she came from France, her ideas still fresh with the newest Paris fashions, she came with that country's soul of genius. From the outside, this

[28] Lucien Perey, *Le roman du gran roi, Louis XIV et Marie Mancini, d'après des lettres et documents inédits* (Paris: Calmann Lévy, 1894), 198.

[29] Ibid., 103.

[30] There is an engraving of the bed in "Letto fatto per la nascita del primogenito del contestabile Colonna. A 1663 alli 7 d'aprile. Gio Paulo Schor da Inspruch inve. et delin," in Alvar González-Palacios, "Bernini as a Furniture Designer," *The Burlington Magazine*, 112, no. 812 (November 1970): 719–23; and another in Windsor Castle, Royal Library, inv. 4457, and a third attributed to a Roman artist in the second half of the seventeenth century at the Cooper-Hewitt Museum of Design in New York.

[31] Mancini, *La verdad en su luz*, 89–91.

> led her to admire stylish clothing and, as the marquise and I unfortunately were missing that here, after a somewhat boring reception she insulted our clothing with the insults they deserved.[32]

As we will see, clothing transmits the soul of the nation, which was very clear in Maria's case. Each time she visited a court, she asked people to send her little adornments and accessories that gave the courts their identity: scented gloves, fans, powders for her hair, stockings, and so on.

After her third son was born and she had decided to stop sharing her husband's bed, she could no longer put up with the Roman court. Successive miscarriages, weak health, her husband's infidelity, alleged attempts of her husband to poison her, and, especially, the example of Hortensia, who left her husband in 1668, encouraged her to leave Rome, the *condestable*, and her three children. She left on May 29, 1672 with Hortensia.[33] Filippo was nine, Marcantonio eight, and Carlo seven.

Leaving her husband nearly turned into a matter of state and was amply reported on in newsletters.[34] Lorenzo sent his agents throughout Europe to inform him promptly about his wife's activities. Maria also kept him apprised of her activities, because despite it all, she corresponded regularly with him. She also wrote frequently to her dear friend Hortensia Stella, whom she had left in charge of her children in Rome and who would become one of Lorenzo's lovers. In all the letters, without ever harming Colonna's image, she justified having left him. Sometimes she said she did so to be with her sister, but other times she confessed she feared for her life. In her memoirs, she justified her decision:

---

[32] Ibid., 119–20.

[33] In her memoirs, Maria alluded to her husband's continual lack of attention to her after she requested not to sleep with him any longer: "echaba de menos en el condestable la acostumbrada fineza, la ternura ordinaria, la estimación sólita, y la confianza primera … no pudiendo, pues, resistir más a tan sensibles pesares, resolví buscarles alivio, y como en la continuación de nuestros baños y paseos habíamos trabado más estrecha amistad que nunca madama Mazarino y yo, quise aprovecharme de su cariño, y le pedí encarecidamente no se fuese a Francia sin llevarme consigo." The two sisters finally did flee from Rome in dramatic fashion: "Partimos, pues, a veinte y nueve de mayo, muy a la ligera, reduciéndose todo mi caudal a setecientos doblones, mis perlas, y unas arracadas de diamantes." Ibid., 154–56 and 159.

[34] Biblioteca Apostólica Vaticana, Berberini Latini, 6375, Avvisi di Roma, June 1, 1672, 118v. "Habbiamo altra scena, e forse più scandalosa di quella, con la fuga della contestabilessa e della Mazzarina sua sorella, e senza sapersene la causa fattasi condurre hier da una muta a Fiumicino presecò colà una filuca da'imbarcarono non si sa per dove. Non hanno con ese loro ch'un cuoco, la bella mora et un'altra damigella; si sono spedite più persone per arrivarle, ma sin a quin non se n'ha nuova. Ecco gli effetti che sanno produrre le donne di spirito troppo livero e che vivono con l'idee ricavate dalla lettura de romanzi."

> All these reasons [her husband's curt and disdainful manner], together with my dislike of Italian customs and the way of life in Rome, where dissimulation and hatred among families is far more prominent than in other courts, forced me to hasten my decision to retire to France, the country where I was educated.[35]

But things would not be easy for her. In her letters, we see how Maria found herself in a web spun by her husband. She wished to return to France, where she hoped Louis XIV would allow her to enter a convent on the outskirts of Paris where she could be closer to her family. But in the end she went to the Lys monastery (in Languedoc-Roussillon, the southeast region of France), where she said she was "an example of virtue, and I believe no one could complain of my conduct and even my enemies will be obliged to praise it."[36] There she led a quiet life and received visits and favors from her sisters and friends, among them the count and countess of Soisson. But when she attempted to move closer to Paris, the monarch ordered her to go to Avenay, to an abbey "three leagues from Reims, where His Majesty (reducing the decreed distance by half) has ordered me to go."[37] She spent three months there, "very lonely, with nothing to do except study with Mr. Boniel, my chaplain, who speaks French, Latin, Italian, and Spanish well."[38] Her extensive correspondence throughout the rest of her life would show she had learned Italian, Spanish, and French well.

After staying in Nevers with her sister, Maria went to Turin in February 1673, where she enjoyed "the protection of His Royal Highness [Carlo Emanuele II of Savoy], which made me very happy. His attentions and manners had always been thus, but particularly then I was not left wanting for anything."[39] She visited the Savoy royal residence, the Venaria Reale, "full of pleasures such that I have never had a more enjoyable time, receiving multiple shows of affection and esteem from His Highness and his royal wife."[40] Maria then lived in the Visitation convent in

---

35 Mancini, *La verdad en su luz*, 158.

36 "Essendo un esempio di virtu; dove credo non vi potete lamentar della mia condotta, essendo tale che i miei nemici stessi saranno obligati di lodarla." AC, MMC-LOC, September 23, 1672.

37 "Abadía distante de tres leguas de Rheims, en la cual su Majestad (bajando la mitad de la distancia decretada) había mandado estuviese." Mancini, *La verdad en su luz*, 216.

38 "Molto solitaria non avendo altra soddisfazione che d'studiare con Mr Boniel mio cappellano il quale possede bene la lingua francese, latina, e italiana et spagnola." AC, MMC-LOC, December 2, 1672.

39 "La protección de su Alteza Real [Charles Emanuel II of Savoy], con la cual tenía yo muy justas razones de estar contenta, habiendo sido durante algún tiempo tales sus atenciones y finezas, y en especial entonces que no me dejaban que desear." Mancini, *La verdad en su luz*, 228–29.

40 "Fértil en todo género de cazas y holguras, de calidad que puedo decir que haber gozado mejor tiempo que entonces, recibiendo muy repetidas veces de su Alteza, y de Madama real, su esposa, todas las demostraciones de cariño, y estimación que yo podía desear." Mancini, *La verdad en su luz*, 231.

Turin, although she had a papal dispensation that allowed her to leave the convent occasionally. In the convent she continued writing to her husband,[41] who was keeping track of her through his agent, Mauricio Bologna, who was on Maria's heels.[42]

Colonna also sent Carlo Emanuele Filiberto d'Este, the marquis of Borgomanero, to persuade her that she would be better off in the Spanish Netherlands, where she would have more freedom. Flanders was within Colonna's realm of interest, because he hoped to obtain an important post in Spanish territories, and Maria agreed to go. In November 1673, despite the bad weather, she and the marquis went over the St. Bernard pass in the French Alps and stopped in Cologne, where she was received by an official of the count of Monterrey, governor of Flanders, who told Maria that a place for her in a convent was being prepared. However, instead of going to a convent, Maria found herself in the castle of Antwerp treated as if she were a prisoner, which was not the agreement she had made with her husband. From there she continued writing to her husband, begging him to free her. He told her she could go to Madrid, where his brother-in-law, the third marquis of los Balbeses, Paolo Spinola Doria (1628–99) would keep an eye on her. The *condestable* also had several business matters in Spain, and he knew that Maria's presence might help him win favors at court, both for him and for his family.

At long last, on May 25, 1674, Maria was ready to leave for Ostend, where she would take a ship to San Sebastián and from there travel to Madrid. She had spent money on "blouses, a dress, and a Spanish-style coat" and on other caprices (*bagatelle*).[43] Once again, she knew clothing could help her adapt to the new lifestyle she would find in Madrid, which would be different from that of Paris and Rome.[44] In any case, she was anxious to reach the Spanish court to meet the queen and seek her favor.

---

41 Mancini, *La verdad en su luz*, 231 and 222–25; AC, MMC-LOC, January 26, 1673: "In questa città [Turin], dove mi ritrovo in un convento e me traterrò fin che Dio minspiri altramente; sarei stata a Nevers con mio fratello e sua moglie se mi fusse stato concesso; ma già che avete mostrato tanta ansietà se scesse fuor di Francia, sono venuta in Italia per darvi questa sodisfactione; et per farvi conoscer la mia indiferenza; assicurandovi ch'in ogni luogo sarò sempre l'istessa per voi. M.M.C."

42 The *condestable* still doubted Maria's intentions on March 3 when she went to Turin: "… circa a quello mi dite poi ch'io sono partita di Francia per goder magior libertà mi meraviglio di questo vostro pensiero, mentre mi sono voluntariamente rinchiusa in un monasteio; se io avessi potuto restar nel Lys non saria uscita di Francia; ma la poca compiacenza del Re ma fatto pigliar questa resolutione; non so perche supponente che io avessi libertà a Nevers mentre nella casa di mio fratello stavo a punto come in un convento." AC, MMC-LOC, Turin, March 1, 1673.

43 "Camicie, abito e manto alla spagnola." AC, MMC-LOC, May 25, 1674.

44 When Maria in 1666 greeted the future empress on her way to Vienna, Maria showed the importance of clothing as an icon of royal power. She wore a "very Spanish" outfit like that she would wear years later when she found refuge in Mariana of Austria's court: "la cual [la emperatriz] llegó a finales de otoño [de 1666], y a quien fui a besar

A Lady *alla francese* in Madrid

On June 12, 1674 Maria reached San Sebastián after a nine-day journey. Earlier, upon her husband's recommendation, she had written to the Admiral of Castile: "as your relative, and more amicable than the rest, as you have assured me; I pray that God makes it so and that I find in Madrid more finesse and courtesy than I have experienced in Flanders."[45]

Don Juan Gaspar Enríquez de Cabrera (1623–91), the tenth Admiral of Castile, was a cultured man and the highest-ranking Spanish nobleman after the monarch. Unlike his father, Juan Alfonso, who had been appointed viceroy of Sicily in 1641 and, three years later, viceroy in Naples, Juan Gaspar never occupied any post outside of Spain. In 1660 he was named the king's *mayordomo mayor* (chief steward), but, disappointed with court, he chose to retire to La Huerta, his residence on the Paseo de Recoletos. There he could look at the paintings by Titian, Tintoretto, and Bassano that his father had acquired in Italy, along with paintings purchased through his agents there. He held literary gatherings, or *tertulias*, where guests included literary figures such as Ribeiro de Barros and artists including Juan de Alfaro, a disciple of Velázquez, and Juan Carreño de Miranda. They wrote poetry and discussed painting.[46] Indeed, her husband did not err; don Juan Gaspar was the Spanish courtier most similar to the sort Maria had known at other courts.

---

la mano, con traje español, y con grandísimo luto, el cual traía por muerte del cardenal [Girolamo] Colonna, que había fallecido en el Finale de una enfermedad que le había dado, acompañando a esta princesa. Me recibió su Majestad con inexplicable agasajo, y me dijo, que en el aire, y en los modos, parecía ser lo que el traje decía (lisonja, con la cual me anteponía a las demás naciones) no habiendo una que no tenga lo que estila, por lo más cumplido y primoroso." Mancini, *La verdad en su luz*, 108–09.

[45] "Come vostro parente, e come più compito del'altri per quanto poi stesso mavete assicurato; Dio faccia che riesca tale, e che trovi maggior finessa et compitesa in Madrid che non ho avuto in Fiandra." AC, MMC-LOC, Madrid, June 12, 1674.

[46] On the Admiral of Castille see José Antonio Álvarez y Baena, *Hijos de Madrid ilustres en Santidad, dignidades, armas, ciencias y artes …* (Madrid: B. Cano, 1789), vol. 3, 263–65. On his collections see Cesáreo Fernández Duro, *El último Almirante de Castilla: don Juan Tomás Enríquez de Cabrera* (Madrid: M. Tello, 1903); Marcus B. Burke, "Private Collections of Italian Art in Seventeenth-Century Spain," (PhD diss., New York University, 1984), vol. 1, 92–94; Fernando Checa and José M. Morán, *El coleccionismo en España: de la cámara de maravillas a la galería de pinturas* (Madrid: Cátedra, 1985), 298–301; Fernando Bouza, *Imagen y propaganda. Capítulos de historia cultural del reinado de Felipe II* (Madrid: Akal, 1998), 206–10; Alejandro Vergara, "The Room of Rubens in the Collection of the X Almirante of Castille," *Apollo*, 396 (1995): 34–39; Marcus B. Burke, Peter Cherry, and Maria L. Gilbert, *Collections of Paintings in Madrid 1601–1755* (Los Angeles: Paul Getty Trust, 1997), 170–74 and 893–962; Javier Portús, *La Sala Reservada del Museo del Prado y el coleccionismo de pintura de desnudo en la Corte española 1554–1838* (Madrid: Museo Nacional del Prado, 1998), 138–40; Javier Portús, "El mecenazgo de la nobleza en Madrid durante el siglo XVII," in *El Madrid de Velázquez y Calderón. Villa y Corte en el siglo XVII*, vol. 1, *Estudios históricos*, eds. Miguel Morán and Bernardo José

She arrived in Madrid after a long trip, worried about what sort of reception she would get, given her husband's interference. In Alcobendas, on the outskirts of Madrid, she received two letters. One was from the queen, Mariana: "Her Majesty treated me with all the honor I could wish for; the other was from the Admiral, who with great generosity gave me the lodging I had requested [at La Huerta], saying he himself would receive me and make his offer in person."[47] The house was located

> at the far east end of Madrid, richly appointed and adorned with an enormous number of the most exquisite and beautiful paintings from Europe, the most celebrated collection of glorious labors of those who emulate nature. Here art triumphs over the arid and contemptible land, and flora has not in its entire domain a wider field on which to show off its sovereignty. Venice, a treasure house of glass, would appear to have given them all for this building, where there are so many, that everything is light, with no breeze, and the wind enters only if one wants it to.[48]

In his collection of paintings were Rubens's *Equestrian Portrait of the Duke of Lerma*, and Ribera's *Martyrdom of St. Andrew*, both from his father's collection, to which Juan Gaspar had added many paintings which he hung on the walls of his home according to careful methods of classification.[49]

García (Madrid: Ayuntamiento de Madrid-Fundación Caja Madrid, 2000), 183–98; Angela Delaforce, "From Madrid to Lisbon and Vienna: The Journey of the Celebrated Paintings of Juan Tomás Enríquez de Cabrera, Almirante de Castilla," *The Burlington Magazine*, 1249 (April 2007): 246–55; Leticia de Frutos, "Juan Gaspar de Cabrera, X Ammiraglio di Castiglia," in *Il collezionismo d'arte a Venezia. Il seicento*, eds. Linda Borean and Stefanie Mason (Venice: Fondazione di Venecia-Marsilio, 2008), 261–62. On the literary gatherings at "La Huerta" see Leticia de Frutos, "Arte, política y literatura entre Lisboa y Madrid: el marqués del Carpio, Ribeiro de Barros y la Corte madrileña (1667–1674)," paper presented at *Portugal, a Europa e Oriente—circulaçao de artistas, modelos e obras. Coloquio de Historia del Arte Fundaçao das Casas de Fronteira e Alorna*, Palacio de Fronteira, Lisbon, March 25, 2010 (forthcoming).

[47] "En que Su Magestad me hacía toda las honras que yo podia desear; y otra del Almirante, con la cual, con gran bizarría, me concedía la casa que le había, añadiendo vendría él mismo a recibirme, y ofrecérmela vocalmente." Mancini, *La verdad en su luz*, 276.

[48] "Casi a los últimos de la parte oriental de Madrid, ricamente alhajada, y adornada de tan grandísimo número de las más exquisitas y ricas pinturas de Europa, que puede preciarse de ser el más célebre depósito de las insignes fatigas de cuantos se singularizaron en aquella émula de la naturaleza. En este sitio triunfa el arte de los desdenes y sequedades del terreno, y no tiene flora en todo su imperio más amplio campo en que ostentar su soberanía. Pródiga Venecia de sus cristales, parece haberlos apurado para el lucimiento de esta fábrica, siendo tantos, que es toda luz sin aire, más que el ambiente, no teniendo los vientos más entrada en ella de las que se les quiere dar." Mancini, *La verdad en su luz*, 278–79.

[49] Today at the Prado and the Szépmüvészati Muzeum in Budapest, respectively; see Burke et al., *Collections*, 424n8–9.

La Huerta was an artistic oasis in 1670s Madrid. Perhaps only the collection of his son-in-law, don Gaspar de Haro y Guzmán (1629–87), the seventh marquis of Carpio, at his home, the San Joaquin Garden, along with the royal collections, could compete with the admiral's. One can imagine Maria in this setting, where she received visits only from her husband's family and a few ladies, and where the days passed slowly. On July 11 she wrote the *condestable* to tell him that she would soon enter the Los Angeles convent:

> Yesterday I had the fortune to kiss the hands of the king and queen, accompanied by the Duchess of Alburquerque and her daughter, and the Marquise of Alcañices, sister of the constable and mother to the wife of the admiral's son, and the Marquise of Santa Cruz, who are among those from whom I receive the greatest courtesies. I hope to soon enter the Convent of los Ángeles, given that the queen has ordered that they receive me, although as they have no spare room it is agreed that I will take a house alongside, half of which will serve for me as a cloister.[50]

Until then, Maria had spent nearly two months enjoying the admiral's company, as she told the *condestable*:

> He treats me as he would a wife; because he loves painting so much, it would go well if you could send him something worthy of both you and of him; if you could find an original by Rafael, I know he has none yet desires one greatly; but you must be sure of its provenance, as he knows painting extremely well and you must only send something perfect.[51]

At that time, the Admiral was expanding his collection and, thanks to his correspondence several years later with his agent in Venice, Vicente Colens, we know that he loved painting.[52] One indication of this is his interest in the works of Rafael. It does not appear the *condestable* sent him the work which

[50] "Hieri abbi la fortuna di baciar le mani alla regina et al re fu acompagnata la dalla duchessa d'Alburquerque, et la figlia queste, et la marquese Alcanisse, sorella del Contestabile et madre della moglie del figlio del Almirante et la marquese Sonta Croce, sono quelle di qui ricebo magior cortesie. Spero che presto entrarò nel convento delli Angeli, havendo la regina ordinato che mi ricevino, ma come non anno habitatione, ci conviene pigliar una casa vicino la quale servirà la meta per me che sarà clausura." AC, MMC-LOC, Madrid, July 11, 1674.

[51] "Il qual mi fa trattar e servire come si fosse sua moglie, e come si diletta molto di quadri, saria bene gli inviasse qualque cosa degno di voi e di lui; se poteste trovar qualque original de Raffaello, so che lui non ha e che lo desidera molto, ma avertite ciò que inviarete che sia originale, perche qui se ne intendono molto bene on (sic) non bisogna mandar miente cosa perfetta." Ibid.

[52] Leticia de Frutos, *Cartas del navegar pintoresco. Correspondencia de pinturas en Venecia* (Madrid: Machado Libros, 2011).

Maria requested, given that upon his death the admiral continued without a single painting by the artist from Urbino.

This was not the only painting Maria asked her husband for as a sign of gratitude toward the admiral. She also mentioned a *Venus* by Correggio, which was too expensive to purchase,[53] and, a year later, in June 1675, she reminded her husband that he should not delay in sending a painting she had requested because her host was "dying for painting."[54]

As she herself recounted in her memoirs, she had spent

> nearly two months in this delicious, pleasant retreat. Fearful that I am a burden on the Admiral, who treats me splendidly, and, at the same time, seeing that … he had not asked the queen to allow me to enter a convent, in accordance with her royal word, I went to speak with Her Majesty and begged her to ask the nuns at Santo Domingo el Real to receive me or give me a place to live between their convent and that of Los Angeles, of the Franciscan Order.[55]

The problem was for the nuns to allow Maria to live with them as the French ladies had done in Paris. For example, Madame de Sablé, whose fears and phobia of death led her to establish her "house" in the Port-Royal convent, and though her deep devotion led her to renounce many pleasures of life, she continued receiving ladies, gentlemen, and intellectuals.[56] This was an option adopted by some orders in France where they lodged women within their walls and gave them a certain degree of autonomy. That perhaps was the sort of life Maria was envisioning when she arrived in Madrid in 1674 and asked the queen to allow her to enter a convent.

At the end of August, Maria moved to a house adjacent to Santo Domingo el Real: "the most beautiful, grandest, and most famous," in the queen's words.[57] But she would not have the freedom to go to Los Angeles whenever she wanted.[58]

---

53 AC, MMC-LOC, Madrid, September 7, 1674.

54 "More per la pittura." Ibid., June 12, 1675.

55 "En este deleitoso, ameno retiro cerca de dos meses, al cabo de los cuales, temiendo ser de embarazo al Almirante, que me regalaba con harta esplendidez, y viendo por otra parte que llevado de su natural poco solícito, no instaba a la reina a que me permitiese entrar en un convento, conforme su real palabra, fui a hablar con su Majestad, y la supliqué mandase a las monjas de santo Domingo el Real me recibiesen, o me diesen una casa suya, situada entre su convento, y el de nuestra Señora de los Ángeles, de la orden de san Francisco." Mancini, *La verdad en su luz*, 279–80.

56 Craveri, *La cultura de la conversación*, 127ff.

57 "Più bello, più grande e più famoso." AC, MMC-LOC, Madrid, August 22, 1674.

58 It was not easy for Maria to move to the convent: "… io seguito a recivere i favori del signor Almirante a causa che mi viene impedita l'entrata nel monasterio degli Angeli per avere necesità d'una casa contigua nella quale vive una dama, e in breve, per ordine della Regina uscirá in tanto obteneme la licenza di poter uscir e di poter entrare nel convento di San Domingo il Reale, altre volte visitato dalle medesime moniche degli Angelo per esservi il passo dal uno altro monasterio." AC, MMC-LOC, July 25, 1674.

Indeed, it would not be easy for Maria to enjoy much freedom; they put a grille and a turnstile lock (*torno*) in her room, and the other side of her house was reserved for don Ferdinando Colonna, who kept a constant watch over her, and for her household.[59] Although in her letters she did not refer to her relations with the nuns, in her memoirs she wrote:

> At first I felt very awkward in this new home, as I did not speak Spanish nor did I know the customs of the country, and if it had not been for doña Vitoria Porcia Orosco, the marquis of Mortara's sister, who at that time was abbess and who spoke Italian reasonably well and was highly refined, I would have had some unhappy spells.[60]

Despite the situation, Maria received visitors, especially the imperial ambassador, Ferdinand Harrach, who had returned to court in 1673 and visited often, at times coinciding with the Venetian ambassador, the Admiral, or the nuncio.[61] They conversed with Maria in her room, perhaps about painting, though Maria certainly tried to take advantage of the circumstance to obtain good positions for her sons in Italy or Germany.

She also tried to obtain permission to leave the convent, as she had done in Turin, but Cardinal Altieri refused.[62] Soon she felt alone, and she even requested permission to return to Italy,[63] though she had no complaint about how the queen

---

[59] Mancini, *La verdad en su luz*, 281–82: "entré, pues, en esta clausura el postrer día de agosto, acompañada del nuncio, hoy cardenal Marescotti, del almirante, y del marqués de Alcañices, y porque yo no diese embarazo, ni le recibiese en mi nuevo domicilio, diéronme la casa contigua, a cuya mitad, destinada para mi cuarto, pusieron rejas y torno, quedando la otra para el abad don Fernando Colonna, y lo demás de la familia."

[60] "Halleme a los principios con harto embarazo en este nuevo hospedaje, por no saber la lengua española, ni las costumbres del país; y si no fuera por doña Vitoria Porcia Orosco, hermana del marqués de Mortara, entonces abadesa, la cual sabe muy razonablemente la lengua italiana, y es discreta en extremo, hubiera tenido malos ratos." Mancini, *La verdad en su luz*, 282.

[61] Österreichisches Staatarchiv-Allgemeines Verwaltungsarchiv, Familienarchiv, Harrach. Hs. 6, vol. 1, mentions visits to Maria on July 1, August 30, September 20, October 4, October 16, and December 27, 1674. My thanks to Laura Oliván for these references, which she used in "Escribir un diario y una hora de baño: vidas privadas en la corte de Madrid (1650–1680)," *Revista de historia moderna*, 30 (2012): 141–58. Oliván is preparing, with Bianca Lindorfer, an edition of the count of Harrach's diaries.

[62] "Me ne so perche il cardinal Altieri doppo averme concessa l'uscita a Turino me la voglia negare a Madrid." AC, MMC-LOC, Madrid, September 7, 1674.

[63] "… ieri scrivete me fixamente la vostra ultima resolutione circa Milano, acció possa partire prontamente, e se avesse dificulta in questa città tanto mi risolvero venire a Bologna per uscir di qua e star più vicino a voi, e non dipender da altri, che certo se vedesse lo stato che sto, e la poca consolatione che ricevo dal Almirante e altri parenti, vi darei pietà. Abiatela in consolarmi quanto prima e crediate che sara meglio per tutti. Adio sono vostra. MMC." AC, MMC-LOC, Madrid, December 25, 1675.

had treated her, a sign of the Colonna family's recognition in Spain.[64] But she missed her children. It had been two years since she had last seen them, and ever since she arrived in Madrid she continually asked her husband to allow one of them to visit her.[65] With the admiral's help, she had begun seeking a position for Marcantonio. There was a vacancy as general of the Flanders galleons and, once in Madrid, he could marry the daughter of a nobleman.[66] Throughout these months, Maria's letters show her looking out for her own interests but also those of her sons and her husband, who was concerned about settling the matter of precedency in the Festival of the Chinea in Rome and was trying to get an important post in Europe, perhaps at the German embassy.

But Maria tried to become integrated. She dressed in Spanish clothing, wearing the heavy farthingale (*guardainfante*), and even demanded that her servants do the same. Nanette, her personal servant, rebelled and refused to wear such an uncomfortable garment.[67] Maria asked her husband to obtain a copy of the *Virgin of the Rosary* for the convent's high altar, and she sent him the measurements. It did not matter if it was not an original, she wrote, as long as "you have some young man produce a good copy of the Madonna of the Rosary; a good imitation will suffice for the church."[68]

Nevertheless, she continued requesting that personal objects be sent to her from Italy and even France, things she needed for her personal care, hygiene, and beauty, such as Arrás powders or spermaceti (whale oil), which she requested several times for her hair.[69] She must have missed what she had left in her old dressing table when she prepared to greet the new queen formally, María Luisa of Orleans, and she had to ask the *condestable* to bring things to her when he came to Spain.[70]

---

[64] "Mi ritrovo tratando in mia casa en el convento di Santo Domingo per comando Della Regina della quale non posso abastanza lodarmi … e del modo che sono stata tratata da questa Maestà potrà conoscere Roma quanto stima si fa della vostra casa e persona." AC, MMC-LOC, Madrid, September 7, 1674.

[65] "Il signor Almirante continua con le medesime cortesie ne vuol permettere che mi faccia le spese da me, io mi sto con desiderio d'aver un figliolo." AC, MMC-LOC, Madrid, August 8, 1674.

[66] AC, MMC-LOC, Madrid, September 7, 1674.

[67] AC, MMC-LOC, Madrid, June 26, 1675.

[68] "Fate copiare da qualche giovane che imiti bene un bone [*sic*] originale della Madonna del Rosario perchè basta che comparisca per la chiesa."AC, MMC-LOC, Madrid, October 2, 1674.

[69] "Y no tengo polvo de arras ni blanco de ballena y así os pido me hagáis merced de enviarme uno y otro cuanto antes." AC, MMC-LOC, Madrid, March 17, 1677.

[70] AC, MMC-LOC, Madrid, October 7, 1679: "… quisiera me hiciérades el gusto de enviarme mis escritorios y tocador, por haber muchas cosas en ellos de que yo necesito para esta función del besamano de la reina, que será preciso luego que llega su Magestad sea yo una de las primeras en darla la obediencia." During the early modern age the practice was to use "dry hygiene," as it was believed that water made the body more vulnerable. This

We know that some of the things she requested from Italy that were quite valued in Spain, such as gloves, fans, and tiaras, were gifts for the ladies who visited her. She also gave presents to the nuns who lodged her, especially relics. The most special gifts were reserved for the queen.[71] That was the case with the agate medallion that her husband sent her and which struck her as the most precious of all. She also asked him to send money so she could buy chocolate for the queen, who was going to visit her at the convent during Lent.[72] Earlier the *condestable* had sent her a painting for the queen.[73]

Presents allowed her to establish relations with some ladies—indeed presents were necessary—but few ladies visited her.[74] Among those who did visit were the duchess of Alburquerque and the marquise of Alcañices with their daughters.[75] Above all she gave them fans, which were exquisite, especially those made in Naples. The women particularly prized fans scented with neroli oil (from oranges), while the men preferred those with flowers.[76]

Everything that came from Italy produced fascination in Spain, which she told her husband months before he arrived in Spain to become viceroy of Aragon, advising him what to bring to gain favor with the nobility. Short gloves and fans from Rome and Naples were greatly valued, she said:

> To satisfy your curiosity and to make sure you choose things that will be appreciated here I can tell you first that the gloves must be short and well-sewn. White gloves should smell of flowers, colored ones of cedar and *carambuco* [acacia farnesiana, or needle bush], and, as these are new, they also will be appreciated in *franchipán*

---

led to the use of hygenic substitutes, such as white under-garments. See María Ángeles Ortego Agustín, "Discursos y prácticas sobre el cuerpo y la higiene en la Edad Moderna," *Cuadernos de historia moderna*, Anejo [supplement] 8 (2009): 67–92.

71 "Per certo squesiti sono i ventagli chi avete fatto ma ce ne vorria una soma per regalare, io fino hora non ho que questo pero se vi è ocassione di mandarmi corone de cocco, qualquna di coralli de lapislazaro e medaglie d'argento, ventagli di Napoli, quelle palle a la nerola da tenere in saccoccia." AC, MMC-LOC, Madrid, September 7, 1674.

72 AC, MMC-LOC, Madrid, November 29, 1674.

73 AC, MMC-LOC, Madrid, May 29, 1675.

74 On January 23, 1675 she wrote to the *condestable*, "Ricordateve in cualque altra occasione di straordinario d'inviarmi guanti, ventagli e anche qualche paio da uomo perche gli ultimi già sono scorti." AC, MMC-LOC, Madrid, January 23, 1675.

75 "La duchessa d'Alburquerque e fliglia, donna Anna de la Queva, desideravano una licenza per entrar nel convento come anche il medesimo dessidera la marquese Alcanissas, et donna Teresa Enriquez sua fliglia, moglie del figlio del Almirante cercate d'averlo in ampia forma per esser signori che lo meritano per la loro qualità e per ricever da loro continuati favori per esser tutti suoi parenti stretti."AC, MMC-LOC, Madrid, July 11, 1674.

76 At this time both men and women used fans. Italy was one of the great producers of fans in the seventeenth century until being surpassed by France at the end of the century. It is no surprise that María requested these prized objects from Italy in order to present them as gifts in Madrid. AC, MMC-LOC, Madrid, March 21, 1675.

> [plumeria rubra]. For the king and don Juan [José of Austria] bring each a box full of gloves and orange blossom soap, but they should be the best ones from your house, and the boxes should be made of special materials. His Highness [Juan José] does not like receiving gifts and anything he gets he immediately sends to His Majesty, and thus you do not have to bring anything valuable. As for the fans, they should be large and painted in different styles, from Naples and Rome, and also in leather of many colors without paint. Also rosaries of various types, but neither too big nor too small, and many medallions. If you have a beautiful *escritorio* [portable desk] with a writing case [*escribanía*] and *bufete* you could bring them, as there will certainly be someone you can give them to ... God be with you and my sons as I wish and is fitting.[77]

Maria also sent presents from Spain. That might have been less a result of her assimilation than her need to remember and be remembered from afar. Because she needed not to forget her children, especially Pippo, she exchanged objects with her husband. She asked him for portraits of their children, which she mentioned in the letter shown at the beginning of this chapter. They arrived by Christmas 1674, though she had been asking for them since she had known she was going to Spain. In a letter from Antwerp castle on May 25, 1674, she said they should be sent to Barcelona, to the address Nanette had given to the countess Stella. In November he wrote that he had sent them in a box with gloves, powders, and *mantega* (*sic*).[78] In return, Maria sent him a portrait of herself to be given to her beloved Hortensia Stella, who was in charge of the children, "made by the most famous painter that there is; it is natural and picturesque, yet I know not whether it will be appreciated by the painters of Rome, although to me it seems fine; while it is somewhat late, tell me your opinion."[79]

---

[77] "Para satisfacer a vuestra curiosidad y para que acertéis la elección de las cosas que allá pueden estar más bien recibidas os diré que primero que los guantes han de ser cortos y sobre todo bien cosidos y el olor de los blancos de flores; los de color, de olor cedrado y otros de calambuco, los cuales por ser nuevos serán estimados también de franchipana, y para el Rey y don Juan [José de Austria] una caja cada uno llena de guantes y de jabón a la Nerola, pero que sean de los ricos y de su casa, advirtiéndoos también que las cajas sean de algún material y hechura extraordinaria que su Alteza no gusta de que le regalen y que todo lo que se le da lo envía al instante a su Majestad y así podéis excusar el traer regalos de valor, en cuanto a los abanicos que sean grandes y de diferentes maneras de Nápoles y de Roma pintados y también otros de cuero sin pintado de todos colores, rosarios de diferente género no muy gruesos, ni muy pequeños, y muchas medallas, si tenéis algún escritorio rico con su bufete y alguna escribanía podréis traerlas que no faltará a quien darlas y para aceite de baldina, mantega a la Nerola y blanco de ballena, y Dios os guarde en compañía de mis hijos como deseo y es menester."AC, MMC-LOC, Madrid, January 28, 1678.

[78] AC, MMC-LOC, Madrid, November 29, 1674. *Manteca* is lard.

[79] "Fatto fal più famoso pittore che sia e'certo che sta naturale e pittoresco non so se il suo modo sarà aprovato di pittori di Roma, ma a me par buono, fuor che è molto tardo ditemene il vostro parere." Ibid.

She warned him it would take time in arriving "because the painter is driving me crazy with his nonchalance."[80] Possibly this was Juan Carreño de Miranda, the best portrait painter at court, who was close to the admiral. In sharp contrast to the portraits of her in low-cut gowns that Voet had painted in Rome, the Spanish portrait surely would have been in the dress she ordered for her visit with the queen and that surprised everyone by being "so Spanish."

She also sent presents to her sons, especially tobacco pouches, boxes, and clay pots (*búcaros*), among which Pippo, her eldest son, whom she adored, could pick first.[81] She also sent a little box inside of which was a scented sponge for cleaning one's teeth in the morning, "which is very good."[82] To the *condestable* she sent shirts, ties, and French-style watches, and she sent her friends other valuable things such as "two fans in the special mail, one to give to the Duchess of Bassaniello and the other to the Princess of Sonnino; they are from India, highly prized and the most beautiful I have ever seen," or cedar fans for the countess Stella.[83]

Despite the good relations she had in Spain and the queen's regard for her, Maria was not integrated into Madrid life. Nevertheless, as in Italy before, though she was enclosed, she continued exercising a powerful attraction on those around her. Despite hiding herself in her clothes, she continued receiving orange blossom gloves and washing her hair with Arrás oils and powders.

Historians and contemporaries have pointed to this woman's extraordinary character and they have highlighted her errant, wandering nature. The circumstances in which she lived made her a witness to life at all the various courts she saw, most importantly those in Paris, Rome, and Madrid. Her memoirs, and especially her abundant correspondence with her husband, her son Pippo, and others of her contemporaries, are firsthand evidence of the differences among these courts. Of particular interest are her letters from Madrid from 1674 to 1702, when she observed one of the most fascinating late seventeenth-century decades, which historians have only recently begun to re-examine and rewrite.

---

80 "Perche il pittore mi fa desperare colla flemma che tiene." AC, MMC-LOC, Madrid, December 30, 1674.

81 "Vi ho mandato per Correggio gentilhuomo venetiano una scatola la quale si è caricato farmi capitar di Venetia per dove parte hora per le poste vi è dentro una corona, e una tabachiera per voi e un buccaro, due scatolette per i imiei ragazzi, Pippo capirá quello vole delle tre cose, e poi, gli altri. Vi è una scatola sembra gialla con dentro una sponja odorosa cola quale si metta [¿] i denti la mattina io me ne servo sempre, è molta bona, e con questo mi ricordo sempre vostra."AC, MMC-LOC, Madrid, October 18, 1674.

82 "é molto buona." Good teeth were considered a sign of beauty; as Baltasar Castiglione wrote, "están muy bien a una mujer los buenos dientes," in *El cortesano* (Madrid: CSIC, 1942), book 1, 82.

83 "Due ventagli per il corriero straordinario ne potrete dare uno alla duchessa di Bassaniello, e l'altro alla principessa de Sonnino, sono d'India stimatissimi e li più belli che siano mai visti."AC, MMC-LOC, Madrid, April 15, 1675.

The life Maria lived in Paris, Rome, and Madrid illustrates exceptionally well the dense network of cultural transfer that characterized the seventeenth century. The complexity of her personal relations allowed her to live at the court of the Sun King, to associate with one of the most emblematic Roman families in Papal Rome, and to live in convents in Paris, Turin, and Madrid. Her life differed greatly depending on where she was; her semi-cloistered existence at the court in Madrid was completely opposed to the life of liberty she had enjoyed in France and Italy. Her story is a rich example of the variety of ways that women lived at different European courts and the important role that women played as cultural mediators.

Bibliography

Álvarez y Baena, José Antonio. *Hijos de Madrid ilustres en Santidad, dignidades, armas, Ciencias y artes*. Madrid: B. Cano, 1789.

Aronson, Nicole. *Madame de Rambouillet ou la magicienne de la Chambre bleue*. Paris: Fayard, 1988.

Bady, René. "François de Sales maître d'honnêteté." *XVIIe siècle*, 78 (1968): 3–20.

Borello, Benedetta. *Trame sovrapposte: la socialità aristocratica e le reti di relazioni femminili a Roma (XVII–XVIII secolo)*. Naples: Edizione scientifiche Italiane, 2003.

Bouza, Fernando. *Imagen y propaganda. Capítulos de historia cultural del reinado de Felipe II*. Madrid: Akal, 1998.

Burke, Marcus B. "Private Collections of Italian Art in Seventeenth-Century Spain." PhD diss., New York University, 1984.

_____ , Peter Cherry, and Maria L. Gilbert. *Collections of Paintings in Madrid 1601–1755*. Los Angeles: Paul Getty Trust, 1997.

Castiglione, Baltasar. *El cortesano*. Madrid: CSIC, 1942.

Celletti, Vincenzo. *I Colonna principi di Paliano*. Milan: Ceschina, 1960.

Chartier, Roger, et al. *L'éducation en France du XVIe au XVIIIe siècle*. Paris: Sedes, 1976.

Checa, Fernando, and José M. Morán. *El coleccionismo en España: de la cámara de maravillas a la galería de pinturas*. Madrid: Cátedra, 1985.

Cholakian, Patricia Frances. *Women and the Politics of Self-Representation in Seventeenth-Century France*. Newark, DE: University of Delaware Press, 2009.

Colonna, Prospero. *I Colonna dagli origini agli inizi del secolo XIX*. Rome, 1927.

Coppi, Antonio. *Memorie colonnesi*. Rome: Salviucci, 1855.

Cousin, Victor. *La société française au XVIIe siècle d'après le Grand Cyrus de Mlle. de Scudéry*. 2 vols. Paris: Didier, 1852.

Craveri, Benedetta. *La civiltà della conversazione*. Milan: Adelphi Edizioni, 2001.

_____ . *La cultura de la conversación*. Translated by César Palma. Madrid: Siruela, 2007.

Delaforce, Angela. "From Madrid to Lisbon and Vienna: The Journey of the Celebrated Paintings of Juan Tomás Enríquez de Cabrera, Almirante de Castilla." *The Burlington Magazine* 1249 (April 2007): 246–55.

De Lucca, Valeria. "'Dalle sponde del Tebro alle rive dell'Adria': Maria Mancini and Lorenzo Onofrio Colonna's Patronage of Music and Theater between Rome and Venice (1659–1675)." PhD diss., Princeton University, 2009.

Feci, Simona. *Pesci fuor d'acqua: donne a Roma in età moderna: diritti e patrimoni*. Rome: Viella, 2004.

Fernández Duro, Cesáreo. *El último Almirante de Castilla: don Juan Tomás Enríquez de Cabrera*. Madrid: M. Tello, 1903.

Frutos, Leticia de. "Juan Gaspar de Cabrera, X Ammiraglio di Castiglia." *In Il collezionismo d'arte a Venezia. Il seicento.* Edited by Linda Borean and Stefanie Mason, 261–64. Venice: Fondazione di Venecia-Marsilio, 2008.

———. "Arte, política y literatura entre Lisboa y Madrid: el marqués del Carpio, Ribeiro de Barros y la Corte madrileña (1667–1674)." Paper presented at *Portugal, a Europa e Oriente—circulaçao de artistas, modelos e obras. Coloquio de Historia del Arte Fundaçao das Casas de Fronteira e Alorna*, Palacio de Fronteira, Lisbon, March 25, 2010.

———. *Cartas del navegar pintoresco. Correspondencia de pinturas en Venecia.* Madrid: Machado Libros, 2011.

Goldsmith, Elizabeth C. "Publishing the Lives of Hortense and Marie Mancini." In *Going Public: Women and Publishing in Early Modern France*. Edited by Elizabeth C. Goldsmith and Dena Goodman, 31–45. Ithaca, NY: Cornell University Press, 1995.

———. *Publishing Women's Life Stories in France, 1647–1720: From Voice to Print*. Aldershot and Burlington, VT: Ashgate, 2001.

———. *The Kings' Mistresses. The Liberated Lives of Marie Mancini, Princess Colonna, and her Sister Hortense, Duchess Mazarin.* New York: Public Affairs, 2012.

———, and Abby Zanger. "The Politics and Poetics of the Mancini Romance: Visions and Revisions of Louis XIV." In *The Rhetorics of Life-Writing in Early Modern Europe: Forms of Biography from Cassandra Fedele to Louis XIV*. Edited by Thomas F. Mayer and Daniel R. Woolf, 341–72. Ann Arbor: University of Michigan Press, 1995.

González-Palacios, Alvar. "Bernini as a Furniture Designer." *The Burlington Magazine*, 112, no. 812 (November 1970): 719–23.

Gozzano, Natalia. *La quadreria di Lorenzo Onofrio Colonna*. Rome: Bulzoni, 2004.

Graziosi, Elisabetta. "Lettere da un matrimonio fallito: Maria Mancini al marito Lorenzo Onofrio Colonna." In *Per lettera. La scrittura epistolare femminile tra archivio e tipografia. Secoli XV–XVII*. Edited by Gabriella Zarri, 535–84. Rome: Viella, 1999.

Harth, Erica. *Cartesian Women. Versions and Subversions of Rational Discourse in the Old Regime*. Ithaca, NY: Cornell University Press, 1992.

Livet, Charles-Louis. *Précieux et précieuses, caractères et moeurs littéraires du XVIIe siècle*. Paris: Didier, 1859.

Mancini, Maria. *La verdad en su luz o verdaderas memorias de María Mancini Colonna*. Zaragoza, 1677.

Mancini, Marie. *La Vérité dans Son Jour, ou les Véritables Mémoires de Mancini, Connétable Colonne*. Edited by Patricia F. Cholakian and Elizabeth C. Goldsmith. New York: Scholars' Facsimiles and Reprints, 1998.

Nikolenko, Lada. "The Beauties' Galleries." *Gazette des Beaux-Arts*, 67 (1966): 19–24.

_____. "The Source of the Mancini-Mazarini Iconography. Catalogue of Portraits in the Chigi d'Ariccia collection." *Gazette des Beaux-Arts*, 76 (1970): 145–58.

Ortego Agustín, María Ángeles. "Discursos y prácticas sobre el cuerpo y la higiene en la Edad Moderna." *Cuadernos de historia moderna*, Anejo [supplement] 8 (2009): 67–92.

Paschini, Pio. *I Colonna*. Rome: Istituto di Studi Romani, 1955.

Perey, Lucien. *Le roman du grand roi, Louis XIV et Marie Mancini, d'après des lettres et documents inédits*. Paris: Calmann Lévy, 1894.

Petrucci, Francesco. *Ferdinand Voet (1639–1689), detto Ferdinando de'ritratti*. Rome: Ugo Bozzi, 2005.

Portús, Javier. *La Sala Reservada del Museo del Prado y el coleccionismo de pintura de desnudo en la Corte española 1554–1838*. Madrid: Museo Nacional del Prado, 1998.

Portús, Javier. "El mecenazgo de la nobleza en Madrid durante el siglo XVII." In *El Madrid de Velázquez y Calderón. Villa y Corte en el siglo XVII*. Vol. 1, *Estudios históricos*. Edited by Miguel Morán and Bernardo José García, 183–98. Madrid: Ayuntamiento de Madrid-Fundación Caja Madrid, 2000.

Poumarède, Géraud. "Mazarin, marieur de l'Europe. Stratégies familiales, enjeux dynastiques et géopolitique au milieu du XVIIe siècle." *Dix-septième siècle*, 43, no. 2 (2009): 201–18.

Rowan, Mary. "Between Salon and Convent: Madame de Rohan, a Precious Abbess." *Papers on French Seventeenth-Century Literature*, 22 (1985): 191–207.

Sales, François de. *Introduzione alla vita devota*. Ed. Benedetta Papàsogli. Milan: Rizzoli, 1986.

Somaize, Antoine Baudeau de. *Le Grand Dictionnaire des prétieuses, historique, poétique, géographique*. Paris: Jean Ribou, 1661.

Tamburini, Elena. *Due teatri per il Principe. Studi sulla commitenza teatrale di Lorenzo Onofrio Colonna*. Rome: Bulzoni, 1997.

Vergara, Alejandro. "The Room of Rubens in the Collection of the X Almirante of Castille." *Apollo*, 396 (1995): 34–39.

Yetano Laguna, Isabel. *Relaciones entre España y Francia desde la paz de los Pirineos (1659) hasta la Guerra de devolución (1667): la embajada del Marqués de La Fuente*. Madrid: Fundación Universitaria Española, 2009.

Chapter 9

The Countess of Harrach and the Cultivation of the Body between Madrid and Vienna*

Laura Oliván Santaliestra

On February 2, 1716, Johanna Theresia Lamberg (see Figure 9.1), the countess of Harrach, died in her palace in Vienna at the age of 77. Two days earlier, after a seizure, the noble lady had ordered medicine from her pharmacy, the White Angel. This medicine included ambergris, the biliary secretion of sperm whales, which was used widely in medicinal perfumes in the seventeenth century.[1]

The countess had introduced the Viennese court to ambergris. She did the same with clay and chocolate; at the age of 77 she continued having a cozy cup of chocolate in the mornings and treating her afternoon guests to chocolate that she herself prepared following several recipes she had acquired during her visits to Madrid.[2] Johanna Theresia also had fragrant clay containers (*búcaros*, or *barros*) that held perfumed water; once the liquid was consumed, the container itself could be eaten bit by bit, a practice that was very common among the ladies of the court in Madrid and Lisbon.[3]

Chocolate, ambergris, and clay, whose taste and aroma further ennobled the bodies of the nobility, appear in the two handwritten recipe books in Spanish owned by the countess that she perhaps kept in one of the portable escritoires from America that she had brought with her from Madrid. These two books contain a dramatic and sometimes unbelievable history of cultural transfer.[4]

---

* This contribution has been translated from the Spanish by Ruth MacKay.

1 Susanne Claudine Pils, *Schreiben über Stadt. Das Wien der Johanna Theresia Harrach, 1639–1716* (Vienna: Franz Deuticke, 2002), 217.

2 Bianca Lindorfer, "Cosmopolitan Aristocracy and the Diffusion of Baroque Culture: Cultural Transfer from Spain to Austria in the Seventeenth Century" (PhD diss., European University Institute, Florence, 2009), 176.

3 On the *barros* and *búcaros* see Natacha Seseña, "El búcaro de las Meninas," in *Velázquez y el arte de su tiempo. V Jornadas de Arte*, ed. Centro de Estudios Históricos (Madrid: Alpuerto, 1991), 39–48; Alfred Morel-Fatio, "Comer barro," Melanges de philologie romane dédies a Carl Wahlund (Macon, 1896), 41–49; Carolina Michaelis de Vasconcellos, "Algunas palavras a respeito de púcaros de Portugal," *Bulletin Hispanique*, 7, no. 2 (1905): 140–96.

4 Österreichisches Staatsarchiv (hereafter ÖStA), Allgemeines Verwaltung Archiv (hereafter AVA), Familien Archiv (hereafter FA) Harrach Handschriften (hereafter Hs.) 482 and 30.

Figure 9.1 Unknown artist, Portrait of Johanna Theresia von Harrach, ca. 1680, oil on canvas, 94 × 74 cm. Rohrau Castle, Austria.

Johanna Theresia Lamberg (1639–1716), the daughter, wife, and mother of imperial ambassadors to Madrid, was an exporter of these products designed to enhance the body, which were developed at the Spanish court and highly valued in Vienna. Emperor Leopold I was very interested in promoting all things Spanish in order to strengthen his candidacy for the Spanish throne after marrying the *infanta* Margarita, Philip IV's daughter, in 1666. The dynastic marriage meant that Spanish culture lived moments of glory in the imperial capital.

Figures such as the countess of Harrach did not miss an opportunity to demonstrate their ties to Madrid, which in her case lasted throughout her life. She was born in 1639, daughter of Maximilian Lamberg. In 1644 she went with her family to Osnabrück, where her father, acting on behalf of Emperor Ferdinand III, negotiated the end of the Thirty Years' War.[5] In 1654 the family moved to Madrid, after Maximilian was appointed ambassador; Johanna was then 14, just five years younger than the queen, Mariana de Austria, the daughter of Ferdinand III. In 1649 Mariana had married her uncle, Philip IV, king of the Hispanic Monarchy. Mariana and Johanna became friends, and their friendship lasted all their lives. Johanna Theresia was named a lady-in-waiting, and in 1661 she married the count of Harrach, extraordinary imperial ambassador in Madrid. After the wedding, the couple returned to Vienna.

In 1665 Philip IV died, leaving his wife as regent during the minority of their son, Charles II, who was just four. The following year, the *infanta* Margarita, Mariana's daughter, married Leopold I. Johanna Theresia served as the new empress's protector, but the empress enjoyed her reign only briefly, dying in 1673. That same year the count of Harrach was appointed imperial ambassador in Madrid, and the couple spent three years there. Johanna Theresia returned to Vienna in 1676, and she and Queen Mariana corresponded by mail. In her late years, Johanna Theresia continued promoting Spanish culture and defending the Austrian side in the War of the Spanish Succession.

Johanna Theresia was closely involved in two important dynastic marriages: that of Mariana of Austria and Philip IV and that of Margarita with Leopold I. She lived in both Madrid and Vienna, making her an important cultural mediator between the two courts.

The Early Years, among *Búcaros* and Perfumes (1653–65)

Along with her mother, Judith Rebecca, and her sister Helena, Johanna was a frequent visitor at the court of Philip IV. The two Lamberg sisters had access to the most intimate quarters of the royal family thanks to the privileged position of imperial ambassadors in Madrid (which included access to the private apartments at the royal Alcázar) and the young queen's family links to the Austrians. The countess of Lamberg and her daughters regularly visited the

[5] Pils, *Schreiben über Stadt*, 18.

Alcázar to see Margarita, who was then four, and the visits were described in letters from the countess of Salvatierra, the little girl's governess (*aya*) in letters to Philip IV.[6] (Philip IV and his wife resided in different palaces throughout the year but because the *infanta* Margarita was still very young, she stayed in the Alcázar with her governess, who regularly wrote the monarchs about their daughter's health.)

The queen and Johanna Theresia grew closer, as they both were born in Central Europe and spoke German. We have little information about Johanna's early years in Madrid, but it seems she adapted perfectly to court life in the Alcázar. Appointed as one of the queen's ladies, she drank chocolate, wore the farthingale (*guardainfante*), dressed with perfumed gloves, ate typical Spanish dishes such as *olla podrida* and tomatoes, and, along with other ladies, enjoyed munching on *búcaros*, the clay pots filled with perfumed water that were believed to keep their skin pale and prevent melancholy and hemorrhages.

In 1659 Johanna Theresia met one of the noblemen in Madrid who knew the most about perfumes: the seventh duke of Montalto. A former viceroy of Sicily and Valencia, Montalto was in Madrid that year in the hope of obtaining a position at court. After failing in his attempt to draw closer to the king, and with his wife suffering from cancer, the duke withdrew to the home of his friend the marquis of Castelrodrigo.[7] After much uncertainty, Montalto was named master of the queen's horse (*caballerizo mayor*), a post he did not much like, as he thought that the ladies of the palace were not going to give him access to Philip IV.[8] During his first years in the queen's household, he assuaged his sorrows with the perfumes prepared by his chamber servant, Francisco.

We know nothing about the relationship between the duke of Montalto and Queen Mariana's favorite lady. It is likely that Johanna had the opportunity to sniff the scents that the queen's master sprinkled on his clothing, his skin, or his hair. They were both present at the queen's court ceremonies, though the duke's low estimation of the queen's attendants, whom he referred to as mules, would not have helped him win the confidence of Johanna Theresia, who had a privileged position among the sovereign's entourage.[9] The Dutch ambassador, Huygens Lodewijck,

---

6 Letter of the countess of Salvatierra to Philip IV, January 24, 1655, in *Correspondencia de la condesa de Salvatierra*, transcribed by the duke of Almazán (1933), unpublished, private collection, 206–07.

7 Duke of Montalto to the marquis of Castelrodrigo, March 14, 1659, Archivo Histórico Nacional (hereafter AHN), Estado, libro 104.

8 Alistair Malcolm, "Spanish Queens and Aristocratic Women at the Court of Madrid, 1598–1665," in *Studies on Medieval and Early Modern Women 4. Victims or Viragos?*, eds. Christine Meek and Catherine Lawless (Dublin: Four Courts, 2005), 160–67. I am grateful to César Esponda for this reference. See also Alistair Malcolm, "La práctica informal del poder. La política de la Corte y el acceso a la Familia Real durante la segunda mitad del reinado de Felipe IV," *Reales sitios*, 38, no. 147 (2001): 45.

9 Montalto to Castelrodrigo, November 18, 1659, AHN, Estado, libro 104, cited in Malcolm, "La práctica informal del poder," 48.

witnessed Johanna's preeminence during a public meal with Mariana on Christmas Day in 1660; following protocol, the queen was to remain silent during the meal, and the fact that she spoke with Johanna Theresia drew Lodewijck's attention: "While the queen ate, three of her ladies of honor stood before her. The one in the middle was the daughter of count Von Lamberg, the former ambassador of the emperor. From time to time, the queen spoke with her ...."[10] Johanna's face was powdered and she wore a broad *guardainfante*; at 21, she was a true Spanish lady.

The following year, in Madrid, she married Ferdinand Bonaventura, count of Harrach. The marriage was arranged by Queen Mariana of Austria, who was eight months pregnant when she attended the wedding of the two Austrian aristocrats in the palace chapel. Afterwards the newlyweds returned to the empire. Mariana gave birth to Charles II on November 6, 1661, and 10 days later she wrote her beloved "Juana" with the news.[11]

For Johanna, Vienna was a foreign city where, to quote Susanne Claudine Pils, she behaved as if she were a tourist.[12] But she was lucky, because her knowledge of Spain would prove very useful. Leopold I was keen to show an interest in Spain while he was negotiating his marriage to the *infanta* Margarita, who would inherit the Spanish throne if Charles II should die.

Johanna soon became a mother; in 1662 her son Karl was born, and in 1664 Josefa was born. That same year Leopold sent the count of Pötting to Madrid to speed up the marriage negotiations with Margarita. Meanwhile, Johanna's close and frequent correspondence with Mariana, which entitled her to consider herself as the queen's *valida*, or favorite, made her stock rise in Vienna.[13]

This may have prompted Leopold, who was Mariana's brother, to send Ferdinand Harrach to Madrid to present the wedding jewels to the imperial bride in fall 1665. The count left for Spain in July 1665. In October the countess of Harrach gave birth to her third child, Franz Anton. Without her husband, and with two other small children, Johanna concentrated on her health and that of her children. On November 4 she wrote to her husband asking that he bring her medical prescriptions from Madrid.[14] She also requested cookbooks and tomato and onion seeds because, she wrote, she knew how to prepare tomatoes "*a la española*."[15]

---

[10] Mauritus Ebben, ed., *Un holandés en la España de Felipe IV. Diario del viaje de Lodewijck Huygens, 1660–1661* (Madrid: Doce Calles, 2012), 188.

[11] Letter of Mariana de Austria to Johanna Theresia Gräfin von Harrach. Madrid, 12 November 1661, ÖStA, AVA-FA, Harrach, Karton (hereafter Kt.) 321, unfol.

[12] Pils, *Schreiben über Stadt*, 78.

[13] ÖStA, AVA-FA Harrach, Kt. 350, TZ 26, November 1665. Cited by Pils, *Schreiben über Stadt*, 20n36.

[14] Cited in Lindorfer, "Cosmopolitan Aristocracy," 179; letter of Johanna Theresia Harrach to Ferdinand Bonaventura Harrach, Vienna, November 4, 1665, Vienna, ÖStA, AVA-FA, Harrach Kt. 350, unfol.

[15] Ibid.

Harrach reached Madrid on November 5, 1665 at a very delicate moment, as Philip IV had died on September 17. Mariana had been named regent for her son, Charles II. On November 22 the count gave the jewels to Margarita, the future empress.[16] While in Madrid, Harrach joined the highest level of the nobility of the Hispanic Monarchy on December 3 when he was named a knight of the Order of the Golden Fleece; his wife and his uncle, Cardinal Adalbert of Harrach, had interceded on his behalf.[17] As an emissary of the emperor, a knight of the Golden Fleece, and husband to the queen's favorite, Harrach would have no difficulty fulfilling his wife's requests.

He began his return to Vienna on December 15. With him he carried chocolate for his wife and his father-in-law, probably along with the handwritten cookbook, *El libro de las conservas y de muchas otras recetas*, which today is in the Harrach archive in Vienna.[18] Manuscript 482 of the Harrach collection is a typical cookbook of the late sixteenth century with one difference: a considerable number of recipes concern the health and care of newborns and their mothers. This must have been useful for the countess, who found herself at a crucial, dangerous, and worrisome, albeit happy, time in her life. The author or collector of the recipes is anonymous, though it is very likely she was a nursemaid, a midwife, or a wet nurse. A recipe entitled "What I gave my children when they were born" indicates the compiler's knowledge of child care.[19]

There are numerous recipes for salves and poultices. During the baroque era, bodies were considered to be very porous, so remedies were often applied directly on the skin; in the case of postpartum women on the breast and belly.[20] Recipes for new mothers include poultice for the breasts made with chamomile oil and lily power; salves made with turpentine, powdered gum, cloves, nutmeg, amber, and musk; a remedy to halt lactation;[21] an omelet for the belly in case of postpartum pain;[22] ointment for the breasts made with parsley juice and green mint; and a

---

16 Miguel Nieto Nuño, ed., *Diario del conde de Pötting, embajador del Sacro Imperio en Madrid (1666–1674)* (Madrid: Ministerio de Asuntos Exteriores, 1990), vol. 1, 153.

17 ÖStA, AVA-FA Harrach, Kt. 338.

18 ÖStA, AVA-FA Harrach Hs. 482. On the taste for chocolate at the imperial court, see Bianca Lindorfer, "Discovering Taste: Spain, Austria, and the Spread of Chocolate Consumption among the Austrian Aristocracy, 1650–1700," *Food and History*, 1 (2009): 35–52.

19 Ibid., 34.

20 Sandra Cavallo, "Health, Beauty and Hygiene," in *At Home in Renaissance Italy*, eds. Marta Ajmar-Wollheim and Flora Dennis (London: Victoria and Albert Museum, 2006), 176.

21 ÖStA, AVA-FA Harrach Hs. 482, 61: "Soak Holland cloth in turpentine, make holes for the nipples and place a cloth over each breast. Then bind the breasts with another Holland cloth to cover the nipples. Maintain the binding in place until the mother no longer has milk. To remove the binding if it is stuck to the skin, soak it in oil to remove without discomfort."

22 Ibid., 35: "Rub the naval with theriac and place the omelet on the belly."

recipe for cloths used by the midwifes of Almansa, waxed to alleviate postpartum pain, made with grease from various animals including bears.[23]

Recipes for babies and children include "What I gave my children when they were born;[24] Aldonza de Bazán's recipe for thyme syrup for epilepsy in babies;[25] a mixture of chamomile oil, fennel juice, and powdered gum that was rubbed on baby girls' bellies when they had a stomach ache;[26] and a mixture made of violet oil, sweet almond oil, and chamomile oil for rubbing on boys' bellies when they had a fever or were constipated.[27]

There also were recipes made with exotic ingredients from America, which conferred great prestige on recipes. Liquid from the guayacán (*lignum vitae*) tree from Mexico, also known as *palo santo*, was used to cure infectious diseases such as syphilis, and another ingredient was known as Drago blood.

The courtly source and audience of the book is evident; there are references to perfumed gloves and aristocratic sweetmeats, along with the ingredients from America. Certain recipes suggest royal provenance, such as "the ointment used by King Alonso" and "water for cleaning His Royal Highness's teeth."

After receiving this book, the countess of Harrach and her acquaintances began to make the recipes, which helped raise the Harrachs' prestige in Viennese court circles. Johanna knew that if they were to triumph, she would have to know the secrets of Spanish culture that were about to arrive with the marriage of Leopold I and Margarita.

The new empress arrived with her entourage in 1666, and the countess received her with great joy. Mariana of Austria had written to Johanna asking her to let her know everything that happened to her daughter.[28] To please the empress, the little girl whom she had played with in the Alcázar, the countess consulted the *Libro de las conservas y muchas otras recetas*.

The Recipe Book of the Seventh Duke of Montalto, Cardinal Moncada (1666–73)

While the countess made these recipes in Vienna, the culture of perfumes blossomed in all its splendor at the court of Madrid. Norbert Elias wrote that the senses of smell

---

[23] Ibid., 64.

[24] Ibid., 30. "If the baby is born strong, do not put him to the breast for six or seven hours. During this time, every so often give him a little of the following syrup on your finger. This will dispel phlegm, and the milk will be received into a clean stomach. Give the baby this syrup for eight or nine days after birth and always before feedings."

[25] Ibid., 9.

[26] Ibid., 86.

[27] Ibid., 87.

[28] ÖStA, AVA-FA Harrach, Kt. 321, May 5, 1666.

and taste lost influence during the early modern age in favor of sight.[29] Though it is true that sight gained in importance, it does not appear that smell and taste ceased being important in court society. During the second half of the sixteenth century, the use of perfumes and perfumed objects grew considerably in Southern Europe. Evelyne Welch has attributed this trend to new commercial practices and the ideas about perfumes that circulated thanks to the printing press and practices of cultural transfer.[30] Perfume bestowed elegance upon the person who wore it, and additionally it had medicinal properties. In the seventeenth-century Madrid court, handkerchiefs, dresses, rooms, curtains, fans, gloves, hair, and jewels were all scented. Ladies and gentlemen both burned perfumed substances in their rooms and refreshed spaces with clay containers of scented water. They perfumed their bodies on the outside but also on the inside, because perfumes were edible; that was the case with scented clay or amber and musk paste, a sweet substance that the nobility loved. To perfume oneself was an act of nobility, a gesture of moral and corporal cleanliness, a cure for melancholy and other diseases that traveled through the air and could easily attack porous, courtly bodies.

The duke of Montalto, the queen's master of the horse who described his lady's ladies as mules, was a true expert in matters of scent. Since the countess of Harrach had left Madrid, the duke had risen; in 1663 he was named the queen's chief steward (*mayordomo mayor*), and in 1665 his son married the daughter of Charles II's governess (*aya*), one of the queen's favorites. The death of Philip IV that same year had turned the queen into regent, which favored the duke, because now he was steward to a regent. The following year he was appointed councilor of state, and in 1667 he was anointed a cardinal, and from then on he would be known as Cardinal Moncada.

Now a man of the church, the duke had not renounced the hedonism of perfumes. His chamber servant and perfumer, Francisco, had copied down many perfume recipes with his master, and a copy of this book years later would end up in the hands of the countess of Harrach. For the time being, Cardinal Moncada amused himself in the vaulted area (*bóveda*) beneath his house making aromatic substances. One of his close friends, the marquis of Grana, visited him in the summer of 1668 and left the following description:

> [It was] a sort of subterranean area that the cardinal had carved out of his house in Madrid as a place where he and his friends could while away the afternoon hours. There was scarce difference with a lady's boudoir; white walls decorated with mirrors, a large marble table with vases of fresh, fragrant flowers, and underneath there were basins filled with sedge grass, which was marvelous.

[29] Norbert Elias, *El proceso de la civilización* (Mexico City: Fondo de Cultura Económica, 1988), 241.

[30] Evelyne Welch, "Scented Buttons and Perfumed Gloves: Smelling Things in Renaissance Italy," in *Ornamentalism. The Art of Renaissance Accessories*, ed. Bella Mirabella (Ann Arbor: University of Michigan Press, 2011), 13–39.

> Against the main wall stood an enormous armoire with several shelves, one of them containing *búcaros* from India, another from Portugal, another of porcelain, all filled with oils and scented water that the cardinal knew how to make. There were Holland linen curtains and a piece of hide on the bed, tanned with amber.[31]

In this *bóveda* Cardinal Moncada met with his friends to chat and have a good time. When visitors came, his perfumer prepared the room:

> At two or three in the afternoon, when the cardinal awoke, his servant Francisco went downstairs to the *bóveda* with two or three silver syringes in his hand; one was filled with oil and the others with delicious flavored waters. Water was sprinkled throughout the room, creating a constant fog that was truly delightful. Then the cardinal came downstairs, accompanied by one or two friends whom he wanted to converse with, such as the marquis of Grana; the first time he invited him there, in the summer of 1668, the cardinal said, "So, here we can speak softly of the whole wide world."[32]

The marquis of Grana was among the emperor's most powerful aides, and supposedly he was in Madrid to conspire against Father Nithard, the Austrian Jesuit who was the favorite of Queen Mariana.[33] The same year he arrived so did Cosimo de' Medici (Cosimo III), who came with Lorenzo Magalotti (1637–1712), a Florentine diplomat, poet, and scientist.[34] Magalotti was fascinated by perfume, and while he was in Madrid he obtained recipes from Castelrodrigo and Cardinal Moncada, though he did not get the book written by the latter's perfumer, Francisco.[35]

Moncada participated in the plot against Nithard that lasted from fall 1668 to March 1669, and as a result he fell out of the queen's favor. His last years were sad and solitary; alone in his *bóveda*, he sniffed perfumes, the very scents that had enabled his political rise, though, according to Francisco, he could not bear the smell of amber.[36] After the cardinal died, in May 1672, Francisco went to work for the cardinal's son, the eighth duke of Montalto, who lived in Brussels. There, in 1673, he coincided with Magalotti.

---

31 Lorenzo Magalotti, *Lettere odorose (1693–1705)* (Milan: Valentino Bompiani, 1943), 36.

32 Ibid.

33 On Grana and his mission in Madrid see Rafaella Pilo Gallisai, "La correspondencia del cardenal Moncada y la conjura contra Nithard," in *La Dinastía de los Austria. Las relaciones entre la monarquía católica y el Imperio*, eds. José Martínez Millán and Rubén González Cuerva (Madrid: Polifemo, 2011), vol. 2, 1080.

34 On Magalotti see Stefano Miniati, "Lorenzo Magalotti: rassegna di studi e nuove prospettive di ricerca," *Annali di storia di Firenze*, 5 (2012): 31–4.

35 Magalotti, *Lettere odorose*, 93.

36 ÖStA, AVA-FA, Harrach Hs. 30, 10v.

From Brussels, Montalto sent Cosimo III some gifts created by Francisco, which was how Magalotti became friends with the perfumer.[37] Both shared an appreciation for scents. Every afternoon, Francisco went to Magalotti's house to create something refined: perfumed gloves, scented waters, or aromatic sweets. Their friendship developed, and one day Francisco brought him his old boss's book of recipes and offered to make him a copy. Magalotti instantly accepted the offer, but before dictating the recipes, Francisco gave him a true lesson in perfume-making:

> You can be sure that scents will resemble perfumers. When the perfumer works, his sleeves are rolled up and his hair is pushed back. When he finishes he becomes a gentleman as he takes the perfumed gloves or the *cazoleta* [a kind of perfume] to the cardinal, the duke, or my lady the duchess ... Sir, it is all glitter, grandeur, and mystery.

They entered the antechamber, and Francisco began dictating the recipes, one by one. Magalotti wrote them down, adding the advice and notes that Francisco made for each one: "This one is worthless, this one I did not like and would not even try, here a half a dram is enough ...."[38]

The copy that Magalotti made that afternoon is the first version of Cardinal Moncada's recipe book in the Harrach archive in Vienna.[39] It contains more than 50 recipes for perfumed waters (amber, musk, rose, orange blossom, etc.); perfumed tablets that were burned; amber, musk, and clay sweets to eat; aromatic waters to drink; perfumed pastes that were set into jewelry; sedge-grass water for porcelain containers; aromatic vinegar; perfumed gloves; and scents for clay jugs. Along with all the recipes are marginal comments dictated by Francisco: "I don't think this one is good";[40] "nothing special";[41] "this much rose does not seem right to me";[42] "I've made this many times";[43] "this one really stinks."[44] Magalotti later added three Italian recipes at the end of the book.

---

[37] Magalotti, *Lettere odorose*, 37.

[38] Ibid., 103.

[39] ÖStA, AVA- FA Harrach Hs. 30. For more on the book, see Laura Oliván Santaliestra and Rafaella Pilo, "Recetario en busca de dueño: Perfumería, medicina y confitería en la Casa del VII duque de Montalto (1635–1666)," *Cuadernos de historia moderna*, 37 (2012): 103–25. In that article we erroneously attribute the collection to Dr. Gabino Farina. Pilo later discovered documentation pointing to the error; in fact it was Francisco who collected them. Magalotti did not remember Francisco's last name; he said it might have been Mercader, but he was not sure.

[40] ÖStA, AVA- FA Harrach Hs. rr, 30, 31v.

[41] Ibid., 31

[42] Ibid., 28.

[43] Ibid., 27v.

[44] Ibid., 24v.

Francisco had copied down all the recipes from 1635 to 1666 as he traveled with the seventh duke of Montalto to Rome, Palermo, Cartagena, Zaragoza, Valencia, and Madrid. Among those who offered up their secrets were the duchess of Terranova, the nuns at the Ascension convent in Palermo, the duke of Nájera, the marquise of Castelrodrigo, the duchess of Montalto, Juan Francisco Andreu (servant to Sor Ana Margarita of Austria, a nun at the Incarnation convent), and famous perfumers including the glover Antonio de Cobos and Francisco Vicar.[45]

And while the Florentine Magalotti wrote down recipes in Brussels in 1673, that same year the life of the count and countess of Harrach was about to change.

The Count and Countess of Harrach, Imperial Ambassadors in Madrid (1673–77)

In early 1673 Leopold I appointed the count of Harrach to be his ambassador in Madrid.[46] The appointment, partly the result of the friendship between the countess and Queen Mariana, caused great joy in the household, only to be quickly followed by the sudden death, on March 12, of Empress Margarita.[47]

Harrach's predecessor, the count of Pötting, heard the sad news in his Madrid house in April, and immediately went to the palace. Father Juan Martínez was the one chosen to tell Mariana that her 19-year-old daughter had died. The queen collapsed in tears, having lost her little girl who so loved chocolate and sipped cool water from perfumed *búcaros*.[48]

Johanna Theresia must have greatly lamented Margarita's death, for she too had a daughter. That unhappy summer, the count and countess and their children traveled to Madrid, and they arrived on October 26. The count and countess of Pötting greeted them, and the countess gave Johanna Theresia an *arroba* of chocolate—a huge amount, equivalent to 12 kilos—with many cups (*jícaras*) and a variety of *búcaros*.[49]

The countess of Harrach lost no time in visiting Queen Mariana. On November 26 she and her daughter Josefa went to see her, carried in a litter. Johanna Theresia

---

45 Magalotti, *Lettere odorose*, 103.

46 Nieto Nuño, *Diario del conde de Pötting*, vol. 2, 322.

47 On Margarita in Vienna, see Laura Oliván Santaliestra, "Giovanne d'anni ma vecchia di giudizio: la emperatriz Margarita en la corte de Viena," in *La dinastía de los Austria*, eds. José Martínez Millán and Rubén González Cuerva, vol. 2, 837–908.

48 On *búcaros*, see the letter of Margarita to the countess of Salvatierra, April 19, 1659, in duke of Almazán, *Correspondencia*, 374 (see n6). See also Laura Oliván Santaliestra, "My Sister is Growing up very Healthy and Beautiful, She Loves Me": The Childhood of the Infantas María Teresa and Margarita María at Court," in *The Formation of the Child in Early Modern Spain*, ed. Grace Coolidge (Burlington, VT: Ashgate, 2014), 165–88.

49 Nieto Nuño, *Diario del conde de Pötting*, vol. 2, 338.

dressed in the Spanish style with a broad *guardainfante*.[50] The queen, dressed in mourning, received her old friend, dressed in Spanish style just as she had been 12 years earlier when Johanna Theresia left the court. Mariana appointed Josefa a *menina* and gave her a diamond watch. The 14-year-old girl would have reminded the queen of her daughter and of Johanna when she entered court, and Mariana fondly called her "Pepa."[51]

The countess of Harrach spent her time as ambassador helping her husband in his diplomatic tasks; she visited the queen at the palace, mediated in the sale of offices, wrote letters, and paid visits. Visiting and receiving was an art among Spanish ladies. Visits were paid in the afternoon, after the main meal. The servant would announce the visitors and lead them through a variety of rooms until reaching the place where the lady of the house awaited: a platform (*estrado*) covered with rugs and pillows where the ladies gathered, in Moorish style, to spend the afternoon sharing stories and secrets. Mariana de Carvajal, a seventeenth-century writer, described the scene in her book *Navidades en Madrid y Noches entretenidas*: "Rugs, pillows, embroidered chairs, large sumptuous escritoires, two silver braziers surrounded with fragrant amber bouquets …."[52]

The platform might be in a bedroom, even the hostess's bedroom, in which case it was referred to as the platform of affection (*estrado del cariño*), because it was there that the most intimate and affectionate visits took place.[53] There the women talked, gossiped, told stories, played the harp, sang, danced, performed theatrical works, read aloud, burned perfumes in the brazier, and relished the aromatic waters in the *búcaros*.[54] When it came time for the late afternoon snack, the lady of the house might offer treats including chocolate, sweets, candies, drinks, and clay. After tasting it all, the women might exchange recipes and gifts: amber-scented gloves, sweets, *búcaros*, strings of candy, even birds from the Indies. The countess of Harrach had learned these customs when she served Queen Mariana, and after returning to Vienna as a married woman she continued meeting with her closest friends in the bedroom and drinking chocolate in bed as she received guests.[55]

Between bits of clay, sips of chocolate, and flowing ambergris, women also negotiated. Aside from pleasantries, the countess of Harrach's receptions had

---

[50] Ferdinand Mencik, ed., *Tagebuch über den Aufenthalt in Spanien in den Jahren 1673–1674* (Vienna: Selbstverlag, 1913), 33.

[51] For a portrait of Josefa at 11 years of age, see Anonymous, *Doña Josepha de Harrach, Menina de la reina dona Mariana de Austria a la edad de once anos*, 1674, Schloss Hrádek, private collection.

[52] Mariana de Carvajal, *Navidades en Madrid y Noches entretenidas* (Seville: Junta de Andalucía, 2010), 23.

[53] Carmen Abad, "El estrado: continuidad de la herencia islámica en los interiores domésticos zaragozanos de las primeras cortes borbónicas," *Artigrama*, 18 (2003): 377.

[54] Sofía Rodríguez Bernis, "Cómo se sentaba la gente en el siglo XVI," *Associació per a l'estudi del moble* (2012): 70–71.

[55] Pils, *Schreiben über Stadt*, 219. ÖStA, AVA- FA, Harrach, Kt. 350, TZ, July 17, 1665.

a political context. On May 30, 1674 she received the duchess of Nájera, who arrived with a bird from the Indies and who wished to persuade the countess to mediate the sale of an office: the position of viceroy of the Indies, which her husband, the duke of Nájera, wanted to purchase.[56]

The countess of Harrach also received other ladies of the palace: on May 24, 1675 the duchess of Medinaceli, whose husband was Charles II's *sumiller de corps*, visited. In early 1676 the duchess of Alburquerque and her daughter, Ana de la Cueva, visited the countess, who received them in her bedroom. The duchess of Alburquerque was married to the chief steward of Charles II, who, in December 1676, had attained his majority. Even so, the queen mother, Mariana, continued governing, and her favorite was still the countess. The duchess of Medinaceli took advantage of her visit to relay palace news from her husband to the count of Harrach.[57] In January 1676 the marquise de la Fuente visited; her husband was a member of the Council of State and the former ambassador to France.[58] The queen's favorite, Fernando de Valenzuela, who was the countess's rival, had been appointed Captain General of Granada, which made it necessary for him to be in Granada from February to May 1676. During this time the countess served as a mediator in the sale of offices.[59]

While he was ambassador to the Spanish court, the count of Harrach grew fond of chocolate, mulled wine, and lemonade, all of which he consumed daily. At auctions, in addition to buying paintings, sculptures, theatrical scripts,[60] and novels[61] he also bought receptacles, such as silver cups (*jícaras*) in which to serve hot chocolate.[62] At the auction of the estate of the deceased count of Peñaranda,[63] Harrach fancied several *chocolateras*, and in the Valenzuela auction (Valenzuela had by then been exiled), he bought *búcaros* for perfumes.[64] Sometimes it was the countess who visited auctions, searching for items for her cushioned platform.

---

[56] Based on notes by the count of Harrach in his diary on May 30 and June 2, 1674. Mencik, *Tagebuch über den Aufenthalt*, 96.

[57] ÖStA, AVA-FA Harrach 6/2. January 23, 1676.

[58] Ibid., January 7, 1676.

[59] Antonio Álvarez-Ossorio Alvariño, *La república de las parentelas. La corte de Madrid y el estado de Milán durante el reinado de Carlos II* (Madrid: Universidad Autónoma de Madrid, 1995), 97.

[60] The couple loved theater, especially the plays of Calderón de la Barca, whose works the countess read aloud. See Pils, *Schreiben über Stadt*, 19. For manuscript copies of Calderón's scripts belonging to the countess, see Jaroslava Kasparova, "Redescubrimiento de dos manuscritos, obra de Pedro Calderón (1600–1681) procedentes de la antigua biblioteca del Castillo de Mlda Vozica," in *Calderón. Protagonista eminente del barroco europeo* (Kassel: Reichenberger, 2002), vol. 2, 21–28.

[61] ÖStA, AVA-FA Harrach Hs. 6/2.

[62] Ibid., 293. January 6, 1676.

[63] Ibid., 231. February 13, 1676.

[64] Ibid., 284. April 24, 1677.

The countess of Harrach ended her sojourn in Madrid on September 3, 1676. That morning, the count bade farewell to her and their children, for they were returning to Vienna. The reasons for her early return are unknown. During the summer of 1676 Madrid was the site of political conspiracies and near civil war as factions tried to push Valenzuela and the queen mother from power and replace them with Don Juan, Carlos II's half-brother.[65] Perhaps it was this political instability that led the count to suggest that his family return to the empire. The count stayed in Madrid until the end of 1677.

Before the countess left, Mariana of Austria gave her friend several presents for the imperial family.[66] For her brother, Leopold, six paintings; for Empress Eleonore (Leopold's new, third wife) a dozen ambergris fans; for the Archduchess Maria Antonia, her granddaughter, a diamond and wooden (*calophyllum*) clock with a portrait inside of Charles II (Mariana hoped to marry her son to her granddaughter), and for her sister, the queen of Poland, amber tanned leather and a wooden rosary.

Her carriages full of presents, the countess and her children left Madrid on September 3, 1676.[67] They were accompanied by several servants, among them a French cook whom her husband had hired.[68] The count wanted his wife to arrive in Vienna prepared to face a new era at the imperial court, where French fashions were now on the rise. Johanna accepted the French cook against her will, especially because she still preferred Spanish food, but she knew that her family stood to gain if she served her Viennese guests French food. She had to adapt to new cultural trends, and for that reason they stopped in Lyon so she could buy clothes and accessories to wear when she met the new empress, Eleonore Magdalena of Neuburg.[69]

The Countess of Harrach in Vienna: Cultural Memories, Castilian Legacies (1677–1716)

On November 27, 1676, Johanna and her children reached Vienna after a three-month journey.[70] The popularity of Spanish culture clearly had diminished since Empress Margarita's death three years earlier, and the countess was well prepared,

---

65 On this issue, see Gabriel Maura y Gamazo, duque de Maura, *Vida y reinado de Carlos II* (Madrid: Aguilar, 1990), 177–81.

66 Handwritten list by the queen of things she sent with the countess. ÖStA, AVA-FA Harrach, Kt. 321.

67 On the journey see Elke Meyer, "Die Reisetagzettel der Johanna Theresia Gräfin Harrach" (master's thesis, University of Vienna, 2013).

68 Lindorfer, "Cosmopolitan Aristocracy," 186.

69 Ibid., 168n653. Also cited in Pils, *Schreiben über Stadt*, 242. ÖStA, AVA-FA Harrach, Kt. 350, Tagzettel, December 9, 1676.

70 Pils, *Schreiben über Stadt*, 89.

making good use of the clothes she had bought in Lyon. In early December she appeared in court dressed in the French style. That month she wrote to her husband, still ambassador in Madrid: "I am quite French, though that may surprise you."[71] Johanna had to give into the ways of court, regardless of her preferences for Spanish things. It was the same for her husband, who, though he dressed in French fashions, remained a "Spanish" gentleman, and two of her children, who, for a carnival organized by the Palffys family, dressed as a Spanish peasant (in the case of Karl) and a Spanish dancer (in the case of Josefa). Both spoke Spanish; Karl studied with the Jesuits, and Josefa played the harp, an instrument typical of the *estrado* setting.[72]

The falling-out with the French cook came quickly.[73] Johanna wrote to her husband complaining that the cook was dirty and a thief, but her husband ignored her and sent another French cook in June 1677.[74] He also employed a French barber and coachman. Johanna's father, Maximilian Lamberg, who was part of the pro-Spanish faction at the Viennese imperial court, said to his daughter, "Your lord has Frenchmen as servants, coachmen, chamberlains, and barbers; you had better take care that he does not turn into a Frenchman himself."[75]

But there was no danger of Harrach becoming French, as it was a facade, and he continued leaning toward Spain. He arrived in Vienna in late 1677 with a collection of Spanish paintings, including an *Immaculate Conception.*[76] Leopold appointed the count—somewhat Frenchified, very cosmopolitan, but still essentially Hispanic—as his master of the horse in 1677.[77]

Lorenzo Magalotti, the Venetian traveler, scientist, and diplomat in the employ of Cosimo III de' Medici, who had obtained a copy of Montalto's book of perfume recipes, had been appointed to the court in 1675. He and the count and countess of Harrach had the same doctor, Franz Billiote, which led to a close friendship between the two parties.[78] The count of Harrach's private correspondence includes a few letters from Magalotti, who in 1678 returned to Florence, from where he wrote of his interest in learning about perfumes from "the countess's perfumer." In exchange, Magalotti offered the count a copy of the Montalto recipe book, an offer that bore fruit only eight years later.[79] The reason for the delay was that he could not find someone capable of copying the book, which was in Spanish; he

---

71 Lindorfer, "Cosmopolitan Aristocracy," 194.

72 Pils, *Schreiben über Stadt*, 155.

73 Lindorfer, "Cosmopolitan Aristocracy," 187.

74 Ibid.

75 Ibid., 188; and Pils, *Schreiben über Stadt*, 124.

76 Javier Ignacio Martínez del Barrio, "La colección de la pintura española de los Harrach," *Anales de historia del arte* (2008): 291–306.

77 Mencik, *Tagebuch über den Aufenhalt*, 3.

78 Cesare Guasto, "Saggi di cartegi diplomatic del Conte Lorenzo Magalotti (1675–1678), *Giornali storico degli archive toscani*, 5 (1861): 263.

79 ÖStA, AVA-FA Harrach, Kt. 279. 13. Magalotti to Harrach, Florence, July 12, 1678.

did not consider it dignified to copy the book himself.[80] Finally, he sent a copy in December 1686 after having asked a friend of a Florentine marquis to copy it.[81]

Years later, in his *Lettere odorose* (1695 and 1705), Magalotti wrote that the countess of Harrach had introduced the Viennese court to the practice of filling clay *búcaros* with perfumed waters:

> At the court of Vienna I saw ladies carrying these *búcaros* made in Estremoz [Portugal] filled with water, fresh carnations, and ambergris ... and, thinking of the countess of Harrach, I believe it was she who introduced these *búcaros* at court, a custom she had learned in Spain when her father and later her husband were ambassadors.[82]

Starting in 1686, Johanna Theresia created some of the perfumes in her recipe book, using the suggestions in the margins written by Francisco, Cardinal Moncada's perfumer. Perhaps she made *cazoleta de monja*, with *búcaros* and amber. The recipe said to cake the clay pots in amber to scent them and then fill them with amber and rose water and bits of clay. According to Francisco's notes, this produced "a lovely fragrance for a small room," and he suggested drinking "the most delicious water with Córdoba amber, and the water in which the *búcaros* are soaked to scent them should be well water."[83]

Despite allowing a portrait to be painted of her in the French style, Johanna never abandoned her links to the Madrid court.[84] She continued writing to Queen Mariana of Austria, who, after a period of disgrace and exile in Toledo (1676–79), returned to the court in Madrid and enjoyed full powers as queen mother. She wrote 141 letters to the countess between 1680 and 1696, when she died.[85]

The countess of Harrach also instructed her daughters in Spanish culture. The eldest, Josefa, was the most Spanish, as she had learned the Spanish language in the three years she spent at the Madrid court as *menina* to the regent queen (1673–76) and could read and sing in Spanish.[86] Though she learned French, she never ceased writing in Spanish. In a portrait of her painted in 1680, Josefa wears Spanish-style jewelry that her mother surely had acquired in Madrid: a string of pearls, a Spanish diamond brooch, and a diamond watch that possibly was the one Mariana had given her upon appointing her *menina* in 1673.[87] In displaying

---

80 Ibid., November 26, 1678.

81 Ibid., December 3, 1686. This is the copy in ÖStA, AVA-FA Harrach Hs. 30.

82 Magalotti, *Lettere odorose*, 35.

83 ÖStA, AVA-FA Harrach, Kt. 30. Cazoleta de monja: "My lady the marquise of Castelrodrigo gave me this recipe in Rome in 1635."

84 Pils, *Schreiben über Stadt*, 243.

85 ÖStA, AVA-FA Harrach, Kt. 321–22.

86 Pils, *Schreiben über Stadt*, 149.

87 Eszter Valyi, "Schmuk und Kleidung auf den Damenporträts der Ahngengalerie Harrach. Ein Beitrag zur Bestimmumg Baroker Adelporträts" (master's thesis, University of Vienna, 2008).

her Spanish jewelry, Josefa wished to show that she was part of a family of imperial ambassadors, a gesture both of prestige and of social advancement.

Josefa later married the count of Kuenburg, in 1682, and went to live in Salzburg, from where she corresponded in Spanish and French with her parents and her brother Aloys, a future imperial ambassador. Of the 34 letters that survive,[88] Josefa wrote 30 to her father, two of which are in French and 28 in Spanish.[89] Three letters to her brother are in French, a sign that French was in ascendance. The one remaining letter is to her mother, in Spanish.

The affection between Josefa and her mother is clear in these letters. In April 1682 the countess of Kuenburg wrote to her father, "my mother left yesterday at 12:30 after eating and she asked me to send you this letter. I am alone and so sad without her."[90] In 1686, when she was pregnant, she wrote to her father, "I humbly beg your excellence to allow my mother to come here and help with the childbirth. I hope your excellence will not deny me this favor."[91] Josefa knew her mother was an expert in home medicine; the countess had been closely involved with the pregnancies of Empress Eleonore and with Archduchess Maria Antonia, and she was familiar with medicinal remedies for newborns and their mothers.[92] That is why Josefa wanted her by her side as she endured the physical pain and the emotions of childbirth. Perhaps the countess prepared a special omelet against after-pains or the cloths used by the midwives of Almansa. Josefa would have nine children.

"Pepa," as Mariana of Austria had called her, was the most Spanish of the countess's children. Johanna left her the escritoire she had brought from Spain, along with her Spanish books (Josefa had to share the German books with her sister Rosa.) Some of the books had the countess's name in them.[93] From her father, Josefa inherited more than 100 theatrical works, including 30 by Calderón de la Barca, which she treasured and took care of, and they have survived to this day.[94]

In her will, Johanna Theresia said she wished to be buried wearing the white Trinitarian habit of an order founded by Spaniards in Vienna in 1689. In her last years, she frequently attended the Alserkirche, a church which had begun to be constructed in 1695 and whose crypt would be the burial site of exiled Spaniards who favored the Austrian side during the War of the Spanish Succession.[95]

---

88 ÖStA, AVA-FA Harrach, Kt. 26.

89 Three letters from her father are in French, so it is possible that she wrote to him in Spanish and he replied in French.

90 Salzburg, April 1682. ÖStA, AVA-FA Harrach, Kt. 262.

91 Salzburg, April 11, 1686. ÖStA, AVA-FA Harrach, Kt. 262.

92 Pils, *Schreiben über Stadt*, 235–38.

93 Pils, *Schreiben über Stadt*, 19.

94 Arnold G. Reichenberger, "The Counts Harrach and the Spanish Theater," in *Homenaje a Rodríguez Moñino: estudios de erudición que le ofrecen sus amigos o discípulos hispanistas norteamericanos* (Madrid: Castalia, 1966), 97–103.

95 Pils, *Schreiben über Stadt*, 19.

The countess, now a widow, died in her Viennese palace, perhaps while she inhaled or tasted ambergris in an effort to stave off the inevitable death. She was one of Spain's most illustrious ambassadors in Vienna.

Recipes, Body Culture, and Political-Social Advancement in the Seventeenth Century

During their stay in Madrid as ambassadors, from 1673 to 1677, the count and countess of Harrach collected furniture, paintings, clothing, dishes for drinking chocolate, escritoires from the Indies, and books which they took with them to Vienna.[96]

Curiously, neither of the two recipe books discussed in this chapter were acquired by the counts while they were ambassadors; that is, at the height of their power (he as ambassador, she as the favorite of the queen regent). The first book, dating from the late sixteenth and early seventeenth century, was obtained by Ferdinand Harrach during his brief stay in Madrid in 1665; the second, put together by the seventh duke of Montalto, Cardinal Moncada, passed to the Harrach family in 1686 via Magalotti. The two recipe books were acquired to be used in Vienna, not Madrid. Some of the recipes were already familiar to the countess, either through word of mouth or from watching ladies of the court make them. The principal reason why the Harrachs acquired these collections of recipes was to preserve the culture centered on the refinement of the body that they remembered from the Spanish court and to reproduce it in their native city. This preservation had a specific political objective, and a more general social one.

The couple wished to display their political relationship to the monarchy of Charles II by cultivating their bodies in the Spanish style through food and perfume, defending the shared interests of Spain and the empire in the 1660s and 1670s and later with the Austrian candidacy for the Spanish succession.

But this interest in another culture had deeper roots, which were related to transformations of the seventeenth-century nobility at a time of intense identity crisis.[97] Faced with the pressure, competition, and criticism of other social groups such as the urban bourgeoisie, the nobility had to reinvent itself by seeking new ways of distinguishing itself. Among other things, it adopted more sophisticated lifestyles that affected both material culture and the care and treatment of bodies. In this world of vanities typical of court society, appearance became highly complex. The nobleman of the Golden Age, anxious to triumph at

---

[96] On the Harrach library see Bianca Lindorfer, "Aristocratic Book Consumption in the Seventeenth Century," in *Books in the Catholic World during the Early Modern Period*, ed. Natalia Maillard (Leiden: Brill, 2013), 145–70.

[97] Ronald G. Asch, *Nobilities in Transition 1550–1700. Courtiers and Rebels in Britain and Europe* (London: Arnold, 2003), 2.

court and desperately holding on to his elite status, tried to construct a lifestyle that was ever more exclusive, modeling his body, adopting more sophisticated social forms, and adopting cosmopolitan practices available only to his own circle.

Norbert Elias's thesis that the nobility was domesticated at court has recently undergone revision, given that courts provided the nobility with substantial possibilities for political-social advancement in addition to offering them the means to achieve cultural hegemony available to no other class.[98] The seventeenth century was a triumphant, not a decadent, period for court nobility.[99]

Ambassadors played a critical role in cultural transfer. When they returned to their home court they would flaunt the exotic and new behaviors they had adopted during their diplomatic missions.[100] In Spain, ambassadors often ended their careers in the Council of State; in the empire, they served in the Palace Council. In obtaining these appointments, perhaps they benefited not only from their successful careers but also from their behavior, their new body culture, their new manners, the glamour that was learned and appreciated in a space of constant cultural renovation.

When she returned to Vienna, the countess thought back to the aromas of her childhood and wanted to recreate the exotic and beloved spaces of the Madrid court, both for fulfillment in her intimate life but also to fascinate her visitors and show off her cosmopolitanism. Johann Theresia Harrach took advantage of her experience to move up the ladder at the Vienna court, marry her children well, and promote her husband, who received important appointments from Leopold I and held them until the emperor died in 1705. The count died in 1706, and his widow supported Archduke Charles during the War of the Spanish Succession as she continued promoting Spanish culture in Vienna. One year after the war ended, with the Bourbons having defeated the Habsburgs, Johanna Theresia died. Possibly one of the last things she did was to taste ambergris.[101]

---

[98] For criticism of Elias's thesis, see Ronald G. Asch, "Adel und Monarchie: Norbert Elias' Höfische Gesellschaft im Lichte der neufern Forschung," in *Höfische Gesellschaft und Zivilisationsprozess. Norbert Elias' Werk in kulturwissenschaftlicher Perspektive*, ed. Claudia Opitz (Cologne: Böhlau, 2005), 119–42. Jeroen Duindam, *Vienna and Versailles: The Courts of Europe's Major Dynastic Rivals, 1550–1780* (Cambridge: Cambridge University Press, 2003), 279–87.

[99] Asch, *Nobilities in Transition*, 3; Ronald G. Asch, "Zwischen defensiver Legitimation und Kultureller Hegemonie," in *Seitenblicke*, 4, no. 2 (2005); Ronald G. Asch and Heinz Duchhardt, eds., *Der Absolutismos—ein Mythos? Strukturwandel monarchischer Herrschaft in West- und Mitteleuropa (ca. 1500–1700)* (Cologne: Böhlau, 1996); Ronald G. Asch and Rudolf Schlögl, *Adel in der Frühen Neuzeit* (Göttingen: Vandenhoeck & Ruprecht, 2007).

[100] Lindorfer, "Cosmopolitan Aristocracy," 68.

[101] ÖStA, AVA-FA Harrach Hs. 30, p. 45v.

Bibliography

Abad, Carmen. "El estrado: continuidad de la herencia islámica en los interiores domésticos zaragozanos de las primeras cortes borbónicas." *Artigrama*, 18 (2003): 375–92.

Álvarez-Ossorio Alvariño, Antonio. *La república de las parentelas. La corte de Madrid y el estado de Milán durante el reinado de Carlos II*. Madrid: Universidad Autónoma de Madrid, 1995.

Asch, Ronald G. *Nobilities in Transition 1550–1700. Courtiers and Rebels in Britain and Europe*. London: Arnold, 2003.

_____. "Adel und Monarchie: Norbert Elias' Höfische Gesellschaft im Lichte der neufern Forschung." In *Höfische Gesellschaft und Zivilisationsprozess. Norbert Elias' Werk in kulturwissenschaftlicher Perspektive*. Edited by Claudia Opitz, 119–42. Cologne: Böhlau, 2005.

_____. "Zwischen defensiver Legitimation und Kultureller Hegemonie." *Zeitenblicke*, 4, no. 2 (2005).

_____, and Heinz Duchhardt, eds. *Der Absolutismos—ein Mythos? Strukturwandel monarchischer Herrschaft in West- und Mitteleuropa (ca. 1500–1700)*. Cologne: Böhlau, 1996.

_____, and Rudolf Schlögl. *Adel in der Frühen Neuzeit*. Göttingen: Vandenhoeck & Ruprecht, 2007.

Carvajal, Mariana de. *Navidades en Madrid y Noches entretenidas*. Seville: Junta de Andalucía, 2010.

Cavallo, Sandra. "Health, Beauty and Hygiene." In *At Home in Renaissance Italy*. Edited by Marta Ajmar-Wollheim and Flora Dennis, 174–87. London: Victoria and Albert Museum, 2006.

Duindam, Jeroen. *Vienna and Versailles: The Courts of Europe's Major Dynastic Rivals, 1550–1780*. Cambridge: Cambridge University Press, 2003.

Ebben, Mauritus, ed. *Un holandés en la España de Felipe IV. Diario del viaje de Lodewijck Huygens, 1660–1661*. Madrid: Doce Calles, 2012.

Elias, Norbert. *El proceso de la civilización*. Mexico: Fondo de Cultura Económica, 1988.

Guasto, Cesare. "Saggi di cartegi diplomatic del Conte Lorenzo Magalotti (1675–1678)." *Giornali storico degli archive toscani*, 5 (1861).

Kasparova, Jaroslava. "Redescubrimiento de dos manuscritos, obra de Pedro Calderón (1600–1681) procedentes de la antigua biblioteca del Castillo de Mlda Vozica." In *Calderón. protagonista eminente del barroco europeo*, vol. 2, 21–28. Kassel: Reichenberger, 2002.

Lindorfer, Bianca. "Cosmopolitan Aristocracy and the Diffusion of Baroque Culture: Cultural Transfer from Spain to Austria in the Seventeenth Century." PhD diss., European University, Florence, 2009.

_____. "Discovering Taste; Spain, Austria, and the Spread of Chocolate Consumption among the Austrian Aristocracy, 1650–1700." *Food and History*, 1 (2009): 35–52.

———. "Aristocratic Book Consumption in the Seventeenth Century." In *Books in the Catholic World during the Early Modern Period*. Edited by Natalia Maillard, 145–70. Leiden: Brill, 2013.

Magalotti, Lorenzo. *Lettere odorose (1693–1705)*. Milan: Valentino Bompiani, 1943.

Malcolm, Alistair. "La práctica informal del poder. La política de la Corte y el acceso a la familia real durante la segunda mitad del reinado de Felipe IV." *Reales sitios*, 147 (2001): 38–48.

———. "Spanish Queens and Aristocratic Women at the Court of Madrid 1598–1665." In *Studies on Medieval and Early Modern Women 4. Victims or Viragos?* Edited by Christine Meek and Catherine Lawless, 160–80. Dublin: Four Courts, 2005.

Martínez del Barrio, Javier Ignacio. "La colección de la pintura española de los Harrach." *Anales de historia del arte* (2008): 291–306.

Maura y Gamazo, Gabriel, duque de Maura. *Vida y reinado de Carlos II*. Madrid: Aguilar, 1990.

Mencik, Ferdinand, ed. *Tagebuch über den Aufenthalt in Spanien in den Jahren 1673–1674*. Vienna: Selbstverlag, 1913.

Meyer, Elke. "Die Reisetagzettel der Johanna Theresia Gräfin Harrach." Master's thesis, University of Vienna, 2013.

Micháelis de Vasconcellos, Carolina. "Algunas palavras a respeito de púcaros de Portugal." *Bulletin Hispanique*, 7, no. 2 (1905): 140–96.

Miniati, Stefano. "Lorenzo Magaotti: rassegna di studi e nuove prospettive di ricerca." *Annali di storia di Firenze*, 5 (2012): 31–47.

Morel-Fatio, Alfred. "Comer barro." In *Mélanges de philologie romane dédiés á Carl Wahlund*, 41–49. Mâcon: Protat frères, 1896.

Nieto Nuño, Miguel, ed. *Diario del conde de Pötting, embajador del Sacro Imperio en Madrid (1666–1674)*. 2 vols. Madrid: Ministerio de Asuntos Exteriores, 1990.

Oliván Santaliestra, Laura. "Giovanne d'anni ma vecchia di giudizio: La emperatriz Margarita en la corte de Viena." In *La dinastía de los Austria. Las relaciones entre la monarquía católica y el Imperio*. Vol. 2. Edited by José Martínez Millán and Rubén González Cuerva, 837–908. Madrid: Polifemo, 2011.

———. "Escribir un diario y una hora de baño: vidas privadas en la corte de Madrid (1650–1680)." *Revista de historia moderna. Anales de la Universidad de Alicante*, 30 (2012): 141–58.

———. "My Sister is Growing up very Healthy and Beautiful, She Loves Me": The Childhood of the Infantas María Teresa and Margarita María at Court." In *The Formation of the Child in Early Modern Spain*. Edited by Grace Coolidge, 165–88. Burlington, VT: Ashgate, 2014.

———, and Rafaella Pilo. "Recetario en busca de dueño: Perfumería, medicina y confitería en la Casa del VII duque de Montalto (1635–1666)." *Cuadernos de historia moderna*, 37 (2012): 103–25.

Pilo, Rafaella. "La correspondencia del cardenal Moncada y la conjura contra Nithard." In *La dinastía de los Austria. Las relaciones entre la monarquía católica y el Imperio*. Vol. 2. Edited by José Martínez Millán and Rubén González Cuerva, 1075–88. Madrid: Polifemo, 2011.

Pils, Susanne Claudine. *Schreiben über Stadt. Das Wien der Johanna Theresia Harrach 1639–1716*. Vienna: Franz Deuticke, 2002.

Reichenberger, Arnold G. "The Counts Harrach and the Spanish Theater." In *Homenaje a Rodríguez-Moñino: estudios de erudición que le ofrecen sus amigos o discípulos hispanistas norteamericanos*, 97–103. Madrid: Castalia, 1966.

Rodríguez Bernis, Sofía. "Cómo se sentaba la gente en el siglo XVI." *Associació per a l'estudi del moble* (2012): 70–71.

Seseña, Natacha. "El búcaro de las Meninas." In *Velázquez y el arte de su tiempo. V Jornadas de Arte*, 39–48. Madrid: Alpuerto, 1991.

Valyi, Eszter. "Schmuk und Kleidung auf den Damenporträts der Ahngengalerie Harrach. Ein Beitrag zur Bestimmumg Baroker Adelporträts." Master's thesis, University of Vienna, 2008.

Welch, Evelyne. "Scented Buttons and Perfumed Gloves: Smelling Things in Renaissance Italy." In *Ornamentalism. The Art of Renaissance Accessories*. Edited by Bella Mirabella, 13–39. Ann Arbor: Michigan University Press, 2011.

EPILOGUE

Chapter 10
Aristocratic Women across Borders, Cultural Transfers and Something More. Why Should We Care?[1]

Bartolomé Yun Casalilla

During recent decades, historians' interest has increased in the border-crossing aspect of the marriages of members of Old Regime royal and noble families. Many factors are behind such a historiographical trend, including an interest in cultural transfers and their roles in Europe's cultural development; the increasingly frequent adoption of a transnational approach to European history; the rise of a new diplomatic history in which cultural mediation is essential; and, last but not least, the gender perspective.[2]

---

[1] This chapter was produced within the framework of the research group *New Atlantic Products. Science, War, Economy and Consumption in the Old Regime, 1492–1824* (P09-HUM 5330), based at the Universidad Pablo de Olavide in Seville and sponsored by the Junta de Andalucía. Some of these ideas were part of the research that I was carrying out at the European University Institute, Florence, and that I have also presented in previous publications and more particularly in my book in progress, *Crossing Borders. Princes and Aristocrats in Western Europe (c. 1500–1700)* (working title).

[2] The literature on the role of cultural transfers as well as on the transnational approach to early modern European history today is very wide. The methodological grounds were established in works such as Michel Espagne, "Sur les limites du comparatisme en histoire culturelle," in *Genèses. Sciences sociales et histoire*, 17 (September 1994): 112–21; Michel Espagne, ed., *L'Ecole normale supérieure et Allemagne* (Leipzig: Leipziger Universitätsverlag, 1995); Michel Espagne, *Les transferts culturels franco-allemands* (Paris: Presses Universitaires de France, 1999); Hans E. Bödeker and Etienne François, eds., *Aufklärung/Lumières und Politik. Zurpolitischen Kultur der deutschen und franzöisischen Aufklärung* (Leipzig: Leipziger Universitätsverlag, 1996); Michel Espagne and Michael Werner, eds., *Transferts: les relations interculturelles dans l'espace franco-allemand (XVIIIe et XIXe siécle)* (Paris: Editions Recherche sur les Civilisations, 1988). For a methodological reflection on transnational history from the perspectives of "*histoire croisée*," see Michael Werner and Bénédicte Zimmermann, "Penser l'histoire croisée: entre empirie et reflexivité," in *De la comparaison à l'histoire croisée*, eds. Michael Werner and Bénédicte Zimmermann (Paris: Seuil, 2004), 15–52; and Robert Muchembled, ed., *Cultural Exchange in Early Modern Europe*, 4 vols. (Cambridge: Cambridge University Press, 2007). For a more recent view see Ann Thomson, Simon Burrows, and Edmon Dziembowski, eds., *Cultural Transfers: France and Britain in the Long Eighteenth Century*

Yet scholars still have much to discover on this subject, and it is also quite possible that future research will depend not on the accumulation of case studies but rather on our ability to give meaning to our findings and connect them with other areas of research. The first step in understanding the implication and historical specificity of these marriages is to examine individual cases in depth using a microanalytical approach. Second, we need to trace links between these marriages and the literature in different historical fields. In other words, only strong contextualization in both history and historiographical traditions will enable us to move beyond anecdotes and interesting stories to the development of a subject that has much to offer not only to cultural and political historians but also to social and even economic historians, as well as scholars interested in the history of religion, war, diplomacy, and other fields. In this respect, this chapter draws upon some of the cases presented in this book as well as on my own research.[3]

(Oxford: Voltaire Foundation, 2010). The theoretical underpinnings of transnational history, which has recently become a fashion, can be understood by reading Christopher A. Bayly, Sven Beckert, Matthew Connelly, Isabel Hofmeyr, Wendy Kozol, and Patricia Seed, "AHR Conversation: On Transnational History," *The American Historical Review*, 5 (December 2006): 30–50. I myself devoted some lines to the subject in Bartolomé Yun Casalilla, "'Localism,' Global History and Transnational History. A Reflection from the Historian of Early Modern Europe," *Historisk Tidskrift*, 127, no. 4 (2007): 659–78. Regarding the new diplomatic history, see Michael J. Levin, *Agents of Empire. Spanish Ambassadors in Sixteenth-Century Italy* (Ithaca, NY: Cornell University Press, 2005); Thomas J. Dandelet, *Spanish Rome, 1500–1700* (New Haven: Yale University Press, 2001); and Heiko Droste, "Diplomacy as Means of Cultural Transfer in Early Modern Times," *Scandinavian Journal of History*, 31, no. 2 (June 2006): 144–50. The gender approach to this subject is widely considered in many recent publications. See for example the many works included in Giulia Calvi and Riccardo Spinelli, eds., *Le donne Medici nel sistema europeo delle corti, XVI–XVIII secolo* (Florence: Edizioni Polistampa, 2008). See also M.J. Rodríguez Salgado, "'Una perfecta princesa'. Casa y vida de la reina Isabel de Valois (1559–1568)," *Cuadernos de historia moderna anejos*, Anejo [supplement] 2 (2003): 39–96, and 28 (2003): 71–98; Bartolomé Bennassar, *Reinas y princesas del Renacimiento a la Ilustración. El lecho, el poder y la muerte* (Barcelona: Paidos, 2006).

[3] Previous works drawn upon for some ideas are Bartolomé Yun Casalilla, "Introducción. Entre el Imperio colonial y la monarquía compuesta. Elites y territorios en la Monarquía Hispánica (ss. XVI y XVII)," in *Las redes del Imperio. Elites sociales en la articulación del imperio español, 1492–1714*, ed. Bartolomé Yun Casalilla (Madrid: Marcial Pons, 2008), 4–38; Bartolomé Yun Casalilla and Ángeles Redondo Álamo, "*'Bem visto tinha* ... 'Entre Lisboa y Capodimonte. La aristocracia castellana en perspectiva 'transnacional' (ss. XVI–XVII)," in ibid., 39–63; Bartolomé Yun Casalilla, "Príncipes más allá de los reinos. Aristocracias, comunicación e intercambio cultural en la Europa de los siglos XVI–XVII," in *Mecenazgo y humanidades en tiempos de Lastanosa. Homenaje a Domingo Indurain*, eds. Aurora Egido and José E. Laplana (Zaragoza: Universidad de Zaragoza, 2008), 51–68; Bartolomé Yun Casalilla and Ángeles Redondo Alamo, "Aristocracias, identidades y espacios políticos en la monarquía compuesta de los Austrias. La Casa de Borja (ss. XVI y XVII)," in *Homenaje a Don Antonio Domínguez Ortíz*, eds. Juan L.

So, what type of men and, more importantly, women, are we studying? In recent decades, research on European royalty and courts has visibly increased. Scholars care about royal marriages and dynastic strategies, about kings' daughters and queens, about princesses such as Maria de' Medici, Isabel of Portugal, Mary Queen of Scots, Anne of Austria, Mary Tudor, and many others. Royal women and their marriages have long and justifiably monopolized historians' attention. Sometimes, however, the reason for this fascination is forgotten: international marriages constituted one of the most powerful forces in Old Regime Europe's political history and was the factor that most closely affected international politics, war, peace treaties, and the formation of the political map, as well as European geopolitics.[4] But the phenomenon does not end there.

Marriages among members of royal or sovereign houses were only one part of a wider practice. Even the marriages of the Tudors, Valois, Stuarts, Habsburgs, Bourbons, and other dynasties, were not marriages just between two royal families. Many princes, high aristocrats, and sovereigns of independent but minor polities intermarried with these great dynasties. That was the case of the Medicis, the Braganzas before ascending to the throne in Portugal, the Gonzagas, Farneses, Sforzas, Lobkowiczes, Dietrichsteins, the Von der Pfalzes, and the Hessen-Kassels, to cite only a few. These aristocratic houses were able to establish marriages with royal families because of the latter's need to break endogamy and the possibilities the former provided in terms of geopolitics, prestige, purity of blood, and antiquity, as well as in terms of strategic political dynamics. Only religious barriers acted as a limit—not an insurmountable obstacle—on the circulation of princes and princesses across boundaries. One should not forget that this was a practice with a sort of spatial dimension. There were areas, such as Italy and the German imperial territories, that from the sixteenth century onward provided a healthy stock of princesses for the great royal dynasties. This development should be more than enough to invite reflection on the wider dimensions of the phenomenon of marriages that crossed political borders.

In Italy, among the many noble families of the Renaissance, the repository of prestige, antiquity, and historical memory (some households claimed to descend from classical Roman times) was truly inexhaustible. These matrimonies offered links to families that had produced popes and cardinals, the most powerful princes

---

Castellano and Miguel L. López-Guadalupe Muñoz (Granada: Universidad de Granada, 2008), 759–72.

[4] Among the books that reflect this phenomenon the best, one needs to cite Lucien Bély, *La société des princes, XVIe–XVIIe siècle* (Paris: Fayard, 1999); Lucien Bély, *Les relations internationales en Europe (XVII–XVIIIe siècles)* (Paris: Presses Universitaires de France, 1992); Lucien Bély, ed., *La presence des Bourbons en Europe, XVIe–XXIe siècle* (Paris: Presses Universitaires de France, 2003). A general acknowledgment of the importance of the dynastic approach to Old Regime politics can be found in the well-known book by Richard Bonney, *The European Dynastic States, 1494–1660* (Oxford: Oxford University Press, 1991).

of Christendom.[5] The fact that ecclesiastical dignitaries remained part of secular society as well as of family and clientele networks was a crucial factor in this regard. Geopolitics also played an important role. From the end of the fifteenth century, convergence and conflict on the Italian peninsula between France and the Hispanic Monarchy, as well as the imperial court, to which feudal obligations linked some Italian polities, situated these families within a very valuable universe of alliances. They provided a source of power with which to control local clienteles and co-opt local alliances. They also provided the possibility of inheriting small states according to the unpredictable game of dynastic succession, thus turning in their favor the area's delicate political equilibrium.

This was also the case of most of the great noble families of the Holy Roman Empire, another crucial region, and, more in particular, of those controlling the emperor's election. Although from the sixteenth century onwards the Habsburgs' predictable transmission of the imperial throne reduced the possibilities of many other families, German households remained attractive for other reasons. This area became a sort of repository for alliances among the Protestant aristocratic elites, which made its families appealing to the leading dynasties in the Netherlands and Britain. The region's geostrategic value was particularly important when it became the apple of discord among the leading European powers during the Thirty Years' War, as it also offered the possibility of acquiring influence in a very politically fragmented area with a delicate equilibrium where sovereigns of small states and high-ranking princes abounded.

Nevertheless, the marriages of the royal dynasties are only the visible tip of a wider phenomenon that deepened its roots in broader aristocratic groups. An analysis of the biographies of the members of the Order of the Golden Fleece is particularly telling. Though the predominance of Catholic and pro-Habsburg families within the group skews the conclusions and cautions against taking this sample as representative of Europe as a whole, it reveals important practices across the continent. As can be seen in Table 10.1, the Order of the Golden Fleece had an important bloc of families from what are today the nation-states of France, Spain, Italy, and Germany, that projected their matrimonial alliances among those same territories. Many of these marriages had cross-border dimensions, particularly in Italy and Germany, which comprised many small polities. They linked families on different sides of the frontiers of kingdoms, such as Castile and Aragon, for example, or city-states and polities, like Genoa, Tuscany, and the Papal States, which would later belong to the same nation-state. But more interestingly, although more precise work remains to be done in order to reach firm conclusions, a considerable proportion of these marriages were from households that bridged distinct imagined communities in formation, such as Spain, France, Italy, and even Germany, in addition to Portugal, which was possibly the most stable and

[5] The literature on this subject is abundant. Among other works and, as a synthesis, see Ronnie Po-Chia Hsia, *The World of Catholic Renewal, 1540–1770 (New Approaches to European History)*, 2nd edn. (Cambridge: Cambridge University Press, 2005), ch. 4.

Table 10.1 Marriages of Members of the Order of the Golden Fleece (1500–25, 1575–1625, 1675–1700)

	Spain	**France**	**Italy**	**Germany**	**Austria**	**Portugal**	**Netherlands**	**Belgium**	**Gt. Britain**	**Others**	**Total (men)**
Spain	**38**	3	3	0	2	1	0	0	0	1	48
France	2	**27**	0	1	3	0	5	7	0	0	45
Italy	9	3	**62**	1	2	2	1	1	0	0	81
Germany	0	12	4	**25**	17	0	2	4	0	6	70
Austria	2	1	5	17	**13**	0	0	0	0	4	42
Portugal	3	0	0	0	1	**1**	0	0	0	0	5
Netherlands	2	8	0	1	0	0	**4**	3	0	3	21
Belgium	1	10	0	2	4	0	4	**8**	0	1	30
Gt. Britain	1	0	0	0	0	0	0	0	**3**	0	4
Others	2	0	4	8	8	1	1	0	0	**5**	29
Total (women)	60	64	78	55	50	5	17	23	3	20	**375**

Source: A. de Ceballos-Escalera, *La Insigne Orden del Toisón de Oro* (Madrid: Palafox & Pezuala, 2000).

permanent proto-national polity of Europe, whose internal political consistency and territorial borders hardly changed from the fifteenth century onward.

These sort of "extroverted" aristocracies were especially present in small polities such as the current territories of Belgium and Holland, which correspond to the Catholic and Protestant Low Countries. In their case, the proportion of cross-border matrimonies was extraordinarily high, similar to what was happening in areas such as Italy or the Holy Roman Empire, which we have camouflaged by grouping them in the framework of present-day nation-states.[6] The small size of the polities, the need for high aristocratic families to differentiate themselves from local lower nobilities (thus avoiding both the weakening of their status and biological decrepitude), the projection of the great powers' interests on many of these territories, and the search for a possible positive outcome in the unpredictable game of inheritances made this strategy a normal practice in these areas even more than in the current territories of Spain and France.

Families from the areas that today are Spain and France, nevertheless, also showed a notable cross-border character. The households from these regions which were increasingly interlinking within their respective polities in formation had their own interest in marrying beyond the territories that would end up defining these nation-states. Marriages between the main Spanish households and the Spínolas, the Medicis, the Gonzagas, the Harrases, the Dietrichsteins, and others show the great attraction of Castilian (or, more generally, Spanish) alliances precisely because they facilitated connections with the top of the Hispanic Monarchy, the most powerful political actor of the time. The French aristocracy was perhaps less extroverted than the aristocracies of the territories comprising present-day Spain, but a notable number of French nobles married into families beyond the kingdom's borders. Our table in this case is misleading in the sense that we have already pointed out, since it includes within France the duchy of Lorraine and other semi-independent estates on the border with the Low Countries. But still, the table registers for the period 1675–1700 houses such as those of the marquis of Conflans, the prince of Rubempré, and the marquis of Richenbourg, which married into families from the Low Countries, the Holy Roman Empire, and others.

Equally telling, and perhaps a more correct way to approach the problem, is the consideration of the matrimonial geopolitics of some of these transnational families. The example of the Borjas, whose Italianization of their name—Borgia—reveals a great deal about their strategies, can be considered in this respect. Originally from Valencia, this household created strong links with Italy in the fifteenth century. During Charles V's reign, the Borjas also established important

---

[6] Obviously, the correct way to study the subject is by differentiating the historical polities in which all these nobles were based or born and by analyzing historical border-crossing relations according to those polities. This, however, requires considering the political units of all Europe across the period as well as the changes taking place within them and in the borders between them. Such an exercise clearly exceeds the ambition and nature of this chapter.

alliances with Portuguese elites to project themselves into Castile and Italy during the second half of the sixteenth century. They would also expand into America, where a secondary branch developed in the seventeenth century.[7]

The phenomenon of border-crossing aristocracies and, consequently, that of princesses traveling across the continent, predated the early modern period but seems to have been especially activated by strong historical forces since the sixteenth century.

One can identify some precipitating factors when some of these marriages are studied in greater detail. Dynastic unions among the first families of Europe, the Habsburgs and the Bourbons in particular, were usually followed by waves of marriages among the nobles of the countries involved in these big family alliances. Thus the marriage of Charles V and Isabel of Portugal reinforced in just a few years a previous tendency to unite the Castilian and the Portuguese aristocracies, a tradition already established in the Middle Ages, as Mafalda Soares da Cunha states in her contribution.[8] The imperial wedding was followed by marriages among members of families such as the Borgias, the Fernández de Castros, and others, who linked their futures to Portuguese households.[9] The reasons are more or less evident: royal marriages at the highest levels caused aristocrats to hope that there would be movement in the administrative structure and new possibilities for social and political advancement. These aristocrats then pursued marriage alliances designed to gain influence in the new system.

These cross-border marriages, as well as family linkages among aristocratic lineages, were not the outcome of haphazard or individual decisions. Furthermore, the careful negotiations among the families involved and the repetitive way in which marriages of members of the same lineage occurred in two, three, and even four generations, point to well-considered and systematic strategies. This practice, common among families within the same polity, was also present in international marriages across political frontiers, sometimes even between different imagined communities in formation. There were various reasons for these cross-border marriages. To begin with, they should not be considered as exceptional cases but rather as normal practice in a world in which the meaning of political frontiers or, to be more precise, the political and jurisdictional implications of borders among different kingdoms, republics, and city-states, were different from present-day nation-states' limits. In some cases, above all among the high noble strata, those cross-border alliances entailed a way to seek social and political promotion, which could include becoming the sovereign of a polity.

Though with very different outcomes, the cases of the Braganzas and the la Trèmoille families are meaningful in this respect. The former had practiced this type of marriage from the sixteenth century. Orienting their matrimonial policy

[7] See Yun Casalilla and Redondo Álamo, "Aristocracias, identidades."

[8] See also Mafalda Soares da Cunha, "Títulos portugueses e redes nobiliarias en la Monarquía Católica," in *Las redes del Imperio*, ed. Yun Casalilla, 205–32.

[9] Yun Casalilla and Redondo Álamo, "Aristocracias, identidades."

outside Portugal was for the Braganzas a way to distinguish themselves from other noble families of their small kingdom, while also satisfying biological needs and social aspirations.[10] This policy was also the motivation for their connections with some of the most powerful Castilian families on the other side of the border such as the Guzmánes. In 1640, don Juan, duke of Braganza, who proclaimed himself king of Portugal after the rebellion which started in December of that year, married the sister of the ninth duke of Medina Sidonia, doña Leonor de Guzmán. This created a strong tie that conditioned the role of the Medina Sidonia family during the political crisis of 1640 and that seems to have been in the background of the duke's conspiracy against Philip IV precisely when don Juan of Portugal was leading the war against the Habsburgs of Madrid. Although Medina Sidonia's plot was quickly suppressed, the use of political links on both sides of the Castilian–Portuguese border seems to have been crucial for the whole story.[11] The la Trèmouilles, of which Henri-Charles, prince of Tarento, was an important member, followed a similar international policy, in their case intermarrying with Protestant families.[12] At the same time, according to the genealogies that the la Trèmouilles commissioned in the seventeenth century, they also intermarried with the Laval family, which gave them the right to claim the crown of Naples. This allowed them to participate in the Westphalia peace negotiations, where they aimed to present their candidacy for the kingdom of Naples. The attempt would prove futile against the interests of the two main houses negotiating at that summit, the Bourbons and the Spanish Habsburgs.[13] Though different in many ways, both cases show that international alliances provided more than one way to marry peers of the same rank when it was difficult to find partners of the same status within the original kingdom or polity. Transnational marriages also offered social promotion as well as a means to play in this peculiar lottery of inheritances characteristic of

---

[10] Leonor Freire Costa and Mafalda Soares da Cunha, *D. Joao IV* (Rio do Mouro: Circulo de Leitores, 2006), 40.

[11] Antonio Domínguez Ortiz, "La conspiración del duque de Medina Sidonia y el Marqués de Ayamonte," in *Crisis y decadencia en la España de los Austrias* (Barcelona: Ariel, 1973), 113–53.

[12] The case of the la Trèmoilles, who in the first generation had linked with other French Protestant families, is even more interesting. Henri-Charles went to the Low Countries, where he would end up losing the support of William of Orange-Nassau, whose daughter he had tried to marry. His failure led to a marriage with Amalia of Hesse-Cassel, also of a Protestant family, but his action made clear his intention to cross political frontiers to establish ties to families with greater possibilities in Europe. The ascension of the Orange-Nassau to the English throne would show that these calculations were correct, thus breaking with a long tradition of French alliances. The story, told by the very same Prince de Tarente, can be found in Henri-Charles de la Trèmoille, *Mémoires de Henri-Charles de la Trèmoille, Prince de Tarente* (Liege: J.F. Bassompierre, 1767), 69.

[13] See Scévole de Sainte-Marthe, *Histoire Généalogique de la Maison de la Trèmoille* (Paris: S. Piget, 1668).

a society in which infant mortality was high and therefore family links created possibilities for legacies and promotion.

This volume, along with a growing scholarly literature, shows how marriages across borders were decisive for the history of cultural contacts among different areas of Europe. The history of these marriages obviously falls under the category of women's history, and the gender approach to history can certainly lead to a better understanding of the implications, context, and effects of these international marriages.[14]

International marriages created optimal conditions for contacts among long-distance societies. This volume pays special attention to this process. With the exception of Mafalda Soares da Cunha's chapter, which focuses on different but no less interesting aspects of marriage, the authors directly or indirectly refer to the role of women and, more generally, to the connections between international marriages and cultural transfers among different regions in Europe. The case of Elisabetta Farnese, studied here by María de los Ángeles Pérez Samper, may be the most explicit in that sense.

It was the cultural and symbolic capital of princes and princesses and their leading role in society that convinced their peers of the high quality of the cultural values and goods they were transmitting. In other words, these members of the European elite engaged, sometimes even unconsciously, in a sort of vicarious consumption that affected first their equals and then the rest of society.[15] Though the theory of the trickle-down effect is obviously an exaggeration, one cannot forget the role of transmission of models of consumption, material culture, and cultural practices and the powerful effects of aristocratic exchanges.

Aristocratic culture and even political culture were propitious for cultural transfers. Exchange of objects and goods was facilitated by practices of gift-giving closely linked to the concept of friendship, one of the cornerstone concepts of early modern European political and social culture.[16] Consequently, gifts and presents easily became the way to intermingle material cultures and fashions. Nobles from

---

[14] Calvi and Spinelli, *Le donne Medici*.

[15] The literature on this aspect is now huge and has been developed in particular by specialists in the history of consumption and material culture. See, for example, the classic essay by Neil McKendrick, "The Consumer Revolution of Eighteenth-Century England," in *The Birth of a Consumer Society. The Commercialization of Eighteenth-Century England*, eds. Neil McKendrick, John Brewer, and John H. Plumb (London: Europa, 1982), 9–33; and Daniel Roche, *La culture des apparences. Une histoire du vêtement (XIIIe–XVIIe siècle)* (Paris: Fayard, 1989). For studies on court life and the consumption of the elites, see, for example, Linda L. Peck, *Consuming Splendour: Society and Culture in Seventeenth-Century England* (Cambridge: Cambridge University Press, 2005).

[16] On the gift as a part of early modern European political culture, see Bartolomé Clavero, *La grâce du don. Antropologie catholique de l'économie moderne* (Paris: Albin Michel, 1996). This book was first published in Spanish as *Antidora: antropología católica de la economía moderna* (Milan: Giuffrè, 1991). See also Natalie Z. Davis, *The Gift in Sixteenth-Century France* (Oxford: Oxford University Press, 2000).

throughout Europe exchanged all types of objects, from fans to jewels, from horses to weapons, from works of art to books, from recipes to portraits, medals, or miniatures. They did so not only to express personal affection, but because gift exchange constituted part of a political and social language.[17] These international marriages were in many cases the channels by which objects circulated in Europe before they became commodities transmitted through mercantile networks. The case of chocolate is but one among others; it circulated among courts from the end of the sixteenth century to become, by the end of the seventeenth century, an internationally traded commodity.[18] Spanish literature, and in particular authors such as Luis de Góngora or even Pedro Calderón de la Barca (not easy authors to comprehend, by the way) and paintings by artists who never left their countries such as Bartolomé Esteban Murillo, traveled from Spain to Austria and even Bohemia thanks to networks of personal contacts and gifts before a market for them arose.[19]

The intermingling of aristocratic habits worked in the same direction. In fact, marriages were not an isolated practice. In her doctoral dissertation on links between the court nobilities of Madrid and Vienna, Bianca Lindorfer demonstrated that, together with trips, diplomatic relationships, and correspondence, marriages were crucial for the spread of Spanish literature and the Spanish language in Austria, as well as for the circulation of art and even recipes. The end result of these contacts was a cosmopolitan aristocratic culture with common features in distant areas of Europe. The cases presented in this volume explore this idea in depth and enrich our knowledge. The forms of cultural mediation identified, moreover, were closely tied to each other. Trips,

---

[17] See some examples in Almudena Pérez de Tudela and Annemarie Jordan Gschwend, "Luxury Goods for Royal Collectors: Exotica, Princely Gifts and Rare Animals Exchanged between the Iberian Courts and Central Europe in the Renaissance (1560–1612)," *Jahrbuch Des Kunsthistorischen Museum Wien* (2001): 1–103; Mark A. Meadow, "Merchants and Marvels. Hans Jacob Fugger and the Origins of the Wunderkammer," in *Merchants and Marvels. Commerce: Science and Art in Early Modern Europe*, eds. Pamela H. Smith and Paula Findlen (New York: Routledge, 2002), 182–200.

[18] The trade in chocolate between different areas of Europe existed already in the sixteenth century. Nevertheless, its massive commerce did not start until these noble networks, in which the gift was a key factor, created a market for such a product. See Bianca M. Lindorfer, "Las redes familiares de la aristocracia austriaca y los procesos de transferencia cultural: entre Madrid y Viena, 1550–1700," in *Las redes del Imperio*, ed. Yun Casalilla, 261–88. On the subsequent diffusion of chocolate, see Irene Fattacciu, "The Resilience and Boomerang Effect of Chocolate: A Product's Globalization and Commodification," in *Global Goods and the Spanish Empire, 1492–1824. Circulation, Resistance and Diversity*, eds. Bethany Aram and Bartolomé Yun Casalilla (Basingstoke: Palgrave Macmillan, 2014). See also the chapter in this book by Laura Oliván.

[19] Bianca M. Lindorfer, "Cosmopolitan Aristocracy and the Diffusion of Baroque Culture: Cultural Transfer from Spain to Austria in the Seventeenth Century" (PhD diss.: European University Institute, Florence, 2009).

particularly the aristocrats' Grand Tour, were often a way to acquire knowledge and establish relationships that could become decisive for obtaining diplomatic posts.[20] Intense correspondence often resulted from those contacts, and long-distance marriages were often the cause or the consequence of such ties among European aristocrats. One of the most important promoters of the Grand Tour, Sir Francis Bacon, suggested that "When a traveler returneth home, let him not leave the countries, where he hath travelled, altogether behind him; but maintain a correspondence by letters, with those of his acquaintance."[21]

Thus, travels, diplomatic contacts, correspondence, and marriages were frequently intertwined, enhancing the role of aristocrats as mediators among different cultures. Nevertheless, the enormous potential of international marriages for cultural exchanges also derives from another, oft-neglected fact. As the cases presented here show, the circulation of women from one area to another in Europe was not an individual but, rather, a collective act. This could also be the case for men's displacements, of course, but was even more frequent and significant for women.[22] Princesses traveled to their new homes with considerable entourages. Furthermore, marriage agreements in many cases stated the obligation of the husband and his entourage to respect the bride's culture and customs, thus enhancing the cross-cultural component of these transfers. One need only consider the case of the *infanta* Catalina Michaela, daughter of Philip II, and her marriage to the duke of Savoy, studied here by Magdalena S. Sánchez, which led to a hybridization of protocol and etiquette at the court of Turin. Eleonora di Toledo's permanent move to Florence was significant for the cultural contacts between Castile and Tuscany precisely because she did not travel alone but with an extensive retinue, which created better conditions for cultural transfers as well as cultural clashes.[23]

---

20 The emphasis on the Grand Tour's importance for cultural encounters is becoming a commonplace in recent literature. For example, see Karin J. MacHardy, "Cultural Capital, Family Strategies and Noble Identity in Early Modern Habsburg Austria, 1579–1620," *Past & Present*, 163 (May 1999): 36–75.

21 Francis Bacon, *Essays, moral, economical, and political. A new ed., with the Latin quotations translated* (London: J. M'Creery, 1819), 79.

22 An interesting contextual biography in this sense is Alessandra Beccucci, "The Art of Politics and the Politics of the Arts. Francesco Ottavio Piccolomini: A Case of Patronage in Thirty Years War Europe" (PhD diss.: European University Institute, Florence, 2012). Regarding the cortèges of princesses, marriage treaties provided for an entourage of servants, friends, and family members travelling with them. See Alessandra Contini, "Il ritorno delle donne nel sistema di corte," in *Le donne Medici*, eds. Calvi and Spinelli, 7. From a wider perspective but on the same subject, see Angelantonio Spagnoletti, "Le donne nel sistema dinastico italiano," in *Le donne Medici*, eds. Calvi and Spinelli, 13–34; and Ángela Muñoz Fernández, "La casa della regina. Un spazio nella Castiglia del Quattrocento," in *Genesis. Rivista della società italiana delle storiche*, 2 (2002): 71–95.

23 Carlos Hernando Sánchez, *Castilla y Nápoles en el siglo XVI. El virrey Pedro de Toledo. Linaje, estado y cultura (1532–1553)* (Salamanca: Junta de Castilla y León, 1994).

Yet, when considering cultural transfers and exchanges, it is also important to avoid one of the leading epistemological problems of transnational history: an excessive emphasis on transference, adoption, and adaptation at the price of forgetting the negative reactions, the resistances to cultural values, goods, and ideas coming from other societies, as well as the role that intercultural contacts played in the rise of local and regional—or even national—cultures based on self-affirmation and the rejection of foreign influences. The examples here are abundant. The correspondence of Liselotte van der Pfalz shows how her life in Paris was crucial for the rise of German patriotic feeling in the deepest corners of her heart long before a German nation-state was even a dream.[24] The same could be said about Maria Mancini regarding the affirmation of her Parisian origins during her difficult years in Rome. Likewise the trips of the two men considered in this book, Philip of Burgundy and Philip II of Spain, provoked similar reactions of self-assertion and conflict. The case of Elisabetta Farnese can also be understood in this context. To what extent did her attempt to compensate for French culture with Italian values, goods, music, and opera entail a reaction against French influence in a person whose origins were ultimately in Italy? Farnese's emphasis on French culture was part of the reason for the negative reaction from the Spanish aristocracy belonging to the so-called Spanish party after Philip V's arrival.[25] In a similar vein, Lindorfer's study of Spanish–Austrian cultural transfers has shown how contacts between Madrid and Vienna were responsible for the creation in Austria of a so-called Spanish party and the spread there of Spanish court culture, but also for the rise of a sort of proto-nationalism among the imperial aristocracy opposed to Spanish influence.[26] The context and the translation into political language of these reactions, with their increasing effects on political life and policy-making, played a very important role. Eleonora di Toledo, who imposed her imprint on Florentine high-society fashion, faced strongest opposition among elites nostalgic for a Republic of Florence.[27] The reason was not only cultural, in the most reductionist sense of the term. It was that many political theorists and social groups identified her with Charles V and the empire, which some considered a negation of republican ideas.

Scholars widely acknowledge the gender component of aristocratic cultural exchanges. Long-distance formative trips such as the Grand Tour were for men, as were diplomacy and war, at least in appearance. Matrimony was obviously a more gender-balanced event. But the intermingling of all these practices created

---

24 Elisabeth-Charlotte d'Orléans, *A Woman's Life in the Court of the Sun King. Letters of Liselotte von der Pfalz, Elisabeth Charlotte, Duchesse d'Orleans, 1652–1722*, trans. and ed. Elborg Forster (Baltimore: Johns Hopkins University Press, 1997).

25 See, among others, Teófanes Egido López, *Opinión pública y oposición al poder en la España del siglo XVIII (1713–1759)*, 2nd edn. (Valladolid: Universidad de Valladolid-Fundación de Historia Moderna, 2002).

26 Lindorfer, "Cosmopolitan Aristocracy."

27 See, among others, Egido López, *Opinión pública*.

a situation in which the role of women was heightened in many ways. Marriage could be an indirect effect of previous knowledge among allied families after displacements led to personal meetings among their members.[28]

But it is also important to consider that, thanks to these marriages, women were even more present in diplomacy and, generally, in the international arena. Diplomacy was not a profession, but a practice. Nor were international negotiations and contacts limited to ambassadors. As a result of their international marriages, displaced women played crucial roles as mediators between different polities. We need to consider that the training of ambassadors and of international mediators in general was not, until the seventeenth century and depending on the countries, something acquired in the public arena but was rather cultural capital acquired within the family. What made the aristocracy the appropriate group for diplomatic relations was a continuous osmosis and reciprocal formation of aristocratic and diplomatic cultures. In this context, one can understand that all these women had assimilated the right type of training and cultural capital thanks to their status and education in the high nobility's *habitus*. In many ways or at least in this particular aspect, the education of male and female members of the family was quite similar. To know court protocol, to behave correctly in the palace, to master the techniques of conversation and writing as well as other components of diplomatic life, formed part of nobles' lives regardless of gender.

The countess of Harrach, studied here by Laura Oliván, offers a good example. In many cases, women were, to begin with, guarantors of international treatises and peace agreements or, to put it rather bluntly, the currency of exchange in the market of loyalties, cooperation, or non-aggression treaties among states. The Bourbon *pactes de famille* in the eighteenth century provide an excellent example. But the practice of exchanging princesses as a way to stamp international treaties had been frequent in Europe for centuries. The case of the exchange of princesses, Anne of Austria from Spain and Elizabeth of Bourbon on the French side, studied elsewhere by Maria José del Rio, provides a vibrant example, celebrated in contemporary iconography.[29] Almost all of the cases presented in this volume illustrate how women could be exchanged or could be the means to cement a peace, something that is certainly visible in the marriage of Eleonora di Toledo and Cosimo de' Medici, studied in this volume by Joan-Lluís Palos.

[28] See for example the already-mentioned attempts of Henri-Charles, prince of Tarento, to wed the eldest daughter of the Prince of Orange as well as the final decision of his family to marry him to princess Amalia of Hesse-Cassel, daughter of the Landgrave of Hesse. The first attempt was a consequence of his own journey to the Netherlands to serve in the army of William Nassau-Orange, a trip that was in part a formative one, to learn the art of war. See la Trèmoille, *Memoires*, 30.

[29] María José del Río Barredo, "Imágenes para una ceremonia de frontera. El intercambio de princesas entre las cortes de Francia y España en 1615," in *La historia imaginada. Construcciones visuales del pasado en la edad moderna*, eds. Joan Lluís Palos and Diana Carrió-Ivernizzi (Madrid: Fernando Villaverde Ediciones, 2008), 153–83.

This last case shows the complexity of the different principles behind this "trade of princesses" and the way their "value" in that "market" was estimated. Eleonora's "value" for Cosimo was precisely to seal his alliance with the emperor Charles V—an alliance that did not prevent Cosimo from acting freely in the international arena in many ways—and to reinforce an aristocratic court and Spanish fashion in Florence, as well as to distance the Medicis from republican Florentines.[30] But more detailed consideration of the case offers interesting historical clues. Eleonora arrived in Florence with huge political capital not only from her lineage but also from the emperor. Her marriage to Cosimo, a man not much inclined to yield and even less prone to give up his appetites without good reason, was not just a result of the power and prestige of don Pedro de Toledo, viceroy of Naples and father of Eleonora. Nor was it exclusively due to the powerful house of Alba, a first-rank Castilian lineage of which don Pedro and Eleonora were members of a secondary branch that was rising thanks to the viceroy's services to the emperor.[31] The marriage also demonstrated Cosimo's commitment to Charles, which, apart from personal feelings and maybe even love toward the duchess, helps explain his respectful behavior toward Eleonora during her life. This obligation would not prevent Cosimo from licentiousness after Eleonora's death, which even gave rise to suspicions of an incestuous relationship with his own daughter, Isabella.[32] Eleonora was, for all of these reasons, a very special case. She could dispose of enormous political capital and, thanks to that, influence life in the Grand Duchy of Tuscany more than many Florentines would have liked. But it is important to consider the notable potential of women like her for mediation among states.

In a study of Italian aristocratic women, Benedetta Borello has shown how women acted as mediators among sometimes distant actors in the concession of favors and patronage.[33] Women were often the "brokers" who mediated between patron and client, as Sharon Kettering demonstrated some years ago.[34] This was also the case in long-distance personal relationships where

[30] See, for example, Roberta Orsi Landini and Bruna Niccoli, *Moda a Firenze 1540–1580. Lo stile di Eleonora di Toledo e la sua influenza* (Florence: Edizione Polistampa, 2005); John R. Hale, *Florence and the Medici* (London: Phoenix, 1977); Andrea M. Gáldy, "L'appartamento di Eleonora di Toledo in Palazzo Vecchio: la scena della nuova Isabella la Catolica," in *Le donne Medici*, ed. Calvi and Spinelli, 615–26; Roberta Orsi Landini, "Eleonora di Toledo e la promozione del gusto: i rivestimenti d'interni," in *Le donne Medici*, ed. Calvi and Spinelli, 626–33.

[31] Hernando Sánchez, *Castilla y Nápoles*.

[32] Hale, *Florence and the Medici*, 139; Caroline P. Murphy, *Isabella de Medici: The Glorious Life and Tragic End of a Renaissance Princess* (London: Faber & Faber, 2008), 189–203.

[33] Benedetta Borello, *Trame sovrapposte: la socialità aristocratica e le reti di relazioni femminili a Roma (17.–18. secolo)* (Rome: Edizioni Scientifiche Italiane, 2003).

[34] Sharon Kettering, *Patrons, Brokers, and Clients in Seventeenth-Century France* (New York: Oxford University Press, 1986).

the capacity to generate trust thanks to personal and sometimes even intimate contacts and feelings was essential.[35] It is not surprising that many sources such as diaries, memoirs, travel books, or chronicles record the role of aristocratic women in organizing marriages. They were, as a matter of fact, matchmakers. To arrange matrimonies, especially in light of the impediments of distance and interculturality, was a practice of high political value. It was the way to put together dynasties and create the most important alliances imaginable. It was a political exercise of central value for the history of Europe, carried out thanks to experience, knowledge of court society and its "who's who," as well as simple *savoir faire*.

Future research will demonstrate the importance of this field for the study of the history of emotions and feelings. Though projected in a cool and Machiavellian way, most of these marriages created situations in which emotions and personal reactions were necessarily explicitly expressed. Letters, one of the main consequences of distance and the displacement of aristocrats, have become a crucial historical source. Letters to and from Madame de Sévigné or the duchess of Orléans, memoirs such as those of Henri-Charles de la Trémoille, travel books such as that of Madame d'Alnois or Cosimo de' Medici, and diaries such as the one written by Ferdinand Bonaventura, count of Harrach, on his trip as imperial ambassador to Madrid, all reveal a complex universe of nostalgia and psychological weakness while reflecting in a very expressive way how strong personalities were built. International marriages, even more than those celebrated between nobles from the same geographic location, also show the tension between individuals and the group or lineage.[36] In this way the new biographical history will cover a heretofore unexplored dimension. As biography leads to life stories in which historians discover new dimensions of the past by looking through different facets of characters and personalities, the transnational breadth of the lives of aristocrats who married across borders and whose memoirs, diaries, and correspondence have survived is becoming evident. In fact, historians are increasingly drawn to these personal biographies which illustrate the cosmopolitan dimension of aristocratic lives and demonstrate how these nobles had a sense of belonging to some particular community. In turn, these sentiments led to a new sense of patriotism, which was sometimes linked to strong feelings of nostalgia.[37]

One can imagine, and this is another dimension to develop in depth in the future, the traumatic world of feelings in which these men and women lived. Bethany Aram presents here a story of violence and love in which one can understand the desperation that contributed to the political incompetence of Queen Juana (the Mad). Aram makes evident that cultural differences strained

[35] Murphy, *Isabella de Medici*.

[36] Jonathan Dewald, *Aristocratic Experience and the Origins of Modern Culture. France 1570–1715* (Berkeley: University of California Press, 1993).

[37] See especially Elisabeth-Charlotte d'Orléans, *A Woman's Life*, 96–97.

the relationship between Juana and her husband, Philip. Yet as dramatic as her life must have been, Queen Juana had the fortune—or perhaps the misfortune—that Philip came to her homeland. This is important because, when reading Aram's text, one has the feeling that some of the couple's problems were inherent to an inversion of gender roles in which the man and his retinue had to emigrate to the woman's lands and cultural milieu. This situation may have been an additional source of conflict not only between the two partners but also among their entourages. Aram shows, for example, that Philip's mistreatment of Juana and his arrogance was a political problem for the Castilian elite. The inverse case, that of the *infanta* Catalina Micaela, is an excellent example of the extent to which different cultural perceptions, prestige, sense of status, and gender roles could create a tense environment in which personal behavior and feelings became an international political problem. Likewise, Anna Santamaría's analysis of the marriage of Philip II and Mary Tudor shows the personal animosity that these alliances could provoke and their impact on feelings, which could become a problem for international relations. Social contexts—such as a woman's infertility—could reshape and even exacerbate human, universal, and ahistorical sentiments, in particular if one considers Mary's desperate desire to have descendants. A personal frustration, infertility, which can be found in any society, had especially dramatic social implications and led to immense frustration in aristocratic societies based on dynastic successions.

Queen Juana's is a special case. She returned to her original cultural, personal, and psychological milieu. But this was rare. The letters of the duchess of Orléans, in practice a prisoner in the intricate and conspiratorial court of Versailles, are an excellent example of how displacement was combined with—and was a source of—strong feelings of nostalgia, paternal and filial love, hate, and suffering, as well as of how these feelings were lived and expressed. No less telling is the case presented here by Leticia de Frutos on Maria Mancini, for whom the clash between the personal *habitus* acquired in Paris and the strictness of the Counter-Reformation court of Rome was the key to the breakdown of a marriage and of plans for a princess's life. It is in this context that we can understand the complex world created by the contrast between personal sentiments and the rigid discipline of extended lineages and family strategies, very hierarchically decided, in which these women were embedded. The outcome of this game was unpredictable. But in many cases, as with Elisabetta Farnese, studied here by Pérez Samper, we confront a sort of social, political, and psychological challenge that was positively faced by women who found it a source of courage and personal development. One could say it is the reason for their historical relevance. Historians are increasingly interested in the way sentiments were managed and the ways in which these women faced psychological threats. We do not need to emphasize to what extent displacement and the need to live in different contexts and milieus were crucial for the forging of these personalities. But quite possibly this type of situation provided one basis for women's increased significance and influence in the cultural and political life so characteristic of the world of eighteenth-century salons.

From the economic historian's perspective, the history of aristocracies, princes, and princesses has never had good press. As part of the reaction in the second half of the twentieth century against *histoire evenementielle* and traditional political and diplomatic history, economic historians have been trapped until recently by nineteenth-century myths of aristocrats' bad management and lack of rationality. Economic historians have started to question such an intellectual framework, and the next frontier for these historians is to understand the links between aristocracies and the political economies and economic institutions so much in vogue today. Nevertheless, economic historians are still not sufficiently interested either in matrimonies or, more specifically, in international marriage strategies. The value of this approach is, however, more than obvious for economic history.

It is difficult to imagine anything that could affect political systems, political stability, and the reproduction of institutional systems—crucial factors for the creation of trust, the reduction of transaction costs, and the containment of risk in international (and domestic) economic activities—more than marriage strategies. But even without imagining historical connections, the positive or negative impact on the economy is not negligible. In many cases, matrimonial links provoked international circulation of economic resources. Dowries, as for example that paid by the la Trémoilles, were not only a way to reconstitute noble economies but also a reason to transfer money and capital across Europe.[38] This was even more important when it came to aristocracies such as the Genoese, where the *nobili vecchi* were also the most influential bankers, for whom matrimony could be a crucial business affair.[39] More importantly, these matrimonies created what we could call federations of international aristocratic estates on different sides of political, and sometimes even religious, borders, whose management was deeply influenced by their disperse and transnational character. The marquis of the Balbases, belonging to the Spínola family and whose estates once extended from Castile to Italy; the la Trémoilles, the Pastranas, the Guises, and many others provide examples of the aristocracy's peculiar managerial conditions and their many problems, particularly due to the twofold character of household patrimony.[40] Though this is not the central point of Soares's chapter, the idea that managing estates extending across international borders could be an economic as well as a political problem can be derived from her analysis.

For all these and many other reasons, it would be a mistake to consider the study of these international marriages and their crucial gender component as a marginal concern. From the viewpoint of social history, cultural and religious

---

38 Sonja Kmec, *Across the Channel. Noblewomen in Seventeenth-Century France and England* (Trier: Kliomedia, 2010), 41.

39 Romano Canossa, *Banchieri genovesi e sovrani spagnoli* (Genoa: Sapere 2000, 1998).

40 On the Guise, see Jonathan Spangler, *The Society of Princes. The Lorraine-Guise and the Conservation of Power and Wealth in Seventeenth-Century France* (Farnham: Ashgate, 2009).

history, and international, diplomatic, and even economic history, not to mention the new biographical turn, one has to acknowledge the importance of this subject, which is far more than a history of cultural transfers. It is, in fact, a fertile crossroads for the understanding of many promising paths of historical research, as well as an arsenal for a richer and more complex comprehension of Old Regime societies. Unfortunately, the subject also can be taken as a set of celebrity notes proper for tabloids and historical gossip. The danger of falling into banalities typical of bad historical novels is more than evident. However, good historians and good historical novelists have the opportunity of using the exceptional nature of these border-crossing lives and the huge amount of information they provide to reach deeper into the social fabric of the Old Regime; that is, into the DNA of European elites during the early modern era. After all, the best way to understand our own era is to consider similarities and differences across time.

Bibliography

Bacon, Francis. *Essays, moral, economical, and political. A new ed., with the Latin quotations translated.* London: J. M'Creery, 1819.

Bayly, Christopher A., Sven Beckert, Matthew Connelly, Isabel Hofmeyr, Wendy Kozol, and Patricia Seed. "AHR Conversation: On Transnational History." *The American Historical Review*, 111, no. 5 (December 2006): 1441–64.

Beccucci, Alessandra. "The Art of Politics and the Politics of the Arts. Francesco Ottavio Piccolomini: A Case of Patronage in Thirty Years War Europe." PhD diss., European University Institute, Florence, 2012.

Bély, Lucien. *Les relations internationales en Europe (XVIIe–XVIIIe siècles).* Paris: Presses Universitaires de France, 1992.

______. *La société des princes, XVIe–XVIIe siècle.* Paris: Fayard, 1999.

______, ed. *La presence des Bourbons en Europe, XVIe–XXIe siècle.* Paris: Presses Universitaires de France, 2003.

Bennassar, Bartolomé. *Reinas y princesas del Renacimiento a la Ilustración. El lecho, el poder y la muerte.* Barcelona: Paidos, 2006.

Bödeker, Hans E., and Etienne François, eds. *Aufklärung/Lumières und Politik. Zurpolitischen Kultur der deutschen und französischen Aufklärung.* Leipzig: Leipziger Universitätsverlag: 1996.

Bonney, Richard. *The European Dynastic States, 1494–1660.* Oxford: Oxford University Press, 1991.

Borello, Benedetta. *Trame sovrapposte: la socialità aristocratica e le reti di relazioni femminili a Roma (17.–18. secolo).* Rome: Edizioni Scientifiche Italiane, 2003.

Calvi, Giulia, and Riccardo Spinelli, eds. *Le donne Medici nel sistema europeo delle corti, XVI–XVIII secolo.* Florence: Edizioni Polistampa, 2008.

Canossa, Romano. *Banchieri genovesi e sovrani spagnoli.* Genoa: Sapere 2000, 1998.

Clavero, Bartolomé. *La grâce du don. Antropologie catholique de l'économie moderne*. Paris: Albin Michel, 1996.

Contini, Alessandra. "Il ritorno delle donne nel sistema di corte." In *Le donne Medici nel sistema europeo delle corti, XVI–XVIII secolo*. Edited by Giulia Calvi and Riccardo Spinelli, 5–12. Florence: Edizioni Polistampa: 2008.

Cunha, Mafalda Soares da. "Títulos portugueses y matrimonios mixtos en la Monarquía Católica." In *Las redes del Imperio. Elites sociales en la articulación de la Monarquía Hispánica, 1492–1714*. Edited by Bartolomé Yun Casalilla, 205–32. Madrid: Marcial Pons, 2009.

Dandelet, Thomas J. *Spanish Rome, 1500–1700*. New Haven: Yale University Press, 2001.

Davis, Natalie Z. *The Gift in Sixteenth-Century France*. Oxford: Oxford University Press, 2000.

De Sainte-Marthe, Scévole. *Histoire Généalogique de la Maison de la Trèmoille*. Paris: S. Piget, 1668.

Dewald, Jonathan. *Aristocratic Experience and the Origins of Modern Culture. France 1570–1715*. Berkeley: University of California Press, 1993.

Domínguez Ortiz, Antonio. "La conspiración del duque de Medina Sidonia y el Marqués de Ayamonte." In *Crisis y decadencia en la España de los Austrias*, 115–53. Barcelona: Ariel, 1973.

D'Orléans, Elisabeth-Charlotte. *A Woman's Life in the Court of the Sun King. Letters of Liselotte von der Pfalz, Elisabeth Charlotte, Duchesse d'Orleans, 1652–1722*. Edited and translated by Elborg Forster. Baltimore: Johns Hopkins University Press, 1997.

Droste, Heiko. "Diplomacy as Means of Cultural Transfer in Early Modern Times." *Scandinavian Journal of History*, 31, no. 2 (June 2006): 144–50.

Egido López, Teófanes. *Opinión pública y oposición al poder en la España del siglo XVIII (1713–1759)*. 2nd edn. Valladolid: Universidad de Valladolid-Fundación de Historia Moderna, 2002.

Espagne, Michel. "Sur les limites du comparatisme en histoire culturelle." *Genèses. Sciences sociales et histoire*, 17 (September 1994): 112–21.

———. *Les transferts culturels franco-allemands*. Paris: Presses Universitaires de France, 1999.

———, ed. *L'Ecole normale supérieure et Allemagne*. Leipzig: Leipziger Universitätsverlag, 1995.

———, and Michael Werner, eds. *Transferts: les relations interculturelles dans l'espace franco-allemand (XVIIIe et XIXe siécle)*. Paris: Editions Recherche sur les Civilisations, 1988.

Fattacciu, Irene. "The Resilience and Boomerang Effect of Chocolate: A Product's Globalization and Commodification." In *Global Goods and the Spanish Empire, 1492–1824. Circulation, Resistance and Diversity*. Edited by Bethany Aram and Bartolomé Yun Casalilla. Basingstoke: Palgrave Macmillan, 2014.

Freire Costa, Leonor, and Mafalda Soares da Cunha. *D. Joao IV*. Rio do Mouro: Circulo de Leitores, 2006.

Hale, John R. *Florence and the Medici*. London: Phoenix, 1977.

Hernando Sánchez, Carlos. *Castilla y Nápoles en el siglo XVI. El virrey Pedro de Toledo. Linaje, estado y cultura (1532–1553)*. Salamanca: Junta de Castilla y León, 1994.

Kmec, Sonja. *Across the Channel. Noblewomen in Seventeenth-Century France and England*. Trier: Kliomedia, 2010.

La Trèmoille, Henri-Charles de. *Mémoires de Henri-Charles de la Trèmoille, Prince de Tarente*. Liege: J.F. Bassompierre, 1767.

Levin, Michael J. *Agents of Empire. Spanish Ambassadors in Sixteenth-Century Italy*. Ithaca, NY: Cornell University Press, 2005.

Lindorfer, Bianca M. 2008. "Las redes familiares de la aristocracia austriaca y los procesos de transferencia cultural: entre Madrid y Viena, 1550–1700." In *Las redes del Imperio. Elites sociales en la articulación del imperio español, 1492–1714*. Edited by Bartolomé Yun Casalilla, 261–88. Madrid: Marcial Pons, 2008.

MacHardy, Karin J. "Cultural Capital, Family Strategies and Noble Identity in Early Modern Habsburg Austria, 1579–1620." *Past & Present*, 163 (May 1999): 36–75.

McKendrick, Neil. "The Consumer Revolution of Eighteenth-Century England." In *The Birth of a Consumer Society. The Commercialization of Eighteenth-Century England*. Edited by Neil McKendrick, John Brewer and John H. Plumb, 9–33. London: Europa, 1982.

Meadow, Mark A. "Merchants and Marvels. Hans Jacob Fugger and the Origins of the Wunderkammer." In *Merchants and Marvels. Commerce, Science and Art in Early Modern Europe*. Edited by Pamela H. Smith and Paula Findlen, 182–200. New York: Routledge: 2002.

Muchembled, Robert, ed. *Cultural Exchange in Early Modern Europe*. Cambridge: Cambridge University Press, 2007.

Muñoz Fernández, Ángela. "La casa della regina. Un spazio nella Castiglia del Quattrocento." *Genesis. Rivista della società italiana delle storiche*, 2 (2002): 71–95.

Murphy, Caroline P. *Isabella de Medici: The Glorious Life and Tragic End of a Renaissance Princess*. London: Faber & Faber, 2008.

Orsi Landini, Roberta, and Bruna Niccoli. *Moda a Firenze 1540–1580, Lo stile di Eleonora di Toledo e la sua influenza*. Florence: Edizione Polistampa, 2005.

Peck, Linda L. *Consuming, Splendour, Society and Culture in Seventeenth-Century England*. Cambridge: Cambridge University Press, 2005.

Pérez de Tudela, Almudena, and Annemarie Jordan Gschwend. "Luxury Goods for Royal Collectors: Exotica, Princely Gifts and Rare Animals Exchanged between the Iberian Courts and Central Europe in the Renaissance (1560–1612)." *Jahrbuch des Kunsthistorischen Museum Wien*, 3 (2001): 1–127.

Po-Chia Hsia, Ronnie. *The World of Catholic Renewal, 1540–1770*. 2nd edn. Cambridge: Cambridge University Press, 2005.

Río Barredo, María José del. "Imágenes para una ceremonia de frontera. El intercambio de princesas entre las cortes de Francia y España en 1615." In *La historia imaginada. Construcciones visuales del pasado en la edad moderna.* Edited by Joan Lluís Palos and Diana Carrió-Ivernizzi, 153–83. Madrid: Fernando Villaverde Ediciones, 2008.

Roche, Daniel. *La culture des apparences.Une histoire du vêtement (XIIIe–XVIIe siècle)*. Paris: Fayard, 1989.

Rodríguez Salgado, M.J. "'Una perfecta princesa.' Casa y vida de la reina Isabel de Valois (1559–1568)." *Cuadernos de historia moderna*, Anejo [supplement] 2 (2003): 39–96, and 28 (2003): 71–98.

Spangler, Jonathan. *The Society of Princes. The Lorraine-Guise and the Conservation of Power and Wealth in Seventeenth-Century France.* Farnham: Ashgate, 2009.

Thomson, Ann, Simon Burrows, and Edmon Dziembowski, eds. *Cultural Transfers: France and Britain in the Long Eighteenth Century.* Oxford: Voltaire Foundation, 2010.

Werner, Michael, and Bénédicte Zimmermann, "Penser l'histoire croisée: entre empirie et reflexivité." In *De la comparaison à l'histoire croisée.* Edited by Michael Werner and Bénédicte Zimmermann. Paris: Seuil, 2004.

Yun Casalilla, Bartolomé. "'Localism,' Global History and Transnational History. A Reflection from the Historian of Early Modern Europe." *Historisk Tidskrift*, 127, no. 4 (2007): 659–78.

———. "Príncipes más allá de los reinos. Aristocracias, comunicación e intercambio cultural en la Europa de los siglos XVI–XVII." In *Mecenazgo y humanidades en tiempos de Lastanosa. Homenaje a Domingo Indurain.* Edited by Aurora Egido and José. E. Laplana, 51–68. Zaragoza: Universidad de Zaragoza, 2008.

———, ed. *Las redes del Imperio. Elites sociales en la articulación del imperio español, 1492–1714.* Madrid: Marcial Pons, 2008.

———, and Ángeles Redondo Alamo. "Aristocracias, identidades y espacios políticos en la monarquía compuesta de los Austrias. La Casa de Borja (ss. XVI y XVII)." In *Homenaje a Don Antonio Domínguez Ortíz.* Edited by Juan L. Castellano and Miguel L. López-Guadalupe Muñoz, 759–72. Granada: Universidad de Granada, 2008.

———, and Ángeles Redondo Álamo. "'*Bem visto tinha …*' Entre Lisboa y Capodimonte. La aristocracia castellana en perspectiva 'trans-nacional' (ss. XVI–XVII)." In *Las redes del Imperio. Elites sociales en la articulación del imperio español, 1492–1714.* Edited by Bartolomé Yun Casalilla, 39–63. Madrid: Marcial Pons, 2008.

Index

Page numbers in **bold** refer to figures in the text.